HUMAN KNOWLEDGE
ITS SCOPE AND LIMITS

HUMAN
KNOWLEDGE

Its Scope and Limits

BERTRAND RUSSELL

with a new Introduction by
John G. Slater

Routledge
Taylor & Francis Group

LONDON AND NEW YORK

First published in 1948

Paperback edition first published in 1992
by Routledge
11 New Fetter Lane, London EC4P 4EE

© 1948 Bertrand Russell
New introduction © 1992 John G. Slater

Reprinted 1997, 2000, 2003

Routledge is an imprint of the Taylor & Francis Group

Printed in Great Britain by
St Edmundsbury Press Ltd, Bury St Edmunds, Suffolk

British Library Cataloguing in Publication Data
Russell, Bertrand
Human Knowledge: Its Scope and Limits. –
New ed
I. Title
121

ISBN 0–415–08302–8

INTRODUCTION

Iɴ his private correspondence Russell was fond of referring to some of his philosophical projects as aiming at the writing of a "big" book. *Human Knowledge: Its Scope and Limits* is Russell's last big book, and its topic – the problem of non-demonstrative inference – has been of central concern to philosophers ever since Hume undermined inductive arguments. At the beginning of his career Russell focused his interest, his talent, and his energies on trying to determine whether there was any certain knowledge. Since nobody claimed that either inductive arguments or any other non-demonstrative arguments for that matter, yielded certain knowledge, he paid little or no attention to these arguments. Beginning with its use in mathematics, he studied demonstrative inference as the likeliest source of knowledge with any claim to certainty. But the mathematics he had been taught, he soon discovered, was built on fallacious proofs, so he was forced back to logic for his starting point.

A logic freed of hidden assumptions would be a useful tool by which to establish mathematical proof on a firm basis. To his great delight he found that many others shared his belief about the importance of a new logic for mathematics; he avidly studied their works and he was soon ready to make original contributions to the development of symbolic logic. As his work proceeded he gradually became convinced that the new logic was not just a tool to be used in improving mathematical proofs, but was itself the very foundation of mathematics. His conviction, and that of Alfred North Whitehead, who had been one of his teachers at Cambridge, that much of mathematics is a branch of symbolic logic, led them to devote a decade of their lives to developing a proof of their thesis. *Principia Mathematica*, published in three large volumes between 1910 and 1913, reports the results of their research in elaborate detail.

When *Principia Mathematica* was finished Russell turned his attention to exploiting what he had learned during its production. He was convinced that a similar method could be applied to other realms of human knowledge with the result that their a priori (certain) and empirical (merely probable) parts could be disentangled. Physics was his first candidate for analysis using the new method. Through a careful study of the writings of physicists, he hoped to discover the minimum vocabulary required in physics, and to state, using only that minimum vocabulary and purely logical terms, the basic relationships of these terms to each other. The model he had in mind is nicely exhibited by the Peano postulates for arithmetic. Using only "zero", "number" and "successor" as undefined mathematical terms, and logical terms, Peano stated five axioms from which, using only logical rules of inference, the ordinary truths of arithmetic are deducible. An important feature of *Principia Mathematica* is the set of definitions that Whitehead and Russell provided for Peano's undefined terms. These definitions are written in purely logical notation, allowing each of them, and, therefore, each of Peano's postulates, to find its proper place in the logical and mathematical system being developed in that book.

Russell expended much thought on this problem of providing a foundation for physics; he called it "the problem of matter". But he did not succeed in cracking it. In the course of his work, he found that progress on the problem of matter required the solution to certain problems in the theory of knowledge, more specifically, the problem of our knowledge of the external world. So he turned his attention in that direction and began to write a "big" book on the theory of knowledge. Wittgenstein turned up during this period and Russell showed him some of his manuscript. The severity of Wittgenstein's criticism led Russell to abandon the book. *Theory of Knowledge: The 1913 Manuscript* was only published in 1984 as Volume 7 of *The Collected Papers of Bertrand Russell*. Although he abandoned one book he soon wrote another dealing with some of the same topics. *Our Knowledge of the External World* was written to be read to a Boston audience during his visit to Harvard in the spring of 1914. Russell had just begun to bring the ideas in that book to bear on the problem of matter, most notably in "The Relation of Sense-Data to Physics" (1914), when the First World War shattered his world.

When he returned to philosophical work after the war his thinking was still dominated by the axiomatic model of *Principia Mathematica*. While studying William James with the intention of refuting him, Russell persuaded himself that James's theory of neutral monism – that both mind and matter are constituted of entities of only one sort, for James it was "experience", for

Russell, "events" – was correct. Mind and matter were merely different configurations of the same basic stuff. With somewhat less persistence than he had shown in mathematics, Russell attempted during the 1920s to discover minimum vocabularies for discussing mind and matter and to propose analyses of some, at least, of these terms in the language of events. Two books, *The Analysis of Mind* (1921) and *The Analysis of Matter* (1927), serve to record his achievements in these projects.

Throughout these studies Russell tended to push questions of empirical knowledge aside. The real gold was a priori knowledge; on such a rock one could build one's philosophy. Empirical knowledge had its uses, but, since it could never be certain, it was outranked by the a priori kind. The axiomatic method, therefore, tended to dominate his thinking. Whenever he tackled a problem, he tried, first of all, to discover its minimum vocabulary, and then, when he experienced some success on that front, he would attempt to formulate the basic propositions linking the various terms of the minimum vocabulary with one another. Success in such an enterprise provides one with a starting point, a set of axioms, from which other truths can be deduced. One's knowledge of the subject being investigated derives from the small set of propositions which serve as premisses in every demonstration. This set of propositions is, in effect, a hostage for the truth of the derived propositions. If a derived proposition is found to be in error, one knows where to look for the source of the error. For most of his life, Russell, like Plato and many later philosophers, fell under the seductive charms of this model of human knowledge.

During the Second World War, which he spent in the United States, Russell came to the conclusion that he could no longer put off dealing with the problem of empirical knowledge. One reason for this change had been simmering in his mind for a long time. During the period he was working on deductive logic he was convinced that the propositions of logic were not only true but also significant. Mathematics was true of the world. His faith in this position had been undermined by Wittgenstein who argued very strenuously that the propositions of logic and mathematics were tautologies, merely formal truths, and, therefore, told us nothing about the world. For a man of Russell's philosophical disposition this was a bitter pill to swallow, and it is doubtful that he ever did swallow it. One immediate consequence of regarding formal truths as tautologies is to increase the importance of contingent truths, for they do refer to the world, and hence are significant.

A second reason has to do with scepticism. Although Russell always prized a sceptical frame of mind, he was not a sceptic in the philosophical sense. Pyrrhonian or Humean scepticism was an insincere philosophy, he believed, because its partisans always preferred bread to stones at meal time. Application of the scientific method has resulted in knowledge about which only theoretical doubt is possible, but Hume's doubts about induction appeared at first glance to taint these results. Since everybody uses induction and other forms of non-demonstrative inference, and everyone has beliefs about the future, what is needed is a canon of non-demonstrative inference; such a canon would serve as a justification for our faith in non-demonstrative inference. In 1943, in an outline which he entitled "Project of Future Work", Russell raised what he regarded as the "main question": "In what circumstances does scientific method allow us to infer the existence of something unobserved from what is observed?" Such an inference is never legitimate in deductive, or demonstrative, logic, but it is in science and in everyday life. A careful analytical study of the actual use of scientific method ought to lead to the formulation of a set of principles which would, collectively, serve as a canon to justify our use of non-demonstrative inference.

Closely related to the second reason is a third: it concerns empiricism as a philosophy. After about 1912 Russell regarded himself as carrying on the work of the great British empiricists, Locke, Berkeley, Hume and Mill, but most of his philosophical work, as we have seen, had to do with the problem of a priori knowledge. The rise of the logical positivists in the 1930s forced him to reconsider his position. They claimed him, along with Hume and Mach and Wittgenstein, as their philosophical ancestor, but, after reading a number of their works and finding some of their positions too extreme for his taste, Russell realized that he had work to do to distinguish his position from logical positivism. The unifying thread he hit upon was an examination of all of those arguments whose conclusions are never certain, given the truth of the premisses, but only probable.

At the end of a long study of the use of non-demonstrative arguments in both science and ordinary life, Russell concluded that five postulates are required to validate arguments of this sort.

They are brought together at the end of the book and the justification for including each of them is summarized. What surprised Russell, and will astonish some readers, is that the principle of induction is not a member of this set of postulates. Russell came to the conclusion, after an extensive study of the role of probability theory in scientific method, that the form of induction used there is demonstrable in probability theory. Therefore, it is unnecessary to assume it as a postulate.

Although the argument of this book proceeds in much the same way as the arguments to be found in his earlier philosophical works, there is one statement in the Preface which seems to call into question the philosophical method which he advocated in "Scientific Method in Philosophy" (1914), written in the flush of the success of *Principia Mathematica*. In that essay, after arguing that "philosophy is the science of the possible", he went on to amplify: "Philosophy, if what has been said is correct, becomes indistinguishable from logic as that word has now come to be used." And there can be no doubt that by "logic" he meant the logic developed in *Principia Mathematica*. It is, therefore, astonishing to find, in the first paragraph of his Preface to *Human Knowledge: Its Scope and Limits*, this long-standing position unceremoniously abandoned: "Logic, it must be admitted, is technical in the same way as mathematics is, but logic, I maintain, is not part of philosophy. Philosophy proper deals with matters of interest to the general educated public, and loses much of its value if only a few professionals can understand what is said." His style of writing often leads him into making statements with more sweep than he probably intends, and in this case he probably intends less than meets the eye. Whatever the truth is on this point, the reader of this book will soon discover that Russell has not abandoned logical analysis as his preferred method, for one finds it used on every page, although, in consideration of those readers unacquainted with modern symbolic logic, he does keep the use of special symbols to a bare minimum. A member of "the general educated public" should, therefore, be able to follow his argument and learn a great deal about the many problems upon which Russell turns his formidable philosophical talent in this important book.

John G. Slater
University of Toronto

PREFACE

THE following pages are addressed, not only or primarily to professional philosophers, but to that much larger public which is interested in philosophical questions without being willing or able to devote more than a limited amount of time to considering them. Descartes, Leibniz, Locke, Berkeley, and Hume wrote for a public of this sort, and I think it is unfortunate that during the last hundred and sixty years or so philosophy has come to be regarded as almost as technical as mathematics. Logic, it must be admitted, is technical in the same way as mathematics is, but logic, I maintain, is not part of philosophy. Philosophy proper deals with matters of interest to the general educated public, and loses much of its value if only a few professionals can understand what is said.

In this book I have sought to deal, as comprehensively as I am able, with a very large question: how comes it that human beings, whose contacts with the world are brief and personal and limited, are nevertheless able to know as much as they do know? Is the belief in our knowledge partly illusory? And, if not, what must we know otherwise than through the senses? Since I have dealt in earlier books with some parts of this problem, I am compelled to repeat, in a larger context, discussions of certain matters which I have considered elsewhere, but I have reduced such repetition to the minimum compatible with my purpose.

One of the difficulties of the subject with which I am concerned is that we must employ words which are common in ordinary speech, such as "belief", "truth", "knowledge", and "perception". Since these words, in their every-day uses, are vague and unprecise, and since no precise words are ready to hand by which to replace them, it is inevitable that everything said in the earlier stages of our inquiry should be unsatisfactory from the point of view that we hope to arrive at in the end. Our increase of knowledge, assuming that we are successful, is like that of a traveller approaching a mountain through a haze: at first only certain large features are discernible, and even they have indistinct boundaries, but gradually more detail becomes visible and edges become sharper. So, in our discussions, it is

5

impossible first to clear up one problem and then proceed to another, for the intervening haze envelops all alike. At every stage, though one part of our problem may be in the focus of attention, all parts are more or less relevant. The different key words that we must use are all interconnected, and so long as some remain vague, others must, more or less, share this defect. It follows that what is said at first is liable to require emendation later. The Prophet announced that if two texts of the Koran appeared inconsistent, the later text was to be taken as authoritative, and I should wish the reader to apply a similar principle in interpreting what is said in this book.

The book has been read in typescript by my friend and pupil Mr. C. K. Hill, and I am indebted to him for many valuable criticisms, suggestions, and emendations. Large parts of the typescript have also been read by Mr. Hiram J. McLendon, who has made a number of useful suggestions.

Part III, Chapter IV, on "Physics and Experience", is a reprint, with few alterations, of a little book with the above title, published by the Cambridge University Press, to whom I owe thanks for permission to reprint it.

CONTENTS

INTRODUCTION

THE central purpose of this book is to examine the relation between individual experience and the general body of scientific knowledge. It is taken for granted that scientific knowledge, in its broad outlines, is to be accepted. Scepticism, while logically impeccable, is psychologically impossible, and there is an element of frivolous insincerity in any philosophy which pretends to accept it. Moreover, if scepticism is to be theoretically defensible it must reject *all* inferences from what is experienced; a partial scepticism, such as the denial of physical events experienced by no one, or a solipsism which allows events in my future or in my unremembered past, has no logical justification, since it must admit principles of inference which lead to beliefs that it rejects.

Ever since Kant, or perhaps it would be more just to say ever since Berkeley, there has been what I regard as a mistaken tendency among philosophers to allow the description of the world to be influenced unduly by considerations derived from the nature of human knowledge. To scientific common sense (which I accept) it is plain that only an infinitesimal part of the universe is known, that there were countless ages during which there was no knowledge, and that there probably will be countless ages without knowledge in the future. Cosmically and causally, knowledge is an unimportant feature of the universe; a science which omitted to mention its occurrence might, from an impersonal point of view, suffer only from a very trivial imperfection. In describing the world, subjectivity is a vice. Kant spoke of himself as having effected a "Copernican revolution", but he would have been more accurate if he had spoken of a "Ptolemaic counter-revolution", since he put Man back at the centre from which Copernicus had dethroned him.

But when we ask, not "what sort of world do we live in?" but "how do we come by our knowledge about the world?" subjectivity is in order. What each man knows is, in an important sense, dependent upon his own individual experience: he knows what he has seen and heard, what he has read and what he has been told, and also what, from these data, he has been able to infer. It is individual, not collective, experience that is here in question, for an inference is required to pass from my data to the acceptance of testimony. If I believe that there is such a place as Semipalatinsk, I believe it because of things that have happened to *me*; and unless certain substantial principles of inference are accepted, I shall have to admit that all these things might have happened to me without there being any such place.

The desire to escape from subjectivity in the description of the world (which I share) has led some modern philosophers astray—at least so it seems to me—in relation to theory of knowledge. Finding its problems distasteful, they have tried to deny that these problems exist. That data are private and individual is a thesis which has been familiar since the time of Protagoras. This thesis has been denied because it has been thought, as Protagoras thought, that, if admitted, it must lead to the conclusion that all knowledge is private and individual. For my part, while I admit the thesis, I deny the conclusion; how and why, the following pages are intended to show.

In virtue of certain events in my own life, I have a number of beliefs about events that I do not experience—the thoughts and feelings of other people, the physical objects that surround me, the historical and geological past of the earth, and the remote regions of the universe that are studied in astronomy. For my part, I accept these beliefs as valid, apart from errors of detail. By this acceptance I commit myself to the view that there are valid processes of inference from events to other events—more particularly, from events of which I am aware without inference to events of which I have no such awareness. To discover what these processes are is a matter of analysis of scientific and common-sense procedure, in so far as such procedure is generally accepted as scientifically valid.

Inference from a group of events to other events can only be justified if the world has certain characteristics which are not logically necessary. So far as deductive logic can show, any collection of events might be the whole universe; if, then, I am ever to be able to infer events, I must accept principles of inference which lie outside deductive logic. All inference from events to events demands some kind of interconnection between different occurrences. Such interconnection is traditionally asserted in the principle of causality or natural law. It is implied, as we shall find, in whatever limited validity may be assigned to induction by simple enumeration. But the traditional ways of formulating the kind of interconnection that must be postulated are in many ways defective, some being too stringent and some not sufficiently so. To discover the minimum principles required to justify scientific inferences is one of the main purposes of this book.

It is a commonplace to say that the substantial inferences of science, as opposed to those of logic and mathematics, are only *probable*—that is to say, when the premisses are true and the inference correct, the conclusion is only *likely* to be true. It is therefore necessary to examine what is meant by "probability". It will be found that there are two different concepts that may be meant. On the one hand, there is mathematical probability: if a class has n members, and m of them have a certain characteristic, the mathematical probability that an unspecified member of this class will have the characteristic in question is m/n. On the other hand, there is a wider and vaguer concept, which I call "degree of credibility", which is the amount of credence that it is rational to assign to a more or less uncertain proposition. Both kinds of probability are involved in stating the principles of scientific inference.

The course of our inquiry, in broad outline, will be as follows.

Part I, on the world of science, describes some of the main features of the universe which scientific investigation has made probable. This Part may be taken as setting the goal which inference must be able to reach, if our data and our principles of inference are to justify scientific practice.

Part II, on language, is still concerned with preliminaries. These are mainly of two sorts. On the one hand, it is important to make clear the meanings of certain fundamental terms, such as "fact" and "truth". On the other hand, it is necessary to examine the relation of sensible experience to empirical concepts such as "red", "hard", "metre", or "second". In addition, we shall examine the relation of words having an essential reference to the speaker, such as "here" and "now", to impersonal words, such as those assigning latitude, longitude, and date. This raises problems, of considerable importance and some difficulty, which are concerned with the relation of individual experience to the socially recognized body of general knowledge.

In Part III, on Science and Perception, we begin our main inquiry. We are concerned, here, to disentangle data from inferences in what ordinarily passes for empirical knowledge.

We are not yet concerned to justify inferences, or to investigate the principles according to which they are made, but we are concerned to show that inferences (as opposed to logical constructions) are necessary to science. We are concerned also to distinguish between two kinds of space and time, one subjective and appertaining to data, the other objective and inferred. Incidentally we shall contend that solipsism, except in an extreme form in which it has never been entertained, is an illogical halfway house between the fragmentary world of data and the complete world of science.

Part IV, on scientific concepts, is concerned to analyse the fundamental concepts of the inferred scientific world, more especially physical space, historical time, and causal laws. The terms employed in mathematical physics are required to fulfil two kinds of conditions: on the one hand, they must satisfy certain formulae; on the other hand, they must be so interpreted as to yield results that can be confirmed or confuted by observation. Through the latter condition they are linked to data, though somewhat loosely; through the former they become determinate as regards certain structural properties. But considerable latitude of interpretation remains. It is prudent to use this latitude in such a way as to minimize the part played by inference as opposed to construction; on this ground, for example, point-instants in space-time are constructed as groups of events or of qualities. Throughout this Part the two concepts of space-time structure and causal chains assume a gradually increasing importance. As Part III was concerned to discover what can be counted as data, so Part IV is concerned to set forth, in a general way, what, if science is to be justified, we must be able to infer from our data.

Since it is admitted that scientific inferences, as a rule, only confer probability on their conclusions, Part V proceeds to the examination of Probability. This term is capable of various interpretations, and has been differently defined by different authors. These interpretations and definitions are examined, and so are the attempts to connect induction with probability. In this matter the conclusion reached is, in the main, that advocated by Keynes: that inductions do not make their conclusions probable unless certain conditions are fulfilled, and that experience alone can never prove that these conditions are fulfilled.

Part VI, on the postulates of scientific inference, endeavours to discover what are the minimum assumptions, anterior to experience, that are required to justify us in inferring laws from a collection of data; and further, to inquire in what sense, if any, we can be said to know that these assumptions are valid. The main logical function that the assumptions have to fulfil is that of conferring a high probability on the conclusions of inductions that satisfy certain conditions. For this purpose, since only probability is in question, we do not need to assume that such-and-such a connection of events occurs always, but only that it occurs frequently. For example, one of the assumptions that appear necessary is that of separable causal chains, such as are exhibited by light-rays or sound-waves. This assumption can be stated as follows: when an event having a complex space-time structure occurs, it frequently happens that it is one of a train of events having the same or a very similar structure. (A more exact statement will be found in Chapter VI of this Part.) This is part of a wider assumption of regularity, or natural law, which, however, requires to be stated in more specific forms than is usual, for in its usual form it turns out to be a tautology.

That scientific inference requires, for its validity, principles which experience cannot render even probable, is, I believe, an inescapable conclusion from the logic of probability. For empiricism, it is an awkward conclusion. But I think it can be rendered somewhat more palatable by the analysis of the concept of "knowledge" undertaken in Part II. "Knowledge", in my opinion, is a much less precise concept than is generally thought, and has its roots more deeply embedded in unverbalized animal behaviour than most philosophers have been willing to admit. The logically basic assumptions to which our analysis leads us are psychologically the end of a long series of refinements which start from habits of expectation in animals, such as that what has a certain kind of smell will be good to eat. To ask, therefore, whether we "know" the postulates of scientific inference, is not so definite a question as it seems. The answer must be: in one sense, yes, in another sense, no; but in the sense in which "no" is the right answer we know nothing whatever, and "knowledge" in this sense is a delusive vision. The perplexities of philosophers are due, in a large measure, to their unwillingness to awaken from this blissful dream.

PART I

THE WORLD OF SCIENCE

Chapter I

INDIVIDUAL AND SOCIAL KNOWLEDGE

SCIENTIFIC knowledge aims at being wholly impersonal, and tries to state what has been discovered by the collective intellect of mankind. In this chapter I shall consider how far it succeeds in this aim, and what elements of individual knowledge have to be sacrificed in order to achieve the measure of success that is possible.

The community knows both more and less than the individual: it knows, in its collective capacity, all the contents of the Encyclopaedia and all the contributions to the Proceedings of learned bodies, but it does not know the warm and intimate things that make up the colour and texture of an individual life. When a man says "I can never convey the horror I felt on seeing Buchenwald" or "no words can express my joy at seeing the sea again after years in a prison camp", he is saying something which is strictly and precisely true: he possesses, through his experience, knowledge not possessed by those whose experience has been different, and not completely capable of verbal expression. If he is a superb literary artist he may create in sensitive readers a state of mind not wholly unlike his own, but if he tries scientific methods the stream of his experience will be lost and dissipated in a dusty desert.

Language, our sole means of communicating *scientific* knowledge, is essentially social in its origin and in its main functions. It is true that, if a mathematician were wrecked on a desert island with a note-book and a pencil, he would, in all likelihood, seek to make his solitude endurable by calculations using the language of mathematics; it is true also that a man may keep a diary which he intends to conceal from all eyes but his own. On a more everyday plane, most of us use words in solitary thinking. Nevertheless the chief purpose of language is communication, and to serve this purpose it must be public, not a private dialect invented by the speaker. It follows that what is most personal in each individual's experience tends to evaporate during the process of translation into language. What is more, the very publicity of language is in large part a delusion. A given form of words will usually be interpreted by competent hearers in such a way as to be true for all of them or false for all of them, but in spite of this it will not have the same meaning for all of them. Differences which do not affect the truth or falsehood of a statement are usually of little practical importance, and are therefore ignored, with the result that we all believe our private world to be much more like the public world than it really is.

This is easily proved by considering the process of learning to understand language. There are two ways of getting to know what a word means: one is by a definition in terms of other words, which is called *verbal* definition; the other is by frequently hearing the word when the object which it denotes is present, which is called *ostensive* definition. It is obvious that ostensive definition is alone possible in the beginning, since verbal definition pre-supposes a knowledge of the words used in the *definiens*. You can learn by a verbal definition that a pentagon is a plane figure with five sides, but a child does not learn in this way the meaning of every-day words such as "rain", "sun", "dinner", or "bed". These are taught by using the appropriate word emphatically while the child is noticing the object concerned. Consequently the meaning that the child comes to attach to the word is a product of his personal experience, and varies according to his circumstances and his sensorium. A child who frequently experiences a mild drizzle will attach a different idea to the word "rain" from that formed by a child who has only experienced tropical torrents. A short-sighted and a long-sighted child will connect different images with the word "bed".

It is true that education tries to depersonalize language, and with a certain measure of success. "Rain" is no longer the familiar phenomenon, but "drops of water falling from clouds towards the earth", and "water" is no longer what makes you wet, but H_2O. As for hydrogen and oxygen, they have verbal definitions which have to be learnt by heart; whether you understand them does not matter. And so, as your instruction proceeds, the world of words becomes more and more separated from the world of the senses; you acquire the art of using words correctly, as you might acquire the art of playing the fiddle; in the end you become such a virtuoso in the manipulation of phrases that you need hardly ever remember that words have meanings. You have then become completely a public character, and even your inmost thoughts are suitable for the encyclopaedia. But you can no longer hope to be a poet, and if you try to be a lover you will find your depersonalized language not very successful in generating the desired emotions. You have sacrificed expression to communication, and what you can communicate turns out to be abstract and dry.

It is an important fact that the nearer we come to the complete abstractness of logic, the less is the unavoidable difference between different people in the meaning attached to a word. I see no reason why there should be any difference at all between two suitably educated persons in the idea conveyed to them by the word "3481". The words "or" and "not" are capable of having exactly the same meaning for two different logicians. Pure mathematics, throughout, works with concepts which are capable of being completely public and impersonal. The reason is that they derive nothing from the senses, and that the senses are the source of privacy. The body is a sensitive recording instrument, constantly transmitting messages from the outside world; the messages reaching one body are never quite the same as those reaching another, though practical and social exigencies have taught us ways of disregarding the differences between the percepts of neighbouring persons. In constructing physics we have emphasized the spatio-temporal aspect of our perceptions, which is the aspect that is most abstract and most nearly akin to logic and mathematics. This we have done in the pursuit of publicity, in order to communicate what is communicable and to cover up the rest in a dark mantle of oblivion.

Space and time, however, as human beings know them, are not in reality so impersonal as science pretends. Theologians conceive God as viewing both space and time from without, impartially, and with a uniform awareness of the whole; science tries to imitate this impartiality with some apparent success, but the success is in part illusory. Human beings differ from the theologians' God in the fact that their space and time have a *here* and *now*. What is here and now is vivid, what is remote has a gradually increasing dimness. All our knowledge of events radiates from a space-time centre, which is the little region that we are occupying at the moment. "Here" is a vague term: in astronomical cosmology the Milky Way may count as "here", in the study of the Milky Way "here" is the solar system, in the study of the solar system "here" is the earth, in geography it is the town or district in which we live, in physiological studies of sensation it is the brain as opposed to the rest of the body. Larger "heres" always contain smaller ones as parts; all "heres" contain the brain of the speaker, or part of it. Similar considerations apply to "now".

Science professes to eliminate "here" and "now". When some event occurs on the earth's surface, we give its position in the space-time manifold by assigning latitude, longitude, and date. We have developed a technique which insures that all accurate observers with accurate instruments will arrive at the same estimate of latitude, longitude, and date. Consequently there is no longer anything personal in these estimates, in so far as we are content with numerical statements of which the meaning is not too closely investigated. Having arbitrarily decided that the longitude of Greenwich and the latitude of the equator are to be zero, other latitudes and longitudes follow. But what is "Greenwich"? This is hardly the sort of term that ought to occur in an impartial survey of the universe, and its definition is not mathematical. The best way to define "Greenwich" is to take a man to it and say: "Here is Greenwich." If some one else has already determined the latitude and longitude of the place where you are, "Greenwich" can be defined by its latitude and longitude relative to that place; it is, for example, so many degrees east and so many degrees north of New York. But this does not get rid of "here", which is now New York instead of Greenwich.

Moreover it is absurd to *define* either Greenwich or New York by its latitude and longitude. Greenwich is an actual place, inhabited by actual people, and containing buildings which ante-date its longitudinal pre-eminence. You can, of course, describe Greenwich, but there always might be another town with the same characteristics. If you want to be *sure* that your description applies to no other place, the only way is to mention its relation to some other place, for instance, by saying that it is so many miles down the Thames from London Bridge. But then you will have to define "London Bridge". Sooner or later you are faced with the necessity of defining some place as "here", and this is an egocentric definition, since the place in question is not "here" for everybody. There may be a way of escape from this con- clusion; at a later stage, we will resume the question. But there is no obvious or easy way of escape, and until one is found all determinations of latitude and longitude are infected with the subjectivity of "here". This means that, although different people assign the same latitude and longitude to a place, they do not, in ultimate analysis, attach the same meaning to the figures at which they arrive.

The common world in which we believe ourselves to live is a construction, partly scientific, partly pre-scientific. We perceive tables as circular or rectangular, in spite of the fact that a painter, to reproduce their appearance, has to paint ellipses or, non-rectangular quadrilaterals. We see a person as of about the same size whether he is two feet from us or twelve. Until our attention is drawn to the facts, we are quite unconscious of the corrections that experience has led us to make in interpreting sensible appearances. There is a long journey from the child who draws two eyes in a profile to the physicist who talks of electrons and protons, but throughout this journey there is one constant purpose: to eliminate the subjectivity of sensation, and substitute a kind of knowledge which can be the same for all percipients. Gradually the difference between what is sensed and what is believed to be objective grows greater; the child's profile with two eyes is still very like what is seen, but the electrons and protons have only a remote resemblance of logical structure. The electrons and protons, however, have the merit that they *may* be what actually exists where there are no sense-organs, whereas our immediate visual data, owing to their subjectivity, are almost certainly not what takes place in the physical objects that we are said to see.

The electrons and protons—assuming it scientifically correct to believe in them—do not depend for their existence upon being perceived; on the contrary, there is every reason to believe that they existed for countless ages before there were any percipients in the universe. But although perception is not needed for their existence, it is needed to give us a reason for believing in their existence. Hundreds of thousands of years ago, a vast and remote region emitted incredible numbers of photons, which wandered through the universe in all directions. At last a very few of them hit a photographic plate, in which they caused chemical changes which made parts of the plate look black instead of white when examined by an astronomer. This tiny effect upon a minute but highly educated organism is our only reason for believing in the existence of a nebula comparable in size, with the Milky Way.

The order for knowledge is the inverse of the causal order. In the order for knowledge, what comes first is the brief subjective experience of the astronomer looking at a pattern of black and white, and what comes last is the nebula, vast, remote, and belonging to the distant past.

In considering the reasons for believing in any empirical statement, we cannot escape from perception with all its personal limitations. How far the information which we obtain from this tainted source can be purified in the filter of scientific method, and emerge resplendently godlike in its impartiality, is a difficult question, with which we shall be much concerned. But there is one thing that is obvious from the start: only in so far as the initial perceptual datum is trustworthy can there be any reason for accepting the vast cosmic edifice of inference which is based upon it.

I am not suggesting that the initial perceptual datum must be accepted as indubitable; that is by no means the case. There are well-known methods of strengthening or weakening the force of individual testimony; certain methods are used in the law courts, somewhat different ones are used in science. But all depend upon the principle that *some* weight is to be attached to every piece of testimony, for it is only in virtue of this principle that a number of concordant testimonies are held to give a high probability. Individual percepts are the basis of all our knowledge, and no method exists by which we can begin with data which are public to many observers.

Chapter II

THE UNIVERSE OF ASTRONOMY

A STRONOMY is the oldest of the sciences, and the contemplation of the heavens, with their periodic regularities, gave men their first conceptions of natural law. But in spite of its age, astronomy is as vigorous as at any former time, and as important in helping us to form a just estimate of man's position in the universe.

When the Greeks began inventing astronomical hypotheses, the apparent motions of the sun and moon and planets among the fixed stars had already been observed for thousands of years by the Babylonians and Egyptians, who had also learned to predict lunar eclipses with certainty and solar eclipses with a considerable risk of error. The Greeks, like other ancient nations, believed the heavenly bodies to be gods, or at any rate each closely controlled by its own god or goddess. Some, it is true, questioned this opinion: Anaxagoras, in the time of Pericles, maintained that the sun was a red-hot stone and that the moon was made of earth. But for this opinion he was prosecuted and compelled to fly from Athens. It is very questionable whether either Plato or Aristotle was equally rationalistic. But it was not the most rationalistic among the Greeks who were the best astronomers; it was the Pythagoreans, to whom superstition suggested what happened to be good hypotheses.

The Pythagoreans, towards the end of the fifth century B.C., discovered that the earth is spherical; about a hundred years later, Eratosthenes estimated the earth's diameter correctly within about fifty miles. Heraclides of Pontus, during the fourth century, maintained that the earth rotates once a day and that Venus and Mercury describe orbits about the sun. Aristarchus of Samos, in the third century, advocated the complete Copernican system, and worked out a theoretically correct method of estimating the distances of the sun and moon. As regards the sun this result, it is true, was wildly wrong, owing to inaccuracy in his data; but a hundred years later Posidonius made an estimate which was about half of the correct figure. This extraordinarily vigorous advance, however, did not continue, and much of it was forgotten in the general decay of intellectual energy during later antiquity.

The cosmos, as it appears, for instance, in Plotinus, was a cosy and human little abode in comparison with what it has since become. The supreme deity regulated the whole, but each star was a subordinate deity, similar to a human being but in every way nobler and wiser. Plotinus finds fault with the Gnostics for believing that, in the created universe, there is nothing more worthy of admiration than the human soul. The beauty of the heavens, to him, is not only visual, but also moral and intellectual. The sun and moon and planets are exalted spirits, actuated by such motives as appeal to the philosopher in his best moments. He rejects with indignation the morose view of the Gnostics (and later of the Manicheans) that the visible world was created by a wicked Demiurge and must be despised by every aspirant to true virtue. On the contrary, the bright beings that adorn the sky are wise and good, and such as to console the philosopher amid the welter of folly and disaster that was overtaking the Roman Empire.

The medieval Christian cosmos, though less austere than that of the Manicheans, was shorn of some elements of poetic fancy that paganism had preserved to the end. The change, however, was not very great, for angels and archangels more or less took the place of the polytheists' celestial divinities. Both the scientific and the poetic elements of the medieval cosmos are set forth in Dante's *Paradiso*; the scientific elements are derived from Aristotle and Ptolemy. The earth is spherical, and at the centre of the universe; Satan is at the centre of the earth, and hell is an inverted cone of which he forms the apex. At the antipodes of Jerusalem is the Mount of Purgatory, at whose summit is the earthly paradise, which is just in contact with the sphere of the moon.

The heavens consist of ten concentric spheres, that of the moon being the lowest. Everything below the moon is subject to corruption and decay; everything from the moon upwards is indestructible. Above the moon, the spheres in their order are those of Mercury, Venus, the Sun, Mars, Jupiter, Saturn and the fixed stars, beyond which is the Primum Mobile. Last of all, above the Primum Mobile, is the Empyrean, which has no motion, and in which there are no times or places. God, the Aristotelian Unmoved Mover, causes the rotation of the Primum Mobile, which, in turn, communicates its motion to the sphere of the fixed stars, and so on downwards to the sphere of the moon. Nothing is said in Dante as to the sizes of the various spheres, but he is able to traverse them all in the space of twenty-four hours. Clearly the universe as he conceived it was somewhat minute by modern standards; it was also very recent, having been created a few thousand years ago. The spheres, which all had the earth at the centre, afforded the eternal abodes of the elect. The elect consisted of those baptized persons who had reached the required standard both in faith and works, together with the patriarchs and prophets who had foreseen the coming of Christ, and a very few pagans who, while on earth, had been miraculously enlightened.

It was against this picture of the universe that the pioneers of modern astronomy had to contend. It is interesting to contrast the commotion about Copernicus with the almost complete oblivion that befell Aristarchus. Cleanthes the Stoic had urged that Aristarchus should be prosecuted for impiety, but the Government was apathetic; perhaps if he had been persecuted, like Galileo, his theories might have won wider publicity. There were, however, other more important reasons for the difference between the posthumous fame of Aristarchus and that of Copernicus. In Greek times astronomy was an amusement of the idle rich—a very dignified amusement, it is true, but not an integrated part of the life of the community. By the sixteenth century, science had invented gunpowder and the mariner's compass, the discovery of America had shown the limitations of ancient geognosis, Catholic orthodoxy had begun to seem an obstacle to material progress, and the fury of obscurantist theologians made the men of science appear as heroic champions of a new wisdom. The seventeenth century, with the telescope, the science of dynamics, and the law of gravitation, completed the triumph of the scientific outlook, not only as the key to pure knowledge, but as a powerful means of economic progress. From this time onwards, science was recognized as a matter of social and not merely individual interest.

The theory of the sun and planets as a finished system was practically completed by Newton. As against Aristotle and the medieval philosophers it appeared that the sun, not the earth, is the centre of the solar system; that the heavenly bodies, left to themselves, would move in straight lines, not in circles; that in fact they move neither in straight lines nor in circles, but in ellipses; and that no action from outside is necessary to preserve their motion. But as regards the origin of the system Newton had nothing scientific to say; he supposed that at the Creation the planets had been hurled by the hand of God in a tangential direction, and had then been left by Him to the operation of the law of gravitation. Before Newton, Descartes had attempted a theory of the origin of the solar system, but his theory proved untenable. Kant and Laplace invented the nebular hypothesis, according to which the sun was formed by the condensation of a primitive nebula, and threw off the planets successively as a result of increasingly rapid rotation. This theory also proved defective, and modern astronomers incline to the view that the planets were caused by the passage of another star through the near neighbourhood of the sun. The subject remains obscure, but no one doubts that, by some mechanism, the planets came out of the sun.

The most remarkable astronomical progress in recent times has been in relation to the stars and the nebulae. The nearest of the fixed stars, Alpha Centauri, is at a distance of about 25×10^{12} miles, or $4 \cdot 2$ light-years. (Light travels 186,000 miles a second; a light-year is the distance it travels in a year.) The first determination of the distance of a star was in 1835; since then, by various ingenious methods, greater and greater distances have been computed. It is believed that the most distant object that can be detected with the most powerful telescope now in existence is about 500 million light-years away.

Something is now known of the general structure of the universe. The sun is a star in the galaxy, which is an assembly of about 300,000 million stars, about 150,000 light-years across and between 25,000 and 40,000 light-years thick. The total mass of the galaxy is about 160,000 million times the mass of the sun; the mass of the sun is about 2×10^{27} tons. The whole of this system is slowly rotating about its centre of gravity; the sun takes about 225 million years to complete its orbit round the milky way.

In the space beyond the milky way, other systems of stars, of approximately the same size as the milky way, are scattered at fairly regular intervals throughout the space that our telescopes can explore. These systems are called extra-galactic nebulae; it is thought that about 30 millions of them are visible, but the census is not yet complete. The average distance between two nebulae is about 2 million light-years. (Most of these facts are taken from Hubble, *The Realm of the Nebulae*, 1936.)

One of the oddest facts about the nebulae is that the lines in their spectra, with very few exceptions, are shifted towards the red, and that the amount of the shift is proportional to the distance of the nebula. The only plausible explanation is that the nebulae are moving away from us, and that the most distant ones are receding most quickly. At a distance of 135 million light-years, this velocity amounts to 14,300 miles per second (Hubble, Plate VIII, p. 118). At a certain distance, the velocity would become equal to the velocity of light, and the nebulae would therefore be invisible however powerful our telescopes might be.

The general theory of relativity has an explanation to offer of this curious phenomenon. The theory maintains that the universe is of finite size—not that it has an edge, outside which there is something which is not part of the universe, but that it is a three-dimensional sphere, in which the straightest possible lines return in time to their starting-point, as on the surface of the earth. The theory goes on to predict that the universe must be either contracting or expanding; it then uses the observed facts about the nebulae to decide for expansion. According to Eddington, the universe doubles in size every 1,300 million years or so. (*New Pathways in Science*, p. 210.) If this is true, the universe was once quite small, but will in time become rather large.

This brings us to the question of the ages of the earth and the stars and the nebulae. On grounds that are largely geological, the age of the earth is estimated at about 3,000 million years. The age of the sun and the other stars is still a matter of controversy. If, in the interior of a star, matter can be annihilated by transforming an electron and a proton into radiation, the stars may be several million million years old; if not, only a few thousand million. (H. Spencer Jones, *Worlds Without End*, p. 231.) On the whole, the latter view seems to be prevailing.

There is even some reason to think that the universe had a beginning in time; Eddington used to maintain that it began in about 90,000 million B.C. This is certainly more than the 4,004 in which our great-grandfathers believed, but it is still a finite period, and raises all the old puzzles as to what was going on before that date.

The net result of this summary survey of the astronomical

world is that, while it is certainly very large and very ancient, there are grounds—though as yet they are very speculative—for thinking that it is neither infinitely large nor infinitely old. The general theory of relativity professes to be able to tell us things about the universe as a whole, by means of an ingenious mixture of observation and reasoning. If this is valid—and I am by no means persuaded that it is—the increase of scale, both in space and time, which has hitherto characterized astronomy, has a limit, and one which we are within measurable distance of reaching. Eddington maintains that the circumference of the universe is of the order of 6,000 million light-years. (*New Pathways in Science*, p. 218.) If so, somewhat better telescopes should enable us to "grasp this sorry scheme of things entire". As we are beginning to see, we may before long be also able to "shatter it to bits". But I do not think we shall be able to "remould it nearer to the heart's desire".

Chapter III

THE WORLD OF PHYSICS

THE most advanced science in the present day, and the one which seems to throw the most light on the structure of the world, is physics. This science virtually begins with Galileo, but in order to appreciate his work it will be well to glance briefly at what was thought before his time.

The scholastics, whose views were in the main derived from Aristotle, thought that there were different laws for celestial and terrestrial bodies, and also for living and dead matter. They held that dead matter, left to itself, would gradually lose any motion it might have, at any rate in the terrestrial sphere. Everything living, according to Aristotle, had some kind of soul. The vegetable soul, possessed by all plants and animals, was only concerned with growth; the animal soul was concerned to cause movements. There were four elements, earth, water, air, and fire, of which earth and water were heavy, while air and fire were light. Earth and water had a natural downward motion, air and fire a natural upward motion. There was also, in the highest heavens, a fifth element, a kind of sublimated fire. There was no suggestion of one set of laws for all kinds of matter, and there was no science of changes in the movements of bodies.

Galileo—and in a lesser degree Descartes—introduced the fundamental concepts and principles which sufficed for physics until the present century. It appeared that the laws of motion are the same for all kinds of dead matter, and probably for living matter also. Descartes held that animals are automata, and that their movements could theoretically be calculated by using the same principles that govern a falling lump of lead. The view that all matter is homogeneous, and that its only scientifically important property is position in space, prevailed practically among physicists, at any rate as a working hypothesis. For theological reasons, human bodies were often (though not always) exempted from the rigid determinism to which physical laws seemed to lead. With this possible exception, scientific orthodoxy came to endorse Laplace's view, that a calculator possessed of sufficient mathematical ability, given the position and velocity and mass of every

29

particle in the universe at a given instant, could calculate the whole past and future of the physical world. If, as some thought, miracles occasionally intervened, these lay outside the purview of science, since they were in their very nature not subject to law. For this reason, even those who believed in miracles had no occasion to lapse from scientific rigour in their calculations.

Galileo introduced the two principles that did most to make mathematical physics possible: the law of inertia, and the parallelogram law. Something must be said about each of these.

The law of inertia, familiar as Newton's first law of motion, states, in Newton's language, that:

"Every body perseveres in its state of rest, or of uniform motion in a right line, unless it is compelled to change that state by forces impressed thereon."

The conception of "force", which was prominent in the work of Galileo and Newton, turned out to be superfluous, and was eliminated from classical dynamics during the nineteenth century. This necessitated a re-statement of the law of inertia. But let us first consider the law in relation to the beliefs prevailing before Galileo.

All terrestrial motions tend to slacken and finally stop. Bowls on even the smoothest bowling-green come to rest after a while; a stone thrown onto ice does not go on sliding for ever. The heavenly bodies, it is true, persist in their orbits, without any discoverable loss of velocity; but their motions are not rectilinear. According to the law of inertia, the retardation of the stone on ice, and the curvilinear orbits of the planets, are not to be explained by anything intrinsic in their own natures, but by the action of the environment.

This principle led to the possibility of regarding the physical world as a causally self-contained system. It soon appeared that in any dynamically independent system—such as the sun and planets are to a very near approximation—the amount of motion, or momentum, in every direction is constant. Thus a universe once in motion will remain in motion for ever, unless stopped by a miracle. Aristotle had thought that the planets needed gods to push them round their orbits, and that movements on earth could be spontaneously initiated by animals. The motions of matter, on this view, could only be accounted for by taking account of non-material causes. The law of inertia changed this, and made it

THE WORLD OF PHYSICS

possible to calculate the motions of matter by means of the laws of dynamics alone.

Technically, the principle of inertia meant that the causal laws of physics should be stated in terms of *acceleration*, i.e. a change of velocity in amount or direction or both. Uniform motion in a circle, which the ancients and the scholastics regarded as "natural" for the heavenly bodies, ceased to be so, since it required a continual change in the direction of motion. The departure from a straight line required a cause, which was found in Newton's law of gravitation.

Acceleration being the second differential of position with respect to time, it followed from the law of inertia that the causal laws of dynamics must be differential equations of the second order, though this form of statement could not be made until Newton and Leibniz had invented the infinitesimal calculus. Throughout all the modern changes in theoretical physics, this consequence of the law of inertia has stood firm. The fundamental importance of *acceleration* is perhaps the most permanent and the most enlightening of all Galileo's discoveries.

The parallelogram law, in Newtonian language, is concerned with what happens when a body is subject to two forces at once. It says that if a body is subject to two forces, one of which is measured, in direction and magnitude, by a line AB, and the other by a line BC, then the effect of their both acting at once is measured by the line AC. This amounts, roughly speaking, to saying that when two forces act simultaneously the effect is the same as if they acted successively. In technical language it means that the equations are linear, which greatly facilitates mathematical calculation.

The law may be interpreted as asserting the mutual independence of different causes acting simultaneously. Take, for example, the question of projectiles, in which Galileo was professionally interested. If the earth did not attract a projectile, it would, according to the law of inertia, continue to move horizontally with uniform velocity (neglecting the resistance of the air). If the projectile had no initial velocity, it would fall vertically with uniform acceleration. To determine where it will in fact be after (say) a second, we may suppose that it first moves horizontally with uniform velocity for a second, and then, starting from rest, falls vertically with uniform acceleration for a second.

31

When the forces to which a body is subject are not constant, the principle does not allow us to take each separately for a finite time, but if the finite time is short the result of taking each separately will be approximately right, and the shorter the time the more nearly right it will be, approaching complete rightness as a limit.

It must be understood that this law is purely empirical; there is no mathematical reason for its truth. It is to be believed in so far as there is evidence for it, and no further. In quantum mechanics it is not assumed, and there are phenomena which seem to show that it is not true in atomic occurrences. But in the physics of large-scale occurrences it remains true, and in classical physics it played a very important role.

From Newton to the end of the nineteenth century, the progress of physics involved no basically new principles. The first revolutionary novelty was Planck's introduction of the quantum constant h in the year 1900. But before considering quantum theory, which is chiefly important in connection with the structure and behaviour of atoms, a few words must be said about relativity, which involved a departure from Newtonian principles much slighter than that of quantum theory.

Newton believed that, in addition to matter, there is absolute space and absolute time. That is to say, there is a three-dimensional manifold of points and a one-dimensional manifold of instants, and there is a three-term relation involving matter, space, and time, namely the relation of "occupying" a point at an instant. In this view Newton agreed with Democritus and the other atomists of antiquity, who believed in "atoms and the void". Other philosophers had maintained that empty space is nothing, and that there must be matter everywhere. This was Descartes' opinion, and also that of Leibniz, with whom Newton (using Dr. Clarke as his mouthpiece) had a controversy on the subject.

Whatever physicists might hold as a matter of philosophy, Newton's view was implicit in the technique of dynamics, and there were, as he pointed out, empirical reasons for preferring it. If water in a bucket is rotated, it climbs up the sides, but if the bucket is rotated while the water is kept still, the surface of the water remains flat. We can therefore distinguish between rotation of the water and rotation of the bucket, which we ought not to be able to do if rotation were merely relative. Since Newton's time other arguments of the same sort have accumulated. Foucault's pendulum, the flattening of the earth at the poles, and the fact that bodies weigh less in low latitudes than in high ones, would enable us to infer that the earth rotates even if the sky were always covered with clouds; in fact, on Newtonian principles we can say that the rotation of the earth, not the revolution of the heavens, causes the succession of night and day and the rising and setting of the stars. But if space is purely relative, the difference between the statements "the earth rotates" and "the heavens revolve" is purely verbal: both must be ways of describing the same phenomena.

Einstein showed how to avoid Newton's conclusions, and make spatio-temporal position purely relative. But his theory of relativity did much more than this. In the special theory of relativity he showed that between two events there is a relation, which may be called "interval", which can be divided in many different ways into what we should regard as a spatial distance and what we should regard as a lapse of time. All these different ways are equally legitimate; there is not one way which is more "right" than the others. The choice between them is a matter of pure convention, like the choice between the metric system and the system of feet and inches.

It follows from this that the fundamental manifold of physics cannot consist of persistent particles in motion, but must consist of a four-dimensional manifold of "events". There will be three co-ordinates to fix the position of the event in space, and one to fix its position in time, but a change of co-ordinates may alter the time-co-ordinate as well as the space co-ordinates, and not only, as before, by a constant amount, the same for all events—as, for example, when dating is altered from the Mohammedan era to the Christian.

The general theory of relativity—published in 1915, ten years after the special theory—was primarily a geometrical theory of gravitation. This part of the theory may be considered firmly established. But it has also more speculative features. It contains, in its equations, what is called the "cosmical constant", which determines the size of the universe at any time. This part of the theory, as I mentioned before, is held to show that the universe is growing either continually larger or continually smaller. The shift towards the red in the spectra of distant nebulae is held to show that they are moving away from us with a velocity proportional to their distance from us. This leads to the conclusion that the universe is expanding, not contracting. It must be understood that, according to this theory, the universe is finite but unbounded, like the surface of a sphere, but in three dimensions. All this involves non-Euclidean geometry, and is apt to seem mysterious to those whose imagination is obstinately Euclidean.

Two kinds of departure from Euclidean space are involved in the general theory of relativity. On the one hand, there are what may be called the small-scale departures (where the solar system, e.g., is regarded as "small"), and on the other hand the large-scale departure of the universe as a whole. The small-scale departures occur in the neighbourhood of matter, and account for gravitation. They may be compared to hills and valleys on the surface of the earth. The large-scale departure may be compared with the fact that the earth is round and not flat. If you start from any point on the earth's surface and travel as straight as you can, you will ultimately return to your starting-point. So, it is held, the straightest line possible in the universe will ultimately return into itself. The analogy with the surface of the earth fails in that the earth's surface is two-dimensional and has regions outside it, whereas the spherical space of the universe is three-dimensional and has nothing outside it. The present circumference of the universe is between 6,000 and 60,000 million light-years, but the size of the universe is doubled about every 1,300 million years. All this, however, must still be regarded as open to doubt.

According to Professor E. A. Milne,[1] there is a great deal more that is questionable in Einstein's theory. Professor Milne holds that there is no need to regard space as non-Euclidean, and that the geometry we adopt can be decided entirely by motives of convenience. The difference between different geometries, according to him, is a difference in language, not in what is described. Where physicists disagree it is rash for an outsider to have an opinion, but I incline to think that Professor Milne is very likely to be in the right.

Quantum theory, in contrast to the theory of relativity, is mainly concerned with the smallest things about which knowledge is possible, namely atoms and their structure. During the nine-

[1] *Relativity Gravitation and World Structure.* By E. A. Milne. Oxford, 1935.

teenth century the atomic constitution of matter became well established, and it was found that the different elements could be placed in a series starting with hydrogen and ending with uranium. The place of an element in this series is called its "atomic number". Hydrogen has the atomic number 1, and uranium 92. There are two gaps in the series at present, so that the number of known elements is 90, not 92; but the gaps may be filled any day, as a number of previously existing gaps have been. In general, but not always, the atomic number increases with the atomic weight. Before Rutherford, there was no plausible theory as to the structure of atoms, or as to the physical properties which caused them to fall into a series. The series was determined by their chemical properties alone, and of these properties no physical explanation existed.

The Rutherford–Bohr atom, as it is called after its two inventors, had a beautiful simplicity, now, alas, lost. But although it has become only a pictorial approximation to the truth, it can still be used when extreme accuracy is not required, and without it the modern quantum theory could never have arisen. It is therefore still necessary to say something about it.

Rutherford gave experimental reasons for regarding an atom as composed of a nucleus carrying positive electricity surrounded by very much lighter bodies, called "electrons", which carried negative electricity, and revolved, like planets, in orbits about the nucleus. When the atom is not electrified, the number of planetary electrons is the atomic number of the element concerned; at all times, the atomic number measures the net positive electricity carried by the nucleus. The hydrogen atom consists of a nucleus and one planetary electron; the nucleus of the hydrogen atom is called a "proton". It was found that the nuclei of other elements could be regarded as composed of protons and electrons, the number of protons being greater than that of the electrons by the atomic number of the element. Thus helium, which is number 2, has a nucleus consisting of four protons and two electrons. The atomic weight is practically determined by the number of protons, since a proton has about 1,850 times the mass of an electron, so that the contribution of the electrons to the total mass is almost negligible.

It has been found that, in addition to electrons and protons, there are two other constituents of atoms, which are called "positrons" and "neutrons". A positron is just like an electron, except that it carries positive instead of negative electricity; it has the same mass as an electron, and probably the same size, in so far as either can be said to have a size. The neutron has no electricity, but has approximately the same mass as a proton. It seems not unlikely that a proton consists of a positron and a neutron. If so, there are three ultimate kinds of constituents in the perfected Rutherford–Bohr atom: the neutron, which has mass but no electricity, the positron, carrying positive electricity, and the electron, carrying an equal amount of negative electricity.

But we must now return to theories which ante-date the discovery of neutrons and positrons.

Bohr added to the Rutherford picture a theory as to the possible orbits of electrons, which, for the first time, explained the lines in the spectrum of an element. This mathematical explanation was almost, but not quite, perfect in the cases of hydrogen and positively electrified helium; in other cases the mathematics was too difficult, but no reason appeared to suppose that the theory would give wrong results if the mathematics could be worked out. His theory made use of Planck's quantum constant h, concerning which a few words must be said.

Planck, by studying radiation, proved that in a light or heat wave of frequency ν the energy must be $h.\nu$ or $2h.\nu$ or $3h.\nu$ or some other integral multiple of $h.\nu$, where h is "Planck's constant", of which the value in C.G.S. units is about $6 \cdot 55 \times 10^{-27}$, and the dimensions are those of action, i.e. energy $\times$ time. Before Planck, it had been supposed that the energy of a wave could vary continuously, but he showed conclusively that this could not be the case. The frequency of waves is the number that pass a given point in a second. In the case of light, the frequency determines the colour; violet light has the highest frequency, red light the lowest. There are other waves of just the same kind as light-waves, but not having the frequencies that cause visual sensations of colour. Higher frequencies than those of violet light are, in order, ultra-violet, X-rays and γ-rays; lower frequencies, infra-red and those used in wireless telegraphy.

When an atom emits light, it does so because it has parted with an amount of energy equal to that in the light-wave. If it emits light of frequency ν, it must, according to Planck's theory, have parted with an amount of energy measured by $h.\nu$ or some integral multiple of $h.\nu$. Bohr supposed that this happened through a planetary electron jumping from a larger to a smaller orbit; consequently the change of orbit must be such as to involve a loss of energy $h.v$ or some integral multiple of this amount. It followed that only certain orbits could be possible. In the hydrogen atom, there would be a smallest possible orbit, and the other possible ones would have 4, 9, 16, . . . times the radius of the minimum orbit. This theory, first propounded in 1913, was found to agree well with observation, and for a time won general acceptance. Gradually, however, it was found that there were facts which it could not explain, so that, though clearly a step on the way to the truth, it could no longer be accepted as it stood. The new and more radical quantum theory, which dates from 1925, is due in the main to two men, Heisenberg and Schrödinger.

In the modern theory there is no longer any attempt to make an imaginative picture of the atom. An atom only gives evidence of its existence when it emits energy, and therefore experimental evidence can only be of changes of energy. The new theory takes over from Bohr the doctrine that the energy in an atom must have one of a discrete series of values involving h; each of these is called an "energy level". But as to what gives the atom its energy the theory is prudently silent.

One of the oddest things about the theory is that it has abolished the distinction between waves and particles. Newton thought that light consisted of particles emitted by the source of the light; Huygens thought that it consisted of waves. The view of Huygens prevailed, and until recently was thought to be definitely established. But new experimental facts seemed to demand that light should consist of particles, which were called "photons". Per contra, De Broglie suggested that matter consists of waves. In the end it was shown that everything in physics can be explained either on the particle hypothesis or on the wave hypothesis. There is therefore no physical difference between them, and either may be adopted in any problem as may suit our convenience. But whichever is adopted, it must be adhered to; we must not mix the two hypotheses in one calculation.

In quantum theory, individual atomic occurrences are not determined by the equations; these suffice only to show that the possibilities form a discrete series, and that there are rules determining how often each possibility will be realized in a large number of cases. There are reasons for believing that this absence

37

of complete determinism is not due to any incompleteness in the theory, but is a genuine characteristic of small-scale occurrences. The regularity which is found in macroscopic phenomena is a statistical regularity. Phenomena involving large numbers of atoms remain deterministic, but what an individual atom may do in given circumstances is uncertain, not only because our knowledge is limited, but because there are no physical laws giving a determinate result.

There is another result of quantum theory, about which, in my opinion, too much fuss has been made, namely what is called Heisenberg's uncertainty-principle. According to this there is a theoretical limit to the accuracy with which certain connected quantities can be simultaneously measured. In specifying the state of a physical system, there are certain pairs of connected quantities; one such pair is position and momentum (or velocity, so long as the mass is constant), another is energy and time. It is of course a commonplace that no physical quantity .can be measured with complete accuracy, but it had always been supposed that there was no theoretical limit to the increase of accuracy obtainable by improved technique. According to Heisenberg's principle this is not the case. If we try to measure simultaneously two connected quantities of the above sort, any increase of accuracy in the measurement of one of them (beyond a certain point) involves a decrease in the accuracy of the measurement of the other. In fact, there will be errors in both measurements, and the product of these two errors can never be less than $h/2\pi$. This means that, if one could be completely accurate, the error in the other would have to be infinite. Suppose, for instance, that you wish to determine the position and velocity of a particle at a certain time: if you get the position very nearly right, there will be a large error in the velocity, and if you get the velocity very nearly right, there will be a large error as to the position. Similarly as regards energy and time: if you measure the energy very accurately, the time when the system has this energy will have a large margin of uncertainty, while if you fix the time very accurately the energy will become uncertain within wide limits. This is not a question of imperfection in our measuring apparatus, but is an essential principle of physics.

There are physical considerations which make this principle less surprising. It will be observed that h is a very small quantity, since it is of the order of 10^{-27}. Therefore wherever h is relevant we are concerned with matters involving very great minuteness. When an astronomer observes the sun, the sun preserves a lordly indifference to his proceedings. But when a physicist tries to find out what is happening to an atom, the apparatus by means of which he makes his observations is likely to have an effect upon the atom. Detailed considerations show that the sort of apparatus best suited for determining the position of an atom is likely to affect its velocity, while the sort of apparatus best suited for determining its velocity is likely to alter its position. Similar arguments apply to other pairs of related quantities. I do not think, therefore, that the uncertainty principle has the kind of philosophical importance that is sometimes attributed to it.

Quantum equations differ from those of classical physics in a very important respect, namely that they are not "linear". This means that when you have discovered the effect of one cause alone, and then the effect of another cause alone, you cannot find the effect of both together by adding the two previous effects. This has very odd results. Suppose, for instance, that you have a screen with a small slit, and you bombard it with particles; some of these will get through the slit. Suppose now you close the first slit and make a second; then some will get through the second slit. Now open both slits at once. You would think that the number getting through both slits would be the sum of the previous numbers, but this turns out not to be the case. The behaviour of the particles at one slit seems to be affected by the existence of the other slit. The equations are such as to predict this result, but it remains surprising. In quantum mechanics there is less independence of causes than in classical physics, and this adds greatly to the difficulty of the calculations.

Both relativity and quantum theory have had the effect of replacing the old conception of "mass" by that of "energy". "Mass" used to be defined as "quantity of matter"; "matter" was, on the one hand "substance" in the metaphysical sense, and on the other hand the technical form of the common-sense notion of "thing". "Energy" was, in its early stages, a state of "matter". It consisted of two parts, kinetic and potential. The kinetic energy of a particle is half the product of the mass and the square of the velocity. The potential energy is measured by the work that would have to be done to bring the particle to its present position from some standard position. (This leaves a constant undetermined, but that is of no consequence.) If you carry a stone from the ground to the top of a tower, it acquires potential energy in the process; if you drop it from the top, the potential energy is gradually transformed into kinetic energy during the fall. In any self-contained system, the total energy is constant. There are various forms of energy, of which heat is one; there is a tendency for more and more of the energy in the universe to take the form of heat. The conservation of energy first became a well-grounded scientific generalization when Joule measured the mechanical equivalent of heat.

Relativity theory and experiment both showed that mass is not constant, as had been held, but is increased by rapid motion; if a particle could move as fast as light, its mass would become infinite. Since all motion is relative, the different estimates of mass formed by different observers, according to their motion relative to the particle in question, are all equally legitimate. So far as this theory is concerned, however, there is still one estimate of mass which may be considered fundamental, namely the estimate made by an observer who is at rest relatively to the body whose mass is to be measured. Since the increase of mass with velocity is only appreciable for velocities comparable with that of light, this case covers practically all observations except those of α and β particles ejected from radio-active bodies.

Quantum theory has made a greater inroad upon the concept of "mass". It now appears that whenever energy is lost by radiation there is a corresponding loss of mass. The sun is held to be losing mass at the rate of four million tons a second. To take another instance: a helium atom, unelectrified, consists (in the language of Bohr's theory) of four protons and four electrons, while a hydrogen atom consists of one proton and one electron. It might have been supposed that, assuming this to be the case, the mass of a helium atom would be four times that of a hydrogen atom. This, however, is not the case: taking the mass of the helium atom as 4, that of the hydrogen atom is not 1, but 1·008. The reason is that energy is lost (by radiation) when four hydrogen atoms combine to form one helium atom—at least so we must suppose, for the process is not one which has ever been observed.

It is thought that the combination of four hydrogen atoms to

THE WORLD OF PHYSICS

form one atom of helium occurs in the interior of stars, and could be made to occur in terrestrial laboratories if we could produce temperatures comparable to those in the interior of stars. Almost all the loss of energy involved in building up elements other than hydrogen occurs in the transition to helium; in later stages the loss of energy is small. If helium, or any element other than hydrogen, could be artificially manufactured out of hydrogen, there would be in the process an enormous liberation of energy in the form of light and heat. This suggests the possibility of atomic bombs more destructive than the present ones, which are made by means of uranium. There would be a further advantage: the supply of uranium in the planet is very limited, and it is feared that it may be used up before the human race is exterminated, but if the practically unlimited supply of hydrogen in the sea could be utilized there would be considerable reason to hope that *homo sapiens* might put an end to himself, to the great advantage of the other less ferocious animals.

But it is time to return to less cheerful topics.

The language of Bohr's theory is still adequate for many purposes, but not for stating the fundamental principles of quantum physics. To state these principles, we must avoid all pictures of what goes on in an atom, and must abandon attempts to say what energy is. We must say simply: there is something quantitative, to which we give the name "energy"; this something is very unevenly distributed in space; there are small regions in which there is a great deal of it, which are called "atoms", and are those in which, according to older conceptions, there was matter; these regions are perpetually absorbing or emitting energy in forms that have a periodic "frequency". Quantum equations give rules determining the possible forms of energy emitted by a given atom, and the proportion of cases (out of a large number) in which each of the possibilities will be realized. Everything here is abstract and mathematical except the sensations of colour, heat, etc., produced by the radiant energy in the observing physicist.

Mathematical physics contains such an immense superstructure of theory that its basis in observation tends to be obscured. It is, however, an empirical study, and its empirical character appears most unequivocally where the physical constants are concerned. Eddington (*New Pathways in Science*, p. 230) gives the following list of the primitive constants of physics:

41

e, The charge of an electron,
m, The mass of an electron,
M, The mass of a proton,
h, Planck's constant,
c, The velocity of light,
G, The constant of gravitation,
λ, The cosmical constant.

These constants appear in the fundamental equations of physics, and it is usually (though not always) held that no one of them can be inferred from the others. Other constants, it is held, are theoretically deducible from these; sometimes the calculation can be actually made, sometimes it is as yet too difficult for the mathematicians. They represent the residuum of brute fact after as much as possible has been reduced to equations. (I am not including brute facts which are merely geographical.)

It should be observed that we are much more certain of the importance of these constants than we are of this or that interpretation of them. Planck's constant, in its brief history since 1900, has been represented verbally in various ways, but its numerical value has not been affected by such changes. Whatever may happen to quantum theory in the future, it is virtually certain that the constant h will remain important. Similarly as regards e and m, the charge and mass of an electron. Electrons may disappear completely from the fundamental principles of physics, but e and m are pretty certain to survive. In a sense it may be said that the discovery and measurement of these constants is what is most solid in modern physics.

Chapter IV

BIOLOGICAL EVOLUTION

WE have been considering hitherto either the universe as a whole, or characteristics in which all parts of the universe are alike. What is said in astronomy and physics, if true, is completely neutral, in the sense that it has no special relation to ourselves or to our spatio-temporal neighbourhood. But we must now turn our attention to more parochial matters. There are things that we can know about our own planet and its parasites which we cannot know about other regions. It may be that life exists elsewhere, or that, in some remote nebula, there is something which, while not life as we know it, is equally complex and equally different from the inorganic substances known to us. But although this may be the case, there is no positive reason to suppose that it is; all that we *know* about life we know from observations on or very near the surface of the earth. In the scientific study of life we are turning our backs on the magnificent vistas of astronomy, and abandoning the search for the minute and intimate knowledge of structure that is to be derived from atomic theory.

Mankind have found it more difficult to be scientific about life than about the heavenly bodies; in the time of Newton, such biology as existed was still deeply infected with superstition. The power of growth possessed by all living things, and the power of apparently spontaneous movement possessed by animals, seemed mysterious. The movements of animals had not the simple regularity of the movements of the heavenly bodies. Moreover we ourselves are alive, and everything that distinguishes us, whether from stocks and stones or from birds and brutes, must, it was thought, be noble, and too grand for the cold detachment of scientific investigation.

The Bible, while it was at first an obstacle to acceptance of the Copernican system, was soon found to allow of interpretations which made it possible for men of exemplary piety, like Newton himself, to accept the verbal inspiration of the Scriptures and also the teachings of astronomy. But in regard to biology it was more difficult to reconcile science and Genesis. If the Bible was accepted literally, the world was created in the year 4004 B.C. or thereabouts; each species of animal was separately created, and Adam and Eve had no parents. Man, alone among animals, was held to have an immortal soul, free will, moral responsibility, and the awful capacity for Sin. The gulf between him and the lower animals was, in consequence, unbridgeable; a creature half human and half simian was inconceivable. To the doctrines derived from Scripture were added others derived from Plato or Aristotle. Man alone was rational, that is to say, he could do sums and understand syllogisms. Every species was immutable, and was a copy of a divine pattern existing in heaven; this is the doctrine implied in Shakespeare's line:

> But in them nature's copy's not eterne.

When geology revealed extinct species, they were supposed to have perished in the flood. All now existing animals of any given species were descended from a pair in the ark, though some naturalists wondered how the sloths could have got from Mount Ararat to South America in the time, and why none of them had lingered *en route*. There was, however, an inconsistent theory that some animals were spontaneously generated by the action of the sun on slime.

As late as the middle of the nineteenth century, men of considerable scientific attainments were troubled by perplexities which now seem astonishing. It was held, for example, that before the Fall there were no beasts of prey; lions and tigers contentedly munched grass, while vultures regaled themselves with fruits and herbs. When geology seemed to show that carnivorous animals had existed before there were human beings, it became difficult to hold that all pain, whether of men or of animals, is a punishment for Adam's sin in eating the apple. Hugh Miller, a competent geologist of the middle of last century, while admitting the evidence, found it deeply disturbing. Geology, altogether, had a hard struggle. Buffon was condemned by the Sorbonne, and compelled to recant, because he maintained that the present mountains and valleys have been produced by "secondary causes", i.e. not directly by God's creative fiat.

The shortness of the time-scale allowed by Genesis was, at first, the most serious obstacle to scientific geology. Those who maintained that sedimentary rocks were produced by processes like those that we see in action at the present day were reduced to fantastic hypotheses, such as that all the chalk was deposited during the few weeks while the Flood was subsiding. Fossils were awkward for everybody; they suggested a greater antiquity than the orthodox could allow, but they afforded evidence for the Flood which so annoyed Voltaire that he invented utterly absurd theories to account for them.

At last it was agreed that the "days" in Genesis meant "ages", and on the basis of this compromise the geologists acquired a certain freedom to theorize. But even then Tennyson was still troubled:

> Are God and Nature then at strife,
> That Nature lends such evil dreams?
> So careful of the type she seems,
> So careless of the single life.
>
> So careful of the type? But no!
> From scarped cliff and quarried stone
> She cries: A thousand types are gone,
> I care for nothing, all must go.

All the earlier battles between science and theology in this field were overshadowed by the great battle over evolution, which began with the publication of Darwin's *Origin of Species* in 1859, and is not yet ended in America. But I shall say no more about these somewhat dusty controversies.

"Evolution" is a word which is often used with an ethical flavour, but science is not improved by an admixture of ethics. If "evolution" is to have no ethical implications, and yet is to be distinguished from mere change, I think it must mean increase of complexity and heterogeneity. In this sense there is reason to believe that there has been evolution also in the inanimate world. The nebular hypothesis, though it will not account for the development of the solar system, accounts admirably for the development of galaxies. At some period, there must have been vast clouds, which gradually condensed into systems of stars. The various elements must have been gradually built up, by processes of which we are now beginning to know something. The building up of chemical compounds is better understood. This process cannot be carried very far except at a moderate temperature, not

45

very different from the temperatures to which we are accustomed; at these temperatures, molecules of a very high degree of complexity can come into existence.

What distinguishes living from dead matter? Primarily, its chemical constitution and cell structure. It is to be supposed that its other characteristics follow from these. The most notable of these others are assimilation and reproduction, which, in the lowest forms of life, are not very sharply distinguished from each other. The result of assimilation and reproduction is that, given a small amount of living matter in a suitable environment, the total amount will quickly increase. A pair of rabbits in Australia quickly become many tons of rabbit. A few measles bacilli in a child quickly become many millions. A few seeds dropped by birds on Krakatoa after volcanic devastation quickly became luxuriant vegetation. So far as animals are concerned, this property of living matter is not fully exhibited, since animals require food that is already organic; but plants can transform inorganic substances into living matter. This is a purely chemical process, but it is one from which, presumably, most of the other peculiarities of living matter, considered as a whole, in some sense follow.

It is an essential feature of living matter that it is not chemically static, but is undergoing continual chemical change; it is, one may say, a natural chemical laboratory. Our blood undergoes one kind of change as it circulates round the body, and an opposite change when it comes in contact with air in the lungs. Food, from the moment of contact with the saliva, undergoes a series of elaborate processes, which end by giving it the chemical structure appropriate to some part of the body.

There is no reason, except the great complexity of the molecules that compose a living body, why such molecules should not be manufactured artificially; nor is there the slightest reason for supposing that, if they were manufactured, they would lack anything distinctive of living matter naturally generated. Aristotle thought that there was a vegetable soul in every plant or animal, and something similar has been widely believed by vitalists. But for this view there has come to be less and less plausibility as organic chemistry has progressed. The evidence, though not conclusive, tends to show that everything distinctive of living matter can be reduced to chemistry, and therefore ultimately to physics. The fundamental laws governing living matter are, in all likelihood, the very same that govern the behaviour of the hydrogen atom, namely the laws of quantum mechanics.

One of the characteristics of living organisms that have seemed mysterious is the power of reproduction. Rabbits generate rabbits, robins generate robins, and worms generate worms. Development from an embryo does not occur in the simplest forms of life; unicellular organisms merely grow till they reach a certain size, and then split. Something of this survives in sexual reproduction: part of the female body becomes an ovum, part of the male body a sperm, but this part is so much less than half that it *seems* qualitatively, and not merely quantitatively, different from the process of splitting into two equal halves. It is not in the splitting, however, that the novelty consists, but in the combination of male and female elements to make a new organism, which, in the natural process of growth, becomes, in time, like its adult parents.

As a consequence of the Mendelian theory, the process of heredity has come to be more or less understood. It appears that in the ovum and in the sperm there are a certain fairly small number of "genes", which carry the hereditary characteristics. The laws of heredity, like those of quantum theory, are discrete and statistical; in general, when grandparents differ in some character, we cannot tell which grandparent a given child will resemble, but we can tell the proportion, out of a large number, that will resemble this one or that as regards the character in question.

In general, the genes carry the parental character, but sometimes there are sports, or "mutants", which differ substantially from the parent. They occur naturally in a small proportion of cases, and they can be produced artificially by X-rays. It is these sports that give the best opportunity for evolution, i.e. for the development of new kinds of animals or plants by descent from old kinds.

The general idea of evolution is very old; it is already to be found in Anaximander (sixth century B.C.), who held that men are descended from fishes. But Aristotle and the Church banished such theories until the eighteenth century. Already Descartes, Kant, and Laplace had advocated a gradual origin for the solar system, in place of sudden creation followed by a complete absence of change. As soon as geologists had succeeded in determining the relative ages of different strata, it became evident from fossils that the more complex forms of life came into existence later than the simpler forms; moreover many forms that existed long ago have completely died out. It was found that the highly differentiated types to which we are accustomed have been preceded by intermediate types. The hypothesis of spontaneous generation formerly widely accepted, was experimentally disproved except as regards the hypothetical origin of the simplest forms of life. All this made it natural to suppose that the various animals and plants existing now or in the past were all descended from a common ancestry, and had become gradually differentiated as a result of variation in hereditable characters.

The doctrine of evolution, in the above sense, is now generally accepted.[1] But the particular motive force which Darwin suggested, namely the struggle for existence and the survival of the fittest, is not nearly so popular among biologists as it was fifty years ago. Darwin's theory was an extension, to the whole of life, of *laissez-faire* economics; now that this kind of economics, and the associated kind of politics, are out of fashion, people prefer other ways of accounting for biological changes. Where such changes have already occurred in part of a given stock, the Darwinian mechanism is still allowed to explain why one side gets the victory in a contest between the mutants and the conservatives. But whereas the earlier Darwinians thought that minute changes occurred, by selection, in each generation, some modern Mendelians lay stress on comparatively large changes occurring only occasionally, and their hope is to find a more or less mechanical theory as to the origin of such changes. The power of altering genes experimentally by X-rays gives hope of progress in this direction.

There are some who hold that the fundamental concept in biology should be that of "organism", and that, on this account, biology can never be reduced to chemistry and physics. This view is derived from Aristotle, and was encouraged by the Hegelian philosophy, though Hegel himself does not use the word "organism". It is, to my mind, an erroneous view, and one which, in so far as it prevails, is a barrier to scientific progress. But as it is still fairly widely advocated, it will be well to examine it.

Let us first try to state the logical essence of the theory. It holds that the body of an animal or plant is a unity, in the sense that

[1] The present state of scientific opinion on this subject may be studied in Julian Huxley's *Evolution: a Modern Synthesis*.

the laws governing the behaviour of the parts can only be stated by considering the place of the parts in the whole. An amputated limb, or an eye removed from its socket, no longer serves the purposes that it served when joined to a body: the limb cannot walk and the eye cannot see. This, of course, is true, but is not a peculiarity of living things: your wireless cannot tell you the news when the current is switched off. And properly speaking it is not the eye that sees; it is the brain, or the mind. The eye is merely a transmitter and transformer of radiant energy. But the "organic" view would hold that the way in which the eye deals with radiant energy cannot be understood without taking account of the rest of the body, and of the body as a single whole.

The opposite view, which I should regard as correct, would say that, to understand what an eye does, you need to know, in addition to its own structure, only the inflow and outflow of energy. The outer surface of the eye is exposed to certain influences from without, which set up processes that are transmitted from the inner surface of the eye to the nerves. The mechanistic view holds that, if an eye is separated from its body, but preserves its structure and chemical constitution, and is provided with artificial nerves to drain away the impulses received from incident light, it will behave as it would if it were still in its proper place. The experiment is one which cannot be fully carried out, because an isolated eye will soon decay, and because, owing to our lack of skill, artificial substitutes for nerves cannot have quite the same properties as actual nerves. But to an increasing extent similar experiments are becoming possible; for instance, frogs' hearts can be kept beating after being extracted from the frogs.

Speaking generally, scientific progress has been made by analysis and artificial isolation. It may be that, as quantum theory suggests, there are limits to the legitimacy of this process, but if it were not usually or approximately valid scientific knowledge would be impossible. It is therefore in any case prudent to adopt the mechanistic view as a working hypothesis, to be abandoned only where there is clear evidence against it. As regards biological phenomena, such evidence, so far, is entirely absent.

To sum up: Life is only *known* to occur on this planet; it is very improbable that it occurs on any other planet of the solar system, and it seems likely that the great majority of stars have no planets. Life, therefore, is almost certainly a very rare phenomenon. Even on the earth it is transitory: at first the earth was too hot, and in the end it will be too cold. Some highly conjectural dates are suggested in Spencer Jones's *Worlds Without End* (p. 19). The age of the earth is probably less than 3,000 million years; the beginnings of life may be placed at about 1,700 million years ago. Mammals began about 60 million years ago; anthropoid apes about 8 million, man about 1 million. It is probable that all forms of life on earth have evolved from unicellular organisms. How these were first formed we do not know, but their origin is no more mysterious than that of helium atoms. There is no reason to suppose living matter subject to any laws other than those to which inanimate matter is subject, and considerable reason to think that everything in the behaviour of living matter is theoretically explicable in terms of physics and chemistry.

Chapter V

THE PHYSIOLOGY OF SENSATION AND VOLITION

FROM the standpoint of orthodox psychology, there are two boundaries between the mental and physical, namely sensation and volition. "Sensation" may be defined as the first mental effect of a physical cause, "volition" as the last mental cause of a physical effect. I am not maintaining that these definitions will prove ultimately satisfactory, but only that they may be adopted as a guide in our preliminary survey. In the present chapter I shall not be concerned with either sensation or volition themselves, since they belong to psychology; I shall be concerned only with the physiological antecedents and concomitants of sensation, and with the physiological concomitants and consequents of volition. Before considering what science has to say, it will be worth while to look at the matter first from a common-sense point of view.

Suppose something is said to you, and in consequence you take some action; for example, you may be a soldier obeying the word of command. Physics studies the sound waves that travel through the air until they reach the ear; physiology studies the consequent event in the ear and nerves and brain, up to the moment when you hear the sound; psychology studies the sensation of hearing and the consequent volition; physiology then resumes the study of the process, and considers the outgoing chain of events from the brain to the muscles and the bodily movement expressing the volition; from that point onward, what happens is again part of the subject-matter of physics. The problem of the relation of mind and matter, which is part of the stock in trade of philosophy, comes to a head in the transition from events in the brain to the sensation, and from the volition to other events in the brain. It is thus a two-fold problem: how does matter affect mind in sensation, and how does mind affect matter in volition? I do not propose to consider this problem at this stage; I mention it now only to show the relevance of certain parts of physiology to questions which philosophy must discuss.

The physiological processes which precede and accompany

sensation are admirably set forth in Adrian's book *The Basis of Sensation: The Action of the Sense Organs* (London, 1928). As every one knows, there are two sorts of nerve fibres, those that carry messages into the brain, and those that carry messages out of it. The former alone are concerned in the physiology of sensation. Isolated nerves can be stimulated artificially by an electric current, and there is good reason to believe that the processes thus set up are essentially similar to those set up naturally in nerves that are still in place in a living body. When an isolated nerve is thus stimulated in an adequate manner, a disturbance is set up which travels along the nerve at a speed of about 220 miles an hour (100 metres a second). Each nerve consists of a bundle of nerve fibres running from the surface of the body to the brain or the spinal chord. The nerve fibres which carry messages to the brain are called "afferent", those which carry messages from the brain are called "efferent". A nerve usually contains both afferent and efferent fibres. Broadly speaking, the afferent fibres start from sense-organs and the efferent fibres end in muscles.

The response of a nerve fibre to a stimulus is of what is called the "all-or-nothing" type, like the response of a gun to pressure on the trigger. A slight pressure on the trigger produces no result, but a pressure which is sufficiently great produces a specific result which is the same however great the pressure may be (within limits). Similarly when a nerve fibre is stimulated very slightly, or for a very brief period (less than ·00001 of a second), there is no result, but when the stimulus is sufficient a current travels along the nerve fibre for a very brief period (a few thousandths of a second), after which the nerve fibre is "tired" and will not transmit another current until it is rested. At first, for two or three thousandths of a second, the nerve fibre is completely refractory; then it recovers gradually. During the period of recovery a given stimulus produces a smaller response, and one which travels more slowly. Recovery is complete after about a tenth of a second. The result is that a constant stimulus does not produce a constant state of excitement in the nerve fibres, but a series of responses with quiescent periods between. The messages that reach the brain are, as Adrian puts it, like a stream of bullets from a machine gun, not like a continuous stream of water.

It is supposed that in the brain, or the spinal column, there is a converse mechanism which reconverts the discrete impulses into a continuous process, but this, so far, is purely hypothetical.

Owing to the discontinuous nature of the response to a stimulus, the response will be exactly the same to a constant stimulus as to one which is intermittent with a frequency adapted to the period of recovery in the nerve. It would seem to follow that there can be no means of knowing whether the stimulus is constant or intermittent. But this is not altogether true. Suppose, for instance, that you are looking at a bright spot of light: if you could keep your eyes absolutely fixed, your sensations would be the same if the light flickered with appropriate rapidity as they would be if the light were steady. But in fact it is impossible to keep the eyes quite still, and therefore fresh unfatigued nerves are perpetually being brought into play.

A remarkable fact, which might seem to put a limit on the informative value of sensations, is, that the response of the nerve fibre is the same to any stimulus of sufficient strength and duration: there is just one message, and only one, that a given nerve fibre can transmit. But consider the analogy of a typewriter: if you press a given letter, only one result occurs, and yet the typewriter as a whole can transmit any information, however complicated.

The mechanism of the efferent nerve fibres appears to be just the same as that of the afferent nerve fibres; the messages that travel from the brain to the muscles have the same jerky character as those that travel from the sense-organs to the brain.

But the most interesting question remains: what goes on in the brain between the arrival of a message by the afferent nerves and the departure of a message by the efferent nerves? Suppose you read a telegram saying "all your property has been destroyed in an earthquake", and you exclaim "heavens! I am ruined". We feel, rightly or wrongly, that we know the psychological links, after a fashion, by introspection, but everybody is agreed that there must also be physiological links. The current brought into the vision centre by the optic nerve must pass thence to the speech centre, and then stimulate the muscles which produce your exclamation. How this happens is still obscure. But it seems clear that, from a physiological point of view, there is a unitary process from the physical stimulus to the muscular response. In man this process may be rendered exceedingly complex by the operation of acquired habits, especially language habits, but in some less highly organized animals the process is simpler and less difficult to study; the reason why the moth approaches the flame, for example, is fairly well understood in physiological terms.

This raises a question of great interest, namely: is the process in the brain, which connects the arrival of the sensory stimulus with the departure of the message to the muscles, completely explicable in physical terms? Or is it necessary to bring in "mental" intermediaries, such as sensation, deliberation, and volition? Could a superhuman calculator, with sufficient knowledge of the structure of a given brain, predict the muscular response to a given stimulus by means of the laws of physics and chemistry? Or is the intervention of mind an essential link in connecting a physical antecedent (the stimulus) with a physical consequent (a bodily movement)?

Until more is known about the brain than is known at present, it will not be possible to answer this question confidently in either sense. But there are already some grounds, though not conclusive ones, for regarding what might be called the materialist answer as the more probable one. There are reflexes, where the response is automatic, and not controlled by volition. From unconditioned reflexes, by the law of habit, conditioned reflexes arise, and there is every reason to regard habit as physiologically explicable. Conditioned reflexes suffice to explain a great part of human behaviour; whether there is a residue that cannot be so explained must remain, for the present, an open question.

At a later stage I shall maintain that there is no such gulf between the mental and the physical as common sense supposes. I shall also maintain that, even if the physiological causal chain from sense-organ to muscle can be set forth in terms which ignore the psychological occurrences in the middle of the chain, that will not prove that volitions are not "causes" in the only valid sense of the word "cause". But both of these contentions require considerable argument and elucidation. For the present, I will only add a few words from the standpoint of scientific common sense.

If—as seems likely—there is an uninterrupted chain of purely physical causation throughout the process from sense-organ to muscle, it follows that human actions are determined in the degree to which physics is deterministic. Now physics is only deterministic as regards macroscopic occurrences, and even in regard to them it asserts only very high probability, not certainty. It might be that, without infringing the laws of physics, intelligence could make improbable things happen, as Maxwell's demon would have defeated the second law of thermo-dynamics by opening the trap-door to fast-moving particles and closing it to slow-moving ones.

On these grounds it must be admitted that there is a bare possibility—no more—that, although occurrences in the brain do not infringe the laws of physics, nevertheless their outcome is not what it would be if no psychological factors were involved. I say there is no more than a bare possibility for several reasons. In the first place, the hypothesis supposes only the microscopic laws preserved, not the macroscopic laws. But the evidence for the macroscopic laws is better than the evidence for the microscopic laws, and very strong grounds would be needed to justify a belief that on some occasion they had failed. In the second place, all the occurrences which illustrate the connection of mind and matter are macroscopic: a volition, for example, results in a perceptible bodily movement, not in a mere atomic change. In the third place, the study of processes in the nerves and brain, so far, has shown physical causation wherever adequate observation was possible: the region as to which there is still ignorance is one where very minute phenomena are concerned, and where observation is very difficult. There is therefore, so far, not the smallest positive reason for supposing that there is anything about physical processes in the brain that involves different macroscopic laws from those of the physics of inanimate matter.

Nevertheless, for those who are anxious to assert the power of mind over matter it is possible to find a loophole. It may be maintained that one characteristic of living matter is a condition of unstable equilibrium, and that this condition is most highly developed in the brains of human beings. A rock weighing many tons might be so delicately poised on the summit of a conical mountain that a child could, by a gentle push, send it thundering down into any of the valleys below; here a tiny difference in the initial impulse makes an enormous difference to the result. Perhaps in the brain the unstable equilibrium is so delicate that the difference between two possible occurrences in one atom suffices to produce macroscopic differences in the movements of muscles. And since, according to quantum physics, there are no physical laws to determine which of several possible transitions a given atom will undergo, we may imagine that, in a brain, the choice between possible transitions is determined by a psychological cause called "volition". All this is *possible*, but no more than possible; there is not the faintest positive reason for supposing that anything of the sort actually takes place.

On the evidence as it exists the most probable hypothesis is that, in the chain of events from sense-organ to muscle, everything is determined by the laws of macroscopic physics. To return to our previous illustration of the man who reads a telegram and exclaims "I am ruined": it seems probable that, if you had a sufficiently minute knowledge of his brain-structure, and if you were a sufficiently good mathematician, you could foretell that when the shapes making the message, on the telegram came into his field of vision they would set up a process ending in certain movements in his mouth, to wit, those producing the sounds which we represent in writing as "I am ruined". It is here assumed that you could make this prophecy without knowing English; it should not be necessary for you to know the meaning either of the telegram or of his exclamation. The difference between a man knowing English and a man not knowing it should, on the physiological side, consist in the presence in one case, and absence in the other, of connections between the afferent nerves when stimulated by the hearing or reading of English words, and the efferent nerves producing the appropriate response. This difference we suppose visible to a hypothetical observer without his having to know the "meaning" either of the stimulus or of the response.

This hypothesis, it must be admitted, does not seem very plausible, and I am far from asserting dogmatically that it is true. The most that can legitimately be asserted, in my opinion, is that it is the right working hypothesis for a man investigating the physiological concomitants of sensation and volition. In so far as it is true, it may help him to make discoveries; if, at some point, it is false, its falsehood is most likely to be discovered by means of experiments suggested by the assumption of its truth. In so far as the hypothesis is true, physiology is a science independent of psychology; if at any point it is false, physiology ceases to be autonomous. As a matter of practical policy, the physiologist does well to assume that his science is autonomous so long as no evidence to the contrary has been discovered.

Chapter VI

THE SCIENCE OF MIND

PSYCHOLOGY as a science has suffered from being entangled with philosophy, and even, until recent times, with theology. The distinction between mind and matter, which was not drawn sharply by the pre-Socratics, became emphatic in Plato, in whom it was connected with religion. Christianity took over this aspect of Platonism, and made it the basis of much theological dogma. Soul and body were different substances; the soul was immortal, while the body decayed at death, though at the resurrection we should acquire a new, incorruptible body. It was the soul that sinned, and that suffered eternal punishment as the result of the Divine justice, or enjoyed eternal bliss as the result of the Divine mercy. The existence of two sorts of substance, material and mental, was accepted by all the leading scholastics; orthodoxy demanded matter just as much as mind, since Christ's Body was required for the dogma of transubstantiation. Gradually the distinction of soul and body, which was at first a recondite metaphysical subtlety, became a part of accepted common sense, until, in our day, it is only a few metaphysicians who dare to question it.

The Cartesians increased the absoluteness of the distinction, by denying all interaction between mind and matter. But their dualism was succeeded by Leibniz's monadology, according to which all substances are souls, and what we call "matter" is only a confused perception of many souls. After him Berkeley, for quite other reasons, also denied the existence of matter, and so did—for yet other reasons—Fichte and Hegel. Meanwhile, especially in eighteenth-century France, there were materialists who denied the existence of the soul while upholding the existence of material substance. Hume alone, among the great philosophers, denied substance altogether, and thus paved the way for modern discussions of the distinction between the mental and the physical.

For my part, before attempting a metaphysical discussion of mind and matter, I should prefer to investigate the distinction between the science of psychology and the science of physics. It is clear that they are different sciences, since in every university

57

they are taught by different men. What physicists have to teach is fairly clear, but what have the psychologists to teach?

There are those among psychologists who take a view which really denies to psychology the status of a separate science. According to this school, psychology consists in the study of human and animal behaviour, and the only thing that distinguishes it from philosophy is its interest in the organism as a whole. The observations upon which the psychologist must rely, according to this view, are such as a man might make on animals other than himself; there is no science, say the adherents of this school, which has data that a man can only obtain by observation of himself. While I admit the importance of what has been learnt by studying behaviour, I cannot accept this view. There are—and I am prepared to maintain this dogmatically—many kinds of events that I can observe when they happen to me, but not when they happen to any one else. I can observe my own pains and pleasures, my perceptions, my desires, my dreams. Analogy leads me to believe that other people have similar experiences, but this is an inference, not an observation. The dentist does not feel my toothache, though he may have admirable inductive grounds for believing that I do.

This suggests a possible definition of psychology, as the science of those occurrences which, by their very nature, can only be observed by one person. Such a definition, however, unless somewhat limited, will turn out to be too wide in one direction, while too narrow in another. When a number of people observe a public event, such as the bursting of a rocket or a broadcast by the Prime Minister, they do not all see or hear exactly the same thing: there are differences due to perspective, distance from the source of the sight or sound, defects in the sense-organs, and so on. Therefore if we were to speak with pedantic accuracy, we should have to say that everything that can be observed is private to one person. There is often, however, such a close similarity between the simultaneous percepts of different people that the minute differences can, for many purposes, be ignored; we then say that they are all perceiving the same occurrence, and we place this occurrence in a public world outside all the observers. Such occurrences are the data of physics, while those that have not this social and public character supply (so I suggest) the data of psychology.

According to this view, a datum for physics is something abstracted from a system of correlated psychological data. When a crowd of people all observe a rocket bursting, they will ignore whatever there is reason to think peculiar and personal in their experience, and will not realize without an effort that there is any private element in what they see. But they can, if necessary, become aware of these elements. One part of the crowd sees the rocket on the right, one on the left, and so on. Thus when each person's perception is studied in its fullness, and not in the abstract form which is most convenient for conveying information about the outside world, the perception becomes a datum for psychology.

But although every physical datum is derived from a system of psychological data, the converse is not the case. Sensations resulting from a stimulus within the body will naturally not be felt by other people; if I have a stomach-ache I am in no degree surprised to find that others are not similarly afflicted. There are afferent nerves from the muscles, which cause sensations when the muscles are used; these sensations, naturally, are only felt by the person concerned. It is only when the stimulus is outside the body of the percipient, and not always even then, that the sensation is one of a system which together constitutes one datum for physics. If a fly is crawling on your hand, the visual sensations that it causes are public, but the tickling is private. Psychology is the science which deals with private data, and with the private aspects of data which common sense regards as public.

To this definition a fundamental objection is raised by a certain school of psychologists, who maintain that "introspection" is not a valid scientific method, and that nothing can be scientifically known except what is derived from public data. This view seems to me so absurd that if it were not widely held I should ignore it; but as it has become fashionable in various circles I shall state my reasons for rejecting it.

To begin with, we need a more precise definition of "public" and "private" data. "Public" data, for the purpose of those who reject introspection, are not only data which in fact are shared by other observers, but also those which might be so shared given suitable circumstances. Robinson Crusoe, on this view, is not being unscientifically introspective when he describes the crops he raised, although there is no other observer to confirm his narrative, for its later parts are confirmed by Man Friday, and its earlier parts might have been. But when he relates how he became persuaded that his misfortunes were a punishment for his previous sinful life, he is either saying something meaningless or telling what words he would have uttered if he had had any one to speak to—for what a man says is public, but what he thinks is private. To maintain that what he says expresses his thought is, according to this school, to say something not scientifically verifiable and therefore something which science should not say. To attempt—as Freud did—to make a science of dreams is a mistake; we cannot know what a man dreams, but only what he says he dreams. What he says he dreams is part of physics, since the saying consists of movements of lips and tongue and throat; but it is a wanton assumption to suppose that what he says in professing to relate his dream expresses an actual experience.

We shall have to define a "public" datum as one which *can* be observed by many people, provided they are suitably placed. They need not all observe it at once, provided there is reason to think that there has been no change meanwhile: two people cannot look down a microscope at the same time, but the enemies of introspection do not mean to exclude data obtained by means of microscopes. Or consider the fact that, if you press one eyeball upwards, everything looks double. What is meant by saying that things "look" double? This can only be interpreted by distinguishing between the visual perception and the physical fact, or else by a subterfuge. You may say: "When I say that Mr. A. is seeing double, I say nothing about his perceptions; what I say means: 'If Mr. A. is asked, he will *say* he is seeing double'." Such an interpretation makes it meaningless to inquire whether Mr. A. is speaking the truth, and impossible to discover what it is that he thinks he is asserting.

Dreams are perhaps the most indubitable example of facts which can only be known by means of private data. When I remember a dream I can relate it, either truly or with embellishments; I can know which I am doing, but others seldom can. I knew a Chinese lady who, after a few lessons in psycho-analysis, began to have perfect text-book dreams; the analyst was delighted, but her friends were sceptical. Although no one except the lady could be sure of the truth, I maintain that the fact as to what she had dreamed was just as definitely such-and-such rather than so-and-so as in the case of a physical phenomenon.

We shall have to say: A "public" datum is one which generates similar sensations in all percipients throughout a certain space-time region, which must be considerably larger than the region occupied by one human body throughout (say) half a second— or rather, it is one which would generate such sensations if suitably placed percipients were present (this is to allow for Robinson Crusoe's crops).

This distinction between public and private data is one which it is difficult to make precise. Roughly speaking, sight and hearing give public data, but not always. When a patient is suffering from jaundice everything looks yellow, but this yellowness is private. Many people are liable to a buzzing in the ears which is sub-jectively indistinguishable from the hum of telegraph wires in a wind. The privacy of such sensations is only known to the percipient through the negative testimony of other people. Touch gives public data in a sense, since different people can successively touch the same object. Smells can be so public as to become grounds of complaint to the sanitary authority. Tastes are public in a lesser degree, for, though two people cannot eat the same mouthful, they can eat contiguous portions of the same viand; but the curate's egg shows that this method is not quite reliable. It is, however, sufficiently reliable to establish a public distinction between good cooks and bad ones, though here introspection plays an essential part, for a good cook is one who causes pleasure to most consumers, and the pleasure of each is purely private.

I have kept this discussion on a common-sense level, but at a later stage I shall resume it, and try to probe more deeply into the whole question of private data as a basis for science. For the present I am content to say that the distinction between public and private data is one of degree, that it depends upon testimony which bears witness to the results of introspection, that physiology would lead to the expectation that sensations caused by a stimulus inside a human body would be private, and, finally, that many of the facts of which each one of us is most certain are known to us by means private to ourselves. Do you like the smell of rotten eggs? Are you glad the war is over? Have you a toothache? These questions are not difficult for you to answer, but no one else can answer them except by inferences from your behaviour, including your testimony.

I conclude, therefore, that there is knowledge of private data, and that there is no reason why there should not be a science of them. This being granted, we can now inquire what psychology in fact has to say.

There is, to begin with, a matter of which the importance is often overlooked, and that is the correlation of physical occurrences with sensation. Physicists and astronomers base their assertions as to what goes on in the outer world upon the evidence of the senses, especially the sense of sight. But not a single one of the occurrences that we are told take place in the physical world is a sensation; how, then, can sensations confirm or confute a physical theory? Let us take an illustration belonging to the infancy of science. It was early discovered that an eclipse of the sun is due to the interposition of the moon, and it was found that eclipses could be predicted. Now what was directly verified when an eclipse occurred was a certain sequence of expected sensations. But the development of physics and physiology has gradually caused a vast gulf between the sensations of an astronomer watching an eclipse and the astronomical fact which he infers. Photons start from the sun, and when the moon is not in the way some of them reach an eye, where they set up the kind of complicated process that we considered in the last chapter; at last, when the process reaches the astronomer's brain, the astronomer has a sensation.

The sensation can only be evidence of the astronomical fact if laws are known connecting the two, and the last stage in these laws must be one connecting stimulus and sensation, or connecting occurrences in the optic nerve or the brain with sensation. The sensation, it should be observed, is not at all like the astronomical fact, nor are the two *necessarily* connected. It would be possible to supply an artificial stimulus causing the astronomer to have an experience subjectively indistinguishable from what we call "seeing the sun". And at best the resemblance between the sensation and the astronomical fact cannot be closer than that between a gramophone record and the music that it plays, or between a library catalogue and the books that it enumerates. It follows that, if physics is an empirical science, whose statements can be confirmed or confuted by observation, then physics must be supplemented by laws connecting stimulus and sensation.

Now such laws belong to psychology. Therefore what is empirically verifiable is not pure physics in isolation, but physics plus a department of psychology. Psychology, accordingly, is an essential ingredient in every part of empirical science.

So far, however, we have not inquired whether there are any laws that connect one mental event with another. The laws of correlation so far considered have been such as connect a physical stimulus with a mental response; what we have now to consider is whether there are any causal laws which are entirely within one mind. If there are, psychology is to that extent an autonomous science. The association of ideas, as it appears for example in Hartley and Bentham, was a law of this kind, but the conditioned reflex and the law of habit, which have taken its place, are primarily physiological and only derivatively psychological, since association is thought to be caused by the creation of paths in the brain connecting one centre with another. We may still state the association of ideas in purely psychological terms, but when so stated it is not a law as to what always happens, but only as to what is apt to happen. It has not therefore the character that science hopes to find in a causal law, or at least used to hope for before the rise of quantum theory.

The same thing may be said of psycho-analysis, which aims at discovering purely mental causal laws. I do not know of any psycho-analytic law which professes to say what will *always* happen in such and such circumstances. When a man, for example, suffers from claustrophobia, psycho-analysis will discover this or that past experience which is held to explain his trouble; but many people will have had the same experience without the same result. The experience in question, accordingly, though it may well be *part* of the cause of the phobia, cannot be its *whole* cause. We cannot, this being the case, find in psychoanalysis any examples of purely psychical causal laws.

In the last chapter we suggested, as a probable hypothesis, the view that all bodily behaviour is theoretically explicable in physical terms, without taking any account of the mental concomitants of physiological occurrences. This hypothesis, it should be observed, in no way decides our present question. If A and B are two events in the brain, and if A causes B, then if *a* is a mental concomitant of A, and *b* of B, it will follow that *a* causes *b*, which is a purely mental causal law. In fact, causal laws are not of the simple form "A causes B", but in their true form the principle remains the same.

Although, at present, it is difficult to give important examples of really precise mental causal laws, it seems pretty certain, on a common-sense basis, that there are such laws. If you tell a man that he is both a knave and a fool, he will be angry; if you inform your employer that he is universally regarded as a swindler and a bloodsucker, he will invite you to seek employment elsewhere. Advertising and political propaganda supply a mass of materials for the psychology of belief. The feeling one has in a novel or a play as to whether the behaviour of the characters is "right" is based upon unformulated knowledge of mental causality, and so is shrewdness in handling people. In such cases, the knowledge involved is pre-scientific, but it could not exist unless there were scientific laws which could be ascertained by sufficient study.

There are a certain number of genuine causal laws of the kind in question, though so far they are mostly concerned with matters that have no great intrinsic interest. Take, for example, after-images: you look fixedly at a bright red object, and then shut your eyes; you see first a gradually fading red image, and then a green image, of approximately the same shape. This is a law for which the evidence is purely introspective. Or again, take a well-known illusion:

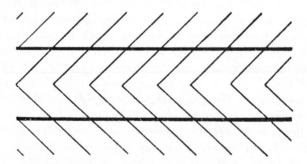

In the figure the two horizontal lines are parallel, but they look as if they approached each other towards the right. This again is a law for which the evidence is purely introspective. In both cases there are physiological explanations, but they do not invalidate the purely psychological laws.

I conclude that, while some psychological laws involve physiology, others do not. Psychology is a science distinct from physics and physiology, and in part independent of them. All the data of physics are also data of psychology, but not vice versa; data belonging to both are made the basis of quite different inferences in the two sciences. Introspection is valid as a source of data, and is to a considerable extent amenable to scientific controls.

There is much in psychology that is genuinely scientific although it lacks quantitative precision. Take, for example, the analysis of our spatial perceptions, and the building up of the common-sense notion of space from its sensational foundations. Berkeley's theory of vision, according to which everything looks flat, is disproved by the stereoscope. The process by which we learn in infancy to touch a place that we see can be studied by observation. So can volitional control: a baby a few months old can be watched learning with delight to move its toes at will, instead of having to look on passively while they wriggle in purely reflex movements. When, in later life, you acquire some skill, such as riding a bicycle, you find yourself passing through stages: at first you will certain movements of your own body, in the hope that they will cause the desired movements of the bicycle, but afterwards you will the movements of the bicycle directly, and the necessary movements of your body result automatically. Such experiences throw much light on the psychology of volition.

Much psychology is involved in connecting sensory stimuli with the beliefs to which they give rise. I am thinking of such elementary occurrences as thinking "there's a cat" when certain coloured patches in motion pass across your field of vision. It is obvious that the same sensory stimulus could be caused otherwise than by a cat, and your belief would then be false. You may see a room reflected in a mirror, and think that it is "real". By studying such occurrences we become aware that a very large part of what we think we perceive consists of habits caused by past experience. Our life is full of expectations of which, as a rule, we only become aware when they are disappointed. Suppose you see half of a horse that is just coming round a corner; you may be very little interested, but if the other half proved to be cow and not horse you would experience a shock of surprise which would be almost unendurable. Yet it must be admitted that such an occurrence is logically possible.

The connection of pleasure and pain and desire with habit-formation can be studied experimentally. Pavlov, whose work nowhere appeals to introspection, put a dog in front of two doors, on one of which he had drawn an ellipse and on the other a circle. If the dog chose the right door he got his dinner; if he chose the wrong one he got an electric shock. Thus stimulated, the dog's progress in geometry was amazingly rapid. Pavlov gradually made the ellipse less and less eccentric, but the dog still distinguished correctly, until the ratio of minor to major axis was reduced to 8: 9, when the poor beast had a nervous breakdown. The utility of this experiment in connection with schoolboys and criminals is obvious.

Or, again, take the question: why do we believe what we do? In former times, philosophers would have said it was because God had implanted in us a natural light by which we knew the truth. In the early nineteenth century they might have said it was because we had weighed the evidence and found a preponderance on one side. But if you ask a modern advertiser or political propagandist he will give you a more scientific and more depressing answer. A large proportion of our beliefs are based on habit, conceit, self-interest, or frequent iteration. The advertiser relies mainly on the last of these, but if he is clever he combines it skilfully with the other three. It is hoped that by studying the psychology of belief, those who control propaganda will in time be able to make anybody believe anything. Then the totalitarian State will become invincible.

In regard to human knowledge there are two questions that may be asked: first, what do we know? and second, how do we know it? The first of these questions is answered by science, which tries to be as impersonal and as dehumanized as possible. In the resulting survey of the universe it is natural to start with astronomy and physics, which deal with what is large and what is universal; life and mind, which are rare and have, apparently, little influence on the course of events, must occupy a minor position in this impartial survey. But in relation to our second question, namely, how do we come by our knowledge, psychology is the most important of the sciences. Not only is it necessary to study psychologically the processes by which we draw inferences, but it turns out that all the data upon which our inferences should be based are psychological in character, that is to say, they are experiences of single individuals. The apparent publicity of our world is in part delusive and in part inferential; all the raw material of our knowledge consists of mental events in the lives of separate people. In this region, therefore, psychology is supreme.

... note, but that in his data what might there to one
should he based on the mechanics, in one word. But to say,
they are equal to a ... equilibrium. The apparent mass,
obscure could be ... its ... definite and all part interessant obtain
... material ... ... masses of model ...s in ...
... ... people. In this region, therefore, the theory of
supposed

PART II

LANGUAGE

Chapter I

THE USES OF LANGUAGE

LANGUAGE, like other things of mysterious importance, such as breath, blood, sex, and lightning, has been viewed superstitiously ever since men were capable of recording their thoughts. Savages fear to disclose their true name to an enemy, lest he should work evil magic by means of it. Origen assures us that pagan sorcerers could achieve more by using the sacred name Jehovah than by means of the names Zeus, Osiris, or Brahma. Familiarity makes us blind to the linguistic emphasis in the Commandment: "Thou shalt not take the *name* of the Lord in vain." The habit of viewing language superstitiously is not yet extinct. "In the beginning was the Word", says our version of St. John's Gospel, and in reading some logical positivists I am tempted to think that their view is represented by this mistranslated text.

Philosophers, being bookish and theoretical folk, have been interested in language chiefly as a means of making statements and conveying information, but this is only one of its purposes, and perhaps not the most primitive. What is the purpose of language to a sergeant-major? On the one hand there is the language of words of command, designed to cause identical simultaneous bodily movements in a number of hearers; on the other hand there is bad language, designed to cause humility in those in whom the expected bodily movements have not been caused. In neither case are words used, except incidentally, to state facts or convey information.

Language can be used to express emotions, or to influence the behaviour of others. Each of these functions can be performed, though with less adequacy, by pre-linguistic methods. Animals emit shrieks of pain, and infants, before they can speak, can express rage, discomfort, desire, delight, and a whole gamut of feelings, by cries and gurgles of different kinds. A sheep dog emits imperatives to his flock by means hardly distinguishable from those that the shepherd employs towards him. Between such noises and speech no sharp line can be drawn. When the dentist hurts you, you may emit an involuntary groan; this does not count as speech. But if he says "let me know if I hurt you", and you then make the very same sound, it has become speech, and moreover speech of the sort intended to convey information. This example illustrates the fact that, in the matter of language as in other respects, there is a continuous gradation from animal behaviour to that of the most precise man of science, and from pre-linguistic noises to the polished diction of the lexicographer.

A sound expressive of emotion I shall call an "interjection". Imperatives and interjections can already be distinguished in the noises emitted by animals. When a hen clucks at her brood of chickens, she is uttering imperatives, but when she squawks in terror she is expressing emotion. But as appears from your groan at the dentist's, an interjection may convey information, and the outside observer cannot tell whether or not it is intended to do so. Gregarious animals emit distinctive noises when they find food, and other members of the herd are attracted when they hear these noises, but we cannot know whether the noises merely express pleasure or are also intended to state "food here".

Whenever an animal is so constructed that a certain kind of circumstance causes a certain kind of emotion, and a certain kind of emotion causes a certain kind of noise, the noise conveys to a suitable observer two pieces of information, first, that the animal has a certain kind of feeling, and second, that a certain kind of circumstance is present. The sound that the animal emits is public, and the circumstance may be public—e.g. the presence of a shoal of fish if the animal is a sea-gull. The animal's cry may act directly on the other members of its species, and *we* shall then say that they "understand" its cry. But this is to suppose a "mental" intermediary between the hearing of the cry and the bodily reaction to the sound, and there is no real reason to suppose any such intermediary except when the response is delayed. Much of the importance of language is connected with delayed responses, but I will not yet deal with this topic.

Language has two primary purposes, expression and communication. In its most primitive forms it differs little from some other forms of behaviour. A man may express sorrow by sighing, or by saying "alas!" or "woe is me!" He may communicate by pointing or by saying "look". Expression and communication are not necessarily separated; if you say "look" because you see a ghost, you may say it in a tone that expresses horror. This applies not only to elementary forms of language; in poetry, and especially in songs, emotion and information are conveyed by the same means. Music may be considered as a form of language in which emotion is divorced from information, while the telephone book gives information without emotion. But in ordinary speech both elements are usually present.

Communication does not consist only of giving information; commands and questions must be included. Sometimes the two are scarcely separable: if you are walking with a child, and you say "there's a puddle there", the command "don't step in it" is implicit. Giving information may be due solely to the fact that the information interests you, or may be designed to influence behaviour. If you have just seen a street accident, you will wish to tell your friends about it because your mind is full of it; but if you tell a child that six times seven is forty-two you do so merely in the hope of influencing his (verbal) behaviour.

Language has two interconnected merits: first, that it is social, and second that it supplies public expression for "thoughts" which would otherwise remain private. Without language, or some pre-linguistic analogue, our knowledge of the environment is confined to what our own senses have shown us, together with such inferences as our congenital constitution may prompt; but by the help of speech we are able to know what others can relate, and to relate what is no longer sensibly present but only remembered. When we see or hear something which a companion is not seeing or hearing, we can often make him aware of it by the one word "look" or "listen", or even by gestures. But if half an hour ago we saw a fox, it is not possible to make another person aware of this fact without language. This depends upon the fact that the word "fox" applies equally to a fox seen or a fox remembered, so that our memories, which in themselves are private, are represented to others by uttered sounds, which are public. Without language, only that part of our life which consists of public sensations would be communicable, and that only to those so situated as to be able to share the sensations in question.

It will be seen that the utility of language depends upon the distinction between public and private experiences, which is important in considering the empirical basis of physics. This distinction, in turn, depends partly on physiology, partly on the persistence of sound-waves and light quanta, which makes possible the two forms of language, speech and writing. Thus language depends upon physics, and could not exist without the approximately separable causal chains which, as we shall see, make physical knowledge possible, and since the publicity of sensible objects is only approximate, language applying to them, considered socially, must have a certain lack of precision. I need hardly say that I am *not* asserting that the existence of language requires a *knowledge* of physics. What I am saying is that language would be impossible if the physical world did not in fact have certain characteristics, and that the *theory* of language is at certain points dependent upon a knowledge of the physical world. Language is a means of externalizing and publicizing our own experiences. A dog cannot relate his autobiography; however eloquently he may bark, he cannot tell you that his parents were honest though poor. A man can do this, and he does it by correlating "thoughts" with public sensations.

Language serves not only to express thoughts, but to make possible thoughts which could not exist without it. It is sometimes maintained that there can be no thought without language, but to this view I cannot assent: I hold that there can be thought, and even true and false belief, without language. But however that may be, it cannot be denied that all fairly elaborate thoughts require words. I can know, in a sense, that I have five fingers, without knowing the word "five", but I cannot know that the population of London is about eight millions unless I have acquired the language of arithmetic, nor can I have any thought at all closely corresponding to what is asserted in the sentence: "the ratio of the circumference of a circle to the diameter is approximately $3 \cdot 14159$". Language, once evolved, acquires a kind of autonomy: we can know, especially in mathematics, that a sentence asserts something true, although what it asserts is too complex to be apprehended even by the best minds. Let us consider for a moment what happens psychologically in such cases.

In mathematics, we start from rather simple sentences which we believe ourselves capable of understanding, and proceed, by rules of inference which we also believe ourselves to understand, to build up more and more complicated symbolic statements, which, if our initial assumptions are true, must be true whatever they may mean. As a rule it is unnecessary to know what they "mean", if their "meaning" is taken to be a thought which might occur in the mind of a superhuman mathematical genius. But there is another kind of "meaning", which gives occasion for pragmatism and instrumentalism. According to those who adopt this view of "meaning", what a complicated mathematical sentence does is to give a rule for practical procedure in certain kinds of cases. Take, for instance, the above statement about the ratio of the circumference of a circle to the diameter. Suppose you are a brewer, and you desire hoops of a given diameter for your beer barrels, then the sentence gives you a rule by which you can find out how much material you will need. This rule may consist of a fresh sentence for each decimal point, and there is therefore no need ever to grasp its significance as a whole. The autonomy of language enables you to forego this tedious process of interpretation except at crucial moments.

There are two other uses of language that are of great importance; it enables us to conduct our transactions with the outer world by means of symbols that have (1) a certain degree of permanence in time, (2) a considerable degree of discreteness in space. Each of these merits is more marked in writing than in speech, but is by no means wholly absent in speech. Suppose you have a friend called Mr. Jones. As a physical object his boundaries are somewhat vague, both because he is continually losing and acquiring electrons, and because an electron, being a distribution of energy, does not cease abruptly at a certain distance from its centre. The surface of Mr. Jones, therefore, has a certain ghostly impalpable quality, which you do not like to associate with your solid-seeming friend. It is not necessary to go into the niceties of theoretical physics in order to show that Mr. Jones is sadly indeterminate. When he is cutting his toe nails, there is a finite time, though a short one, during which it is doubtful whether the parings are still part of him or not. When he eats a mutton chop, at what moment does it become part of him? When he breathes out carbon dioxide, is the carbon part of him until it passes his nostrils? Even if we answer in the affirmative, there is a finite time during which it is questionable whether certain molecules have or have not passed beyond his nostrils. In these and other ways, it is doubtful what is part of Mr. Jones and what is not. So much for spatial vagueness.

There is the same problem as regards time. To the question "what are you looking at?" you may answer "Mr. Jones", although at one time you see him full-face, at another in profile, and at another from behind, and although at one time he may be running a race and at another time dozing in an arm-chair. There is another question, namely "what are you thinking of?" to which you may also answer "Mr. Jones", though what is actually in your mind may be very different on different occasions: it may be Mr. Jones as a baby, or Mr. Jones being cross because his breakfast is late, or Mr. Jones receiving the news that he is to be knighted. What you are experiencing is very different on these various occasions, but for many practical purposes it is convenient to regard them as all having a common object, which we suppose to be the meaning of the name "Mr. Jones". This name, especially when printed, though it cannot wholly escape the indefiniteness and transience of all physical objects, has much less of both than Mr. Jones has. Two instances of the printed words "Mr. Jones" are much more alike than (for instance) the spectacle of Mr. Jones running and the memory of Mr. Jones as a baby. And each instance, if printed, changes much more slowly than Mr. Jones does: it does not eat or breathe or cut its toe nails. The name, accordingly, makes it much easier than it would otherwise be to think of Mr. Jones as a single quasi-permanent entity, which, though untrue, is convenient in daily life.

Language, as appears from the above discussion of Mr. Jones, though a useful and even indispensable tool, is a dangerous one, since it begins by suggesting a definiteness, discreteness, and quasi-permanence in objects which physics seems to show that they do not possess. The philosopher, therefore, is faced with the difficult task of using language to undo the false beliefs that it suggests. Some philosophers, who shrink from the problems and uncertainties and complications involved in such a task, prefer to treat language as autonomous, and try to forget that it is intended to have a relation to fact and to facilitate dealings with the environment. Up to a point, such a treatment has great advantages: logic and mathematics would not have prospered as they have done if logicians and mathematicians had continually remembered that symbols should mean something. "Art for art's sake" is a maxim which has a legitimate sphere in logic as in painting (though in neither case does it give the whole truth). It may be that singing began as an incident in courtship, and that its biological purpose was to promote sexual intercourse;

but this fact (if it be a fact) will not help a composer to produce good music. Language is useful when you wish to order a meal in a restaurant, but this fact, similarly, is of no importance to the pure mathematician.

The philosopher, however, must pursue truth even at the expense of beauty, and in studying language he must not let himself be seduced by the siren songs of mathematics. Language, in its beginnings, is pedestrian and practical, using rough and ready approximations which have at first no beauty and only a very limited degree of truth. Subsequent refinements have too often had aesthetic rather than scientific motives, but from the inquiry upon which we are about to embark aesthetic motives must, however reluctantly, be relentlessly banished.

Chapter II

OSTENSIVE DEFINITION

"OSTENSIVE definition" may be defined as "any process by which a person is taught to understand a word otherwise than by the use of other words". Suppose that, knowing no French, you are shipwrecked on the coast of Normandy: you make your way into a farmhouse, you see bread on the table, and, being famished, you point at it with an inquiring gesture. If the farmer thereupon says *"pain"*, you will conclude, at least provisionally, that this is the French for "bread", and you will be confirmed in this view if the word is not repeated when you point at other kinds of eatables. You will then have learnt the meaning of the word by ostensive definition. It is clear that, if you know no French and your teacher knows no English, you must depend upon this process during your first lessons, since you have no linguistic means of communication.

The process of ostensive definition, however, is better exemplified when the learner knows no language at all than when he already possesses a language of his own. An adult knows that there are words, and will naturally suppose that the French have a way of naming bread. His knowledge takes the form: " '*Pain*' means 'bread' ". It is true that, when you were shipwrecked, it was by means of actual bread that you acquired this knowledge, but if you had been shipwrecked with a dictionary the actual bread would not have been necessary. There are two stages in the acquisition of a foreign language, the first that in which you only understand by translating, the second that in which you can "think" in the foreign language. In the first stage you know that *"pain"* means "bread", in the second stage you know that it means bread. The infant, possessing as yet no language, has to begin with the second stage. His success does credit to the capacities of the infant mind.

Knowing a language has two aspects, passive and active: passive when you understand what you hear, active when you can speak yourself. Dogs to some degree achieve the former, and children usually achieve it some time before the latter.

Knowing a language does not mean a capacity for explicit explanation of what its words signify; it means that hearing the words
has appropriate effects, and using them has appropriate causes.
I have sometimes, in the course of travel, watched a quarrel
springing up between two men whose language I did not understand, and it was difficult not to feel their mounting excitement
ridiculous. But probably the first was accusing the second of
being the offspring of parents who were not married, and the
second was retorting that the first's wife was unfaithful. If I had
understood, the effect of the insult and the cause of the retort
would have been obvious. As this example illustrates, a person
knows a language when hearing certain sounds has certain effects
and uttering them has certain causes. The process by which,
in the infant, the establishment of these causal laws is begun,
is the process of ostensive definition.

Ostensive definition, in its earliest form, requires certain
conditions. There must be a feature of the environment which is
noticeable, distinctive, emotionally interesting, and (as a rule)
frequently recurring, and the adult must frequently utter the
name of this feature at a moment when the infant is attending
to it. Of course there are risks of error. Suppose the child has
milk in a bottle. You may each time say "milk" or each time say
"bottle". In the former case the child may think "milk" is the
right word for a bottle of water; in the latter case, he may think
"bottle" the right word for a glass of milk. To avoid such errors,
you should in theory apply Mill's inductive canons, remembering
that induction is a bodily habit, and only by courtesy a logical
process. Instead of saying merely "milk" or merely "bottle",
you should say "bottle of milk"; you should then, on appropriate
occasions, say "glass of milk" and "bottle of water". In time,
by the use of Mill's canons, the infant, if he survives, will learn
to speak correctly. But I am not giving practical pedagogic
advice; I am merely exemplifying a theory.

The passive part in ostensive definition is merely the familiar
business of association or the conditioned reflex. If a certain
stimulus A produces in a child a certain reaction R, and is frequently experienced in conjunction with the word B, it will happen
in time that B will produce the reaction R, or some part of it.
As soon as this has happened, the word B has acquired a "meaning" for the child: it "means" A. The meaning may not be quite

what the adult intended: the adult may have intended "bottle" and the child may understand the word as meaning milk. But that does not prevent the child from possessing a word that has meaning; it only signifies that the child's language is not yet correct English.

When an experience causes violent emotion, repetition may be unnecessary. If a child, after learning to understand "milk", is given milk so hot as to scald his mouth, and you say "hot", he may ever after understand this word. But when an experience is uninteresting, many repetitions may be necessary.

The active part in the learning of language requires other capacities, which however, are of less philosophic interest. Dogs cannot learn human speech because they are anatomically incapable of producing the right sounds. Parrots, though they can produce more or less the right sounds, seem incapable of acquiring the right associations, so that their words do not have meaning. Infants, in common with the young of the higher animals, have an impulse to imitate adults of their own species, and therefore try to make the sounds that they hear. They may, on occasion, repeat sounds like a parrot, and only subsequently discover the "meaning" of the sounds. In that case the sounds cannot count as words until they have acquired meaning for the child. For every child it is a discovery that there are words, i.e. sounds with meaning. Learning to utter words is a joy to the child, largely because it enables him to communicate his wishes more definitely than he had been able to do by crying and making gestures. It is owing to this pleasure that children go through the mental labour and muscular practice involved in learning to talk.

In general, though not universally, repetition is necessary for an ostensive definition, for ostensive definition consists in the creation of a habit, and habits, as a rule, are learned gradually. The exceptional cases are illustrated by the proverbs "once bit, twice shy" and "the burnt child dreads the fire". Apart from such unusually emotional matters, the words that have ostensive definitions denote frequently recurring features of the environment, such as the members of the family, foods, toys, pet animals, etc. This involves the process of recognition, or something of the kind. Although a child's mother looks somewhat different on different occasions, he thinks of her (when he begins to think) as always the same person, and feels no difficulty in applying the same name to her various epiphanies. Language, from the start, or rather from the start of reflection on language, embodies the belief in more or less permanent persons and things. This is perhaps the chief reason for the difficulty of any philosophy which dispenses with the notion of substance. If you were to tell a child that his mother is a series of sensible impressions, connected by similarity and causal relations, but without material identity, and if by a miracle you could make him understand what you meant, he would consider you demented and be filled with indignation. The process called "recognition" is therefore one that demands investigation.

Recognition, as a physiological or psychological occurrence, may or may not be veridical. It fails in an every-day sense to be veridical when we mistake one of two twins for the other, but it may be metaphysically misleading even when it is correct from the standpoint of common sense. Whether there is anything identical, and if so what, between two different appearances of Mr. A, is a dark and difficult question, which I shall consider in connection with proper names. For the moment I wish to consider recognition as a process which actually occurs, without regard to its interpretation.

The first stage in the development of this process is repetition of a learnt reaction when the stimulus is repeated. It must be a *learnt* reaction, since recognition must grow out of a process involving something, in later reactions to a given stimulus, which was not present in the first reaction. Suppose, for instance, you give a child a glass of milk containing bitter medicine: the first time he drinks the doctored milk and makes a face, but the second time he refuses the milk. This is subjectively something like recognition, even if the second time he is mistaken in supposing that the milk contains medicine. It is clear that this process may be purely physiological, and that it involves only similarity, not identity, in stimulus and response. The learning of words by ostensive definition can be brought wholly within this primitive stage. The child's world contains a number of similar stimuli to which he has learnt to respond by similar noises, namely those that are instances of the word "milk"; it contains also another set of similar stimuli to which he has learnt to respond by instances of the word "mother". In this there is nothing involving any beliefs or emotions in the child.

81

It is only as a result of subsequent reflection that the child, now become a philosopher, concludes that there is one word, "mother", and one person, Mother. I believe this first step in philosophy to be mistaken. The word "mother", I should say, is not a single entity, but a class of similar noises; and Mother herself is also not a single entity, but a class of causally connected occurrences. These speculations, however, are irrelevant to the process of ostensive definition, which, as we have just seen, requires only the very first stage on the road towards what would usually count as recognition, namely similar learnt responses to similar stimuli.

This primitive form of recognition is relevant in the analysis of memory and in explaining the similarity of an idea to an impression (to borrow Hume's phraseology). When I remember a past event, I cannot make it itself occur again, though I may be able to make a similar event occur. But how do I know that the new event is similar to the old one? Subjectively, I can only know by comparing an idea with an impression: I have an idea of the past event and an impression of the present event, and I perceive that they are similar. But this is not sufficient, since it does not prove that my idea of the past event is similar to my impression of the *past* event when it existed. This, in fact, cannot be proved, and is in some sense one of the premisses of knowledge. But although it cannot be strictly proved, it can be in various ways confirmed. You may describe Mr. A while he is present, and your description may be recorded on a dictaphone. You may later describe him from memory, and compare your new description with the dictaphone record. If they agree closely, your memory may be accepted as correct.

This illustration depends upon a fact which is fundamental in this subject, namely, that we apply the same words to ideas as to the impressions which are their prototypes. This explains the possibility of learning a word ostensively by means of a single sensible occurrence. I saw Disraeli once, and once only, and was told, at the moment, "that's Dizzy". I have since very frequently remembered the occurrence, with the name "Dizzy" as an essential part of the memory. This has made it possible for a habit to be formed by repetition of the idea (in Hume's sense), although the impression has never been repeated. It is obvious that ideas differ from impressions in various ways, but their similarity to their prototypes is vouched for by the fact that they cause the same words. The two questions, "what are you looking at?" and "what are you thinking of?" may, on two different occasions, be answered identically.

Let us consider the different kinds of words that are commonly learnt by means of ostensive definitions. What I have in mind is a logical form of the grammatical doctrine of parts of speech.

We have already had occasion for a preliminary consideration of proper names. I shall say no more about them at present, as they will be the subject of a separate chapter.

Next come names of species: man, woman, cat, dog, etc. A species of this sort consists of a number of separate individuals, having some recognizable degree of likeness to each other. In biology before Darwin, "species" was a prominent concept. God had created a pair of each species, and different species could not interbreed, or, in the exceptional cases when they could, such as horse and ass, the offspring was sterile. There was an elaborate hierarchy of genera, families, orders, etc. This kind of classification, which was and is convenient in biology, was extended by the scholastics to other regions, and impeded logic by creating the notion that some ways of classifying are more correct than others. As regards ostensive definition, different experiences will produce different results. Most children learn the word "dog" ostensively; some learn in this way the kinds of dogs, collies, St. Bernards, spaniels, poodles, etc., while others, who have little to do with dogs, may first meet with these words in books. No child learns the word "quadruped" ostensively, still less the word "animal" in the sense in which it includes oysters and limpets. He probably learns "ant", "bee", and "beetle" ostensively, and perhaps "insect", but if so he will mistakenly include spiders until corrected.

Names of substances not obviously collections of individuals, such as "milk", "bread", "wood", are apt to be learnt ostensively when they denote things familiar in every-day life. The atomic theory is an attempt to identify this class of objects with the former, so that milk, for instance, is a collection of milky individuals (molecules), just as the human race is a collection of men, women, and children. But to unscientific apprehension such names of substances are not to be assimilated to species composed of separate individuals.

Next come qualities: red, blue, hard, soft, hot, cold, etc. Many of these are usually learnt ostensively, but the less common ones, such as vermilion, may be described by their similarities and differences.

Names of certain relations, such as "up", "down", "right", "left", "before", "after", are usually learnt ostensively. So are such words as "quick" and "slow".

There are a number of words of the sort that I call "ego-centric", which differ in meaning according to the speaker and his position in time and space. Among these the simple ones are learnt ostensively, for instance "I", "you", "here", "now". These words raise problems which we will consider in a later chapter.

All the words I have mentioned hitherto belong to the public world. A spectator can see when a certain feature of the public environment is attracting a child's attention, and then mention the name of this feature. But how about private experiences, such as stomach-ache, pain, or memory? Certainly some words denoting private kinds of experience are learnt ostensively. This is because the child shows in behaviour what he is feeling: there is a correlation between e.g. pain and tears.

There are no *definite* limits to what can be learnt by ostensive definition. "Cross", "crescent", "swastika" can be learnt in this way, but not "chiliagon". But the point where this method of learning becomes impossible depends upon the child's experience and capacity.

The words so far mentioned are all capable of being used as complete sentences, and are in fact so used in their most primitive employment. "Mother", "dog", "cat", "milk", and so on, may be used alone to express either recognition or desire. "Hard", "soft", "hot", "cold" would be more naturally used to express recognition than desire, and usually to express recognition accompanied by surprise. If the toast is uneatable because it is old you may say "hard"; if a ginger biscuit has lost its crispness by exposure to air you may say "soft". If the bath scalds you, you say "hot"; if it freezes you, you say "cold". "Quick" is frequently used by parents as an imperative; "slow" is used similarly on roads and railways where there is a curve. The words "up" and "down" are habitually used as complete sentences by lift-boys; "in" and "out" are similarly used at turnstiles.

"Before" and "after" are used as complete sentences in advertisements of hair-restorers. And so on and so on. It is to be noted that not only substantives and adjectives, but adverbs and prepositions, may on occasion be used as complete sentences.

I think the elementary uses of a word may be distinguished as indicative, imperative, and interrogative. When a child sees his mother coming, he may say "mother!"; this is the indicative use. When he wants her, he calls "mother!"; this is the imperative use. When she dresses up as a witch and he begins to pierce the disguise, he may say "mother?"; this is the interrogative use. The indicative use must come first in the acquisition of language, since the association of word and object signified can only be created by the simultaneous presence of both. But the imperative use very quickly follows. This is relevant in considering what we mean by "thinking of" an object. It is obvious that the child who has just learnt to call his mother has found verbal expression for a state in which he had often been previously, that this state was associated with his mother, and that it has now become associated with the word "mother". Before language, his state was only partially communicable; an adult, hearing him cry, could know that he wanted something, but had to guess what it was. But the fact that the word "mother!" expresses his state shows that, even before the acquisition of language, his state had a relation to his mother, namely the relation called "thinking of". This relation is not created by language, but antedates it. What language does is to make it communicable.

"Meaning" is a word which must be interpreted somewhat differently according as it is applied to the indicative or the imperative. In the indicative, a word A means a feature B of the environment if, (1) when B is emphatically present to attention, A is uttered, or there is an impulse to utter A, and (2) when A is heard it arouses what may be called the "idea" of B, which shows itself either in looking for B or in behaviour such as would be caused by the presence of B. Thus in the indicative a word "means" an object if the sensible presence of the object causes the utterance of the word, and the hearing of the word has effects analogous, in certain respects, to the sensible presence of the object.

The imperative use of a word must be distinguished according as it is heard or uttered. Broadly speaking, an imperative heard

—e.g. the word of command in the army—is understood when it causes a certain kind of bodily movement, or an impulse towards such a movement. An imperative uttered expresses a desire, and therefore requires the existence of an "idea" of the intended effect. Thus while it "expresses" something in the speaker, it "means" the external effect which it commands. The distinction between what is "meant" and what is "expressed" is essential in this use of words.

We have been concerned, in this chapter, only with the most primitive uses of the most primitive words. We have not considered the use of words in narrative or in hypothesis or in fiction, nor have we examined logical words such as "not", "or", "all", and "some"; we have not inquired how learners acquire the correct use of such words as "than" or "of", which do not denote recognizable features of any sensible environment. What we have decided is that a word may become associated with some notable feature of the environment (in general, one that occurs frequently), and that, when it is so associated, it is also associated with something that may be called the "idea" or "thought" of this feature. When such an association exists, the word "means" this feature of the environment; its utterance can be caused by the feature in question, and the hearing of it can cause the "idea" of this feature. This is the simplest kind of "meaning", out of which other kinds are developed.

Chapter III

PROPER NAMES

THERE is a traditional distinction between "proper" names and "class" names, which is explained as consisting in the fact that a proper name applies, essentially, to only one object, whereas a class name applies to all objects of a certain kind, however numerous they may be. Thus "Napoleon" is a proper name, while "man" is a class name. It will be observed that a proper name is meaningless unless there is an object of which it is the name, but a class name is not subject to any such limitation. "Men whose heads do grow beneath their shoulders" is a perfectly good class name, although there are no instances of it. Again, it may happen that there is only one instance of a class name, e.g. "satellite of the earth". In such a case, the one member may have a proper name ("the moon"), but the proper name does not have the same meaning as the class name, and has different syntactical functions. E.g. we can say: " 'Satellite of the earth' is a unit class", but we cannot say "the moon is a unit class", because it is not a class, or at any rate not a class of the same logical type as "satellite of the earth", and if taken as a class (e.g. of molecules) it is many, not one.

Many difficult questions arise in connection with proper names, Of these there are two that are especially important: first, what is the precise definition of proper names? second, is it possible to express all our empirical knowledge in a language containing no proper names? This second question, we shall find, takes us to the heart of some of the most ancient and stubborn of philosophical disputes.

In seeking a definition of "proper name", we may approach the subject from the point of view of metaphysics, logic, physics, syntax, or theory of knowledge. I will say a few preliminary words about each of these.

A. *Metaphysical.*—It is fairly obvious that proper names owe their existence in ordinary language to the concept of "substance" —originally in the elementary form of "persons" and "things". A substance or entity is named, and then properties are assigned to it. So long as this metaphysic was accepted, there was no

87

difficulty as to proper names, which were the designations of such substances as were sufficiently interesting. Sometimes, it is true, we should give a name to a collection of substances, such as France or the sun. But such names, strictly speaking, were not necessary. In any case, we could extend our definition to embrace collections of substances.

But most of us, nowadays, do not accept "substance" as a useful notion. Are we then to adopt, in philosophy, a language without proper names? Or are we to find a definition of "proper name" which does not depend on "substance"? Or are we to conclude that the conception of "substance" has been too hastily rejected? For the present, I merely raise these questions, without attempting to answer them. All that I want to make clear at the moment is that proper names, as ordinarily understood, are ghosts of substances.

B. *Syntactical.*—It is clear that a syntactical definition of "proper name" must be relative to a given language or set of languages. In the languages of daily life, and also in most of those employed in logic, there is a distinction between subject and predicate, between relation-words and term-words. A "name" will be, in such languages, "a word which can never occur in a sentence except as a subject or a term-word". Or again: a proper name is a word which may occur in *any* form of sentence not containing variables, whereas other words can only occur in sentences of appropriate form. Sometimes it is said that some words are "syncategorimatic", which apparently means that they have no significance by themselves, but contribute to the significance of sentences in which they occur. According to this way of speaking, proper names are not syncategorimatic, but whether this can be a definition is a somewhat doubtful question. In any case, it is difficult to get a clear definition of the term "syncategorimatic".

The chief inadequacy of the above syntactical point of view is that it does not, in itself, help us to decide whether it is possible to construct languages with a different kind of syntax, in which the distinctions we have been considering would disappear.

C. *Logical.*—Pure logic has no occasion for names, since its propositions contain only variables. But the logician may wonder, in his unprofessional moments, what constants could be substituted for his variables. The logician announces, as one of his principles, that, if "fx" is true for every value of "x", then "fa"

is true, where "*a*" is any constant. This principle does not mention a constant, because "any constant" is a variable; but it is intended to justify those who want to *apply* logic. Every application of logic or mathematics consists in the substitution of constants for variables; it is therefore essential, if logic or mathematics is to be applied, to know what sort of constants can be substituted for what sort of variables. If any kind of hierarchy is admitted among variables, "proper names" will be "constants which are values of variables of lowest type". There are, however, a number of difficulties in such a view. I shall not therefore pursue it further.

D. *Physical.*—There are here two points of view to be considered. The first is that a proper name is a word designating any continuous portion of space-time which sufficiently interests us; the second is that, this being the function of proper names, they are unnecessary, since any portion of space-time can be described by its co-ordinates. Carnap (*Logical Syntax*, pp. 12–13) explains that latitude and longitude, or space-time co-ordinates, can be substituted for place-names. "The method of designation by proper names is the primitive one; that of positional designation corresponds to a more advanced stage of science, and has considerable methodological advantages over the former." In the language he employs, co-ordinates, he says, replace such words as "Napoleon" or "Vienna". This point of view deserves full discussion, which I shall undertake shortly.

E. *Epistemological.*—We have here, first, a distinction not identical with that between proper names and other words, but having perhaps some connection with it. This is the distinction between words having a verbal definition and words having only an ostensive definition. As to the latter, two points are obvious: (1) not all words can have verbal definitions; (2) it is largely arbitrary which words are to have only ostensive definitions. E.g. if "Napoleon" is defined ostensively, "Joseph Bonaparte" may be defined verbally as "Napoleon's oldest brother". However, this arbitrariness is limited by the fact that, in the language of a given person, ostensive definitions are only possible within the limits of his experience. Napoleon's friends might (subject to limitations) define him ostensively, but we cannot, since we can never say truly "*that* is Napoleon". There is obviously here a problem connected with that of proper names; how closely, I shall not discuss at present.

We have, it is clear, a number of problems to consider, and, as is apt to happen in philosophy, it is difficult to be clear as to what precisely the problems are. I think we shall do best if we begin with Carnap's substitution of co-ordinates for proper names. The question we have to consider is whether such a language can express the whole of our empirical knowledge.

In Carnap's system, a group of four numbers is substituted for a space-time point. He illustrates by the example "Blue x_1, x_2, x_3, x_4, meaning "the position (x_1, x_2, x_3, x_4) is blue", instead of "Blue (a)" meaning "the object a is blue". But now consider such a sentence as "Napoleon was in Elba during part of 1814". Carnap, I am sure, will agree that this sentence is true, and that its truth is empirical, not logical. But if we translate it into his language it will become a logical truth. "Napoleon" will be replaced by "all quartets of numbers enclosed within such-and-such boundaries"; so will "Elba", and so will "1814". We shall then be stating that these three classes of quartets have a common part. This, however, is a fact of logic. Clearly this is not what we meant. We give the name "Napoleon" to a certain region, not because we are concerned with topology, but because that region has certain characteristics which make it interesting. We may defend Carnap by supposing, adopting a schematic simplification, that "Napoleon" is to mean "all regions having a certain quality say N", while "Elba" is to mean "all regions having the quality E". Then "Napoleon spent some time in Elba" will become: "The regions having the quality N and those having the quality E overlap." This is no longer a fact of logic. But it has interpreted the proper names of ordinary language as disguised predicates.

But our schematic simplification is too violent. There is no quality, or collection of qualities, present wherever Napoleon was and absent wherever he was not. As an infant, he did not wear a cocked hat, or command armies, or fold his arms, while all these things were also done, at times, by other people. How, then, are we to define the word "Napoleon"? Let us continue to do our best for Carnap. In the moment of baptism, the priest decides that the name "Napoleon" is to apply to a certain small region in his neighbourhood, which has a more or less human shape, and that it is to apply to other future regions connected with this one, not only by continuity, which is not sufficient to secure material identity, but by certain causal laws, those, namely, which lead us to regard a body on two occasions as that of the same person. We may say: Given a temporally brief region having the characteristics of a living human body, it is an empirical fact that there are earlier and later regions connected with this one by physical laws, and having more or less similar characteristics; the total of such regions is what we call a "person", and one such region was called "Napoleon". That naming is retro-active appears from a plaque on a certain house in Ajaccio saying: "Ici Napoleon fut conçu."

This may be accepted as an answer to the objection that, on Carnap's view, "Napoleon was once in Elba" would be a proposition of logic. It leaves, however, some very serious questions. We saw that "Napoleon" cannot be defined simply by qualities, unless we are to hold it impossible that there should be two exactly similar individuals. One of the uses of space-time, however, is to differentiate similar individuals in different places. Carnap has his sentences "Blue (3)", "Blue (4)", etc., meaning "the place 3 is blue", "the place 4 is blue", etc. We can, it is supposed, distinguish blue in one place from blue in another. But how are the places distinguished? Carnap takes space-time for granted, and never discusses how space-time places are differentiated. In fact, in his system, space-time regions have the characteristics of substance. The homogeneity of space-time is assumed in physics, and yet it is also assumed that there are different regions, which can be distinguished. Unless we are to accept the objectionable metaphysics of substance, we shall have to suppose the regions distinguished by differences of quality. We shall then find that the regions need no longer be regarded as substantial, but as bundles of qualities.

Carnap's co-ordinates, which replace names, are, of course, not assigned quite arbitrarily. The origin and the axes are arbitrary, but when they are fixed, the rest proceeds on a plan. The year which we call "1814" is differently named by the Mohammedans, who date from the Hejira, and by the Jewish era, which dates from the Creation. But the year we call "1815" will have the next number, in any system, to that given to what we call "1814". It is because co-ordinates are not arbitrary that they are not names. Co-ordinates *describe* a point by its relations to the origin and the axes. But we must be able to say "*this* is the origin". If we are to be able to say this, we must be able to *name* the origin, or to describe it in some way, and at first sight it might be thought that any possible way would be found to involve names. Take, for instance, longitude. The origin of longitude is the meridian of Greenwich, but it might equally well be any other meridian. We cannot define "Greenwich" as "longitude 0°, latitude 52°", because, if we do, there is no means of ascertaining where longitude 0° is. When we say "longitude 0° is the longitude of Greenwich", what we say is satisfactory because we can go to Greenwich and say "*this* is Greenwich". Similarly, if we live at (say) longitude 40° W., we can say "the longitude of *this* place is 40° W.", and then we can define longitude 0° by relation to *this* place. But unless we have a way of knowing *some* places otherwise than by latitude and longitude, latitude and longitude become unmeaning. When we ask "what are the latitude and longitude of New York?" we are not asking the same sort of question as we should be if we descended into New York by a parachute and asked "what is the name of this city?" We are asking: "How far is New York west of Greenwich and north of the equator?" This question supposes New York and Greenwich known and already named.

It would be possible to assign a finite number of co-ordinates at haphazard, and then they would all be names. When (as is always done) they are assigned on a principle, they are descriptions, defining points by their relations to the origin and the axes. But these descriptions fail for the origin and the axes themselves, since, as regards them, the numbers *are* assigned arbitrarily. To answer the question "where is the origin?" we must have some method of identifying a place without mentioning its co-ordinates. It is the existence of such methods that is presupposed by the use of proper names.

I conclude, for the moment, that we cannot wholly dispense with proper names by means of co-ordinates. We can perhaps reduce the number of proper names, but we cannot avoid them altogether. Without proper names we can express the whole of theoretical physics, but no part of history or geography; this, at least, is our provisional conclusion so far, but we shall find reason to modify it later.

Let us consider a little further the substitution of descriptions for names. Somebody must be the tallest man now living in the United States. Let us suppose he is Mr. A. We may then, in place of "Mr. A", substitute "the tallest man now living in the

United States", and this substitution will not, as a rule, alter the truth or falsehood of any sentence in which it is made. But it will alter the statement. One may know things about Mr. A that one does not know about the tallest man in the United States, and vice versa. One may know that Mr. A lives in Iowa, but not that the tallest man in the United States lives in Iowa. One may know that the tallest man in the United States is over ten years old, but one may not know whether Mr. A is man or boy. Then there is the proposition "Mr. A is the tallest man in the United States." Mr. A may not know this; there may be a Mr. B who runs him close. But Mr. A certainly knows that Mr. A is Mr. A. This illustrates once more that there are some things which cannot be expressed by means of descriptions substituted for names.

The names of persons have verbal definitions in terms of "this". Suppose you are in Moscow and some one says "that's Stalin", then "Stalin" is defined as "the person whom you are now seeing" —or, more fully: "that series of occurrences, constituting a person, of which *this* is one". Here "this" is undefined, but "Stalin" is defined. I think it will be found that every name applied to some portion of space-time can have a verbal definition in which the word "this", or some equivalent, occurs. This, I should say, is what distinguishes the name of an historical character from that of an imaginary person, such as Hamlet. Let us take a person with whom we are not acquainted, say Socrates. We may define him as "the philosopher who drank the hemlock", but such a definition does not assure us that Socrates existed, and if he did not exist, "Socrates" is not a name. What does assure us that Socrates existed? A variety of sentences heard or read. Each of these is a sensible occurrence in our own experience. Suppose we find in the *Encyclopaedia* the statement "Socrates was an Athenian philosopher". The sentence, while we see it, is a *this*, and our faith in the *Encyclopaedia* leads us to say "this is true". We can define "Socrates" as "the person described in the *Encyclopaedia* under the name 'Socrates'". Here the name "Socrates" is experienced. We can of course define "Hamlet" in a similar way, but some of the propositions used in the definition will be false. E.g. if we say "Hamlet was a Prince of Denmark who was the hero of one of Shakespeare's tragedies", this is false. What is true is: " 'Hamlet' is a word which Shakespeare pretends to be the name of a Prince of Denmark". It would thus seem to

93

follow that, apart from such words as "this" and "that", every name is a description involving some *this*, and is only a name in virtue of the truth of some proposition. (The proposition may be only "this is a name", which is false if this is "Hamlet".)

We must consider the question of minimum vocabularies. I call a vocabulary a "minimum" one if it contains no word which is capable of a verbal definition in terms of the other words of the vocabulary. Two minimum vocabularies dealing with the same subject-matter may not be equal; there may be different methods of definition, some of which lead to a shorter residuum of undefined terms than others do. The question of minimum vocabularies is sometimes very important. Peano reduced the vocabulary of arithmetic to three words. It was an achievement in classical physics when all units were defined in terms of the units of mass, length, and time. The question I wish to discuss is: What characteristics must belong to a minimum vocabulary by means of which we can define all the words used in expressing our empirical knowledge or beliefs, in so far as such words have any precise meaning? More narrowly, to revert to a former example, what sort of minimum vocabulary is needed for "Napoleon was in Elba during part of 1814" and kindred statements? Perhaps, when we have answered this, we shall be able to define "names". I assume, in the following discussion, that such historical-geographical statements are not analytic, that is to say, though they are true as a matter of fact, it would not be logically impossible for them to be false.

Let us revert to the theory, which is suggested by what Carnap says, that "Napoleon" is to be defined as a certain region of space-time. We objected that, in that case, "Napoleon was for a time in Elba" is analytic. It may be retorted: yes, but to find out what is not analytic you must inquire why we give a name to the portion of space-time that was Napoleon. We do so because it had certain peculiar characteristics. It was a person, and when adult it wore a cocked hat. We shall then say: "This portion of space-time is a person, and in its later portions it wears a cocked hat; that portion of space-time is a small island; this and that have a common part". We have here three statements, the first two empirical, the third analytic. This seems unobjectionable. It leaves us with the problem of assigning co-ordinates, and also with that of defining such terms as "person" and "island". Such terms as "person" and "island" can obviously be defined in terms of qualities and relations; they are general terms, and not (one would say) such as lead to proper names. The assigning of co-ordinates requires the assigning of origin and axes. We may, for simplicity, ignore the axes and concentrate on the origin. Can the origin be defined?

Suppose, for example, you are engaged in planetary theory, not merely in a theoretical spirit, but with a view to the testing of your calculations by observations. Your origin, in that case, will have to be defined by something observable. It is universally agreed that absolute physical space-time is not observable. The things we can observe are, broadly speaking, qualities and spatio-temporal relations. We can say "I shall take the centre of the sun as my origin". The *centre* of the sun is not observable, but the sun (in a sense) is. It is an empirical fact that I frequently have an experience which I call "seeing the sun", and that I can observe what seem to be other people having a similar experience. "The sun" is a term which can be defined by qualities: round, hot, bright, of such-and-such apparent size, etc. It happens that there is only one object in my experience having these qualities, and that this object persists. I can give it a proper name, "the sun", and say "I shall take the sun as my origin". But since I have defined the sun by its qualities, it does not form part of a minimum vocabulary. It seems to follow that, while the words for qualities and spatio-temporal relations may form part of my minimum vocabulary, no words for physical spatio-temporal regions can do so. This is, in fact, merely a way of stating that physical spatio-temporal position is relative, not absolute.

Assuming this correct so far, the question arises whether we need names for qualities and spatio-temporal relations. Take colours, for example. It may be said that they can be designated by wave-lengths. This leads to Carnap's contention that there is nothing in physics which cannot be known to a blind man. So far as theoretical physics is concerned, this is obviously true. It is true also, up to a point, in the empirical field. *We see* that the sky is blue, but a race of blind men could devise experiments showing that transverse waves of certain wave-lengths proceed from it, and this is just what the ordinary physicist *quâ* physicist, is concerned to assert. The physicist, however, does not trouble to assert, and the blind man cannot assert, the proposition: "When light of a certain frequency strikes a normal eye, it causes a sensation of blue." This statement is not a tautology; it was a discovery, made many thousands of years after words for "blue" had been in common use.

The question whether the word "blue" can be defined is not easy. We might say: "Blue" is the name of colour-sensations caused by light of such-and-such frequencies. Or we might say: "Blue" is the name of those shades of colour which, in the spectrum, come between violet and green. Either of these definitions might enable us to procure for ourselves a sensation of blue. But when we had done so, we should be in a position to say: "So *that* is *blue*." This would be a discovery, only to be made by actually experiencing blue. And in this statement, I should say, "that" is in one sense a proper name, though of that peculiar sort that I call "egocentric".

We do not usually give names to smells and tastes, but we could do so. Before going to America, I knew the proposition "the smell of a skunk is disagreeable". Now I know the two propositions: "*that* is the smell of a skunk", and "*that* is disagreeable". Instead of "that", we might use a name, say "pfui", and should do so if we often wished to speak of the smell without mentioning skunks. But to any one who had not had the requisite experience, the name would be an abbreviated description, not a name.

I conclude that names are to be applied to what is experienced, and that what is experienced does not have, essentially and necessarily, any such spatio-temporal uniqueness as belongs to a space-time region in physics. A word must denote something that can be *recognized*, and space-time regions, apart from qualities, cannot be recognized, since they are all alike. They are in fact logical fictions, but I am ignoring this for the moment.

There are occurrences that I experience, and I believe there are others that I do not experience. The occurrences that I experience are all complex, and can be analysed into qualities with spatial and temporal relations. The most important of these relations are compresence, contiguity, and succession. The words that we use to designate qualities are not precise; they all have the sort of vagueness that belongs to such words as "bald" and "fat". This is true even of the words that we are most anxious to make precise, such as "centimetre" and "second". Words designating qualities *must* be defined ostensively, if we are to be able to express observations; as soon as we substitute a verbal definition, we cease to express what is observed. The word "blue," for instance, will mean "a colour like *that*", where *that* is a blue patch. How like *that* it must be to be blue, we cannot state with any precision.

This is all very well, but how about such words as "this" and "that", which keep on intruding themselves? We think of the word "this" as designating something which is unique, and can only occur once. If, however, "this" denotes a bundle of compresent qualities, there is no logical reason why it should not recur. I accept this. That is to say, I hold that there is no class of empirically known objects such that, if x is a member of the class, the statement "x precedes x" is logically impossible.

We are accustomed to think that the relation "precedes" is asymmetrical and transitive.[1] "Time" and "event" are both concepts invented with a view to securing these properties to the relation "precedes". Most people have discarded "time" as something distinct from temporal succession, but they have not discarded "event". An "event" is supposed to occupy some continuous portion of space-time, at the end of which it ceases, and cannot recur. It is clear that a quality, or a complex of qualities, may recur; therefore an "event", *if* non-recurrence is logically necessary, is not a bundle of qualities. What, then, is it, and how is it known? It will have the traditional characteristics of substance, in that it will be a subject of qualities, but not defined when all its qualities are assigned. And how do we know that there is any class of objects the members of which *cannot* recur? If we are to know this, it might seem that it must be a case of synthetic *a priori* knowledge, and that if we reject the synthetic *a priori*, we must reject the impossibility of recurrence. We shall, of course, admit that, if we take a sufficiently large bundle of qualities, there will be no empirical instance of recurrence. Nonrecurrence of such bundles may be accepted as a law of physics, but not as something necessary.

The view that I am suggesting is that an "event" may be defined as a complete bundle of compresent qualities, i.e. a bundle

[1] I.e. that if A precedes B, B does not precede A, and if A precedes B and B precedes C, then A precedes C.

having the two properties (a) that all the qualities in the bundle are compresent, (b) that nothing outside the bundle is compresent with *every* member of the bundle. I assume that, as a matter of empirical fact, no event recurs; that is to say, if a and b are events, and a is earlier than b, there is some qualitative difference between a and b. For preferring this theory to one which makes an event indefinable, there are all the reasons commonly alleged against substance. If two events were exactly alike, nothing could ever lead us to suppose that they were two. In taking a census, we could not count one apart from the other, for, if we did, that would be a difference between them. And from the standpoint of language, a word must denote something that can be recognized, and this requires some recognizable quality. This leads to the conclusion that words such as "Napoleon" can be defined, and are therefore theoretically unnecessary; and that the same thing would be true of words designating events, if we were tempted to invent such words.

I conclude that, if we reduce our empirical vocabulary to a minimum, thereby excluding all words that have verbal definitions, we shall still need words for qualities, compresence, succession, and observed spatial relations, i.e. spatial relations which can be discriminated within a single sensible complex. It is an empirical fact that, if we form a complex of all the qualities that are all compresent with each other, this complex is found, so far as our experience goes, not to precede itself, i.e. not to recur. In forming the time-series, we generalize this observed fact.

The nearest approach to proper names in such a language will be the words for qualities and complexes of compresent qualities. These words will have the syntactical characteristics of proper names, but not certain other characteristics that we expect, for example that of designating a region which is spatio-temporally continuous. Whether, in these circumstances, such words are to be called "names", is a matter of taste, as to which I express no opinion. What are commonly called proper names— e.g. "Socrates"—can, if I am right, be defined in terms of qualities and spatio-temporal relations, and this definition is an actual analysis. Most subject-predicate propositions, such as "Socrates is snub-nosed", assert that a certain quality, named by the predicate, is one of a bundle of qualities named by the subject— this bundle being a unity in virtue of compresence and causal relations. Proper names in the ordinary sense, if this is right, are misleading, and embody a false metaphysic.

Note.—The above discussion of proper names is not intended to be conclusive. The subject will be resumed in other contexts, especially in Part IV, Chapter VIII.

Chapter IV

EGOCENTRIC PARTICULARS

I GIVE the name "egocentric particulars" to words of which the meaning varies with the speaker and his position in time and space. The four fundamental words of this sort are "I", "this", "here", and "now". The word "now" denotes a different point of time on each successive occasion when I use it; the word "here" denotes a different region of space after each time when I move; the word "I" denotes a different person according to who it is that utters it. Nevertheless there is obviously *some* sense in which these words have a constant meaning, which is the reason for the use of the words. This raises a problem, but before considering it let us consider what other words are egocentric, and especially what words are really egocentric although intended not to be so.

Among obviously egocentric words are "near" and "far", "past", "present", and "future", "was", "is", and "will be", and generally all forms of verbs involving tense. "This" and "that" are obviously egocentric; in fact, "this" might be taken as the only egocentric word not having a nominal definition. We could say that "I" means "the person experiencing this", "now" means "the time of this", and "here" means "the place of this". The word "this" is, in a sense, a proper name, but it differs from true proper names in the fact that its meaning is continually changing. This does not mean that it is ambiguous, like (say) "John Jones", which is at all times the proper name of many different men. Unlike "John Jones", "this" is at each moment the name of only one object in one person's speech. Given the speaker and the time, the meaning of "this" is unambiguous, but when the speaker and the time are unknown we cannot tell what object it denotes. For this reason, the word is more satisfactory in speech than in print. If you hear a man say "this is an age of progress", you know what age he refers to; but if you read the same statement in a book it may be what Adam said when he invented the spade or what was said by any later optimist. You can only decide what the statement means by finding out when it was written, and in this sense its meaning is not self-contained but requires elucidation by extraneous information.

One of the aims of both science and common sense is to replace the shifting subjectivity of egocentric particulars by neutral public terms. "I" is replaced by my name, "here" by latitude and longitude, and "now" by date. Suppose I am walking with a friend on a dark night, and we lose touch with each other: he calls out "where are you?" and I reply "here I am". Science will not accept such language; it will substitute "At 11.32 p.m. on January 30, 1946, B.R. was at longitude 4° 3′ 29″ W. and at latitude 53° 16′ 14″ N". This information is impersonal: it gives a prescription by which a qualified person who possesses a sextant and a chronometer, and has the patience to wait for a sunny day, can determine where I was, which he may proclaim in the words "here is where he was". If the matter is of sufficient importance, say in a trial for murder, this elaborate procedure may be worth the trouble it involves. But its appearance of complete impersonality is in part deceptive. Four items are involved: my name, the date, latitude, and longitude. In regard to each of these there is an element of egocentricity which is concealed by the fact that, for most purposes, it has no *practical* importance.

From a practical point of view, the impersonality is complete. Two competent persons, given time and opportunity, will both accept or both reject a statement of the form: "At time t, A was at longitude B, latitude C." Let us call this statement "P". There is a procedure for determining date, latitude, and longitude, which, if correctly observed, leads different people to the same result, in the sense that, if both say truly "he was here five minutes ago", they must be in each other's presence. This is the essential merit of scientific terminology and scientific technique. But when we examine closely the meanings of our scientific terms we find that the subjectivity we sought to avoid has not been wholly banished.

Let us begin with my name. We substitute "B.R." for "I" or "you" or "he", as the case may be, because "B.R." is a public appellation, appearing on my passport and my identity card. If a policeman says "who are you?" I might reply by saying "look! this is who I am", but this information is not what the policeman wants, so I produce my identity card and he is satisfied. But essentially I have only substituted one sensible impression for another. In looking at the identity card the policeman acquires a certain visual impression, which enables him to say "the name of the accused is B.R." Another policeman, looking at the same identity card, will utter what is called the "same" sentence, that is to say, he will emit a series of noises closely similar to those emitted by the first policeman. It is this similarity, mistakenly regarded as identity, which is the merit of the name. If the two policemen had had to describe my appearance, the first, delaying me at the end of an all-day walk in the rain, might say "he was a furious red-faced tramp", while the other might say "he was a benign old gentleman in evening dress". The name has the merit of being less variable, but it remains something known only through the sensible impressions of individuals, of which no two are exactly alike. We always come back to *"this* is his name", where *this* is a present occurrence. Or rather, to be exact, "his name is a class of sensible occurrences all very similar to *this*". We secure, by our procedure, a method of providing sets of closely similar occurrences, but we do not wholly escape from "this".

There is involved here a principle of considerable scope and importance, which deserves a more detailed exposition, to which we must now devote ourselves.

Let us begin with a homely illustration. Suppose you are acquainted with a certain Mrs. A, and you know that her mother, whom you have never met, is called Mrs. B. What does the name "Mrs. B" mean for you? Not what it means for those who know her, still less what it means for her herself. It must mean something definable in terms of your experience, as must every word that you can use understandingly. For every word that you can understand must either have a nominal definition in terms of words having ostensive definitions, or must itself have an ostensive definition; and ostensive definitions, as appears from the process by which they are effected, are only possible in relation to events that have occurred to you. Now the name "Mrs. B" is something that you have experienced; therefore when you speak of Mrs. B you may be mentally defining her as "the lady whose name is 'Mrs. B' ". Or, if one were to concede (what would not be strictly accurate) that you are acquainted with Mrs. A, you might define "Mrs. B" as "the mother of Mrs. A". In this way, although Mrs. B is outside your experience, you can interpret sentences in which her name occurs in such a way that your lack of experience does not prevent you from knowing if the sentences are true.

We can now generalize the process involved in the above illustration. Suppose there is some object a which you know by experience, and suppose you know (no matter how) that there is just one object to which a has a known relation R, but there is no such object in your experience. (In the above case, a is a Mrs. A, and R is the relation of daughter to mother.) You can then give a name to the object to which a has the relation R; let the name be "b". (In our illustration it was "Mrs. B".) It then becomes easy to forget that b is unknown to you although you may know multitudes of true sentences about b. But in fact, to speak correctly, you do *not* know sentences about b; you know sentences in which the name "b" is replaced by the phrase "the object to which a has the relation R". You know also that there are sentences about the actual object b which are verbally identical with those that you know about the object to which a has the relation R—sentences pronounced by other people in which "b" occurs as a name—but although you can describe these sentences, and know (within common-sense limits) which are true and which false, you do not know the sentences themselves. You may know that Mrs. A's mother is rich, but you do not know what Mrs. B knows when she says "I am rich".

The result of this state of affairs is that our knowledge *seems* to extend much further beyond our experience than it actually does. We may perhaps distinguish, in such cases as we have been considering, between what we can assert and what we *intend*. If I say "Mrs. B is rich", I *intend* something about Mrs. B herself, but what I actually assert is that Mrs. A has a rich mother. Another person may know of Mrs. B, not as the mother of Mrs. A, but as the mother of another daughter Mrs. C. In that case, when he says "Mrs. B is rich", he means "Mrs. C has a rich mother", which is not what I meant. But we both *intend* to say something about Mrs. B herself, though in this neither of us is successful. This does not matter in practice, as the things we respectively say about Mrs. A's mother or Mrs. C's mother would be true of Mrs. B if only we could say them. But although it does not matter in practice, it matters greatly in theory of knowledge. For in fact everybody except myself is to me in the position of Mrs. B;

so are the sun and moon, my house and garden, my dog and my cat, Stalin and the King. All these are only known to me by description, not by acquaintance. And the description has to be in terms of my own experiences. So much for names. We must next consider dates, in the endeavour to interpret our statement P.

When I know a date, how can the date be defined in terms of my own experience, or, in other words, in terms which have for me an ostensive definition? Take, to begin with, the definition of "1946". The public definition is "1946 years after the official date of the birth of Christ". It is agreed that this cannot be the actual date of His birth, since Herod died in 4 B.C. Therefore "1946" really means: a certain number of years after the time when the Christian era was fixed. That is to say, if in a certain year it was decided that the year should count as the year n A.D., then "1946" means "$1946-n$ years after that year". This, we said, is the *public* meaning, but it is obviously not my private meaning, since I do not know what year that was. What I know through my own experience is that this year is called "1946" in the newspaper and in my diary and in letters, and generally wherever a date is to be expected; I can also remember that last year was called "1945". I know what is meant by "A.D.", and am therefore aware that the date is said to have a connection with certain historical events of which I know through reading the Bible.

In analysing the subjective meaning of a date, we come ultimately to some experience of my own, either in present perception or in memory. Sometimes this process is obvious: I want to know what day of the week it is, my diary tells me that I dined with so-and-so on Wednesday, and my memory tells me that I dined with him yesterday, whence I infer that to-day is Thursday. Or I may hear the church bells and infer that it is Sunday. When I believe that to-day is January 30, 1946, I do so because I have seen the date in the newspaper, or because I remember that yesterday was the 29th, or for some such reason.

Similar things are to be said about latitude and longitude. Even the words that we most desire to render scientifically impersonal require for their interpretation personal experiences of the interpreter. This is concealed from our notice by what may be called "verbal" thought. The year 1946 is a difficult object to think about, but the word "1946" is easy. I cannot in any obvious sense experience 1946, but I experience "1946" whenever I hear or read it. What I call "verbal" thought is characterized by using the name of an object as a means of describing it. When we mean to think about Napoleon, we substitute the description "the man whose name was 'Napoleon' ". We can experience the name "Napoleon", and often we are unconscious of having used "the man called 'Napoleon' " as a substitute for "Napoleon". Owing to this unconscious substitution we never realize that about Napoleon himself we know literally nothing, since we are not acquainted with him.

To return to egocentric particulars, the problems that they raise are specially important in relation to space and time. The quality "red" (say) has no essential privacy; it is possible to doubt whether the sort of sensation that I call "red" is similar to that which another man calls by the same name, but there is no positive ground for supposing a difference. On the other hand, what I call "here" is of necessity different from what anybody else calls "here", and what I now call "now" is of necessity different from what I call "now" on another occasion, and from what another man calls "now" at other times. This is the sharp point, in language, of the essential privacy of each individual's experience. Like Leibniz's monads, we each mirror the world from our own personal point of view. But in fact Leibniz did not carry his monadism far enough, since he applied it only spatially. Not only is a man private from other people, but he is also private from his past and future selves. It is not "here" alone that is private, but also "now"; in fact "here-now" is what is fundamental in our present problem. I-here-now know certain things; in some degree, however inadequately, I mirror the universe by the present contents of my mind. But is this possible? And how is it possible? And how far is it possible? These are some of the fundamental problems with which the present work is concerned. Continued analysis gradually narrows us down from the astronomical universe to the mind of the astronomer, and from his mind as exemplified in his whole life to his mind as it exists in a single moment. But from this pin-point, this tiny camera obscura, if (as we all in fact believe) the astronomer really knows what he is thought to know, we can throw the light of knowledge over vast stretches of time and space, and discover the unreality of the walls of our supposed subjective prison. In this process of escape the interpretation of egocentric particulars is a very essential step.

Before attempting a precise account of egocentric words, let us briefly survey the picture of the world to which subsequent discussions will lead us.

There is one public space, namely the space of physics, and this space is occupied by public physical objects. But public space and public objects are not sensible; they are arrived at by a mixture of inference and logical construction. Sensible spaces and sensible objects differ from one person to another, though they have certain affinities to each other and to their public counter-parts.

There is one public time,[1] in which not only physical events, but mental events also, have their place. There are also private times, which are those given in memory and expectation.

My whole private space is "here" in physical space, and my whole private time is "now" in public time. But there are also private "heres" and "nows" in private spaces and times.

When your friend calls out in the dark "where are you?" and you answer "here I am", the "here" is one in physical space, since you are concerned to give information which will help another to find you. But if, when alone, you are looking for a lost object, and on finding it you exclaim "here it is", the "here" may be either in public space or in your private space. Of course ordinary speech does not distinguish between public and private space. Broadly, "here" is where my body is—my physical body if I mean "here" in physical space, and my percept of my body if I mean "here" in my private space. But "here" may be much more narrowly localized, for instance if you are pointing out a thorn in your finger. One might say (though this would not quite accord with usage) that "here" is the place of whatever sensible object is occupying my attention. This, though not quite the usual meaning of the word, is the concept which most needs discussing in connection with the word "here".

"Now" has a similar two-fold meaning, one subjective and one objective. When I review my life in memory, some of the things

---

[1] This is subject to limitations connected with relativity. But as language and theory of knowledge are concerned with inhabitants of the earth, these may be ignored, since no two people have a relative velocity comparable to that of light.

I remember seem a long time ago, others more recent, but all are in the past as compared with present percepts. This "pastness", however, is subjective: what I am remembering, I remember *now*, and my recollecting is a present fact. If my memory is veridical, there was a fact to which my recollection has a certain relation, partly causal, partly of similarity; this fact was objectively in the past. I maintain that, in addition to the objective relation of before-and-after, by which events are ordered in a public time-series, there is a subjective relation of more-or-less-remote, which holds between memories that all exist at the same objective time. The private time-series generated by this relation differs not only from person to person, but from moment to moment in the life of any one person. There is also a future in the private time-series, which is that of expectation. Both private and public time have, at each moment in the life of a percipient, one peculiar point, which is, at that moment, called "now".

It is to be observed that "here" and "now" depend upon perception; in a purely material universe there would be no "here" and "now". Perception is not impartial, but proceeds from a centre; our perceptual world is (so to speak) a perspective view of the common world. What is near in time and space generally gives rise to a more vivid and distinct memory or percept than what is far. The public world of physics has no such centre of illumination.

In defining egocentric particulars, we may take "this" as fundamental, in a sense in which "this" is not distinguished from "that". I shall attempt an ostensive definition of "this", and thence a nominal definition of the other egocentric particulars.

"This" denotes whatever, at the moment when the word is used, occupies the centre of attention. With words which are not egocentric, what is constant is something about the object indicated, but "this" denotes a different object on each occasion of its use: what is constant is not the object denoted, but its relation to the particular use of the word. Whenever the word is used, the person using it is attending to something, and the word indicates this something. When a word is not egocentric, there is no need to distinguish between different occasions when it is used, but we must make this distinction with egocentric words, since what they indicate is something having a given relation to the particular use of the word.

We may define "I" as "the person attending to this", "now" as "the time of attending to this", and "here" as "the place of attending to this". We could equally well take "here-now" as fundamental; then "this" would be defined as "what is here-now", and "I" as "what experiences this".

Can two persons experience the same "this", and if so, in what circumstances? I do not think this question can be decided by logical considerations: *a priori*, either answer would be possible. But taking the question empirically, it has an answer. When the "this" concerned is what common sense takes to be a percept of a physical object, difference of perspective makes a difference in the percept unavoidable, if the same physical object is concerned in the two cases. Two people looking at one tree, or listening to the song of one bird, are having somewhat different percepts. But two people looking at different trees might, theoretically, have exactly similar percepts, though this would be improbable. Two people may see exactly the same shade of colour, and are likely to do so if each is looking at a continuous band of colours, e.g. those of the rainbow. Two people looking at a square table will not see exactly similar quadrilaterals, but the quadrilaterals they see will have certain geometrical properties in common.

It thus appears that two people are more likely to have the same "this" if it is somewhat abstract than if it is fully concrete. In fact, broadly speaking, every increase of abstractness diminishes the difference between one person's world and another's. When we come to logic and pure mathematics, there need be no difference whatever: two people can attach exactly the same meaning to the word "or" or the word "371,294". This is one reason why physics, in its endeavour to eliminate the privacy of sense, has grown progressively more abstract. This is also the reason for the view, which has been widely held by philosophers, that all true knowledge is intellectual rather than sensible, and that the intellect liberates while the senses keep us in a personal prison. In such views there is an *element* of truth, but no more, except where logic and pure mathematics are concerned; for in all empirical knowledge liberation from sense can be only partial. It can, however, be carried to the point where two men's interpretations of a given sentence are nearly certain to be both true or both false. The securing of this result is one of the aims (more or less unconscious) governing the development of scientific concepts.

Chapter V

SUSPENDED REACTIONS: KNOWLEDGE AND BELIEF

WE have been concerned hitherto with what may be called the "exclamatory" use of language, when it is used to denote some interesting feature of a man's present experience. So long as this use alone is in question, a single word can function as a sentence in the indicative. When Xenophon's Ten Thousand exclaimed "Sea! Sea!" they were using the word in this way. But a single word may also be used in other ways. A man found dying of thirst in the desert may murmur "water!" and is then uttering a request or expressing a desire; he may see a mirage and say "water?"; or he may see a spring and assert "water". Sentences are needed to distinguish between these various uses of words. They are needed also—and this is perhaps their main use—to express what may be called "suspended reactions". Suppose you intend to take a railway journey to-morrow, and you look up your train to-day: you do not propose, at the moment, to take any further action on the knowledge you have acquired, but when the time comes you will behave in the appropriate manner. Knowledge, in the sense in which it does not merely register present sensible impressions, consists essentially of preparations for such delayed reactions. Such preparations may in all cases be called "beliefs", but they are only to be called "knowledge" when they prompt *successful* reactions, or at any rate show themselves related to the facts with which they are concerned in some way which distinguishes them from preparations that would be called "errors".

It is important not to exaggerate the role of language. In my view, there is in pre-linguistic experience something that may be called "belief", and that may be true or false; there are also, I should say, what may be called "ideas". Language immensely increases the number and complexity of possible beliefs and ideas, but is not, I am convinced, necessary for the simplest beliefs and ideas. A cat will watch for a long time at a mousehole, with her tail swishing in savage expectation; in such a case, one should say (so I hold) that the smell of mouse stimulates the "idea" of the rest of what makes up an actual mouse. The objection to such language comes, it seems to me, from an unduly intellectualist conception of what is meant by the word "idea". I should define an "idea" as a state of an organism appropriate (in some sense) to something not sensibly present. All desire involves ideas in this sense, and desire is certainly pre-linguistic. Belief also, in an important sense, exists in the cat watching the mousehole, belief which is "true" if there is a mouse down the hole and "false" if not.

The word "mouse", by itself, will not express the different attitudes of the cat while waiting for her prey and when seizing it; to express these different attitudes further developments of language are necessary. Command, desire, and narrative all involve the use of words describing something not sensibly present, and to distinguish them from each other and from the indicative various linguistic devices are necessary.

Perhaps the necessity to assume "ideas" as existing ante-cedently to language may be made more evident by considering what it is that words express. The dying man in the desert who murmurs "water!" is clearly expressing a state in which a dying animal might be. How this state should be analysed is a difficult question, but we all, in a sense, know the meaning of the word "thirst", and we all know that what this word means does not depend for its existence upon there being a word to denote it. The word "thirst" denotes a desire for something to drink, and such a desire involves, in the sense already explained, the presence of the "idea" of drink. What would commonly be called a man's "mental" life is entirely made up of ideas and attitudes towards them. Imagination, memory, desire, thought, and belief all involve ideas, and ideas are connected with suspended reactions. Ideas, in fact, are parts of causes of actions, which become complete causes when a suitable stimulus is applied. They are like explosives waiting to be exploded. In fact, the similarity may be very close. Trained soldiers, hearing the word "fire!" (which already existed in them as an idea) proceed to cause explosions. The similarity of language to explosives lies in the fact that a very small additional stimulus can produce a tremendous effect. Consider the effects which flowed from Hitler's pronouncing the word "war!"

It is to be observed that words, when learnt, can become substitutes for ideas. There is a condition called "thinking of" this or that, say water when you are in the desert. A dog appears, from its behaviour, to be capable of being in this condition; so does an infant that cannot yet speak. When this condition exists, it prompts behaviour having reference to water. When the word "water" is known, the condition may consist (mainly, not wholly) in the presence of this word, either overtly pronounced or merely imagined. The word, when understood, has the same causal efficacy as the idea. Familiar knowledge is apt to be purely verbal; few schoolboys go beyond the words in reciting "William the Conqueror 1066". Words and ideas are, in fact, interchangeable; both have meaning, and both have the same kind of causal relations to what they mean. The difference is that, in the case of words, the relation to what is meant is in the nature of a social convention, and is learnt by hearing speech, whereas in the case of ideas the relation is "natural", i.e. it does not depend upon the behaviour of other people, but upon intrinsic similarity and (one must suppose) upon physiological processes existing in all human beings, and to a lesser extent in the higher animals.

"Knowledge", which is, in most forms, connected with sus-pended reactions, is not a precise conception. Many of the difficulties of philosophers have arisen from regarding it as precise. Let us consider various ways of "knowing" the same fact. Suppose that, at 4 p.m. yesterday, I heard the noise of an explosion. When I heard it, I "knew" the noise in a certain sense, though not in the sense in which the word is usually employed. This sense, in spite of being unusual, cannot be discarded, since it is essential in explaining what is meant by "empirical verification". Immediately afterwards, I may say "that was loud!" or "what was that noise?" This is "immediate memory", which differs only in degree from sensation, since the physiological disturbance caused by the noise has not yet wholly subsided. Immediately before the explosion, if I have seen the train fired which leads to a charge of explosive, I may be in a state of tense expectation; this is, in a sense, akin to immediate memory, but directed to the near future. Next comes true memory: I now remember the bang I heard yesterday. My state is now made up of ideas (or images) or words, together with belief and a context which dates the occurrence remembered. I can imagine a bang just like the one that I remember, but when I do this, belief and dating are absent. (The word "belief" is one which I shall discuss later.) Imagined events are not included in knowledge or error, because of the absence of belief.

Sensation, immediate expectation, immediate memory, and true memory all give knowledge which is, in some degree and with appropriate limitations, independent of extraneous evidence. But most of the knowledge of people with any degree of education is not of any of these kinds. We know what we have been told or have read in books or newspapers; here words come first, and it is often unnecessary to realize what the words mean. When I believe "William the Conqueror 1066", what I am really believing (as a rule) is: "the words 'William the Conqueror 1066' are true". This has the advantage that the words can be made sensible whenever I choose; the Conqueror is dead, but his name comes to life whenever I pronounce it. It has also the advantage that the name is public and the same for all, whereas the image (if any) employed in thinking of William will differ from person to person, and is sure to be too concrete. If (e.g.) we think of him on horseback, that will not suit "William was born at Falaise", because he was not born on horseback.

Sentences heard in narrative are, of course, not necessarily understood in this purely verbal manner; indeed a purely verbal understanding is essentially incomplete. A child reading an exciting adventure story will "live through" the adventures of the hero, particularly if the hero is of about the same age as the reader. If the hero leaps a chasm, the child's muscles will grow taut; if the hero sees a lion about to spring, the child will hold his breath. Whatever happens to the hero, the child's physiological condition is a reproduction, on a smaller scale, of the physiological condition of the hero. In adult life, the same result can be produced by good writing. When Shakespeare's Antony says "I am dying, Egypt, dying", we experience something which we do not experience when we see in *The Times* a notice of the death of some person unknown to us. One difference between poetry and bald statement is that poetry seeks to take the reader behind the words to what they signify.

The process called "verification" does not absolutely *necessitate* (but often involves) an imaginative understanding of words, but only a comparison of words used in advance with words used when the fact concerned becomes sensible. You say "this litmus paper will turn red"; I, later, say "this litmus paper has turned red". Thus I *need* only pass outside the purely verbal region when I use a sentence to express a present sensible fact.

"Knowledge" is a vague concept for two reasons. First, because the meaning of a word is always more or less vague except in logic and pure mathematics; and second, because all that we count as knowledge is in a greater or less degree uncertain, and there is no way of deciding how much uncertainty makes a belief unworthy to be called "knowledge", any more than how much loss of hair makes a man bald.

"Knowledge" is sometimes defined as "true belief", but this definition is too wide. If you look at a clock which you believe to be going, but which in fact has stopped, and you happen to look at it at a moment when it is right, you will acquire a true belief as to the time of day, but you cannot be correctly said to have knowledge. The correct definition of "knowledge" need not concern us at the moment; what concerns us now is belief.

Let us take some simple sentence expressing something that is or may be a sensible fact, such as "a loud bang is (or has been, or will be) taking place". We will suppose it a fact that such a bang occurs at a place P at time t, and that the belief to be considered refers to this particular bang. That is to say we will amend our sentence to "a loud bang occurs at place P at time t". We will call this sentence S. What sort of thing is happening to me when I believe this sentence, or rather when I believe what it expresses?

There are a number of possibilities. First, I may be at or near the place P at the time t, and may hear the bang. In that case, at time t I have direct sensible knowledge of it; ordinary language would hardly call this "belief", but for our purposes it is better to include it in the scope of the word. Obviously this sort of knowledge does not require words. No more does the immediate memory that subsists while I am still shaken by the noise. But how about more remote memory? Here, also, we may have no words, but an auditory image accompanied by a feeling which could be (but need not be) expressed in the words "that occurred". Immediate expectation also does not need words. When you watch a door about to be slammed by the wind, your body and mind are in a state of expectation of noise, and if no noise resulted you would experience a shock of surprise. This immediate expectation is different from our ordinary expectations about events that are not imminent. I expect that I shall get up to-morrow morning, but my body is not in that unpleasant condition in which it will be to-morrow morning when I am expecting to get up in a moment. I doubt whether it is possible, without words, to expect any event not in the *immediate* future. This is one of the differences between expectation and memory.

Belief about something outside my own experience seems usually only possible through the help of language, or some rudimentary beginning of language. Sea-gulls and cannibals have a "food-cry", which in the cannibals is meant to give information, but in the sea-gulls may be a spontaneous expression of emotion, like a groan when the dentist hurts you. A noise of this sort is a word to the hearer, but not to the utterer. An animal's behaviour may be affected by signs which have no analogy with language, for instance when it is in search of water in an unknown region. If a thirsty animal runs persistently down into a valley, I should be inclined to say that it "believes" there is water there, and in such a case there would be non-verbal belief in something that is as yet outside the animal's experience. However, I do not wish to become involved in a controversy as to the meaning of words, so I will not insist upon the view that such behaviour shows "belief".

Among human beings, the usual way of acquiring beliefs as to what has not been, and is not just about to be, experienced is through verbal testimony. To revert to our sentence S, some person whom we believe to be truthful pronounces it in our presence, and we then believe what the sentence asserts. I want to inquire what is actually occurring in us while we are believing the sentence.

We must, of course, distinguish a belief as a habit from the same belief when it is active. This distinction is necessary in regard to all habits. An acquired habit consists in the fact that a certain stimulus, whenever it occurs, now produces a certain reaction which it did not produce in the animal in question until the animal had had certain experiences. We must suppose that, even in the absence of the stimulus concerned, there is some difference between an animal that has a certain habit and one that lacks it. A man who understands the word "fire" must differ in some way from a man who does not, even when he is not hearing the word. We suppose the difference to be in the brain, but its nature is hypothetical. However, it is not a habit as a permanent character of an organism that concerns us, but the *active* habit, which is only displayed when the appropriate stimulus is applied. In the case we are investigating, the stimulus is the sentence S; or rather, since the sentence may have been never heard before, and may therefore have had no chance to generate a habit, the stimulus is the succession of the words composing S, each of which, we are supposing, is familiar to the hearer, and has already generated the habit which constitutes understanding of its meaning.

It may happen, when we hear a sentence, that we do not trouble to think what it means, but merely believe "this sentence is true". With certain kinds of sentences, this is the usual reaction; for example, when we are told someone's address and we only wish to write to him. If we wish to go and see him, the meaning of the words becomes important, but for sending him a letter the words alone are sufficient. When we believe "this sentence is true", we are not believing what the sentence asserts; if the sentence is in a language unknown to us, we may believe that it is true without being able to find out what it asserts—for example, if it is a sentence in a Greek Testament and we know no Greek. I shall therefore ignore this case, and consider what happens when, hearing S, we believe what S asserts.

Let us somewhat simplify the sentence, and suppose that, when I am walking with a friend, he says: "There was an explosion here yesterday." I may believe him, or understand him without believing. Let us suppose that I believe him, and that I believe what his words assert, not merely that the words are true. The most important word in the sentence is "explosion". This word, when I am actively understanding it, rouses in me faint imitations of the effects of hearing an actual explosion—auditory images, images of nervous shock, etc. Owing to the word "here", these images are combined in my mental picture with the surrounding scenery. Owing to the word "yesterday", they are combined with recollections of yesterday's experiences. All this, so far, is involved in understanding the sentence, whether or not it is believed. I incline to the view that believing a sentence is a simpler occurrence than understanding without belief; I think the primitive reaction is belief, and that understanding without belief involves inhibition of the impulse to belief. What distinguishes belief is readiness for any action that may be called for if what is asserted is a fact. Suppose for instance that an acquaintance of mine has disappeared, and is known to have been hereabouts yesterday, then belief may prompt me to search for signs of his remains, which I shall not do if I understand without believing. If no such action is called for, there is at least the action of repeating what I have been told whenever it may seem appropriate to do so.

From all this it appears that, when I believe what a certain sentence asserts, the words, having had their intended effect, need no longer be present to me. All that need exist is a state of mind and body appropriate to the fact that the sentence asserts.

It is an error to suppose that beliefs consist *solely* in tendencies to actions of certain kinds. Let us take an analogy; a belief may be compared to a cistern plus a pipe plus a tap. The tap *can* be turned on, and the belief *can* influence action, but neither happens without an additional stimulus. When a man is believing something, there must exist in him either appropriate words or appropriate images, or, at the very least, appropriate muscular adjustments. Any of these, given certain additional circumstances (which correspond to turning on the tap), will produce action, and this action may be such as to show an outside observer what it is that is being believed; this is particularly the case if the action consists in pronouncing appropriate words. The impulse to action, given the right stimulus, is inherent in the presence of words, images, or muscular adjustments. To entertain an idea vividly and not act upon it is difficult. If, alone at night, you read a story in which a man is stabbed in the back, you will have an impulse to press your chair tight against the wall. Booth the actor (the brother of Lincoln's assassin), on one occasion when he was playing Macbeth under the influence of liquor, refused to be killed, and chased Macduff murderously all through the stalls. It is unwise to read a ghost story just before walking through a churchyard at midnight. As these examples show, when an idea is entertained without belief, the impulse to belief is not absent, but is inhibited. Belief is not something added to an idea previously merely entertained, but something subtracted from an idea, by an effort, when the idea is considered without being accepted.

Another example is the difficulty that uneducated people feel about hypotheses. If you say "let us suppose so-and-so and see what comes of the supposition", they will tend either to believe what you suppose, or to think that you are wasting your time. For this reason, *reductio ad absurdum* is a form of argument that is repugnant to those who are not familiar with logic or mathematics; if the hypothesis is going to be proved false, they cannot make themselves hypothetically entertain it.

I do not wish to exaggerate the scope of pre-linguistic belief: only very simple and primitive matters can be dealt with in the absence of words. Words are public, permanent (when written), and capable of being created at will. These merits make it possible to have more complicated habits based on words than any that could be based on wordless ideas or images. By acquiring verbal habits we can prepare ourselves for actual situations when they arise. What is more, knowledge can be externalized in books of reference, and need then only exist in human beings when it is wanted. Consider the telephone book: no one wants to know all its contents, or indeed any except at certain moments. The people who compile the book may never use it, and the immense majority of those who use it have had no hand in compiling it. This kind of socialized potential knowledge is only rendered possible by language, in fact by *written* language. All that the user of the telephone needs to know is a simple prescription for deriving appropriate action from the appropriate entry in the book. By such devices we diminish enormously the amount of knowledge that it is necessary to carry in our heads.

All generalized knowledge is of this sort. Suppose the geography book tells me that Semipalatinsk is a province and city of Central Asia, in the territory of the U.S.S.R. This knowledge will remain purely verbal unless I have occasion to go to Semipalatinsk, but if this should happen there are rules by which the words of the book show me how to produce desired experiences. In such a case I may be said to understand the words if I know what action they prescribe when I have desires connected with what the words mean, or, in an extreme case, merely a desire to know what the words mean. You may feel a longing to see the Altai Mountains, knowing nothing about them except that that is their name. In that case, the guide book shows you what you must do in order to know the proposition: "*These* are the Altai Mountains." When you have learnt arithmetic you can deal with all the innumerable occasions on which you have to count your change in shops, but in learning arithmetic you need not be thinking of its applications. In such ways the province of purely verbal knowledge becomes wider and wider, and at last it becomes easy to forget that verbal knowledge must have some relation to sensible experience. But except through such relation we cannot define empirical truth and falsehood, and to forget it is therefore fatal to any hope of a sound philosophy.

Chapter VI

SENTENCES

I WANT in this chapter to consider sentences as opposed to words, and to ask in what consists the understanding of words that do not denote objects, but occur only as parts of sentences. We saw that the one word "water" may be used to express what, if fully expressed, requires different sentences. It may mean "here is water"; it may mean "I want water"; it may, if pronounced with an interrogative inflexion, mean "is this water?" Obviously such ambiguity is not desirable, especially in writing, where differences of inflexion are difficult to indicate. We therefore need such words as "here is", "I want", "is this". It is the function of such words that forms the theme of this chapter.

Consider the following sentences: "there is fire here", "there was fire here", "there will be fire here", "is there fire here?" "I want fire here", "there is no fire here". These sentences are respectively present, past, future, interrogative, optative, and negative, but all deal with the same object, namely fire.

The word "fire" may be caused in me in various ways. When it is caused by the sensible presence of fire, I communicate the fact by the sentence "there is fire here"; when by the memory, by the sentence "there was fire here". But I may use this sentence, not to express a memory, but to report what I have been told, or to state an inference from charred embers. In the former case, the word "fire" is caused in me by my hearing the word; in the latter case, by my seeing something which I know to be an effect of fire. Thus when I say "there was fire here", my state of mind may be one of several very different possibilities. In spite of these subjective differences, however, what I am asserting is the same in all the different cases. If my assertion is true, a certain occurrence took place here, and the occurrence in virtue of which it is true is the same whether the occurrence is remembered or known through testimony or inferred from present traces of past combustion. It is for this reason that we use the same words in these various cases, for a sentence in the indicative is concerned, not to express a state of mind (though it always does so), but to assert a fact other than that expressed by the sentence. But we will postpone the explicit consideration of truth and falsehood to a later chapter.

Similar subjective ambiguities exist in connection with the sentence "there will be fire here". In a situation in which you experience immediate expectation of fire, your subjective state is analogous to memory, except in the vital point of being directed to the future. But as a rule statements about the future are inferences. You may see a damp haystack fermenting and infer that it will burn, or you may have been told that at some future date there is to be a bonfire here. But again these various possibilities make no difference to what is asserted when you say "there will be fire here".

"Is there fire here?" may be a form of imperative, or a suggestion for investigation. This sentence does not make an assertion, but shows a desire to be able to make one. The difference from "there is a fire here" is not in anything having an external reference, but in our attitude to what has such a reference. We may say that there is an "idea" called "fire-here-now"; when we preface these words by "there is" we assert this idea, whereas when we preface them by "is there" we "actively consider" them, i.e. we are concerned to find out whether or not to assert them. I speak of "outward reference" in a preliminary way, as the concept is a difficult one, demanding considerable discussion.

"I want fire here" is a sentence in the indicative, asserting that I feel a certain desire, but it is commonly used as if it were an *expression* of desire, not an *assertion* of it. Strictly speaking, desire ought to be expressed by "would there were a fire here" or "Oh for a fire here!" This is more easily and naturally expressed in a language which, like Greek, has an optative mood. The sentence "Oh for a fire!" asserts nothing, and is therefore neither true nor false. It *expresses* a desire, and a person hearing me pronounce it may infer that I feel a desire, but it does not *assert* that I feel a desire. Similarly when I say "there is a fire here" I *express* a belief, and the hearer can infer that I have this belief, but I do not *assert* that I have a belief.

When I say "there is not a fire here", what may be called the "content" is the same as when I say "there is fire here", but this content is denied instead of being asserted.

Reviewing the above sentences, but omitting those referring to past or future, we find that, considering what they express, they all have the same core, namely "fire-here-now". The ideas expressed by "fire", "here", and "now" may be called "indicative" ideas, that is to say, they can all indicate features of a sensible experience. Taken all together, they constitute one complex indicative idea. An indicative idea sometimes indicates, and sometimes does not; if there is a fire here now, "fire-here-now" indicates that fire, but if there is not a fire, "fire-here-now" indicates nothing. Towards an indicative idea we may have various attitudes: assertive, interrogative, optative, or negative. These attitudes are expressed by the words "there is", "is there", "oh for", and "there is not" respectively. (I do not pretend that this list of possible attitudes is exhaustive.) These attitudes, which are *expressed* by the above words, can also be *asserted*, but we then need indicative words for them; the words are "belief", "doubt", "desire", "disbelief". This leads to new sentences, all of which are assertions, but about my state of mind, not about fire. The sentences are: "I believe there is a fire here now", "I wonder if there is a fire here now", "I hope there is a fire here now", and "I disbelieve that there is a fire here now".

It is evident that "there-is", "is-there", "oh-for", and "there-is-not" should each be regarded as one word, and as expressing different attitudes on the part of the speaker to one and the same idea. It is not their function to indicate objects, as names do; the fact that the word "not" can be used significantly does not imply that there is an object called "not" in some Platonic heaven. For the understanding of language it is essential to realize that, while some necessary words mean objects, others do not.

Words that mean objects may be called "indicative" words. I include among such words not only names, but words denoting qualities such as "white", "hard", "warm", and words denoting perceptible relations such as "before", "above", "in". If the sole purpose of language were to describe sensible facts, we could content ourselves with indicative words. But, as we have seen, such words do not suffice to express doubt, desire, or disbelief. They also do not suffice to express logical connections, e.g. "if that is so, I'll eat my hat", or "if Wilson had been more tactful, America would have joined the League of Nations". Nor do they suffice for sentences needing such words as "all" and "some", "the" and "a". The significance of words of this kind can only be explained by explaining the significance of sentences in which they occur. When you want to explain the word "lion," you can take your child to the Zoo and say "look, that's a lion." But there is no Zoo where you can show him *if* or *the* or *nevertheless*, for these are not indicative words. They are needed in sentences, but only in sentences not concerned exclusively with the assertion of single facts. It is because we need such sentences that words which are not indicative are indispensable.

Chapter VII

EXTERNAL REFERENCE OF IDEAS
AND BELIEFS

THE kind of external reference with which we shall be concerned in this chapter is not that by which experiences are interpreted as percepts of external objects, as when, for instance, a visual sensation produces in me a condition called "seeing a table". This kind of external reference will be considered in connection with the interpretation of physics and the evidence for its truth. What we are now concerned with is a reference of one part of my mental life to another, and only derivatively to things not forming part of my experience.

We are in the habit of saying that we think *of* so-and-so and that we believe *in* such-and-such. It is the meaning of "of" and "in" in such phrases that I wish to discuss, as a necessary preliminary to the definition of "truth" and "falsehood".

We considered in an earlier chapter the process of ostensive definition as the source of the meanings of words. But we then found that a given word can "mean" an idea as well as a sensible experience; this happens, notably, when the word is used to express a memory. When the same word can be used to denote an idea or a sensible experience, that is a sign that the idea is an idea "of" the sensible experience. But obviously the relation expressed by this word "of" is one which can exist independently of language, and is, in fact, presupposed in the use of the same word for an idea and a sensible experience.

The relation with which we are concerned is perhaps seen most clearly in the case of memory. Suppose you have lately seen something horrible—say a friend run over and killed by a lorry. You will have a constantly recurring picture of the event in your mind, not only as pure imagination, but as something that you know actually occurred. As the dreadful swift sequence overwhelms you once more, you may say to yourself "yes, that really happened". But in what sense can this be true? For your recollections are *now*, and consist of images, not of sensations, still less of actual motor lorries. The sense in which it is nevertheless true is what we have to elucidate.

Images occur in two ways, as imagination and as recollection. I have sometimes, under the influence of fatigue or fever, seen the faces of people of whom I was fond, not with the benign expression to which I was accustomed, but horribly grimacing and grotesque. These painful images did not command belief unless my temperature was high enough to cause delirium. Even in deliberate recollection there are often imaginative accretions which are not believed, but these do not count as memories. Whatever counts as a memory consists of images or words which are felt as referring to some earlier experience. Since it is clear that words can only express memories because a given word can apply both to an image (or idea) and to a sensible occurrence, it is clear that we must first consider non-verbal memory, with a view to discovering what is the relation of an idea to a sensible experience which leads us to use the same word for both. I shall therefore, for the present, exclude memories expressed in words, and consider only those that come as images accompanied by the belief or feeling that they refer to a previous occurrence.

Suppose I am asked to describe the furniture of my room. I may go to my room and record what I see, or I may call up a picture of my room and record what I see with my mind's eye. If I am a good visualizer and my room is one which I have inhabited for some time, the two methods will give results that, at least in broad outline, will be indistinguishable. It is easy, in this way, to test the accuracy of my memory. But before it is tested I implicitly believe it. Some memories are not capable of being tested at all thoroughly, for instance if you have been the sole spectator of a murder; nevertheless your evidence will be accepted unless there is reason to suspect you of perjury. At present, it is not the trustworthiness of memory that concerns us, but the analysis of the occurrence.

What is involved in saying that A is an "image" or "idea" of B? First, there must be resemblance; more particularly, if both are complex, there must be resemblance of structure. Second, B must play a certain definite part in the causation of A. Third, A and B must have certain effects in common, for example, they can cause the same words to occur to a person who experiences them. When these three relations exist, I shall say that B is the "prototype" of A.

But if A is a recollection of B, something more is involved.

For in this case A is felt or believed to be pointing to something other than itself, and this something is, in fact, B. We should *like* to say that A is felt to be pointing to B, but this we have no right to say, since B is not itself present to the person recollecting; what is present is only A, as B's representative. We must say, therefore, that, in memory as opposed to pure imagination, there is the belief: "A is related to *something* as idea to prototype", where the relation of idea to prototype is defined by the three characteristics mentioned in the preceding paragraph. I do not mean, of course, that an ordinary memory belief has the explicitness suggested by the above analysis. I mean only that, in memory, an idea is vaguely felt to point beyond itself, and that the above is an account of what may be the actual state of affairs when this vague feeling is justifiable.

When B is the prototype of A, we say that A is an image "of" B. This is a definition of this use of the word "of".

It is obvious that A may be an image of B without the person concerned being aware of the fact. It is also obvious that A may have many prototypes. If I tell you I met a negro in an English country lane, the word "negro" may call up in your mind an image vaguely compounded of many negroes whom you have seen; in this case they must all count as prototypes of your image. In general, even when an image has only one prototype, it will usually be vaguer than its prototype. If, for example, you have an image of a shade of colour, various shades that you can distinguish when sensibly present might all serve as its prototypes. This, incidentally, supplies an answer to Hume's query: Could you imagine a shade of colour you had never seen, if it was intermediate between two very similar shades that you had seen? The answer is that you could not form so precise an image, even of a colour that you had seen, but that you could form a vague image, equally appropriate to the shade that you had not seen and to the two similar shades that you had seen.

It will be seen that, according to the above theory, the external reference of an idea or image consists in a belief, which, when made explicit, may be expressed in the words: "this has a prototype". In the absence of such a belief (which, when it exists, is usually a somewhat vague feeling), although there may be in fact a prototype there is no external reference. This is the case of pure imagination.

In the case of a memory-belief, if what is said to be remembered is an experience of the person remembering, the above kind of external reference is the only kind required. But as a rule there is also another kind, namely that which, at the beginning of this chapter, we declined to consider. Suppose I remember "I saw an elephant yesterday". There is involved not only my experience of yesterday, but belief in an animal having an independent existence, not only when I saw it, but also before and after. All this depends upon animal inference in the sense to be considered in Part III, involving a reference external, not only to my present experience, but to the whole of my experience. This kind of external reference, however, takes us beyond the subject of the present chapter.

Chapter VIII

TRUTH: ELEMENTARY FORMS

TRUTH and falsehood, in so far as they are public, are attributes of sentences, either in the indicative or in the subjunctive or conditional. In the present chapter, which will consider only the simpler examples of truth, I shall confine myself to sentences in the indicative. In addition to sentences there are some other ways of making public statements, maps, for instance, and graphs. There are also conventional devices for reducing a sentence to one essential word, as is done in telephone books and railway time tables. But for our purposes we may, without any important loss of generality, confine ourselves to fully expressed sentences. And until we have considered logical words, which will be the subject of the next two chapters, we must confine ourselves to sentences in the indicative.

But in order to define "truth" and "falsehood" we must go behind sentences to what they "express" and what they "indicate".

A sentence has, to begin with, a property which I shall call "signification". This is the property which is preserved in an accurate translation. "Two and two make four" has the same signification as "deux et deux font quatre". Signification is also preserved when the wording is changed; e.g. "A is the husband of B", "B is the wife of A", "A is a male who is married to B", "A is married to B, who is a female", all have the same signification. It is obvious that when two sentences have the same signification both are true or both are false; therefore whatever distinguishes truth from falsehood is to be sought rather in the signification of sentences than in sentences themselves.

Some sentences which, at first sight, appear to be correctly constructed, are in fact nonsense, in the sense that they have no signification. Such, if interpreted literally, are "necessity is the mother of invention" and "procrastination is the thief of time". A very important part of logical syntax consists of rules for avoiding nonsense in constructing sentences. But for the present we are concerned with sentences that are too simple to run the risk of being nonsensical.

To arrive at what a sentence "signifies", the easiest way is to ask ourselves what is in common between a sentence in one language and its translation into another. Suppose that on a given occasion I say to an Englishman "I am hot" and to a Frenchman "j'ai chaud", the two sentences express the same state of mind and body, and are made true (or false) by the same fact. The signification of a sentence would thus seem to have two aspects: on the one hand it "expresses" the condition of the person uttering it, and on the other hand it points outside this present condition to something in virtue of which it is true or false. What an asserted sentence expresses is a *belief*; what makes it true or false is a *fact*, which is in general distinct from the belief. Truth and falsehood are external relations, that is to say, no analysis of a sentence or a belief will show whether it is true or false. (This does not apply to logic and mathematics, where truth or falsehood, as the case may be, follows from the form of the sentence. But I am for the present ignoring logical truth.) Consider e.g. the sentence "I am an uncle", and suppose you know that your sister in India is due to have a child, but you do not know whether the child has yet been born. No analysis of the sentence or of your state of mind will show whether the sentence is true or false, since its truth or falsehood depends upon events in India as to which you are in ignorance. But although understanding the sentence does not enable you to know whether it is true or false, it does enable you to know what sort of fact would make it true and what sort would make it false; this, therefore, is part of the signification of a sentence, or is at least inseparably connected with the signification, although the actual truth or falsehood (as the case may be) is not.

If "truth" and "falsehood" had been defined, we could say that two sentences are to have, by definition, the same "signification" if whatever possible state of affairs makes one of them true also makes the other true, and vice versa. But, as we shall see, it is not clear that "truth" and "falsehood" can be defined without first defining "signification".

There are, we said, two sides to signification, which we may call subjective and objective respectively. The subjective side has to do with the state of the person uttering the sentence, while the objective side has to do with what would make the sentence true or false. Let us begin by considering the subjective side.

When we say that a sentence is true, we mean that a person

asserting it will be speaking truly. A person may pronounce a sentence without intending to assert it: when an actor says "this is I, Hamlet the Dane", no one believes him, but no one accuses him of lying. This shows that the subjective side in the analysis of signification is essential. When we say that a sentence is "true", we mean to say something about the state of mind of a person uttering or hearing it with belief. It is in fact primarily beliefs that are true or false; sentences only become so through the fact that they can express beliefs. It is therefore in beliefs that the subjective side of the signification of sentences is to be sought.

We may say that two sentences have the same signification if they express the same belief. But we must, having said this, explain in what sense two people (or one person at different times) can have the same belief, and by what tests we can discover when this is the case. For practical purposes we may say that two people who speak the same language have the same belief if they accept the same sentence as expressing it; and when two people speak different languages, their beliefs are the same if a competent interpreter regards the sentence in which one of them expresses his belief as a translation of that used by the other. But this criterion is not theoretically sufficient, since infants that cannot speak must be allowed to have beliefs, and so (I should say) must animals.

"Belief", as I wish to use the word, denotes a state of mind or body or both, in which an animal acts with reference to something not sensibly present. When I go to the station in expectation of finding a train, my action expresses a belief. So does the action of a dog excited by the smell of fox. So does that of a bird in a room, which flies against the window panes in the hope of getting out. Among human beings, the only action by which a belief is expressed is, very often, the pronouncing of appropriate words.

It will be seen that, according to the above definition of "belief", it is closely connected with meaning and with ostensive definition. Words have "meaning" when there is an association or a conditioned reflex connecting them with something other than themselves—this, at least, applies to indicative words. I say "look, there's a fox", and you act as you would do if you smelt a fox. I say "fox" when I see a fox, because a fox suggests the word "fox" as well as vice versa. When, the fox having just disappeared, I utter the word "fox", and when you, having not yet seen the animal, hear the word, there is "belief" in the sense defined above. So there is when, without speaking, you look for the fox. But it is only when action is suspended that belief becomes a definite state of mind—for instance when you have just looked up a train that you mean to take to-morrow. When immediate action is called for, energy may be drained into the muscles, and "belief" may be shown as merely a characteristic of bodily movements. But it must be remembered that shouting "fox" or "tally-ho" is a bodily movement; we cannot therefore deny that bodily movements may express beliefs.

External reference, which we discussed in the last chapter, exists in all indicative words when used in the way in which the use of words begins. It exists also in non-verbal behaviour, as when a dog scratches at a rabbit-hole because he has seen a rabbit go down the hole. But when behaviour is non-verbal it is difficult for the observer, and often for the agent, to say what, exactly, it is that the behaviour refers to. Words, like balances and thermometers, are instruments of precision, though often not very good ones; but that to which they give precision can exist, and be apprehended vaguely, without their help.

To put the matter schematically, with a more or less unreal simplification: the presence of a stimulus A causes a certain kind of behaviour, say B; as a result of experience, something else, say C, may cause B in the absence of A. In that case, C may be said to cause "belief" in A, and "belief" in A may be said to be a feature of the behaviour B. When words come in, all this becomes more precise. The sight of a fox (A) causes you to pronounce the word "fox" (B); you may learn the trail of a fox in snow (C), and, seeing it, say "fox". You are then "believing" A because of C. And if the trail *was* made by a fox, your belief is true.

That which has external reference—the belief or idea or bodily movement—is in some cases public and in others private. It is public when it consists in overt behaviour, including speech; it is private when it consists of images or "thoughts". (The meaning of "public" and "private" in this connection will be explained in Part III.) When an occurrence in an organism has external reference, the only feature *always* present is the causal one explained in the last paragraph, namely that the occurrence has some of the effects that would result from the sensible presence of that which is its external reference. We will give the name "representational occurrence" to anything that happens in an organism and has external reference.

In addition to the essential causal relation by which "representational occurrence" is defined, further relations exist in certain kinds of such occurrences. In a memory image there is resemblance to what is represented (i.e. remembered). In other images there is likely also to be resemblance, though of a less exact kind. If somebody tells you "your son has been killed by falling over a precipice", you are likely to have a very vivid image which will be correct in some respects but not in others. But words (except when onomatopoeic) have no resemblance to what they mean, and therefore verbal beliefs cannot be judged true or false by likeness to, or difference from, what they assert. Verbal behaviour is only one form of bodily behaviour that is representational; another form is that of the dog scratching at the rabbit-hole. We may say quite generally that bodily behaviour, when representational, need not have any resemblance to that to which it refers.

Nevertheless, in the case of explicit language, there is often a *structural* resemblance between a sentence and what it asserts. Suppose you see a fox eat a goose, and afterwards you say "the fox ate the goose". The original occurrence was a relation between a fox and a goose, while the sentence creates a relation between the word "fox" and the word "goose", namely that the word "ate" comes between them. (Cf. Wittgenstein's *Tractatus*.) This possible structural similarity between a sentence and what it asserts has a certain importance, but not, I think, an importance which is fundamental.

The above account of what makes a representational occurrence "true" is, I think, correct when it is applicable, but there are various extensions which give "truth" a wider scope.

Let us begin with memory. You may recollect an event which calls for no present action, and in that case the above definition of "true" is not applicable. Your memory, if it is in images, may then be "true" in the sense of being like the event. And even if no *present* action is called for, there may be future situations in which your memory has practical importance, and it may now be called "true" if it will then fulfil the test.

But what is of more importance is what may be called "derivative" meaning, which is a property of sentences whose several words have "primary" meaning. Suppose that, for a given child, the words "cat", "dog", and "hate" have primary meaning, in the sense that they have been learnt by ostensive definition. Then the sentence "cats hate dogs" has a meaning which does not have to be learnt by a fresh process of either ostensive or nominal definition. It is, moreover, a sentence which can never be verified by one sensible occurrence; in this it differs from "there will be a loud noise in a moment". Only in Plato's heaven could we see THE CAT hating THE DOG. Here on earth, the facts in virtue of which the sentence is true are many, and cannot all be experienced at one time. The relation of the sentence to the facts in virtue of which it is true is derivative from a number of other sentences, each of the form: "This is a cat and that is a dog, and this hates that." (I am taking "hate" as a characteristic of overt behaviour; I am doing this not as a theory, but for purposes of illustration.) We have here three sentences, (a) "this is a cat", (b) "that is a dog", (c) "this hates that". Each of these can be directly caused by the present sensible facts, given that the observer has learnt English. A sufficient number of such sentences, or of the corresponding observations or beliefs, will, in most people, in time cause the sentence "cats hate dogs", of which the meaning follows by the laws of syntax from the meanings of sentences of the forms (a), (b), and (c). It is in this sense that the meaning of such sentences is "derivative". For the present, having observed that the meaning of most sentences is derivative, I wish to confine myself to sentences of which the meaning is primary.

Let us consider the sentence "this is a cat", uttered when a cat is sensibly present. Hitherto I have been considering "truth" and "falsehood" as ideas only applicable to representations of things not sensibly present, and if we adhered strictly to this view our sentences (a), (b), and (c), when uttered, would be neither true nor false. This way of using the words would, however, be inconvenient, and I should prefer to say that (a), (b), and (c) are true or false.

If, in the presence of an animal, I say "this is a cat", what are the possibilities of falsehood? There is, first, deliberate lying: I may be talking to a blind man, and wish him to think it a cat when it is really a rabbit. We may exclude this case, on the ground that the words I utter do not express a belief, and on the further ground that the word "cat" is not caused by what I see, but by some ulterior motive. Then there is the case where I do not see distinctly, owing to darkness or bad eyesight, and when some one turns on another light I say "oh, I see it was not a cat". In this case what I see must have some likeness to a cat, and if I had said "this is something resembling a cat" I should have spoken truly. Then there is the case of insufficient knowledge of the language, leading me to give the name "cat" to what is officially called a puma. In this case there is only social error: my language is not correct English, but in the language that I speak my statement is true. Finally, I may be suffering from *delirium tremens* and see a cat where there is nothing, at least from a public point of view. In the absence of such unusual possibilities, my statement "this is a cat" will be true.

When there is a cat, and I say "there is a cat", what is the relation of what I say to the actual present quadruped? There is a causal relation: the sight of the cat causes the word "cat", but this, as we saw in the case of indistinct vision, is not enough to insure truth, since something not a cat may cause the word "cat". When I say "this is a cat", I am asserting the existence of something which is not merely a momentary visual experience of my own, but lives and breathes and mews and purrs and is capable of feline joys and sorrows. All this is erroneous in the case of *delirium tremens*. Let us therefore take a simpler example, say "this is blue". This statement need not imply anything beyond an experience private to me, and is therefore not liable to the kind of error that afflicts the drunkard. In this case, the only possibility of error is ignorance of the language, leading me to call "blue" what others would call "violet". This is social error, not intellectual error; what I am believing is true, but my words are ill chosen. In this case, therefore, the possibility of genuine falsehood in my statement seems to be at a minimum.

We may say generally: an indicative word is true when it is caused by what it means, assuming that the word is used in what may be called the exclamatory manner, as when people shout "fire!" or "murder!" In developed speech, we usually drop this way of using indicative words, and, instead, preface the word by "this is". Thus the statement "this is blue" is true if it is caused by what "blue" means. This is in fact a tautology. But most words, such as "cat" and "dog", mean not only what can be a momentary percept, but also the habitual concomitants of this kind of percept. If these are only usual but not invariable concomitants, there may be error in using the word that the percept causes; this is the case of the victim of *delirium tremens*, and also of Isaac when he mistook Jacob for Esau. Most words embody animal inductions which are usually true, but not always; this applies, more particularly, to names of objects or kinds of objects, such as our friends or the various species of animals. Whenever such words are employed as a result of a percept there is, therefore, some possibility of error, though often only a very slight one.

We may now say, as a definition: A sentence of the form "this is A" is called "true" when it is caused by what "A" means. We may say further that a sentence of the form "that was A" or "there will be A" is "true" if "this is A" was, or in the second case will be, true in the above sense. This covers all sentences asserting what are, were, or will be, facts of perception, and also those in which, from a percept, we correctly infer its usual concomitants by animal inference, in so far, at least, as such concomitants can form part of the meaning of an indicative word. This covers all the factual premisses of empirical knowledge. It does not cover general statements, such as "dogs bark", nor yet principles of inference, whether deductive or non-demonstrative. These cannot be adequately considered until we have dealt with the meaning of logical words such as "or" and "all". The above, moreover, is only a definition of "truth", not of "falsehood". "Falsehood" remains to be dealt with later.

There is one important observation to be made about our definitions of "meaning" and "truth", and that is that both depend upon an interpretation of "cause" which, according to modern physics, might seem to be crude and only partially applicable to natural processes. If this view is adopted, it follows that whatever defects belong to this old-fashioned notion of "cause" belong also to the notions of "meaning" and "truth" as we have interpreted them. I do not think, however, that this is a very serious objection. Both concepts, on other grounds, are necessarily somewhat vague and inexact, and these other grounds do much more to prevent precision than is done by modern physics. Such propositions as "lightning causes thunder", "micro-organisms cause fevers", "wounds cause pain", although they have not the certainty formerly attributed to them, and even if (what for reasons that will appear later, I do not believe) "cause" is a rough-and-ready notion belonging to a certain stage of science, not a fundamental category as used to be thought, nevertheless express in a convenient form truths about the usual though not invariable course of nature, and as such are still useful except where, as in quantum physics, the last refinement of accuracy is sought in spite of its complication and its consequent uselessness for most purposes of prediction. If human behaviour could be calculated by the physicists, we should have no need of such concepts as "meaning", "belief", and "truth". But in the meantime they remain useful, and up to a point they can be freed from ambiguity and vagueness. Beyond this point it would be useless to attempt to go, if "cause" is in fact not a fundamental concept of science. But if, as I hold, the concept of "cause" is indispensable, then the above considerations do not arise, or at any rate arise only in a modified form.

Chapter IX

LOGICAL WORDS AND FALSEHOOD

IN the preceding Chapter we dealt with the truth of beliefs and sentences in cases where this depends only upon observation and not upon inference from previous knowledge. In this Chapter we have to begin the inquiry into sentences of kinds that can be proved or disproved when suitable data derived from observation are known. Where such sentences are concerned, we no longer have to consider the relation of beliefs or sentences to something which is in general neither a belief nor a sentence; we have instead to consider only syntactical relations between sentences, in virtue of which the indubitable or probable truth or falsehood of a certain sentence follows from the truth or falsehood of certain others.

In such inferences there are certain words, which I shall call "logical" words, of which one or more always occur. These words are of two kinds, which may be called respectively "conjunctions" and "general words", though not quite in the usual grammatical sense. Examples of conjunctions are "not", "or", "and", "if-then". Examples of general words are "all" and "some". (Why "some" is called a "general" word will appear as we proceed.)

By the use of conjunctions we can make various simple inferences. If "p" is true, "not-p" is false; if "p" is false, "not-p" is true. If "p" is true, "p or q" is true; if "q" is true, "p or q" is true. If "p" is true and "q" is true, "p and q" is true. And so on. Sentences containing conjunctions I shall call "molecular" sentences, the "p" and "q" which are conjoined being conceived as the "atoms". Given the truth or falsehood of a set of propositions, the truth or falsehood of every molecular proposition constructed out of the set follows by syntactical rules, and requires no fresh observation of facts. We are, in fact, in the domain of logic.

Given that we know about "p", both what is involved in believing "p" and what would make "p" true or false, what can we say about "not-p"?

Given a sentence "p", we may either believe or disbelieve it. Neither of these is the primary use of a sentence; the primary use is to express belief in something else. If, feeling a drop on my nose, I say "it is raining", that is what may be called "primary" assertion, in which I pay no attention to the sentence, but use it to refer directly to something else, namely the rain. This kind of assertion has no corresponding negative. But if you say to me "is it raining?" and I then look out of the window, I may answer "yes" or "no", and the two answers are, so to speak, at the same level. In this case I am presented first with a sentence, and afterwards, because of the sentence, with a meteorological fact which enables me to say "yes" or "no". If I answer "yes", I am not saying "it is raining", but "the sentence 'it is raining' is true"; for what was presented to me by your question was a sentence, not a meteorological fact. If I answer "no", I am saying "the sentence 'it is raining' is false". This suggests that *perhaps* I could interpret "it is not raining" as meaning "the sentence 'it is raining' is false".

There are, however, two difficulties about such a view. The first is that it will make it very difficult to see what we mean by "false"; the second is that it makes it almost impossible to understand how a sentence containing the word "not" can be found true by observation. When, in answer to your question, I look out of the window, I do not merely not observe that it is raining, for I could have achieved this without looking out; in some sense I observe that it is not raining, but what this sense can be is obscure.

How do I know what I assert when I say "it is not raining"? I may say: "I saw the whole sky was blue, and I know it does not rain when the sky is blue". But how do I know this? Because I have often simultaneously observed facts which I could assert in the two sentences "the sky is blue" and "it is not raining". So I cannot in this way explain how I come to know negative facts.

In what sense, if any, are there negative facts, as opposed to true sentences containing the words "not"? Let us put the matter as follows: Imagine a person who knew everything that can be stated without using the word "not" or some equivalent; would such a person know the whole course of nature, or would he not? He would know that a buttercup is yellow, but he would not know that it is not blue. We may say that the purpose of knowledge is to describe the world, and that what makes a judgment of perception true (or false) is in general something that would still be a fact if there were no judgments in the world. The yellowness of the buttercup may be taken to be such a fact, and must be mentioned in a complete description of the world. But would there be the buttercup's not-blueness if there were no judgments? And must we, in a complete description of the buttercup, mention all the colours that it is not?

Let us consider a case where perception leads us as directly as possible to a very simple negative judgment. Suppose you take sugar thinking it is salt; when you taste it you are likely to exclaim "this is *not* salt". In such a case there is a clash between idea and sensation: you have the idea of the taste of salt, and the sensation of the taste of sugar, and a shock of surprise because the two are so different. Perception only gives rise to a negative judgment when the correlative positive judgment had already been made or considered. When you look for something lost, you say "no, it's not there"; after a flash of lightning you may say "I have not heard the thunder". If you saw an avenue of beeches with one elm among them, you might say "that's not a beech". If some one says the whole sky is blue, and you descry a cloud on the horizon, you may say "that is not blue". All these are very obvious negative judgments resulting, fairly directly, from perception. Yet, if I see that a buttercup is yellow, I hardly seem to be adding to my knowledge by remarking that it is not blue and not red. What, then, is meant, in the way of objective fact, by a true negative judgment?[1]

In all spontaneous negative perceptive judgments the experience which leads to the judgment is, in its essential core, of one and the same kind. There is an image or idea of a sensation of a certain sensational class, and there is a sensation of the same class but different from that of which there was an idea. I look for blue, and I see red; I expect the taste of salt, and I get the taste of sugar. Here everything is positive: idea of blue, sensation of red, experience of difference. When I say "difference" I do not mean mere logical non-identity, such as exists (e.g.) between a colour

[1] In what follows I am concerned to show that it is possible to define the truth of negative judgments without assuming that there are negative facts. I profess only to construct one theory which secures this result; I do not contend that there is no alternative theory which might be equally satisfactory.

and a taste; I mean the sort of difference that is felt between two colours. This sort of difference is a matter of degree. We can pass from blue to red by a series of intermediate shades, each of which is subjectively indistinguishable from the next. We can say that between two shades of colour there is a "great" difference, which would be meaningless if said of a colour and a taste. Two shades of colour have a certain kind of incompatibility: when I see blue in a certain direction, I do not simultaneously see red in that direction. Other kinds of sensation have a similar incompatibility; at any rate this is true of sensations of touch: if I feel a given part of the body tickled, I do not simultaneously feel it thumped.

When, as a result of perception, I say "this is not blue", I may be interpreted as meaning "this is a colour differing from blue", where "differing" is the positive relation that might be called "dissimilarity", not abstract non-identity. At any rate, it may be taken that this is the fact in virtue of which my judgment is true. We have to distinguish between what a judgment expresses and what it states, i.e. what makes it true or false. Thus when I say truly "this is not blue", there is, on the subjective side, consideration of "this is blue", followed by rejection, while on the objective side there is some colour differing from blue. In this way, so far as colour judgments are concerned, we escape the need of negative facts as what make negative judgments true.

But there remains a difficulty, and a very serious one. The above theory only succeeds in virtue of the incompatibility of different colours, i.e. of the fact that if I see red in a given direction I do not simultaneously see blue in that direction. This reintroduces "not", which we were trying to get rid of. If I could see both blue and red simultaneously in a given direction, then "this is red" would not be a ground for "this is not blue". The impossibility of seeing two colours simultaneously in a given direction *feels* like a logical impossibility, not like an induction from experience; but this is only one of various hypotheses that are *prima facie* possible. Suppose that, in a given direction from my eye, there were a source of red light, and also a source of blue light directly behind it; I should then have some colour sensation, which might not be either red or blue, but would be of some single shade of colour. It would seem that the different shades of colour are the only sensations of their kind that are physiologically possible, and that there is nothing analogous to hearing a chord in music.

Let us examine the hypothesis that the incompatibility of red and blue is logical, and ask ourselves whether this helps us in eliminating "not" from the objective world. We are now supposing it a tautology to say: "if there is red at a given moment in a given direction in the visual field, there is not blue in that direction at that time". More simply, though less accurately, we may state our supposition as saying: "It is logically impossible that 'this is red' and 'this is blue' should both be true of a given 'this'." But this supposition, whether true or false, will not help us. Two positive predicates, as Leibniz pointed out in proving that God is possible, cannot be logically incompatible. Therefore our supposition requires us to regard either "red" or "blue" or both as complex, and one at least must contain a "not" in its definition. For, given two complex predicates P and Q, they will only be *logically* incompatible if one of them contains a constituent A and the other contains a constituent not-A. In this sense "healthy" and "ill" are incompatible, and so are "alive" and "dead". But there can never be logical incompatibility except what is ultimately derived from the incompatibility of two propositions p and not-p. Therefore we cannot eliminate "not" from the objective world if we suppose red and blue to be *logically* incompatible.

Let us examine more carefully the view that the incompatibility of red and blue has a physiological source. That is to say, we are to suppose that a stimulus of a certain kind causes a sensation of red, while a stimulus of another kind causes a sensation of blue. I incline to think this the best theory, but we then have to explain the incompatibility of the two kinds of stimuli. As a matter of physics, this incompatibility may be taken to arise from the fact that each light-quantum has one definite amount of energy, together with the quantum laws connecting energy and frequency. The difficulty here is that it is not enough to say of a given light quantum that it has such-and-such an amount of energy; we must also be able to say that it does *not* have also some other amount. This is always regarded as so self-evident that it is never even stated. In classical physics analogous principles might have had a logical basis, but in quantum physics the incompatibility seems synthetic.

Let us make a new start in the endeavour to eliminate negative facts. Given a single indicative sentence, such as "this is red", we may have towards it two attitudes, belief and disbelief. Both are "positive" in the sense that they are actual states of the organism, which can be described without the word "not". Each is capable of being "true", but the "truth" of a disbelief is not quite the same thing as that of a belief. We considered in a previous Chapter what is meant by the "truth" of a perceptive belief: "this is red" is "true" if it is caused by something red. We did not then define what makes the corresponding disbelief "true". Let us now address ourselves to this question.

If disbelief in "this is red" is a judgment of perception—which is the case that we are considering—then "this" must be a colour. It is only in logic or philosophy that we are concerned to disbelieve in the redness of smells or sounds, and such disbelief belongs to a later stage than that which has to be considered in relation to our present problem. I shall therefore assume that when, as a judgment of perception, we disbelieve "this is red", we are always perceiving that it is some other colour. We may therefore say that a disbelief in "this is red" is "true" when it is caused by something having to red the relation of positive dissimilarity which we considered earlier. (This is a sufficient, not a necessary, condition.)

We must now interpret the law of contradiction. We must not say " 'this is red' and 'this is not red' cannot both be true", since we are concerned to eliminate "not". We must say "A disbelief in the sentence 'the belief that this is red and the disbelief that this is red are both true' is always true". It seems that in this way we can replace "not" and "falsehood" by "disbelief" and "the truth of a disbelief". We then reintroduce "not" and "false-hood" by definitions: the words "this is not blue" are defined as expressing disbelief in what is expressed by the words "this is blue". In this way the need of "not" as an indefinable constituent of facts is avoided.

The above theory may be summarized as follows: As a matter of logic, if any propositions containing the word "not" are known, there must be, among uninferred propositions, some that are of the form "not-p" or of the form "p implies not-q". It seems that a judgment "this is not red" may be a judgment of perception, provided "this" is a colour other than red. The judgment may be interpreted as disbelief in "this is red", disbelief being a state just as positive as belief. A sufficient (not necessary) condition for the truth of disbelief in "this is red" is that the disbelief should be caused by a "this" having to red the relation of positive dissimilarity.

There is another sufficient, not necessary, test of truth in certain cases. "This is blue" is "true" if a person whose belief is expressed by these words will, in suitable circumstances, have a "quite-so" feeling, and is "false" if he will get a "how-surprising" feeling. To every belief there is a corresponding disbelief. A person "disbelieves" what is expressed by "this is blue" if he will be surprised if "this is blue" is true, and have a "quite-so" feeling if "this is blue" is false. The words "this is not blue" (to repeat) express disbelief in what is expressed by "this is blue". Speaking generally, "not-p" must be defined by what it *expresses*.

The purpose of this theory is to explain how negative sentences can be true, and can be known, without its being necessary to assume that there are facts which can only be asserted in sentences containing the word "not".

All empirical negative judgments are derived from negative judgments of perception of the type of "this is not blue". Suppose you see an animal at a distance, which at first you take to be a dog, but which, on a nearer approach, turns out to be a fox. This depends upon perception of shape, and perception of shape depends upon the fact that where you see one colour you do not see another. The moment when you say "that is not a dog, but a fox" is the moment when you see something that you did not expect, say the fox's brush. When your surprise is analysed it comes down to some such judgment of perception as "this is not green but brown", where the fox's brush unexpectedly hides the grass.

There is more to be said about negation, in connection with general propositions, and also with logic. But the above analysis seems adequate where negative judgments of perception are concerned, and generally in all cases in which observation leads us to assert a sentence containing the word "not".

We must now attempt a similar treatment of the word "or".

In the case of "or" it is even more obvious than in the case of "not" that what makes "p or q" true is not a fact containing some constituent corresponding to "or". Suppose I see an animal and say "that was a stoat or a weasel". My statement is true if it was a stoat, and true if it was a weasel; there is not a third kind of animal, stoat-or-weasel. In fact, my statement expresses partial knowledge combined with hesitation; the word "or" expresses my hesitation, not something objective.

But it is possible to raise objections to this view. It may be said that the word "stoat" denotes a class of animals, not all exactly alike, and that the same is true of the word "weasel". The phrase "stoat or weasel", it may be said, merely denotes another class of animals, which, like each of the previous classes, is composed of individuals having common characteristics combined with differences. There might easily be one word for stoat-or-weasel, say "stosel", and we could then say "that was a stosel". This would assert, without "or", the same fact previously asserted with that word.

Or, to take a simpler instance: there are many shades of blue, having different names; there is navy-blue, aquamarine, peacock-blue, and so on. Suppose we have a set of shades of blue, which we will call b_1, b_2, and so on, and suppose everything blue is of one of these shades. Then the statement "this is b_1, or b_2, or etc.", is precisely equivalent to "this is blue", but the first statement contains "or" while the other does not.

Such facts, however, rightly interpreted, confirm the view that the meaning of "or" is subjective. The word "or" can be eliminated without making any difference to the fact that makes a sentence true or false, but not without making a difference to the state of mind of a person asserting the sentence. When I say "that is a stoat or a weasel", I may be supposed to add "but I don't know which"; when I say "that is a stosel", this addition is absent, though it might still be true if I made it. In fact "or" expresses conscious partial ignorance, although in logic it is capable of other uses.

There is in this respect a difference between the standpoint of logic and that of psychology. In logic, we are only interested in what makes a sentence true or false; in psychology, we are also interested in the state of mind of the person uttering the sentence with belief. In logic, "p" implies "p or q", but in psychology the state of mind of a person asserting "p" is different from that of a person asserting "p or q", unless the person concerned is a logician. Suppose I am asked "what day was it you went to

London?" I may reply "Tuesday or Wednesday, but I don't remember which". If I know that it was Tuesday, I shall not reply "Tuesday or Wednesday", in spite of the fact that this answer would be true. In fact we only employ the word "or" when we are uncertain, and if we were omniscient we should express our knowledge without the use of this word—except, indeed, our knowledge as to the state of mind of those aware of a greater or less degree of ignorance.

The elimination of disjunctive "facts" is not so difficult as the elimination of negative "facts". It is obvious that, although I may believe truly that to-day is Tuesday or Wednesday, there is not, in addition to Tuesday and Wednesday, another day of the week, called "Tuesday-or-Wednesday". What I believe is true because to-day is Tuesday, or because to-day is Wednesday. Here "or" appears again, and it is true that we cannot define "or". But what we cannot define is not a characteristic of the non-cognitive world, but a form of partial cognition.

Someone might argue: "When I believe 'p or q' I am clearly believing *something*, and this something is neither 'p' nor 'q', therefore there must be something objective which is what I am believing". This argument would be fallacious. We decided that when I am said to be believing "not-p" I am really disbelieving "p"; that is to say, there is a sentence not containing the word "not", which denotes a certain content that I may believe or disbelieve, but when the word "not" is added the sentence no longer expresses merely a content, but also my attitude towards it. The case of "or" is closely analogous. If I assert "to-day is Tuesday or Wednesday", there are two sentences, "to-day is Tuesday" and "to-day is Wednesday", each of which denotes a certain content. My disjunctive assertion expresses a state of mind in which neither of these contents is either affirmed or denied, but there is hesitation between the two. The word "or" makes the sentence one which no longer denotes a single content, but expresses a state of mind towards two contents.

When an indicative sentence is asserted, there are three things concerned. There is the cognitive attitude of the assertor—belief, disbelief and hesitation, in the cases so far considered; there is the content or contents denoted by the sentence; and there is the fact or facts in virtue of which the sentence is true or false, which I will call the "verifier" or "falsifier" of the sentence. In the

sentence "To-day is Tuesday or Wednesday", the cognitive attitude is hesitation, the contents are two, namely the significations
of "to-day is Tuesday" and "to-day is Wednesday"; the verifier
may be the fact that it is Tuesday or the fact that it is Wednesday,
or the falsifier may be that it is a different day of the week.

A sentence containing no logical words can only express belief.
If we knew all true sentences containing no logical words, and
also knew that they *were* all, every other true sentence could be
obtained by logical inference. A sentence not in the list would
become true by insertion of the word "not". A sentence in which
two sentences are connected by the word "or" would be true if
either component sentence occurred in the list. A sentence in
which two sentences are connected by the word "and" would be
true if both component sentences occurred in the list. The same
kind of logical proof would be possible for sentences containing
the logical words "all" and "some", as will be shown in the next
Chapter.

Thus if we give the name "atomic sentence" to one not containing logical words, we should need, as premisses for omniscience
(*a*) a list of all true atomic sentences, (*b*) the sentence "all true
atomic sentences occur in the above list". We could then obtain
all other true sentences by logical inference.

But the above method fails without (*b*), when we wish to establish the truth of a sentence containing the word "all" or the
falsehood of a sentence containing the word "some". We can,
no doubt, find substitutes for (*b*) but they will all contain, as it
does, the word "all". It seems to follow that our knowledge must
embrace premisses containing this word, or, what is equivalent,
asserting the falsehood of sentences containing the word "some".
This brings us to the explicit consideration of the words "all"
and "some", which will be the subject of the next Chapter.

Chapter X

GENERAL KNOWLEDGE

B Y "general knowledge" I mean knowledge of the truth or falsehood of sentences containing the word "all" or the word "some" or logical equivalents of these words. The word "some" might be thought to involve less generality than the word "all", but this would be a mistake. This appears from the fact that the negation of a some-sentence is an all-sentence, and vice-versa. The negation of "some men are immortal" is "all men are mortal", and the negation of "all men are mortal" is "some men are immortal". Thus any person who disbelieves a some-sentence must believe an all-sentence, and vice versa.

The same element of universality in a some-sentence appears from a consideration of its meaning. Suppose I say "I met a negro in the lane". My statement is true if I met any member of the whole class of negroes; thus the whole class is relevant, just as much as it would be if I said "all negroes are of African descent". Suppose you wanted to disprove my statement, there would be two things you could do. First, you could go through the whole class of negroes and prove that none of them were in the lane; secondly, you could go through the class of people I met, and prove that none of them were black. In either case a complete enumeration of some class is necessary.

But as a rule a class cannot be completely enumerated. No one can enumerate the class of negroes. If it is to be possible to enumerate the class of people I met in the lane, we must be able to know, concerning any member of the human race, whether or not I met him in the lane. If I know, on a basis of perception, that I met A, B, and C, and no one else, then I must be supposed to know the general proposition "all human beings other than A, B, and C were not met by me". This raises in an acute form the question of negative judgments of perception which we considered in the preceding Chapter. It also makes it evident that there are difficulties in disproving some-sentences, and correlatively in proving all-sentences.

But before considering further the truth or falsehood of such sentences, let us first examine what they signify.

It is clear that the sentence "all men are mortal" can be understood by a person who is unable to give a list of all human beings. If you understand the logical words involved, and also the predicates "man" and "mortal", you can fully *understand* the sentence, whether or not you can know its truth. Sometimes you can quite certainly know the truth of such a sentence although enumeration of the class concerned is impossible; an example is "all primes other than 2 are odd". This of course is a tautology; so is the statement "all widows have been married", which is not known by means of an enumeration of widows. In order to understand a general sentence, only *intensions* need be understood; the cases in which *extensions* are known are exceptional.

Further: when an intension is first given, enumeration of the corresponding extension is only possible through a universal negative. Given, e.g. that A, B, C . . . inhabit a certain village, this only gives the extension of "inhabitant of this village" if we know "no human being except A, B, C . . . inhabits this village". Thus unless a class is *defined* by enumeration, it can only be enumerated by the help of some negative all-sentence which must be supposed known.

Although, in pure logic, an all-proposition cannot be proved except by means of premisses which are all-propositions, there are many all-propositions which we all believe for reasons derived from observation. Such are "dogs bark", "men are mortal", "copper conducts electricity". The conventional view is that such propositions are inductive generalizations, which are probable, but not certain, when their premisses are known. We are supposed to know from observation "A is a dog and A barks", "B is a dog and B barks", and so on; we are also supposed not to know any proposition of the form "X is a dog and X does not bark". It is supposed to follow that probably all dogs bark. I am not concerned at the moment with the validity of such inferences, but only with the fact that knowledge of the principle guaranteeing their validity, if it exists, is general knowledge, and of a sort which cannot be based on observation. Induction, therefore, even if valid, does not help us to understand how we come by general knowledge.

There are three chief methods of arriving at general propositions. Sometimes they are tautologies, such as "all widows are female"; sometimes they result from induction; sometimes they are proved by complete enumeration, e.g. "everybody in this room is male". I shall begin by considering complete enumeration.

From the point of view of knowledge, though not of logic, there is an important difference between positive and negative general propositions, namely that some general negative propositions seem to result from observation as directly as "this is not blue", which we considered in the preceding Chapter. In *Through the Looking-Glass* the king says to Alice "who do you see coming along the road?", and she replies "I see nobody coming", to which the king retorts: "What good eyes you must have! It's as much as I can do to see somebody by this light". The point, for us, is that "I see nobody" is *not* equivalent to "I do not see somebody". The latter statement is true if my eyes are shut, and affords no evidence that there is not somebody; but when I say "I see nobody", I mean "I see, but I do not see somebody", which is *prima facie* evidence that there is not somebody. Such negative judgments are just as important as positive judgments in building up our empirical knowledge.

Consider, for example, such a statement as "this village has 623 inhabitants". Census officials make such statements confidently on a basis of enumeration. But enumeration involves not only 623 propositions of the form "this is a human being", but also an indefinite number of propositions of the form "this is not a human being", and finally some assurance that I have enough such propositions to be fairly sure that no one has been overlooked. Jenghiz Khan believed the proposition "all the inhabitants of Merv have been killed", but he was wrong, because some had crept into hiding-places that he overlooked. This was an actual source of error; another possible source would have been if some grotesque and long-immured prisoner had been wrongly judged by him to be a gorilla.

Suppose you are a Gestapo officer engaged in a search, and you satisfy yourself that at a certain time a certain house contained just five people. What is involved in arriving at this knowledge? Whenever you perceive a human being in any part of the house, you cause him to come to a certain room; when you are satisfied that none are left, you count those whom you can see, and find that there are five of them. This requires that, in the first place, you should have a number of judgments "I see a man in this direction" and "I see in that direction something which is not a man". It requires in the second place the judgment "in the process that I went through, any man in the house would have been perceived". This second judgment is very likely to be mistaken for common-sense reasons, and we may ignore it, but the other requires examination.

When you answer "no" to such questions as "is there a man there?" "do you hear a noise?" "does that hurt?" you are asserting a universal negative, and yet your answer *seems* to result as directly from perception as if you had answered "yes". This must depend upon the kind of incompatibility discussed in the previous Chapter. You are seeing something, but its shape differs from that of a human being; your auditory consciousness is in the state of listening, but not of hearing; in the part of the body concerned you are feeling something other than pain. It is only in virtue of incompatibility that a positive percept gives rise to a universal negative: where I see blue, I can assert that I see no shade of red, provided the area involved is sufficiently small. Such universal negatives based on perception raise great difficulties, but without them most of our empirical knowledge would be impossible, including, as we have seen, everything statistical and everything arrived at by enumerating the members of a class defined by intension, such as "the inhabitants of this village" or "the people now in this room". We must therefore somehow find a place in our theory of knowledge for universal negatives based on perception.

I will, however, for the moment, leave this problem aside to examine whether there are general *facts*, as opposed to true general propositions; and, if general facts are rejected, what it is that makes general propositions true, when they are true. If this question has been decided, it may become easier to discover how true general propositions come to be known.

Are there general *facts*? We may re-state this question in the following form: Suppose I knew the truth or falsehood of every sentence not containing the word "all" or the word "some" or an equivalent of either of these words; what, then, should I not know? Would what I should not know be only something about my knowledge and belief, or would it be something that involves no reference to knowledge or belief? I am supposing that I can say "Brown is here", "Jones is here", "Robinson is here", but not "some men are here", still less "exactly three men are here" or "every man here is called 'Brown' or 'Jones' or 'Robinson' ". And I am supposing that, though I know the truth or falsehood of every sentence of a certain sort, I do not know that my knowledge has this completeness. If I knew my list to be complete I could infer that there are three men here, but, as it is, I do not know that there are no others.

Let us try to make clear exactly what is involved. When the Antarctic Continent was discovered, something became known which had been there before anybody knew it; the knowing was a relation between a percipient and something which was independent of perception and generally of the existence of life. Is there anything analogous in the case of true all-sentences and some-sentences, e.g. "there are volcanoes in the Antarctic"?

Let us give the name "first-order omniscience" to knowledge of the truth or falsehood of every sentence not containing general words. "Limited first-order omniscience" will mean similar complete knowledge concerning all sentences of a certain form, say the form "x is human". We are to inquire what is *not* known to a person with first-order omniscience.

Can we say that the only thing he does not know is that his knowledge has first-order completeness? If so, this is a fact about his knowledge, not about facts independent of knowledge. It might be said that he knows everything except that there is nothing more to know; it would seem that no fact independent of knowing is unknown to him.

Let us take a case of limited first-order omniscience. Consider sentences of the form "x is human" and "x is mortal", and let us suppose that a certain wise man knows whether these sentences are true or false, for every value of "x" for which the sentences are significant, but does not know (what is in fact true) that there are no other values of "x" for which the sentences are significant. Suppose A, B, C . . . Z are the values of "x" for which "x is human" is true, and suppose that for each of these values "x is mortal" is true. Then the statements "A is mortal", "B is mortal" . . . "Z is mortal", taken together, are *in fact* equivalent to "all men are mortal", that is to say, if one is true so is the other, and *vice versa*. But our wise man cannot know this equivalence. In any case, the equivalence involves the conjunction of "A is mortal", "B is mortal" . . . "Z is mortal", that is to say, it involves a sentence built up by repeated use of the word "and", which is to be interpreted on the same lines as the word "or".

The relation of "and" and "or" is peculiar. When I assert "p and q", I can be regarded as asserting "p" and asserting "q", so that the "and" of "p and q" seems unnecessary. But if I deny "p and q", I am asserting "not-p or not-q", so that "or" seems necessary for interpreting the *falsehood* of a conjunction. Conversely, when I deny "p or q", I am asserting "not-p and not-q", so that conjunction is needed to interpret the *falsehood* of disjunction. Thus "and" and "or" are interdependent; either can be defined in terms of the other plus "not". In fact, "and", "or" and "not" can all be defined in terms of "not-p or not-q", and also in terms of "not-p and not-q".

It is obvious that all-sentences are analogous to conjunctions, and some-sentences to disjunctions.

Continuing with "all men are mortal", let us allow our wise man to understand "and" and "or" and "not", but let us still suppose him incapable of "some" and "all". Let us further suppose, as before, that A, B, C . . . Z are all the men there are, and that our wise man knows "A is mortal and B is mortal and . . . and Z is mortal"; but since he does not know the word "all", he does not know "A, B, C . . . Z are all the men there are". Let us call this proposition "P". The question that concerns us is: what, precisely, does he not know in not knowing P?

In mathematical logic, P is interpreted as: "Whatever x may be, either x is not human or x is A or x is B or . . . x is Z". Or it may be interpreted as: "Whatever x may be, the conjunction 'x is human and x is not A and x is not B and . . . x is not Z' is false." Either of these is a statement about everything in the universe, and it seems preposterous to suppose that we can know about all the things in the universe. In the case of "all men" there is real doubt, since there *may* be men on a planet of some other star. But how about "all the men in this room"?

We will now suppose that A, B, C are all the men in this room, that I know "A is in the room", "B is in the room", "C is in the room", that I understand "and" and "or" and "not", but not "all" or "some", so that I cannot know "A and B and C are all the men in this room". We will call this proposition "Q". What do I not know in not knowing Q?

Mathematical logic still brings in everything in the universe in interpreting Q, which it enunciates in the form: "Whatever x may be, either x is not in the room or x is not human or x is A or x is B or x is C"; or "Whatever x may be, if x is not A and x is not B and x is not C, then x is not human or x is not in the room". But in this case the logistical interpretation, however convenient technically, seems obviously preposterous psychologically, for in order to know who is in the room I obviously need not know anything about what is outside the room. How, then, is Q to be interpreted?

In practice, if I have seen A and B and C, and wish to be sure of Q, I look in cupboards, under tables, and behind curtains, and from time to time I say "there is no one in this part of the room". Theoretically, I could divide the volume of the room into a number of smaller volumes, each just large enough to contain a small human being; I could examine each volume, and say "no one here" except where I found A and B and C. In the end, we must be able to say "I have examined all parts of this room" if we are to be justified in asserting Q.

The statement "no one here" is analogous to "this is not blue", which we considered in the preceding Chapter. It is *not* an indefinitely extended conjunction: "Brown is not here and Jones is not here and Robinson is not here and . . .", through a catalogue of the human race. What it does is to deny a *character* which is common to places where there are human beings, and which we assert when we say "some one is here", say in playing hide-and-seek. This raises no new problem. The universal is now in "I have examined all parts of the room" or some equivalent.

The universal that we require may be stated as follows: "If I go through a certain process, every person in the room will become perceptible at some stage of the process." The process must be one that can be actually carried out; we should never be justified in saying "there are just three uranium atoms in this room", but human beings, fortunately, are never microscopic. Our universal may be put in the form: "If I perform a certain series of acts $A_1, A_2, \ldots A_n$, every human being within a certain volume V will be perceived during at least one of these acts." This involves an almost inextricable tangle of logical, physical, metaphysical, and psychological elements, and as we are concerned at the moment only with the logical elements it will be better to choose another example to begin with.

Let us take: "I have just heard six pips on the wireless." This may be interpreted as: "During a brief recent period of time, I had exactly six closely similar auditory sensations of a certain well-defined sort, namely the sort called 'pips'." I may give proper names to each of these, say P_1, P_2. ... P_6. Then I say: "P_1, and P_2 and ... and P_6 were all the pips I heard in the period from the time t_1 to the time t_2." We will call this statement "R".

It is fairly obvious that what distinguishes R from the conjunction "I heard P_1 and I heard P_2 and ... and I heard P_6" is negative: it is the knowledge that I heard no other pips. Let us consider this. Suppose I agree to listen for pips throughout a period of five seconds, at the beginning and end of which you say "now". Immediately afterwards, you say "did you hear any pips"? and I say "no". This, though logically a universal, may be psychologically a single negative judgment of perception, like "I don't see any blue sky" or "I don't feel any rain". In such judgments (to repeat) we have the suggested idea of a quality and the sensation of a different quality which causes us to disbelieve the suggested idea. There is here no multiplicity of instances, but a specious present in which one quality is present and another is felt to be absent. We know "I did not hear pippiness" and we translate this into "I heard no pips". The plurality of "pips" is that of events as opposed to qualities—a subject considered above in connection with proper names.

We can extend such negative judgments beyond the specious present, because there is no sharp boundary between sensation and immediate memory, or between immediate memory and true memory. You say "do you hear a pip", and I reply, not by a sharp "no", but by a long-drawn out "no–o–o–o". In this way my negation can apply to a period of ten seconds or so. By immediate memory and true memory it can have its temporal scope extended indefinitely, so as to justify such a statement as "I watched all night without seeing a single aeroplane". When such statements are legitimate, we can say "between the time t_1 and the time t_2 I saw exactly six planes", because we can divide the period into smaller ones, in six of which we say "I saw a plane", and in the others we say "I saw no plane". These various judgments are then assembled in memory, and give rise to the enumerative judgment "in the whole period I saw just six planes".

If the above theory is correct, negative judgments of perception are not themselves universal: they say (e.g.) "I did not hear pippiness", not "I heard no pips". The judgment "I heard no pips" follows logically, for a pip is a complex of which pippiness is a constituent. The inference is like that from "I saw no one" to "I saw no processions". A procession is a crowd of human beings, and one man may at different times form part of many processions, but processions cannot exist without human beings. We can, therefore, from absence of the quality called "humanity", logically infer the absence of processions. In like manner, from absence of noisiness we can infer absence of noises.

If the above theory is correct, enumerative empirical judgments depend upon universal negative judgments logically inferable from negative perceptive judgments concerned with single qualities, such as "I do not see blue". Our problem, so far as such judgments are concerned, is therefore solved by the preceding theories as to "not" and as to proper names.

The above, however, is only one of the ways in which we arrive at general propositions. It is the way that is appropriate when complete enumeration is possible, i.e. when there is some property P of which we can say: "$a_1, a_2, \ldots a_n$ are all the subjects of which P can be truly asserted". It is applicable in arriving at "this village has 323 inhabitants", or "all the inhabitants of this village are called Jones" or "all mathematical logicians whose names begin with Q live in the United States". What we have been discussing is: "what is involved in the possibility of complete enumeration"? But there are multitudes of general propositions in which we all believe although complete enumeration is either practically or theoretically impossible. These are of two kinds, tautologies and inductions. Of the former kind are "all pentagons are polygons", "all widows have had husbands", etc. Of the latter kind are "all men are mortal", "all copper conducts electricity", etc. Something must be said about each of these kinds.

Tautologies are primarily relations between properties, not between the things that have the properties. Pentagonality is a property of which polygonality is a constituent; it may be defined as polygonality plus quintuplicity. Thus whoever asserts pentagonality necessarily asserts polygonality at the same time. Similarly "x is a widow" means "x had a husband who is dead", and therefore asserts, incidentally, "x had a husband". We have seen that an element of tautology comes in when we seek to interpret

154

such judgments as "I have heard no pips". The strictly empirical element is "I have not heard pippiness"; "pips" are defined as "complexes of which pippiness is a constituent". The inference from "not pippiness" to "no pips" is thus tautological. I shall say no more about tautological general propositions, since the subject belongs to logic, with which we are not concerned.

It remains to consider inductive generalizations—not their justification, but their significance, and what facts are necessary if they are to be true.

That all men are mortal could, theoretically, be proved by the enumerative method: some world-governing Caligula, having made a complete census, might extirpate his subjects and then commit suicide, exclaiming with his last breath: "Now I *know* that all men are mortal". But in the meantime we have to rely upon less conclusive evidence. The most important question is whether such generalizations, when not proved by complete enumeration, are to be regarded as asserting a relation of intensions, whether certain or probable, or only a relation of extensions. And further: where there is a relation of intensions such as to justify "all A is B", must this be a *logical* relation making the generalization tautological, or is there an extra-logical relation of intensions, of which we acquire probable knowledge by induction?

'Take "copper conducts electricity". This generalization was arrived at inductively, and the induction consisted of two parts. On the one hand, there were experiments with different bits of copper; on the other hand, there were experiments with a variety of substances, showing that, in every case that had been tested, each element has a characteristic behaviour as regards the conduction of electricity. The same two stages exist in establishing the induction "dogs bark". On the one hand, we hear a number of dogs barking; on the other hand, we observe that each species of animal, if it makes a noise at all, makes a noise characteristic of the species. But there is a further stage. The copper atom has been found to have a certain structure, and from this structure, together with the general laws of physics, the conduction of electricity can be inferred. If we now *define* copper as "what has a certain atomic structure", there is a relation between the intension "copper" and the intension "conductivity", which becomes logical if the laws of physics are assumed. There is now, however, a concealed induction, namely that what appears as copper by the tests that were applied before the modern theory of atomic structure is also copper by the new definition. (This need only be true in general, not universally.) This induction itself could, theoretically, be replaced by deductions from the laws of physics. The laws of physics themselves are partly tautologies, but in their most important parts they are hypotheses that are found to explain great numbers of subordinate inductions.

The same sort of thing may be said about "dogs bark". From the anatomy of a dog's throat, as from that of any musical wind instrument, it should be possible to infer that only certain sorts of sounds can issue from it. We thus replace the rather narrow inductive evidence derived from listening to dogs by the much wider evidence upon which the theory of sound depends.

In all such cases the principle is the same. It is this: Given a mass of phenomena, everything about them except an initial space-time distribution follows tautologically from a small number of general principles, which we therefore take to be true.

We are concerned at present, not with the validity of the grounds for these general principles, but with the character of what they assert, i.e. whether they assert relations of intension or purely extensional relations of class-inclusion. I think we must decide in favour of the former interpretation. When an induction seems plausible, that is because a relation between the intensions involved strikes us as not unlikely. "Logicians whose names begin with Q live in the United States" may be proved by complete enumeration, but will not be believed on inductive grounds, because we can see no reason why a Frenchman named (say) Quételet should abandon his native country as soon as he became interested in logic. On the other hand, "dogs bark" is readily accepted on inductive grounds, because we expect a possible answer to the question "what sort of noise do dogs make?" What induction does, in suitable cases, is to make a relation of intensions probable. It may do this even in cases where the general principle suggested by induction turns out to be a tautology. You may notice that $1 + 3 = 2^2$, $1 + 3 + 5 = 3^2$, $1 + 3 + 5 + 7 = 4^2$, and be led to conjecture that the sum of the first n odd numbers is always n^2; when you have framed this hypothesis, it is easy to prove it deductively. How far ordinary scientific inductions, such as "copper conducts electricity", can be reduced to tautologies, is a very difficult question, and a very ambiguous one. There are various possible definitions of "copper", and the answer may depend upon which of these definitions we adopt. I do not think, however, that relations between intensions, such as justify statements of the form "all A is B", can *always* be reduced to tautologies. I am inclined to believe that there are such intensional relations that are only discoverable empirically, and that are not, either practically or theoretically, capable of logical demonstration.

It is necessary, before leaving this subject, to say something about some-propositions, or existence-propositions as they are called in logic. The statement "some A is B" is the negation of "all A is not B" (i.e. "no A is B"), and "all A is B" is the negation of "some A is not B". Thus the truth of some-sentences is equivalent to the falsehood of related all-sentences, and vice versa. We have considered the truth of all-sentences, and what we have said applies to the falsehood of some-sentences. Now we wish to consider the truth of some-sentences, which involves the falsehood of correlative all-sentences.

Suppose I met Mr. Jones, and I say to you "I met a man". This is a some-sentence: it asserts that, for *some* value of x, "I met x and x is human" is true. I know that the x in question is Mr. Jones, but you do not. What I know enables me to infer the truth of "I met a man". There is here a distinction of some importance. If I know that the sentences "I met Jones" and "Jones is a man" are true, it is a substantial inference that the sentence "I met a man" is true. But if I know that I met Jones, and also that Jones is a man, then I am already knowing that I met a man. To know that the sentence "I met Jones" is true is not the same thing as to know that I met Jones. I can know the latter, but not the former, if I do not know English; I can know the former, but not the latter, if I hear it pronounced by a person for whose moral character I have the highest respect, but again I know no English.

Suppose you hear the door-bell, and you infer that there is a caller. While you do not know who it is, you are in a certain state of mind, in which belief and uncertainty are combined. When you find out who it is, the element of uncertainty disappears, but the element of belief remains, together with the new belief "it is Jones". Thus the inference from "a has the property P" to "something has the property P" consists merely in isolating and attending to a portion of the total belief expressed in asserting "a has the property P". I think something of the same sort may be said about all deductive inference, and that the difficulty of such inference, when it exists, is due to the fact that we are believing that a sentence is true rather than what the sentence asserts.

The transition from sentences expressing judgments of perception to some-sentences, e.g. from "there's Jones" to "there's somebody", thus offers no difficulty. But there are a number of some-sentences in which we all believe, but which are not arrived at in this simple way. We often know that *something* has the property P, although there is no definite thing *a* of which we can say "*a* has the property P". We know, for instance, that some one was Mr. Jones's father, but we may be unable to say who he was. No one knows who was Napoleon III's father, but we all believe that some one was. If a bullet whizzes past you when no one is in sight, you say "some one fired at me". As a rule, in such cases, you are making an inference from a general proposition. Everyone has a father, therefore Mr. Jones has a father. If you believe that everything has a cause, many things will be only known to you as "the something that caused this". Whether such generalizations are the only source of some-sentences not directly derived from perception, or whether, on the contrary, there must be some-sentences among the premisses of our knowledge, is a question which, for the present, I will leave open.

There is a school, of which Brouwer is the founder, which holds that a some-sentence may be neither true nor false. The stock example is "there are three consecutive 7's in the decimal expression of π". So far as this has been worked out, no three consecutive 7's have occurred. If they occur at a later point, this may in time be discovered; but if they never occur, this can never be discovered. I have discussed this question in the "Inquiry into Meaning and Truth", where I came to the conclusion that such sentences are always either true or false if they are syntactically significant. As I see no reason to change this view, I shall refer the reader to that book for a statement of my grounds, and I shall assume, without further argument, that all syntactically correct sentences are either true or false.

Chapter XI

FACT, BELIEF, TRUTH, AND KNOWLEDGE

THE purpose of this chapter is to state in dogmatic form certain conclusions which follow from previous discussions, together with the fuller discussions of "An Inquiry into Meaning and Truth". More particularly, I wish to give meanings, as definite as possible, to the four words in the title of this chapter. I do not mean to deny that the words are susceptible of other equally legitimate meanings, but only that the meanings which I shall assign to them represent important concepts, which, when understood and distinguished, are useful in many philosophical problems, but when confused are a source of inextricable tangles.

A. FACT

"Fact", as I intend the term, can only be defined ostensively. Everything that there is in the world I call a "fact". The sun is a fact; Caesar's crossing of the Rubicon was a fact; if I have toothache, my toothache is a fact. If I make a statement, my making it is a fact, and if it is true there is a further fact in virtue of which it is true, but not if it is false. The butcher says: "I'm sold out, and that's a fact"; immediately afterwards, a favoured customer arrives, and gets a nice piece of lamb from under the counter. So the butcher told two lies, one in saying he was sold out, and the other in saying that his being sold out was a fact. Facts are what make statements true or false. I should like to confine the word "fact" to the minimum of what must be known in order that the truth or falsehood of any statement may follow analytically from those asserting that minimum. For example, if "Brutus was a Roman" and "Cassius was a Roman" each assert a fact, I should not say that "Brutus and Cassius were Romans" asserted a new fact. We have seen that the questions whether there are negative facts and general facts raise difficulties. These niceties, however, are largely linguistic.

I mean by a "fact" something which is there, whether anybody thinks so or not. If I look up a railway time-table and find that there is a train to Edinburgh at 10 a.m., then, if the time-table is correct, there is an actual train, which is a "fact". The statement in the time-table is itself a "fact", whether true or false, but it only *states* a fact if it is true, i.e. if there really is a train. Most facts are independent of our volitions; that is why they are called "hard", "stubborn", or "ineluctable". Physical facts, for the most part, are independent, not only of our volitions, but even of our existence.

The whole of our cognitive life is, biologically considered, part of the process of adaptation to facts. This process is one which exists, in a greater or less degree, in all forms of life, but is not commonly called "cognitive" until it reaches a certain level of development. Since there is no sharp frontier anywhere between the lowest animal and the most profound philosopher, it is evident that we cannot say precisely at what point we pass from mere animal behaviour to something deserving to be dignified by the name of " knowledge". But at every stage there is adaptation, and that to which the animal adapts itself is the environment of *fact*.

B. BELIEF

"Belief", which we have next to consider, has an inherent and inevitable vagueness, which is due to the continuity of mental development from the amoeba to *homo sapiens*. In its most developed form, which is that most considered by philosophers, it is displayed by the assertion of a sentence. After sniffing for a time, you exclaim: "Good heavens! the house is on fire." Or, when a picnic is in contemplation, you say: "Look at those clouds: there will be rain." Or, in a train, you try to subdue an optimistic fellow-passenger by observing: "Last time I did this journey we were three hours late." Such remarks, if you are not lying, express beliefs. We are so accustomed to the use of words for expressing beliefs that it may seem strange to speak of "belief" in cases where there are no words. But it is clear that even when words are used they are not of the essence of the matter. The smell of burning first makes you believe that the house is on fire, and then the words come, not as *being* the belief, but as a way of putting it into a form of behaviour in which it can be communicated to others. I am thinking, of course, of beliefs that are not very complicated or refined. I believe that the angles of a polygon add up to twice as many right angles as the figure has sides diminished by

four right angles, but a man would need super-human mathematical intuition to be able to believe this without words. But the
simpler kind of belief, especially when it calls for action, may be
entirely unverbalized. When you are travelling with a companion,
you may say: "We must run; the train is just going to start." But
if you are alone you may have the same belief, and run just as
fast, without any words passing through your head.

I propose, therefore, to treat belief as something that can be
pre-intellectual, and can be displayed in the behaviour of animals.
I incline to think that, on occasion, a purely bodily state may
deserve to be called a "belief". For example, if you walk into
your room in the dark, and someone has put a chair in an unusual
place, you may bump into it, because your body believed there
was no chair there. But the parts played by mind and body
respectively in belief are not very important to separate for our
present purposes. A belief, as I understand the term, is a certain
kind of state of body or mind or both. To avoid verbiage, I shall
call it a state of an organism, and ignore the distinction of bodily
and mental factors.

One characteristic of a belief is that it has external reference,
in the sense defined in a previous chapter. The simplest case,
which can be observed behaviouristically, is when, owing to a
conditioned reflex, the presence of A causes behaviour appropriate
to B. This covers the important case of acting on information
received: here the phrase heard is A, and what it signifies is B.
Somebody says "look out, there's a car coming", and you act as
you would if you saw the car. In this case you are believing what
is signified by the phrase "a car is coming".

Any state of an organism which consists in believing something
can, theoretically, be fully described without mentioning the
something. When you believe "a car is coming", your belief
consists in a certain state of the muscles, sense-organs, and emotions, together perhaps with certain visual images. All this, and
whatever else may go to make up your belief, could, in theory,
be fully described by a psychologist and physiologist working
together, without their ever having to mention anything outside
your mind and body. Your state, when you believe that a car is
coming, will be very different in different circumstances. You
may be watching a race, and wondering whether the car on which
you have put your money will win. You may be waiting for the

return of your son from captivity in the Far East. You may be trying to escape from the police. You may be suddenly roused from absent-mindedness while crossing the street. But although your total state will not be the same in these various cases, there will be something in common among them, and it is this something which makes them all instances of the belief that a car is coming. A belief, we may say, is a collection of states of an organism bound together by all having, in whole or part, the same external reference.

In an animal or a young child, believing is shown by an action or series of actions. The beliefs of the hound about the fox are shown by his following the scent. But in human beings, as a result of language and of the practice of suspended reactions, believing often becomes a more or less static condition, consisting perhaps in pronouncing or imagining appropriate words, together with one of the feelings that constitute different kinds of belief. As to these, we may enumerate: first, the kind of belief that consists in filling out sensations by animal inferences; second, memory; third, expectation; fourth, the kind of belief generated unreflectingly by testimony; and fifth, the kind of belief resulting from conscious inference. Perhaps this list is both incomplete and in part redundant, but certainly perception, memory, and expectation differ as to the kinds of feeling involved. "Belief", therefore, is a wide generic term, and a state of believing is not sharply separated from cognate states which would not naturally be described as believings.

The question what it is that is believed when an organism is in a state of believing is usually somewhat vague. The hound pursuing a scent is unusually definite, because his purpose is simple and he has no doubt as to the means; but a pigeon hesitating whether to eat out of your hand is in a much more vague and complex condition. Where human beings are concerned, language gives an illusory appearance of precision; a man may be able to express his belief in a sentence, and it is then supposed that the sentence is what he believes. But as a rule this is not the case. If you say "look, there is Jones", you are believing something, and expressing your belief in words, but what you are believing has to do with Jones, not with the name "Jones". You may, on another occasion, have a belief which *is* concerned with words. "Who is that very distinguished man who has just come in? That is Sir

Theophilus Thwackum." In this case it is the name you want. But as a rule in ordinary speech the words are, so to speak, transparent; they are not what is believed, any more than a man is the name by which he is called.

When words merely *express* a belief which is about what the words mean, the belief indicated by the words is lacking in precision to the degree that the meaning of the words is lacking in precision. Outside logic and pure mathematics, there are no words of which the meaning is precise, not even such words as "centimetre" and "second". Therefore even when a belief is expressed in words having the greatest degree of precision of which empirical words are capable, the question as to what it is that is believed is still more or less vague.

This vagueness does not cease when a belief is what may be called "purely verbal", i.e. when what is believed is that a certain sentence is true. This is the sort of belief acquired by schoolboys whose education has been on old-fashioned lines. Consider the difference in the schoolboy's attitude to "William the Conqueror, 1066" and "next Wednesday will be a whole holiday". In the former case, he knows that that is the right form of words, and cares not a pin for their meaning; in the latter case, he acquires a belief about next Wednesday, and cares not a pin what words you use to generate his belief. The former belief, but not the latter, is "purely verbal".

If I were to say that the schoolboy is believing that the sentence "William the Conqueror, 1066" is "true", I should have to add that his definition of "truth" is purely pragmatic: a sentence is "true" if the consequences of uttering it in the presence of a master are pleasant; if they are unpleasant, it is "false".

Forgetting the schoolboy, and resuming our proper character as philosophers, what do *we* mean when we say that a certain sentence is "true"? I am not yet asking what is meant by "true"; this will be our next topic. For the moment I am concerned to point out that, however "true" may be defined, the significance of "this sentence is true" must depend upon the significance of the sentence, and is therefore vague in exactly the degree in which there is vagueness in the sentence which is said to be true. We do not therefore escape from vagueness by concentrating attention on purely verbal beliefs.

Philosophy, like science, should realize that, while complete precision is impossible, techniques can be invented which gradually diminish the area of vagueness or uncertainty. However admirable our measuring apparatus may be, there will always remain some lengths concerning which we are in doubt whether they are greater than, less than, or equal to, a metre; but there is no known limit to the refinements by which the number of such doubtful lengths can be diminished. Similarly, when a belief is expressed in words, there will always remain a band of possible circumstances concerning which we cannot say whether they would make the belief true or false, but the breadth of this band can be indefinitely diminished, partly by improved verbal analysis, partly by a more delicate technique in observation. Whether complete precision is or is not theoretically possible depends upon whether the physical world is discrete or continuous.

Let us now consider the case of a belief expressed in words all of which have the greatest attainable degree of precision. Suppose, for the sake of concreteness, that I believe the sentence: "My height is greater than 5 ft. 8 ins. and less than 5 ft. 9 ins." Let us call this sentence "S". I am not yet asking what would make this sentence true, or what would entitle me to say that I know it; I am asking only: "What is happening in me when I have the belief which I express by the sentence S?" There is obviously no one correct answer to this question. All that can be said definitely is that I am in a state such as, if certain further things happen, will give me a feeling which might be expressed by the words "quite so", and that, now, while these things have not yet happened, I have the idea of their happening combined with the feeling expressed by the word "yes". I may, for instance, imagine myself standing against a wall on which there is a scale of feet and inches, and in imagination see the top of my head between two marks on this scale, and towards this image I may have the feeling of assent. We may take this as the essence of what may be called "static" belief, as opposed to belief shown by action: static belief consists in an idea or image combined with a yes-feeling.

C. TRUTH

I come now to the definition of "truth" and "falsehood". Certain things are evident. Truth is a property of beliefs, and derivatively of sentences which express beliefs. Truth consists in a certain relation between a belief and one or more facts other than the belief. When this relation is absent, the belief is false. A sentence may be called "true" or "false" even if no one believes it, provided that, if it were believed, the belief would be true or false as the case may be.

So much, I say, is evident. But what is not evident is the nature of the relation between belief and fact that is involved, or the definition of the possible fact that will make a given belief true, or the meaning of "possible" in this phrase. Until these questions are answered we have no adequate definition of "truth".

Let us begin with the biologically earliest form of belief, which is to be seen among animals as among men. The compresence of two kinds of circumstance, A and B, if it has been frequent or emotionally interesting, is apt to have the result that, when A is sensibly present, the animal reacts as it formerly reacted to B, or at any rate displays some part of this reaction. In some animals this connection may be sometimes innate, and not the result of experience. But however the connection may be brought about, when the sensible presence of A causes acts appropriate to B, we may say that the animal "believes" B to be in the environment, and that the belief is "true" if B is in the environment. If you wake a man up in the middle of the night and shout "fire!" he will leap from his bed even if he does not yet see or smell fire. His action is evidence of a belief which is "true" if there is fire, and "false" otherwise. Whether his belief is true depends upon a fact which may remain outside his experience. He may escape so fast that he never acquires sensible evidence of the fire; he may fear that he will be suspected of incendiarism and flee the country, without ever inquiring whether there was a fire or not; nevertheless his belief remains true if there was the fact (namely fire) which constituted its external reference or significance, and if there was not such a fact his belief remained false even if all his friends assured him that there had been a fire.

The difference between a true and false belief is like that between a wife and a spinster: in the case of a true belief there is a fact to which it has a certain relation, but in the case of a false belief there is no such fact. To complete our definition of "truth" and "falsehood" we need a description of the fact which would make a given belief true, this description being one which applies to nothing if the belief is false. Given a woman of whom we do not know whether she is married or not, we can frame a description which will apply to her husband if she has one, and to nothing if she is a spinster. Such a description would be: "the man who stood beside her in a church or registry office while certain words were pronounced". In like manner we want a description of the fact or facts which, if they exist, make a belief true. Such fact or facts I call the "verifier" of the belief.

What is fundamental in this problem is the relation between sensations and images, or, in Hume's terminology, between impressions and ideas. We have considered in a previous chapter the relation of an idea to its prototype, and have seen how "meaning" develops out of this relation. But given meaning and syntax, we arrive at a new concept, which I call "significance", and which is characteristic of sentences and of complex images. In the case of single words used in an exclamatory manner, such as "fire!" or "murder!" meaning and significance coalesce, but in general they are distinct. The distinction is made evident by the fact that words must have meaning if they are to serve a purpose, but a string of words does not necessarily have significance. Significance is a characteristic of all sentences that are not nonsensical, and not only of sentences in the indicative, but also of such as are interrogative, imperative, or optative. For present purposes, however, we may confine ourselves to sentences in the indicative. Of these we may say that the significance consists in the description of the fact which, if it exists, will make the sentence true. It remains to define this description.

Let us take an illustration. Jefferson had a belief expressed in the words: "There are mammoths in North America." This belief might have been true even if no one had seen one of these mammoths; there might, when he expressed the belief, have been just two in an uninhabited part of the Rocky Mountains, and they might soon afterwards have been swept by a flood down the Colorado River into the sea. In that case, in spite of the truth of his belief, there would have been no evidence for it. The actual mammoths would have been facts, and would have been, in the above sense, "verifiers" of the belief. A verifier which is not experienced can often be described, if it has a relation known by experience to something known by experience; it is in this way that we understand such a phrase as "the father of Adam", which describes nothing. It is in this way that we understand Jefferson's belief about mammoths: we know the sort of facts that would have made his belief true, that is to say, we can be in a state of mind such that, if we had seen mammoths, we should have exclaimed: "Yes, that's what I was thinking of."

The significance of a sentence results from the meanings of its words together with the laws of syntax. Although meanings must be derived from experience, significance need not. I know from experience the meaning of "man" and the meaning of "wings", and therefore the significance of the sentence "There is a winged man", although I have no experience of what this sentence signifies. The significance of a sentence may always be understood as in some sense a description. When this description describes a fact, the sentence is "true"; otherwise it is "false".

It is important not to exaggerate the part played by convention. So long as we are considering beliefs, not the sentences in which they are expressed, convention plays no part at all. Suppose you are expecting to meet some person of whom you are fond, and whom you have not seen for some time. Your expectation may be quite wordless, even if it is detailed and complex. You may hope that he will be smiling, you may recall his voice, his gait, the expression of his eyes; your total expectation may be such as only a good painter could express, in paint, not in words. In this case you are expecting an experience of your own, and the truth or falsehood of your expectation is covered by the relation of idea and impression: your expectation is "true" if the impression, when it comes, is such that it might have been the prototype of your previous idea if the time-order had been reversed. This is what we express when we say: "That is what I expected to see." Convention is concerned only in the translation of belief into language, or (if we are told something) of language into belief. Moreover the correspondence of language and belief, except in abstract matters, is usually by no means exact: the belief is richer in detail and context than the sentence, which picks out only certain salient features. You *say* "I shall see him soon", but you *think* "I shall see him smiling, but looking older, friendly, but shy, with his hair untidy and his shoes muddy"—and so on, through an endless variety of detail of which you may be only half aware.

The case of an expectation is the simplest from the point of view of defining truth and falsehood, for in this case the fact upon which truth or falsehood depends is about to be experienced. Other cases are more difficult.

Memory, from the standpoint of our present problem, is closely analogous to expectation. A recollection is an idea, while the fact recollected was an impression; the memory is "true" if the recollection has to the fact that kind of resemblance which exists between an idea and its prototype.

Consider, next, such a statement as "you have a toothache". In any belief concerning another person's experience there may be the same sort of extra-verbal richness that we have seen to be frequent in regard to expectations of our own experiences; you may, having recently had toothache, feel sympathetically the throbbing pangs that you imagine your friend to be suffering. Whatever wealth or paucity of imagination you may bring to bear, it is clear that your belief is "true" in proportion as it resembles the fact of your friend's toothache—the resemblance being again of the sort that can subsist between idea and prototype.

But when we pass on to something which no one experiences or has experienced, such as the interior of the earth, or the world before life began, both belief and truth become more abstract than in the above cases. We must now consider what can be meant by "truth" when the verifying fact is experienced by no one.

Anticipating coming discussions, I shall assume that the physical world, as it is independently of perception, can be known to have a certain structural similarity to the world of our percepts, but cannot be known to have any qualitative similarity. And when I say that it has structural similarity, I am assuming that the ordering relations in terms of which the structure is defined are spatio-temporal relations such as we know in our own experience. Certain facts about the physical world, therefore—those facts, namely, which consist of space-time structure—are such as we can imagine. On the other hand, facts as to the qualitative character of physical occurences are, presumably, such as we cannot imagine.

Now while there is no difficulty in supposing that there are unimaginable *facts*, there cannot be *beliefs*, other than general beliefs, of which the verifiers would be unimaginable. This is an important principle, but if it is not to lead us astray a little care is necessary as regards certain logical points. The first of these is that we may know a general proposition although we do not know any instance of it. On a large pebbly beach you may say, probably with truth: "There are pebbles on this beach which no one will ever have noticed." It is quite certainly true that there are finite integers which no one will ever have thought of. But it is self-contradictory to suppose such propositions established by giving instances of their truth. This is only an application of the principle that we can understand statements about all or some of the members of a class without being able to enumerate the members. We understand the statement "all men are mortal" just as completely as we should if we could give a complete list of men; for to understand this statement we need only understand the concepts "man" and "mortal" and what is meant by being an instance of them.

Now take the statement: "There are facts which I cannot imagine." I am not considering whether this statement is true; I am only concerned to show that it is intelligible. Observe, in the first place, that if it is not intelligible, its contradictory must also be not intelligible, and therefore not true, though also not false. Observe, in the second place, that to understand the statement it is unnecessary to be able to give instances, any more than of the unnoticed pebbles or the numbers that are not thought of. All that is necessary is to understand the words and the syntax, which we do. The statement is therefore intelligible; whether it is true is another matter.

Take, now, the following statement: "There are electrons, but they cannot be perceived." Again I am not asking whether the statement *is* true, but what is meant by supposing it true or believing it to be true. "Electron" is a term defined by means of causal and spatio-temporal relations to events that we experience, and to other events related to them in ways of which we have experience. We have experience of the relation "parent", and can therefore understand the relation "great-great-great-grandparent", although we have no experience of this relation. In like manner we can understand sentences containing the word "electron", in spite of not perceiving anything to which this word is applicable. And when I say we can understand such sentences, I mean that we can imagine facts which would make them true.

The peculiarity, in such cases, is that we can imagine *general* circumstances which would verify our belief, but cannot imagine the particular facts which are instances of the general fact. I cannot imagine any particular fact of the form: "n is a number which will never have been thought of", for, whatever value I give to n, my statement becomes false by the very fact of my giving that value. But I can quite well imagine the general fact which gives truth to the statement: "There are numbers which will never have been thought of." The reason is that general statements are concerned with intensions, and can be understood without any knowledge of the corresponding extensions.

Beliefs as to what is not experienced, as the above discussion has shown, are not as to unexperienced individuals, but as to classes of which no member is experienced. A belief must always be capable of being analysed into elements that experience has made intelligible, but when a belief is set out in logical form it often suggests a different analysis, which would seem to involve components not known by experience. When such psychologically misleading analysis is avoided, we can say, quite generally: Every belief which is not merely an impulse to action is in the nature of a picture, combined with a yes-feeling or a no-feeling; in the case of a yes-feeling it is "true" if there is a fact having to the picture the kind of similarity that a prototype has to an image; in the case of a no-feeling it is "true" if there is no such fact. A belief which is not true is called "false".

This is a definition of "truth" and "falsehood".

D. KNOWLEDGE

I come now to the definition of "knowledge". As in the cases of "belief" and "truth", there is a certain inevitable vagueness and inexactitude in the conception. Failure to realize this has led, it seems to me, to important errors in the theory of knowledge. Nevertheless, it is well to be as precise as possible about the unavoidable lack of precision in the definition of which we are in search.

It is clear that knowledge is a sub-class of true beliefs: every case of knowledge is a case of true belief, but not vice versa. It is very easy to give examples of true beliefs that are not knowledge. There is the man who looks at a clock which is not going, though he thinks it is, and who happens to look at it at the moment when it is right; this man acquires a true belief as to the time of day, but cannot be said to have knowledge. There is the man who believes, truly, that the last name of the Prime Minister in 1906 began with a B, but who believes this because he thinks that Balfour was Prime Minister then, whereas in fact it was Campbell-Bannerman. There is the lucky optimist who, having bought a ticket for a lottery, has an unshakeable conviction that he will win, and, being lucky, does win. Such instances can be multiplied indefinitely, and show that you cannot claim to have known merely because you turned out to be right.

What character in addition to truth must a belief have in order to count as knowledge? The plain man would say there must be sound evidence to support the belief. As a matter of common sense this is right in most of the cases in which doubt arises in practice, but if intended as a complete account of the matter it is very inadequate. "Evidence" consists, on the one hand, of certain matters of fact that are accepted as indubitable, and, on the other hand, of certain principles by means of which inferences are drawn from the matters of fact. It is obvious that this process is unsatisfactory unless we know the matters of fact and the principles of inference not merely by means of evidence, for otherwise we become involved in a vicious circle or an endless regress. We must therefore concentrate our attention on the matters of fact and the principles of inference. We may then say that what is known consists, first, of certain matters of fact and certain principles of inference, neither of which stands in need of extraneous evidence, and secondly, of all that can be ascertained by applying the principles of inference to the matters of fact. Traditionally, the matters of fact are those given in perception and memory, while the principles of inference are those of deductive and inductive logic.

There are various unsatisfactory features in this traditional doctrine, though I am not at all sure that, in the end, we can substitute anything very much better. In the first place, the doctrine does not give an intensional definition of "knowledge", or at any rate not a *purely* intensional definition; it is not clear what there is in common between facts of perception and principles of inference. In the second place, as we shall see in Part III, it is very difficult to say what are facts of perception. In the third place, deduction has turned out to be much less powerful than was formerly supposed; it does not give new knowledge, except as to new forms of words for stating truths in some sense already known. In the fourth place, the methods of inference that may be called in a broad sense "inductive" have never been satisfactorily formulated; when formulated, even if completely true, they only give probability to their conclusions; moreover, in any possibly accurate form, they lack self-evidence, and are only to be believed, if at all, because they seem indispensable in reaching conclusions that we all accept.

There are, broadly speaking, three ways that have been suggested for coping with the difficulties in defining "knowledge". The first, and oldest, is to emphasize the concept of "self-evidence". The second is to abolish the distinction between premisses and conclusions, and to say that knowledge is constituted by the coherence of a whole body of beliefs. The third and most drastic is to abandon the concept of "knowledge" altogether and substitute "beliefs that promote success"—and here "success" may perhaps be interpreted biologically. We may take Descartes, Hegel, and Dewey as protagonists of these three points of view.

Descartes holds that whatever I conceive clearly and distinctly is true. He believes that, from this principle, he can derive not only logic and metaphysics, but also matters of fact, at least in theory. Empiricism has made such a view impossible; we do not think that even the utmost clarity in our thoughts would enable us to demonstrate the existence of Cape Horn. But this does not dispose of the concept of "self-evidence": we may say that what he says applies to conceptual evidence, but that there is also perceptual evidence, by means of which we come to know matters of fact. I do not think we can entirely dispense with self-evidence. If you slip on a piece of orange peel and hit your head with a bump on the pavement, you will have little sympathy with a philosopher who tries to persuade you that it is uncertain whether you are hurt. Self-evidence also makes you accept the argument that if all men are mortal and Socrates is a man, then Socrates is mortal. I do not know whether self-evidence is anything except a certain firmness of conviction; the essence of it is that, where it is present, we cannot help believing. If, however, self-evidence is to be accepted as a guarantee of truth, the concept must be carefully distinguished from others that have a subjective resemblance to it. I think we must bear it in mind as relevant to the definition of "knowledge", but as not in itself sufficient.

Another difficulty about self-evidence is that it is a matter of degree. A clap of thunder is indubitable, but a very faint noise is not; that you are seeing the sun on a bright day is self-evident, but a vague blur in a fog may be imaginary; a syllogism in *Barbara* is obvious, but a difficult step in a mathematical argument may be very hard to "see". It is only for the highest degree of self-evidence that we should claim the highest degree of certainty.

The coherence theory and the instrumentalist theory are habitually set forth by their advocates as theories of *truth*. As such they are open to certain objections which I have urged elsewhere. I am considering them now, not as theories of *truth*, but as theories of *knowledge*. In this form there is more to be said for them.

Let us ignore Hegel, and set forth the coherence theory of knowledge for ourselves. We shall have to say that sometimes two beliefs cannot both be true, or, at least, that we sometimes believe this. If I believe simultaneously that A is true, that B is true, and that A and B cannot both be true, I have three beliefs which do not form a coherent group. In that case at least one of the three must be mistaken. The coherence theory in its extreme form maintains that there is only one possible group of mutually coherent beliefs, which constitutes the whole of knowledge and the whole of truth. I do not believe this; I hold, rather, to Leibniz's multiplicity of possible worlds. But in a modified form the coherence theory can be accepted. In this modified form it will say that all, or nearly all, of what passes for knowledge is in a greater or less degree uncertain; that, if principles of inference are among the *prima facie* materials of knowledge, then one piece of *prima facie* knowledge may be inferrible from another, and thus acquires more credibility than it had on its own account. It may thus happen that a body of propositions, each of which has only a moderate degree of credibility on its own account, may collectively have a very high degree of credibility. But this argument depends upon the possibility of varying degrees of intrinsic credibility, and is therefore not a *pure* coherence theory. I shall consider this matter in more detail in Part V.

With respect to the theory that we should substitute for "knowledge" the concept "beliefs that promote success", it is sufficient to point out that it derives whatever plausibility it may possess from being half-hearted. It assumes that we can know (in the old-fashioned sense) what beliefs promote success, for if we cannot know this the theory is useless in practice, whereas its purpose is to glorify practice at the expense of theory. In practice, obviously, it is often very difficult to know what beliefs promote success, even if we have an adequate definition of "success".

The conclusion to which we seem to be driven is that knowledge is a matter of degree. The highest degree is found in facts of perception, and in the cogency of very simple arguments. The next highest degree is in vivid memories. When a number of beliefs are each severally in some degree credible, they become more so if they are found to cohere as a logical whole. General principles of inference, whether deductive or inductive, are usually less obvious than many of their instances, and are psychologically derivative from apprehension of their instances. Towards the end of our inquiry I shall return to the definition of "knowledge", and shall then attempt to give more precision and articulation to the above suggestions. Meanwhile let us remember that the question "what do we mean by 'knowledge'?" is not one to which there is a definite and unambiguous answer, any more than to the question "what do we mean by 'baldness'?"

PART III

SCIENCE AND PERCEPTION

INTRODUCTION

WE come now to an inquiry which proceeds in the opposite order from that of our initial survey of the universe. In that survey we were attempting to be as far as possible impartial and impersonal; it was our aim to come as near as our capacities permit to describing the world as it might appear to an observer of miraculous perceptive powers viewing it from without. We were concerned with what we *know* rather than with what *we* know. We attempted to use an order in our description which ignored, for the moment, the fact that we are part of the universe, and that any account which we can give of it depends upon its effects upon ourselves, and is to this extent inevitably anthropocentric. We accordingly began with the system of galaxies, and passed on, by stages, to our own galaxy, our own little solar system, our own tiny planet, the infinitesimal specks of life upon its surface, and finally, as the climax of insignificance, the bodies and minds of those odd beings that have imagined themselves the lords of creation and the end and aim of the whole vast cosmos.

But this survey, which seems to end in the pettiness of Man and all his concerns, is only one side of the truth. There is another side, which must be brought out by a survey of a different kind. In this second kind of survey, which is now to occupy our attention, we ask no longer what the universe is, but how we come to know whatever we do know about it. In this survey Man again occupies the centre, as in the Ptolemaic astronomy. What we know of the world we know by means of events in our own lives, events which, but for the power of thought, would remain merely private. The little dots that an astronomer sees on a photographic plate are to him signs of vast galaxies separated from him by hundreds of thousands of light-years. All the immensities of space and all the abysses of time are mirrored in his thought, which, in a sense, is as vast as they are. Nothing is too great or too small for his intellect to comprehend, nothing is too distant in time or space for him to assign to it its due weight in the structure of the cosmos. In power he is nearly as feeble as his minuteness suggests, but in contemplation he is boundless, and the equal of all that he can understand.

It is my purpose in the following Parts to discuss, first our data, and then the relation of science to the crude material of experience. The data from which scientific inferences proceed are private to ourselves; what we call "seeing the sun" is an event in the life of the seer, from which the astronomer's sun has to be inferred by a long and elaborate process. It is evident that, if the world were a higgledy-piggledy chaos, inferences of this kind would be impossible; but for causal interconnectedness, what happens in one place would afford no indication of what has happened in another, and my experiences would tell me nothing of events outside my own biography. It is the process from private sensation and thought to impersonal science that will now concern us. The road is long and rugged, and the goal must be kept in view if the journey is not to seem wearisome. But until we have traversed this road neither the scope nor the essential limitations of human knowledge can be adequately understood.

The inferences upon which we implicitly rely in this investigation, of which the explicit logic will be considered in Part VI, differ from those of deductive logic and mathematics in being not demonstrative, i.e. in being inferences which, when the premisses are true and the reasoning correct, do not insure the truth of the conclusion, though they are held to make the conclusion "probable" in some sense and in some degree. Except in mathematics, almost all the inferences upon which we actually rely are of this sort. In some cases the inference is so strong as to amount to *practical* certainty. A page of typescript which makes sense is assumed to have been typed by someone, although, as Eddington points out, it may have been produced accidentally by a monkey walking on a typewriter, and this bare possibility makes the inference to an intentional typist non-demonstrative. Many inferences which are accepted by all men of science are much less nearly certain, for instance, the theory that sound is transmitted by waves. There is a gradation in the probability assigned to different inferences by scientific common sense, but there is no accepted body of principles according to which such probabilities are to be estimated. I should wish, by analysing scientific procedure, to systematize the rules of such inference. The ideal would be the kind of systematization which has been achieved in relation to deductive logic.

It has been customary to regard all inference as deductive or inductive, and to regard probable inference as synonymous with inductive inference. I believe that, if ordinarily accepted scientific inferences are to be accepted as valid, we shall have need of other principles in addition to induction if not in place of it.

We may take three questions as typical of those that I wish to investigate. These three are as to the best available grounds for believing: (1) that the world existed yesterday, (2) that the sun will rise to-morrow, (3) that there are sound-waves. I am not asking whether these beliefs are true, but what, assuming them true, are the best reasons for believing them. And generally: why should we believe things asserted by science but not verified by present perception? The answer, if I am not mistaken, is by no means simple.

Chapter I

KNOWLEDGE OF FACTS
AND KNOWLEDGE OF LAWS

WHEN we examine our beliefs as to matters of fact, we find that they are sometimes based directly on perception or memory, while in other cases they are inferred. To common sense this distinction presents little difficulty: the beliefs that arise immediately from perception appear to it indubitable, and the inferences, though they may sometimes be wrong, are thought, in such cases, to be fairly easily rectified except where peculiarly dubious matters are concerned. I know of the existence of my friend Mr. Jones because I see him frequently: in his presence I know him by perception, and in his absence by memory. I know of the existence of Napoleon because I have heard and read about him, and I have every reason to believe in the veracity of my teachers. I am somewhat less certain about Hengist and Horsa, and much less certain about Zoroaster, but these uncertainties are still on a common-sense level, and do not seem, at first sight, to raise any philosophical issue.

This primitive confidence, however, was lost at a very early stage in philosophical speculation, and was lost for sound reasons. It was found that what I know by perception is less than has been thought, and that the inferences by which I pass from perceived to unperceived facts are open to question. Both these sources of scepticism must be investigated.

There is, to begin with, a difficulty as to what is inferred and what is not. I spoke a moment ago of my belief in Napoleon as an inference from what I have heard and read, but there is an important sense in which this is not quite true. When a child is being taught history, he does not argue: "My teacher is a person of the highest moral character, paid to teach me facts; my teacher says there was such a person as Napoleon; therefore probably there was such a person." If he did, he would retain considerable doubt, since his evidence of the teacher's moral character is likely to be inadequate, and in many countries at many times teachers have been paid to teach the opposite of facts. The child in fact, unless he hates the teacher, spontaneously believes what he is told.

When we are told anything emphatically or authoritatively, it is an effort not to believe it, as any one can experience on April Fools' day. Nevertheless there is still a distinction, even on a common-sense level, between what we are told and what we know for ourselves. If you say to the child "how do you know about Napoleon?" the child may say "because my teacher told me". If you say "how do you know your teacher told you"? the child may say "why, of course, because I heard her". If you say "how do you know you heard her"? he may say "because I remember it distinctly". If you say "how do you know you remember it"? he will either lose his temper or say "well, I do remember it". Until you reach this point, he will defend his belief as to a matter of fact by belief in another matter of fact, but in the end he reaches a belief for which he can give no further reason.

There is thus a distinction between beliefs that arise spontaneously and beliefs for which no further reason can be given. It is the latter class of beliefs that are of most importance for theory of knowledge, since they are the indispensable minimum of premisses for our knowledge of matters of fact. Such beliefs I shall call "data". In ordinary thinking they are *causes* of other beliefs rather than *premisses* from which other beliefs are inferred; but in a critical scrutiny of our beliefs as to matters of fact we must, wherever possible, translate the causal transitions of primitive thinking into logical transitions, and only accept the derived beliefs to the extent that the character of the transitions seems to justify. For this there is a common-sense reason, namely, that every such transition is found to involve some risk of error, and therefore data are more nearly certain than beliefs derived from them. I am not contending that data are ever completely certain, nor is this contention necessary for their importance in theory of knowledge.

There is a long history of discussions as to what was mistakenly called "scepticism of the senses". Many appearances are deceptive. Things seen in a mirror may be thought to be "real". In certain circumstances, people see double. The rainbow seems to touch the ground at some point, but if you go there you do not find it. Most noteworthy in this connection are dreams: however vivid they may have been, we believe, when we wake up, that the objects which we thought we saw were illusory. But in all these cases the core of data is not illusory, but only the derived beliefs.

My visual sensations, when I look in a mirror or see double, are exactly what I think they are. Things at the foot of the rainbow do really look coloured. In dreams I have all the experiences that I seem to have; it is only things outside my mind that are not as I believe them to be while I am dreaming. There are in fact no illusions of the senses, but only mistakes in interpreting sensational data as signs of things other than themselves. Or, to speak more exactly, there is no evidence that there are illusions of the senses.

Every sensation which is of a familiar kind brings with it various associated beliefs and expectations. When (say) we see and hear an aeroplane, we do not merely have a visual sensation and the auditory sensation of a whirring noise; spontaneously and without conscious thought we interpret what we see and hear and fill it out with customary adjuncts. To what an extent we do this becomes obvious when we make a mistake, for example when what we thought was an aeroplane turns out to be a bird. I knew a road, along which I used often to go in a car, which had a bend at a certain place, and a white-washed wall straight ahead. At night it was very difficult not to see the wall as a road going straight on up a hill. The right interpretation as a house and the wrong interpretation as an up-hill road were both, in a sense, inferences from the sensational datum, but they were not inferences in the logical sense, since they occurred without any conscious mental process.

I give the name "animal inference" to the process of spontaneous interpretation of sensations. When a dog hears himself called in tones to which he is accustomed, he looks round and runs in the direction of the sound. He may be deceived, like the dog looking into the gramophone in the advertisement of "His Master's Voice". But since inferences of this sort are generated by the repeated experiences that give rise to habit, his inference must be one which has usually been right in his past life, since otherwise the habit would not have been generated. We thus find ourselves, when we begin to reflect, expecting all sorts of things that in fact happen, although it would be logically possible for them not to happen in spite of the occurrence of the sensations which give rise to the expectations. Thus reflection upon animal inference gives us an initial store of scientific laws, such as "dogs bark". These initial laws are usually somewhat unreliable, but they help us to take the first steps towards science.

Every-day generalizations, such as "dogs bark", come to be explicitly believed after habits have been generated which might be described as a pre-verbal form of the same belief. What sort of habit is it that comes to be expressed in the words "dogs bark"? We do not expect them to bark at all times, but we do expect that, *if* they make a noise, it will be a bark or a growl. Psychologically, induction does not proceed as it does in the text-books, where we are supposed to have observed a number of occasions on which dogs barked, and then proceeded consciously to generalize. The fact is that the generalization, in the form of a habit of expectation, occurs at a lower level than that of conscious thought, so that, when we begin to think consciously, we find ourselves believing the generalization, not, explicitly, on the basis of the evidence, but as expressing what is implicit in our habit of expectation. This is a history of the belief, not a justification of it.

Let us make this state of affairs somewhat more explicit. First comes the repeated experience of dogs barking, then comes the habit of expecting a bark, then, by giving verbal expression to the habit, comes belief in the general proposition "dogs bark". Last comes the logician, who asks, not "why do I believe this"? but "what reason is there for supposing this true"? Clearly the reason, if any, must consist of two parts: first, the facts of perception consisting of the various occasions on which we have heard dogs bark; second, some principle justifying generalization from observed instances to a law. But this logical process comes historically after, not before, our belief in a host of common-sense generalizations.

The translation of animal inferences into verbal generalizations is carried out very inadequately in ordinary thinking, and even in the thinking of many philosophers. In what counts as perception of external objects there is much that consists of habits generated by past experience. Take, for example, our belief in the permanence of objects. When we see a dog or a cat, a chair or a table, we do not suppose that we are seeing something which has a merely momentary existence; we are convinced that what we are seeing has a past and a future of considerable duration. We do not think this about everything that we see; a flash of lightning, a rocket, or a rainbow is expected to disappear quickly. But experience has generated in us the expectation that ordinary solid objects, which can be touched as well as seen, usually persist, and can be seen and touched again on suitable occasions. Science reinforces this belief by explaining away apparent disappearances as transformations into gaseous forms. But the belief in quasi-permanence, except in exceptional cases, antedates the scientific doctrine of the indestructibility of matter, and is itself antedated by the animal expectation that common objects can be seen again if we look in the right place.

The filling out of the sensational core by means of animal inferences, until it becomes what is called "perception", is analogous to the filling out of telegraphic press messages in newspaper offices. The reporter telegraphs the one word "King", and the newspaper prints "His Gracious Majesty King George VI". There is some risk of error in this proceeding, since the reporter may have been relating the doings of Mr. Mackenzie King. It is true that the context would usually reveal such an error, but one can imagine circumstances in which it would not. In dreams, we fill out the bare sensational message wrongly, and only the context of waking life shows us our mistake.

The analogy to abbreviated press telegrams is very close. Suppose, for instance, you see a friend at the window of an incoming train, and a little later you see him coming towards you on the platform. The physical causes of your perceptions (and of your interpretation of them) are certain light-signals passing between him and your eyes. All that physics, by itself, entitles you to infer from the receipt of these signals is that, somewhere along the line of sight, light of the appropriate colours has been emitted or reflected or refracted or scattered. It is obvious that the kind of ingenuity which has produced the cinema could cause you to have just these sensations in the absence of your friend, and that in that case you would be deceived. But such sources of deception cannot be frequent, or at least cannot have been frequent hitherto, since, if they were, you would not have formed the habits of expectation and belief in context that you have in fact formed. In the case supposed, you are confident that it is your friend, that he has existed throughout the interval between seeing him at the window and seeing him on the platform, and that he has pursued a continuous path through space from the one to the other. You have no doubt that what you saw was something solid, not an intangible object like a rainbow or a cloud. And so, although the message received by the senses contains (so to speak) only a few key words, your mental and physical habits cause you, spontaneously and without thought, to expand it into a coherent and amply informative dispatch.

This expansion of the sensational core to produce what goes by the somewhat question-begging name of "perception" is obviously only trustworthy in so far as our habits of association run parallel to processes in the external world. Clouds looked down upon from a mountain may look so like the sea or a field of snow that only positive knowledge to the contrary prevents you from so interpreting your visual sensations. If you are not accustomed to the gramophone, you will confidently believe that the voice you hear on the other side of the door proceeds from a person in the room that you are about to enter. There is no obvious limit to the invention of ingenious apparatus capable of deceiving the unwary. We know that the people we see on the screen in the cinema are not really there, although they move and talk and behave in a manner having some resemblance to that of human beings; but if we did not know it, we might at first find it hard to believe. Thus what we seem to know through the senses may be deceptive whenever the environment is different from what our past experience has led us to expect.

From the above considerations it follows that we cannot admit as data all that an uncritical acceptance of common sense would take as given in perception. Only sensations and memories are truly data for our knowledge of the external world. We must exclude from our list of data not only the things that we consciously infer, but all that is obtained by animal inference, such as the imagined hardness of an object seen but not touched. It is true that our "perceptions", in all their fullness, are data for psychology: we do in fact have the experience of believing in such-and-such an object. It is only for knowledge of things outside our own minds that it is necessary to regard only sensations as data. This necessity is a consequence of what we know of physics and physiology. The same external stimulus, reaching the brains of two men with different experiences, will produce different results, and it is only what these different results have in common that can be used in inferring external causes. If it is objected that the truth of physics and physiology is doubtful, the situation is even worse; for if they are false, nothing whatever as to the outer world can be inferred from my experiences. I am, however, throughout this work, assuming that science is broadly speaking true.

If we define "data" as "those matters of fact of which, independently of inference, we have a right to feel most nearly certain", it follows from what has been said that all my data are events that happen to me, and are, in fact, what would commonly be called events in my mind. This is a view which has been characteristic of British empiricism, but has been rejected by most Continental philosophers, and is not now accepted by the followers of Dewey or by most of the logical positivists. As the issue is of considerable importance, I shall set forth the reasons which have convinced me, including a brief repetition of those that have already been given.

There are, first, arguments on the common-sense level, derived from illusions, squinting, reflection, refraction, etc., but above all from dreams. I dreamed last night that I was in Germany, in a house which looked out on a ruined church; in my dream I supposed at first that the church had been bombed during the recent war, but was subsequently informed that its destruction dated from the wars of religion in the sixteenth century. All this, so long as I remained asleep, had all the convincingness of waking life. I did really have the dream, and did really have an experience intrinsically indistinguishable from that of seeing a ruined church when awake. It follows that the experience which I call "seeing a church" is not conclusive evidence that there is a church, since it may occur when there is no such external object as I suppose in my dream. It may be said that, though when dreaming I may *think* that I am awake, when I wake up I *know* that I am awake. But I do not see how we are to have any such certainty; I have frequently dreamt that I woke up; in fact once, after ether, I dreamt it about a hundred times in the course of one dream. We condemn dreams, in fact, because they do not fit into a proper context, but this argument can be made inconclusive, as in Calderon's play, *La Vida es Sueño*. I do not believe that I am now dreaming, but I cannot prove that I am not. I am, however, quite certain that I am having certain experiences, whether they be those of a dream or those of waking life.

We come now to another class of arguments, derived from physics and physiology. This class of arguments came into philosophy with Locke, who used it to show that secondary qualities are subjective. This class of arguments is capable of being used to throw doubt on the truth of physics and physiology, but I will deal with them on the hypothesis that science, in the main, is true.

We experience a visual sensation when light waves reach the eye, and an auditory sensation when sound waves reach the ear. There is no reason to suppose that light waves are at all like the experience which we call seeing something, or sound waves at all like the experience which we call hearing a sound. There is no reason whatever to suppose that the physical sources of light and sound waves have any more resemblance to our experiences than the waves have. If the waves are produced in unusual ways, our experience may lead us to infer subsequent experiences which it turns out that we do not have; this shows that even in normal perception interpretation plays a larger part than common sense supposes, and that interpretation sometimes leads us to entertain false expectations.

Another difficulty is connected with time. We see and hear now, but what (according to common sense) we are seeing and hearing occurred some time ago. When we both see and hear an explosion, we see it first and hear it afterwards. Even if we could suppose that the furniture of our room is exactly what it seems, we cannot suppose this of a nebula millions of light-years away, which looks like a speck but is not much smaller than the milky way, and of which the light that reaches us now started before human beings began to exist. And the difference between the nebula and the furniture is only one of degree.

Then there are physiological arguments. People who have lost a leg may continue to feel pain in it. Dr. Johnson, disproving Berkeley, thought the pain in his toe when he kicked a stone was evidence for the existence of the stone, but it appears that it was not even evidence for the existence of his toe, since he might have felt it even if his toe had been amputated. Speaking generally, if a nerve is stimulated in a given manner, a certain sensation results, whatever may be the source of the stimulation. Given sufficient skill, it ought to be possible to make a man see the starry heavens by tickling his optic nerve, but the instrument used would bear little resemblance to the august bodies studied by astronomers.

The above arguments, as I remarked before, may be interpreted sceptically, as showing that there is no reason to believe that our sensations have external causes. As this interpretation concedes what I am at present engaged in maintaining, namely that sensations are the sole data for physics, I shall not, for the moment, consider whether it can be refuted, but shall pass on to a closely similar line of argument which is related to the method of Cartesian doubt. This method consists in searching for data by provisionally rejecting everything that it is found possible to call in question.

Descartes argues that the existence of sensible objects might be uncertain, because it would be possible for a deceitful demon to mislead us. *We* should substitute for a deceitful demon a cinema in technicolour. It is, of course, also possible that we may be dreaming. But he regards the existence of our thoughts as wholly unquestionable. When he says "I think, therefore I am", the primitive certainties at which he may be supposed to have arrived are particular "thoughts", in the large sense in which he uses the term. His own existence is an inference from his thoughts, an inference whose validity does not at the moment concern us. In the context, what appears certain to him is that there is doubting, but the experience of doubting has no special prerogative over other experiences. When I see a flash of lightning I may, it is maintained, be uncertain as to the physical character of lightning, and even as to whether anything external to myself has happened, but I cannot make myself doubt that there has been the occurrence which is called "seeing a flash of lightning", though there may have been no flash outside my seeing.

It is not suggested that I am certain about all my own experiences; this would certainly be false. Many memories are dubious, and so are many faint sensations. What I am saying—and in this I am expounding part of Descartes' argument—is that there are some occurrences that I cannot make myself doubt, and that these are all of the kind that, if we admit a not-self, are part of the life of my self. Not all of them are sensations; some are abstract thoughts, some are memories, some are wishes, some are pleasures or pains. But all are what we should commonly describe as mental events in me.

My own view is that this point of view is in the right in so far as it is concerned with data that are matters of fact. Matters of fact that lie outside my experience can be made to seem doubtful, unless there is an argument showing that their existence follows from matters of fact within my experience together with laws of whose certainty I feel reasonably convinced. But this is a long question, concerning which, at the moment, I wish to say only a few preliminary words.

Hume's scepticism with regard to the world of science resulted from (a) the doctrine that all my data are private to me, together with (b) the discovery that matters of fact, however numerous and well-selected, never logically imply any other matter of fact. I do not see any way of escaping from either of these theses. The first I have been arguing; I may say that I attach especial weight in this respect to the argument from the physical causation of sensations. As to the second, it is obvious as a matter of syntax to any one who has grasped the nature of deductive arguments. A matter of fact which is not contained in the premisses must require for its assertion a proper name which does not occur in the premisses. But there is only one way in which a new proper name can occur in a deductive argument, and that is when we proceed from the general to the particular, as in "all men are mortal, therefore Socrates is mortal". Now no collection of assertions of matters of fact is logically equivalent to a general assertion, so that, if our premisses concern only matters of fact, this way of introducing a new proper name is not open to us. Hence the thesis follows.

If we are not to deduce Hume's scepticism from the above two premisses, there seems to be only one possible way of escape, and that is to maintain that, among the premisses of our knowledge, there are some general propositions, or there is at least one general proposition, which is not analytically necessary, i.e. the hypothesis of its falsehood is not self-contradictory. A principle justifying the scientific use of induction would have this character. What is needed is some way of giving probability (not certainty) to the inferences from known matters of fact to occurrences which have not yet been, and perhaps never will be, part of the experience of the person making the inference. If an individual is to know anything beyond his own experiences up to the present moment, his stock of uninferred knowledge must consist not only of matters of fact, but also of general laws, or at least a law, allowing him to make inferences from matters of fact; and such law or laws must, unlike the principles of deductive logic, be synthetic, i.e. not proved true by their falsehood being self-contradictory. The only alternative to this hypothesis is complete scepticism as to all the inferences of science and common sense, including those which I have called animal inferences.

Chapter II

SOLIPSISM

THE doctrine called "solipsism" is usually defined as the belief that I alone exist. It is not one doctrine unless it is true. If it is true, it is the assertion that I, Bertrand Russell, alone exist. But if it is false, and I have readers, then for you who are reading this chapter it is the assertion that you alone exist. This is a view suggested by the conclusions reached in the preceding chapter, to the effect that all my data, in so far as they are matters of fact, are private to me, and that inferences from one or more matters of fact to other matters of fact are never logically demonstrative. These conclusions suggest that it would be rational to doubt everything outside my own experience, such as the thoughts of other people and the existence of material objects when I am not seeing them. It is this view that we are now to examine.

We must begin by giving more precision to the doctrine, and by distinguishing various forms that it may take. We must not state it in the words "I alone exist", for these words have no clear meaning unless the doctrine is false. If the world is really the common-sense world of people and things, we can pick out one person and suppose him to think that he is the whole universe. This is analogous to the people before Columbus, who believed the Old World to be the total of land on this planet. But if other people and things do not exist, the word "myself" loses its meaning, for this is an exclusive and delimiting word. Instead of saying "myself is the whole universe", we must say "data are the whole universe". Here "data" may be defined by enumeration. We can then say: "this list is complete; there is nothing more". Or we can say: "there is not known to be anything more". In this form, the doctrine does not require a prior definition of the Self, and what it asserts is sufficiently definite to be discussed.

We may distinguish two kinds of solipsism, which I shall call "dogmatic" and "sceptical" respectively. The dogmatic kind, in the above statement, says "there is nothing beyond data", while the sceptical kind says "there is not known to be anything beyond data". No grounds exist in favour of the dogmatic form, since it is just as difficult to disprove existence as to prove it, when what is concerned is something which is not a datum. I shall therefore say no more about dogmatic solipsism, and shall concentrate on the sceptical form.

The sceptical form of the doctrine is difficult to state precisely. It is not right to say, as we did just now, "nothing is known except data", since some one else might know more; there is the same objection as there is to dogmatic solipsism. If we emend our statement by saying "nothing is known *to me* except the following (giving a list of data)", we have again introduced the Self, which, as we saw, we must not do in defining our doctrine. It is not altogether easy to evade this objection.

I think we can state the problem with which solipsism is concerned as follows: "The propositions $p_1, p_2, \ldots p_n$ are known otherwise than by inference. Can this list be made such that from it other propositions, asserting matters of fact, can be inferred?" In this form we do not have to state that our list is complete, or that it embraces all that some one person knows.

It is obvious that if our list consists entirely of propositions asserting matters of fact, then the answer to our question is in the negative, and sceptical solipsism is true. But if our list contains anything in the nature of laws the answer may be different. These laws, however, will have to be synthetic. Any collection of matters of fact is logically capable of being the whole; in pure logic, any two events are compossible, and no collection of events implies the existence of other events.

But before pursuing this line of thought let us consider different forms of solipsism.

Solipsism may be more drastic or less drastic; as it becomes more drastic it becomes more logical and at the same time more unplausible. In its least drastic form, it accepts all my mental states that are accepted by common sense or by orthodox psychology, i.e. not only those of which I am directly aware, but also those that are inferred on purely psychological grounds. It is generally held that at all times I have many faint sensations that I do not notice. If there is a ticking clock in the room, I may notice it and be annoyed by it, but as a rule I am quite unaware of it, even if it is easily audible whenever I choose to listen to it. In such a case one would naturally say that I am having auditory sensations of which I am not conscious. The same may be said, at most times, of objects in the periphery of my field of vision. If they are important objects, such as an enemy with a loaded revolver, I shall quickly become aware of them and bring them into the centre of my visual field: but if they are uninteresting and motionless I shall remain unaware of them. Nevertheless it seems natural to suppose that I am in some sense seeing them.

The same sort of considerations apply to lapses of memory. If I look at an old diary, I find dinner engagements noted that I have completely forgotten, but I find it hard to doubt that I had the experience which common sense would describe as going to a dinner party. I believe that I was once an infant, although no trace of that period survives in my explicit memory.

Such inferred mental states are allowed by the least drastic form of solipsism. It merely refuses to allow inferences to anything other than myself and my mental states.

This, however, is illogical. The principles required to justify inferences from mental states of which I am aware to others of which I am not aware are exactly the same as those required for inferences to physical objects and to other minds. If, therefore, we are to secure the logical safety of which solipsism is in search, we must confine ourselves to mental states of which we are now aware. Buddha was admired because he could meditate while tigers roared around him; but if he had been a consistent solipsist he would have held that the noise of roaring ceased as soon as he ceased to notice it.

We thus arrive at a second form of solipsism, which says that the universe consists, or perhaps consists, of only the following items; and then we enumerate whatever, at the moment of speaking, we perceive or remember. And this will have to be confined to what I actually notice, for what I *could* notice is inferred. At the moment, I notice my dog asleep, and as a plain man I am convinced that I could have noticed him any time this last hour, since he has been consistently (so I believe) in my field of vision, but I have in fact been quite unaware of him. The thoroughgoing solipsist will have to say that when, during the last hour, my eye absent-mindedly rested on the dog, nothing whatever occurred in me in consequence; for to argue that I had a sensation which I did not notice is to allow an inference of the forbidden kind.

In regard to memory, the results of this theory are extremely odd. The things that I am recollecting at one moment are quite different from those that I am recollecting at another, but the thoroughgoing solipsist should only admit what I am remembering now. Thus his world will be one of disjointed fragments which change completely from moment to moment—change, I mean, not as to what exists now, but as to what did exist in the past.

But we have not done with the sacrifices which the solipsist must make to logic if he is to feel safe. It is quite clear that I can have a recollection without the thing remembered having happened; as a matter of logical possibility, I might have begun to exist five minutes ago, complete with all the memories that I then had. We ought therefore to cut out events remembered, and confine the solipsist's universe to present percepts, including percepts of present states of mind which purport to be recollections. With regard to present percepts, this most rigorous type of solipsist (if he exists) accepts the premiss of Descartes' *cogito*, with some interpretation. What he admits can only be correctly stated in the form: "A, B, C, . . . occur." To call A, B, C, . . . "thoughts" adds nothing except for those who reject solipsism. What distinguishes the consistent solipsist is the fact that the proposition "A occurs", if it comes in his list, is never inferred. He rejects as invalid all inferences from one or more propositions of the form "A occurs" to other propositions asserting the occurrence of something, whether named or described. The conclusions of such inferences, he maintains, may or may not happen to be true, but can never be known to be true.

Having now stated the solipsist position, we must inquire what can be said for and against it.

The argument for sceptical solipsism is as follows: From a group of propositions of the form "A occurs", it is impossible to infer by deductive logic any other proposition asserting the occurrence of something. If any such inference is to be valid, it must depend upon some non-deductive principle such as causality or induction. No such principle can be shown to be even probable by means of deductive arguments from a group of propositions of the form "A occurs". (I shall be concerned in a later chapter with the proof of this assertion.) For example, the validity of induction cannot be inferred from the course of events except by assuming induction or some equally questionable postulate.

Therefore if, as empiricists maintain, all our knowledge is based on experience, it must be not only based on experience, but confined to experience; for it is only by assuming some principle or principles which experience cannot render even probable that anything whatever can be proved by experience except the experience itself.

I think this argument proves that we have to choose between two alternatives. Either we must accept sceptical solipsism in its most rigorous form, or we must admit that we know, independently of experience, some principle or principles by means of which it is possible to infer events from other events, at least with probability. If we adopt the first alternative, we must reject far more than solipsism is ordinarily thought to reject; we cannot know of the existence of our own past or future, or have any ground for expectations as to our own future, if it occurs. If we adopt the second alternative, we must partially reject empiricism; we must admit that we have knowledge as to certain general features of the course of nature, and that this knowledge, though it may be caused by experience, cannot be logically inferred from experience. We must admit also that, if we have such knowledge, it is not yet explicit; causality and induction, in their traditional forms, cannot be quite true, and it is by no means clear what should be substituted for them. It thus appears that there are great difficulties in the way of accepting either alternative.

For my part, I reject the solipsist alternative and adopt the other. I admit, what is of the essence of the matter, that the solipsist alternative cannot be disproved by means of deductive arguments, provided we grant what I shall call "the empiricist hypothesis", namely that what we know without inference consists solely of what we have experienced (or, more strictly, what we are experiencing) together with the principles of deductive logic. But we cannot know the empiricist hypothesis to be true, since that would be knowledge of a sort that the hypothesis itself condemns. This does not prove the hypothesis to be false, but it does prove that we have no right to assert it. Empiricism may be a true philosophy, but if it is it cannot be known to be true; those who assert that they know it to be true contradict themselves. There is therefore no obstacle *ab initio* to our rejecting the empiricist hypothesis.

As against solipsism it is to be said, in the first place, that it is psychologically impossible to believe, and is rejected in fact even by those who mean to accept it. I once received a letter from an eminent logician, Mrs. Christine Ladd Franklin, saying that she was a solipsist, and was surprised that there were no others. Coming from a logician, this surprise surprised me. The fact that I cannot believe something does not prove that it is false, but it does prove that I am insincere and frivolous if I pretend to believe it. Cartesian doubt has value as a means of articulating our knowledge and showing what depends on what, but if carried too far it becomes a mere technical game in which philosophy loses seriousness. Whatever anybody, even I myself, may argue to the contrary, I shall continue to believe that I am not the whole universe, and in this every one will in fact agree with me, if I am right in my conviction that other people exist.

The most important part of the argument as to solipsism is the proof that it is only tenable in its most drastic form. There are various half-way positions which are not altogether unplausible, and have in fact been accepted by many philosophers. Of these the least drastic is the view that there can never be good grounds for asserting the existence of something which no one experiences; from this we may, with Berkeley, infer the unreality of matter while retaining the reality of mind. But this view, since it admits the experiences of others than myself, and since these experiences are only known to me by inference, considers that it is possible to argue validly from the existence of certain occurrences to the existence of others; and if this is admitted, it will be found that there is no reason why the inferred events should be experienced. Exactly similar considerations apply to the form of solipsism which believes that oneself has a past and a probable future; this belief can only be justified by admitting principles of inference which lead to the rejection of every form of solipsism.

We are thus reduced to the two extreme hypotheses as alone logically defensible. Either, on the one hand, we know principles of non-deductive inference which justify our belief, not only in other people, but in the whole physical world, including the parts which are never perceived but only inferred from their effects; or, on the other hand, we are confined to what may be called "solipsism of the moment", in which the whole of my knowledge is limited to what I am now noticing, to the exclusion of my past and probable future, and also of all those sensations to which, at this instant, I am not paying attention. When this alternative is clearly realized, I do not think that anybody would honestly and sincerely choose the second hypothesis.

If solipsism of the moment is rejected, we must seek to discover what are the synthetic principles of inference by the knowledge of which our scientific and common-sense beliefs are to be justified in their broad outlines. To this task we shall address ourselves in Part VI. But it will be well first to make a survey, on the one hand of data, and on the other hand of scientific beliefs interpreted in their least questionable form. By analysing the results of this survey we may hope to discover the premisses which, consciously or unconsciously, are assumed in the reasonings of science.

Chapter III

PROBABLE INFERENCE
IN COMMON-SENSE PRACTICE

A "PROBABLE" inference (to repeat what has already been said) is one in which, when the premisses are true and the reasoning correct, the conclusion is nevertheless not certain but only probable in a greater or less degree. In the practice of science there are two kinds of inferences: those that are purely mathematical, and those that may be called "substantial". The inference from Kepler's laws to the law of gravitation as applied to the planets is mathematical, but the inference from the recorded apparent motions of the planets to Kepler's laws is substantial, for Kepler's laws are not the only hypotheses logically compatible with observed facts. Mathematical inference has been sufficiently investigated during the last half-century. What I wish to discuss is non-mathematical inference, which is always only probable.

I shall, broadly speaking, accept as valid any inference which is part of the accepted body of scientific theory, unless it contains some error of a specific kind. I shall not consider the arguments for scepticism concerning science, but shall analyse scientific inference on the hypothesis that it is in general valid.

My concern in this chapter will be mainly with pre-scientific knowledge as embodied in common sense.

We must bear in mind the distinction between inference as understood in logic and what may be called "animal inference". By "animal inference" I mean what happens when an occurrence A causes a belief B without any conscious intermediary. When a dog smells a fox he becomes excited, but we do not think that he says to himself: "This smell has in the past been frequently associated with the neighbourhood of a fox; therefore there is probably a fox in the neighbourhood now." He acts, it is true, as he would if he went through this reasoning, but the reasoning is performed by the body, through habit, or the "conditioned reflex" as it is called. Whenever A has, in the animal's past experience, been frequently associated with B, where B is something of emotional interest, the occurrence of A tends to cause behaviour appropriate to B. There is here no *conscious* connection of A and B; there is, we may say, A-perception and B-behaviour. In old-fashioned language, it would be said that the "impression" of A causes the "idea" of B. But the newer phraseology, in terms of bodily behaviour and observable habit, is more precise and covers a wider field.

Most substantial inferences in science, as opposed to merely mathematical inferences, arise, in the first place, from analysis of animal inferences. But before developing this aspect of our subject, let us consider the scope of animal inference in human behaviour.

The practical (as opposed to the theoretical) understanding of language comes under the head of animal inference. Understanding a word consists practically of (*a*) the effects of hearing it, and (*b*) the causes of uttering it. You understand the word "fox" if, when you hear it, you have an impulse to act in a manner appropriate to the presence of a fox, and when you see a fox, you have an impulse to say "fox". But you do not need to be aware of this connection between foxes and the word "fox"; the inference from the word to the fox or from the fox to the word is an animal inference. It is otherwise with erudite words, such as "dodecahedron". We learn the meaning of such words through a verbal definition, and in such cases the connection of word and meaning begins by being a conscious inference before it becomes a habit.

Words are a particular case of *signs*. We may say that, to a given organism O, a member of a class of stimuli A is a *sign*[1] of some member of a class of objects B if the occurrence to O of a stimulus of class A produces a reaction appropriate to an object of class B. But this is not yet quite precise. Before seeking further precision, let us consider a concrete example, say "no smoke without fire".

There are various stages to be gone through before this proverb can be enunciated. First, there must be repeated experience of both smoke and fire, either simultaneously or in close temporal succession. Originally, each produced its own reaction, (say) smoke that of sniffing, and fire that of running away. But in time a habit is formed, and smoke produces the reaction of running away. (I am assuming an environment where forest fires are frequent.) Some ages after the first formation of this habit, two

---

[1] Or, more correctly, a "subjective sign".

new habits are formed: smoke leads to the word "smoke", and fire leads to the word "fire". Where these three habits exist— smoke causing a reaction appropriate to fire, smoke causing the word "smoke" and fire causing the word "fire"—the materials exist for the formation of a fourth habit, that of the word "smoke" causing the word "fire". When this habit exists in a reflective philosopher, it may cause the sentence "no smoke without fire". Such, at least, is a bare outline of a very complex process.

In the above example, when all these habits exist, smoke is a sign of fire, the word "smoke" is a sign of smoke, and the word "fire" is a sign of fire. Perhaps it may be assumed that the sign-relation is often transitive, i.e. that, if A is a sign of B and B is a sign of C, then A is a sign of C. This will not be invariably the case, but it will tend to happen if the sign-relations of A and B, B and C are very firmly established in the animal's organism. In that case, when the word "smoke" is a sign of smoke, and smoke is a sign of fire, the word "smoke" will be, derivatively, a sign of fire. If fire causes the word "fire", the word "smoke" will thus have become, derivatively, a cause of the word "fire".

Let us set up a definition: An organism O has an "idea" of a kind of object B when its action is appropriate to B although no object of the kind B is sensibly present. This, however, requires some limitation. An "idea" need not produce *all* the reactions that would be produced by the object; this is what we mean by saying that an idea may be faint, or not vividly imagined. There may be nothing but the word "B". Thus we shall say that the idea of B is present to O whenever O shows *some* reaction appropriate to B and to nothing else.

We can now say that A is a sign of B when A causes the "idea" of B.

We have used the word "appropriate", and this word needs further definition. It must not be defined teleologically, as "useful to the organism" or what not. The reaction "appropriate" to B is primarily the reaction caused by the sensible presence of B, independently of acquired habits. A cry of pain on contact with something very hot is an appropriate reaction in this sense. But we cannot altogether exclude acquired habits from our definition of appropriate reactions. To say "fox" when you see a fox is appropriate. We may make a distinction: there is no situation to which, apart from acquired habits, we react by saying "fox".

We may therefore decide to include among "appropriate" re-actions those which, as a result of habit, occur in the presence of the object B, but do not occur spontaneously as reactions to anything except B, and do not occur as habitual reactions to any-thing other than B except as a result of a combination of habits.

The above discussion gives the definition of what may be called a "subjective" sign, when A causes the idea of B. We may say that A is an "objective" sign of B when A is in fact followed or accompanied by B, and not only by the idea of B. We may say roughly that there is error on the part of an organism whenever a subjective sign is not also an objective sign; but such a statement is not correct without qualification.

Qualification is required because we must distinguish an idea accompanied by belief from one merely entertained. If you had two friends called Box and Cox, it is probable that the sight of Box would cause the idea of Cox, but not the belief in the presence of Cox. I think that entertaining an idea without belief is a more complex occurrence than entertaining it with belief. An idea is or involves (I will not argue which) an impulse to a certain kind of action. When the impulse is uninhibited, the idea is "believed"; when inhibited, the idea is merely "entertained". In the former case we may call the idea "active", in the latter "suspended". Error is only connected with *active* ideas. Thus there is error when a subjective sign produces an active idea, although there is no such sequence between the sign and the object of the idea.

Error, according to this view, is pre-intellectual; it requires only bodily habits. There is error when a bird flies against a pane of glass which it does not see. We all, like the bird, entertain rash beliefs which may, if erroneous, lead to painful shocks. Scientific method, I suggest, consists mainly in eliminating those beliefs which there is positive reason to think a source of shocks, while retaining those against which no definite argument can be brought.

In what I have been saying I have been assuming causal laws of the form "A causes B", where A and B are classes of occurrences. Such laws are perhaps never wholly true. True laws can only be expressed in differential equations. But it is not necessary that they should be exactly true. What we need is only: "In a good deal more than half the cases in which A occurs, B occurs simul-taneously or soon afterwards." This makes B *probable* whenever

A has occurred, and that is as much as we should demand. I have assumed that if, in the history of a given organism, A has often been followed by B, A will be accompanied or quickly followed by the "idea" of B, i.e. by an impulse to the actions which would be stimulated by B. This law is inevitably vague. If A and B are emotionally interesting to the organism, one case of their conjunction may suffice to set up a habit; if not, many may be needed. The conjunction of 54 and 6 times 9 has, for most children, little emotional interest; hence the difficulty of learning the multiplication table. On the other hand, "once bit twice shy" shows how easily a habit is formed when the emotional interest is strong.

As appears from what we have been saying, science starts, and must start, from rough and ready generalizations which are only approximately true, many of which exist as animal inferences before they are put into words. The process is as follows: A is followed by B a certain number of times; then A is accompanied by the expectation of B; then (probably much later) comes the explicit judgment "A is a sign of B"; and only then, when multitudes of such judgments already exist, can science begin. Then comes Hume, with his query as to whether we ever have reason to regard A as an objective sign of B, or even to suppose that we shall continue to think it a sign of B. This is a sketch of the psychology of the subject; it has no *direct* bearing on its logic.

The distinction between animal inference and scientific inference, I repeat, is this: In animal inference, the percept A causes the idea of B, but there is no awareness of the connection; in scientific inference (whether valid or invalid) there is a belief involving both A and B, which I have expressed by "A is a sign of B". It is the occurrence of a single belief expressing a connection of A and B that distinguishes what is commonly called inference from what I call animal inference. But it is important to notice that the belief expressing the connection is, in all the most elementary cases, preceded by the habit of animal inference.

Take, as an example, the belief in more or less permanent objects. A dog, seeing his master on different occasions, reacts in a way which has some constant features; this is the observable fact which we express by saying that the dog "recognizes" his master. When the dog looks for his absent master, something more than recognition is involved. It is difficult not to use unduly intellectualist language to describe what occurs in such a case.

One might be tempted to say that there is a desire to replace an idea of an object by an impression of it, but this is the sort of phrase that seems to say much and really says little. The simplest observable fact about desire in animals is restless behaviour until a certain situation arises, and then relative quiescence. There are also physiological facts about the secretions of the glands, such as Pavlov employed. I am not *denying* that dogs have experiences more or less similar to those which we have when we feel desire, but this is an inference from their behaviour, not a datum. What we observe can be summed up by saying that a certain part of the dog's behaviour is unified by reference to his master, as a planet's behaviour is unified by reference to the sun. In the case of the planet, we do not infer that it "thinks" about the sun; in the case of the dog, most of us do make the corresponding inference. But that is a difference with which we need not be concerned as yet.

When we come to language, it is natural to have a single word for those features of the environment which are connected together in the kind of way in which appearances of the dog's master are connected together for the dog. Language has proper names for the objects with which we are most intimately associated, and general names for other objects. Proper names embody a common-sense metaphysic, which, as animal inference, antedates language. Consider such children's questions as "Where's mother?" "Where's my ball?" These imply that mothers and balls, when not sensibly present, nevertheless exist somewhere, and can probably be made sensible by suitable action. This belief in permanent or quasi-permanent objects is based upon recognition, and thus implies memory in some sense. However that may be, it is clear that, by the time a child begins to speak, he has a habit of similar reactions to a certain group of stimuli, which, when reflected upon, becomes a belief in persistent common-sense objects. Much the same must have been true of mankind when developing language. The metaphysic of more or less permanent objects underlies the vocabulary and syntax of every language, and is the basis of the concept of substance. The only point about it that I am concerned to make at the moment is that it results from intellectualizing the animal inference involved in recognition.

I come now to memory. What I wish to say about memory is, that its general though not invariable trustworthiness is a premiss of scientific knowledge, which is necessary if science is to be accepted as mainly true, but is not capable of being made even probable by arguments which do not assume memory. More precisely: When I remember something, it is probable that what I remember occurred, and I can form some estimate of the degree of probability by the vividness of my recollection.

Let us first make clear what is meant logically by saying that memory is a premiss of knowledge. It would be a mistake to set up a general statement of the form: "What is remembered probably occurred." It is rather each instance of memory that is a premiss. That is to say, we have beliefs about past occurrences which are not inferred from other beliefs, but which, nevertheless, we should not abandon except on very cogent grounds. (By "we", here, I mean people versed in scientific method and careful as to what they believe.) The cogent grounds must necessarily involve one or more scientific laws, and also matters of fact, which may be either perceived or remembered. When Macbeth's witches vanish, he doubts whether he ever saw them, because he believes in the persistence of material objects. But although any memory may come to be thought mistaken, it always has a certain weight, which makes us accept it in the absence of contrary evidence.

A few words must be said at this point about scientific laws as opposed to particular facts. It is only by assuming laws that one fact can make another probable or improbable. If I remember that at noon yesterday I was in America, but five minutes earlier I was in Kamchatka, I shall think that one of my memories must be mistaken, because I am firmly persuaded that the journey cannot be performed in five minutes. But why do I think this? As an empiricist, I hold that laws of nature should be inferred inductively from particular facts. But how am I to establish particular facts about how long a journey has taken? It is clear that I must rely partly on memory, since otherwise I shall not know that I have taken a journey. The ultimate evidence for any scientific law consists of particular facts, together with those principles of scientific inference which it is my purpose to investigate. When I say that memory is a premiss, I mean that, among the facts upon which scientific laws are based, some are admitted solely because they are remembered. They are admitted, however, only as probable, and any one of them may be rejected later, after scientific laws have been discovered which make the particular memory improbable. But this improbability is only arrived at by assuming that most memories are veridical.

The necessity of memory as a premiss may be made evident by asking the question: what reason have we for rejecting the hypothesis that the world came into existence five minutes ago? If it had begun then just as, in fact, it then was, containing people with the habits and supposed memories that in fact people then had, there would be no possible way of finding out that they had only just begun to exist. Yet there is nothing logically impossible in the hypothesis. Nothing that is happening now logically implies anything that happened at another time. And the laws of nature by which we infer the past are themselves, as we have seen, dependent upon memories for the evidence in their favour. Consequently remembered facts must be included with perceived facts as part of our data, though we may as a rule assign a lower degree of credence to them than we do to facts of present perception.

There is a distinction to be made here, which is not without importance. A recollection is a present fact: I remember now what I did yesterday. When I say that memory is a premiss, I do not mean that from my present recollection I can infer the past event recollected. This may be in some sense true, but is not the important fact in this connection. The important fact is that the past occurrence is itself a premiss for my knowledge. It cannot be inferred from the present fact of my recollecting it except by assuming the general trustworthiness of memory, i.e. that an event remembered probably did take place. It is this that is the memory-premiss of knowledge.

It must be understood that, when I say that this or that is a premiss, I do not mean that it is certainly true; I mean only that it is something to be taken account of in arriving at the truth, but not itself inferred from something believed to be true. The situation is the same as that in a criminal trial in which the witnesses contradict each other. Each witness has a certain *prima facie* weight, and we have to seek a consistent system embracing as many of their statements as possible.

I come now to another source of knowledge, namely testimony. I do not think that the general truthfulness of testimony needs to be a premiss in the finished structure of scientific knowledge, but it is a premiss in the early stages, and animal inference makes us prone to believe it. Moreover I think we shall find that, in the finished structure of science, there is a general premiss which is needed to secure the probable trustworthiness of testimony as well as certain other things.

Let us first consider common-sense arguments, such as would have weight in a law court. If twelve people, each of whom lies as often as he speaks the truth, independently testify to a certain occurrence, the odds are 4095 to 1 that they are testifying truly. This may be taken as practical certainty, unless the twelve people all have a special motive for lying. This may happen. If two ships have a collision at sea, all the sailors on one ship swear one thing, and all the sailors on the other swear the opposite. If one of the ships has been sunk with all hands, there will be unanimous testimony, about which, nevertheless, lawyers experienced in such cases will feel sceptical. But we need not pursue such arguments, which are a matter for lawyers rather than philosophers.

The common-sense practice is to accept testimony unless there is a positive reason against doing so in the particular case concerned. The cause, though not the justification, of this practice is the animal inference from a word or sentence to what it signifies. If you are engaged in a tiger hunt and somebody exclaims "tiger" your body will, unless you inhibit your impulses, get into a state very similar to that in which it would be if you saw a tiger. Such a state *is* the belief that a tiger is in the neighbourhood; thus you will be believing the testimony of the man who said "tiger". The creation of such habits is half of learning the English language; the other half is the creation of the habit of saying "tiger" when you see one. (I am omitting niceties of grammar and syntax.) You can, of course, learn to inhibit the impulse to belief; you may come to know that your companion is a practical joker. But an inhibited impulse still exists, and if it ceased to exist you would cease to understand the word "tiger". This applies even to such dry statements as "tigers are found in India and Eastern Asia". You may think you hear this statement without any of the emotions appropriate to tigers, and yet it may cause during the following night a nightmare from which you wake in a cold sweat, showing that the impulses appropriate to the word "tiger" survived subconsciously.

It is this primitive credulity about testimony which causes the success of advertising. Unless you are an unusually sophisticated person, you will, if you are told often and emphatically that so-and-so's soaps or politics are the best, in the end come to believe it, with the result that so-and-so becomes a millionaire or a dictator as the case may be. However, I do not want to stray into politics, so I will say no more about this aspect of the belief in testimony.

Testimony must be distinguished from information as to the meaning of a word, though the distinction is not always easy. You learn the correct use of the word "cat" because your parents say "cat" when you are noticing a cat. If they were not sufficiently truthful for this—if, when you are noticing a cat, they said some-times "dog", sometimes "cow", sometimes "crocodile"—you could never learn to speak correctly. The fact that we do learn to speak correctly is a testimonial to the habitual veracity of parents. But while, from the parent's point of view, his utterance of the word "cat" is a statement, from the child's point of view it is merely a step in the acquisition of language-habits. It is only after the child knows the meaning of the word "cat" that your utterance of the word is a statement for him as well as for you.

Testimony is very important in one respect, namely, that it helps to build up the distinction between the comparatively public world of sense and the private world of thought, which is already well established when scientific thinking begins. I was once giving a lecture to a large audience when a cat stalked in and lay down at my feet. The behaviour of the audience persuaded me that I was not suffering from a hallucination. Some of our exper-iences, but not all, appear from the behaviour of others (including testimony) to be common to all who are in a certain neighbourhood and are making use of normal senses. Dreams have not this public character; no more do most "thoughts". It must be noticed that the public character of (say) a clap of thunder is an inference, originally an animal inference. I hear thunder, and a person standing beside me says "thunder". I infer that he heard thunder, and until I become a philosopher I make this inference with my body, i.e. my mind emerges believing that he heard the thunder without having gone through a "mental" process. When I become a philosopher I have to examine the body's inferential propensities, including the belief in a public world which it has inferred from observing behaviour (especially speech-behaviour) similar to its own.

From the point of view of the philosopher, the interesting question is not only whether the testimony you hear is intended to be truthful, but whether it has any intention of conveying information. There are here various stages towards meaninglessness. When you hear an actor on the stage say "I have supped full with horrors", you do not think he is complaining about rationing, and you know that his statements are not intended to be believed. When you hear a soprano voice on a phonograph lamenting her lover's faithlessness in anguished tones, you know that there is no lady in the box, and that the lady who made the record was not expressing her own emotions, but only intending to give you pleasure in the contemplation of an imaginary sorrow. Then there was the Scotch ghost in the eighteenth century, which kept on repeating: "Once I was hap-hap-happy but noo I am meeserable", which turned out to be a rusty spit. Lastly, there are the people in dreams, who say all sorts of things that, when we wake up, we are convinced nobody did say.

For all these reasons, we cannot accept testimony at its face value. The question arises: why should we accept it at all?

We depend here, as we do when we believe in sound waves and light waves, upon an inference going beyond our experience. Why should not everything that seems to us to be testimony be like either the creakings of the rusty spit or the conversation of people in dreams? We cannot refute this hypothesis by reliance upon experience, for our experience may be exactly the same whether the hypothesis is true or false. And in any inference beyond future as well as past experience we cannot rely upon induction. Induction argues that, if A has been frequently *found* to be followed by B, it will probably be *found* to be followed by B next time. This is a principle which remains entirely within experience, actual or possible.

In the case of testimony, we depend upon *analogy*. The behaviour of other people's bodies—and especially their speech behaviour—is noticeably similar to our own, and our own is noticeably associated with "mental" phenomena. (For the moment it does not matter what we mean by "mental".) We therefore argue that other people's behaviour is also associated with "mental" phenomena. Or rather, we accept this at first as an animal inference, and invent the analogy argument afterwards to rationalize the already existing belief.

Analogy differs from induction—at least as I am using the words—by the fact that an analogical inference, when it passes outside experience, cannut be verified. We cannot enter into the minds of others to observe the thoughts and emotions which we infer from their behaviour. We must therefore accept analogy—in the sense in which it goes beyond experience—as an independent premiss of scientific knowledge, or else we must find some other equally effective principle.

The principle of analogical inference will have to be more or less as follows: Given a class of cases in which A is accompanied or succeeded by B, and another class of cases in which it cannot be ascertained whether B is present or not, there is a probability (varying according to circumstances) that in these cases also B is present.

This is not an accurate statement of the principle, which will need various limitations. But the necessary further refinements would not make much difference in relation to the problem with which we are concerned.

A further step away from experience is involved in the inference to such things as sound waves and light waves. Let us concentrate on the former. Suppose at a point O, from which many roads radiate, you place a charge of gunpowder, and at a certain moment you cause it to explode. Every hundred yards along these roads you station an observer with a flag. A person in a stationary balloon observes all the observers, who have orders to wave their flags when they hear the noise of the gunpowder exploding. It is found that those who are equidistant from O all wave their flags at the same moment, while those who are further from O wave their flags later than those who are nearer; moreover, the time that elapses between the seen explosion and the waving of a given observer's flag is proportional to his distance from O. It is inferred by science (common sense concurring) that some process travels outward from O, and that, therefore, something connected with the sound is happening, not only where there are observers, but also where there are none. In this inference we pass outside all experience, not only outside our personal experience as in the case of testimony. We cannot therefore interpret science wholly in terms of experience, even when we include all experience.

The principle used in the above inference may be called, provisionally, the principle of spatio-temporal continuity in causal laws. This is the same thing as denial of action at a distance. We cannot believe that sounds arrive successively at successive observers unless something has travelled over the intervening space. If we deny this, our world becomes altogether too staccato to be credible. The basis of our belief, presumably, is the continuity of all observed motions; thus perhaps analogy can be stretched to cover this inference. However, there is much to be said before we can be clear as to the principle governing such inferences. I therefore leave the further consideration of this subject for a later chapter.

So far, I have been concerned in collecting rough and ready examples of elementary scientific inference. It remains to give precision to the results of our preliminary survey.

I will end with a summary of the results of our present discussion.

When we begin to reflect, we find ourselves possessed of a number of habits which may be called "animal inferences". These habits consist of acting in the presence of A more or less as we should in the presence of B, and they result from the past conjunction of A and B in our experience. These habits, when we become conscious of them, cause such beliefs as "A is always (or usually) followed by B". This is one of the main sources of the stock of beliefs with which we start when we begin to be scientific; in particular, it includes the understanding of language.

Another pre-scientific belief which survives in science is the belief in more or less permanent objects, such as people and things. The progress of science refines this belief, and in modern quantum theory not very much remains of it, but science could hardly have been created without it.

The general, though not universal, trustworthiness of memory is an independent postulate. It is necessary to much of our knowledge, and cannot be established by inference from anything that does not assume it.

Testimony is, like memory, part of the sources of our primitive beliefs. But it need not itself be made into a premiss, since it can be merged in the wider premiss of *analogy*.

Finally, to infer such things as sound waves and light waves we need a principle which may be called spatio-temporal causal continuity, or denial of action at a distance. But this last principle is complicated, and demands further discussion.

Chapter IV

PHYSICS AND EXPERIENCE

THE question to be discussed in this Chapter is one which, in my opinion, has been far too little considered. It is this: Assuming physics to be broadly speaking true, can we know it to be true, and, if the answer is to be in the affirmative, does this involve knowledge of other truths besides those of physics? We might find that, if the world is such as physics says it is, no organism could know it to be such; or that, if an organism can know it to be such, it must know some things other than physics, more particularly certain principles of probable inference.

This question becomes acute through the problem of perception. There have, from the earliest times, been two types of theory as to perception, one empirical, the other idealist. According to the empirical theory, some continuous chain of causation leads from the object to the percipient, and what is called "perceiving" the object is the last link in this chain, or rather the last before the chain begins to lead out of the percipient's body instead of into it. According to the idealist theory, when a percipient happens to be in the neighbourhood of an object a divine illumination causes the percipient's soul to have an experience which is like the object.

Each of these theories has its difficulties.

The idealist theory has its origin in Plato, but reaches its logical culmination in Leibniz, who held that the world consists of monads which never interact, but which all go through parallel developments, so that what happens to me at any instant has a similarity to what is happening to you at the same instant. When you think you move your arm, I think I see you moving it; thus we are both deceived, and no one before Leibniz was sufficiently acute to unmask the deception, which he regards as the best proof of God's goodness. This theory is fantastic, and has had few adherents; but in less logical forms portions of the idealistic theory of perception are to be found even among those who think themselves most remote from it.

Philosophy is an offshoot of theology, and most philosophers, like Malvolio, "think nobly of the soul". They are therefore pre-

211

disposed to endow it with magical powers, and to suppose that the relation between perceiving and what is perceived must be something utterly different from physical causation. This view is reinforced by the belief that mind and matter are completely disparate, and that perceiving, which is a mental phenomenon, must be totally unlike an occurrence in the brain, which is all that can be attributed to physical causation.

The theory that perceiving depends upon a chain of physical causation is apt to be supplemented by a belief that to every state of the brain a certain state of the mind "corresponds", and vice versa, so that, given either the state of the brain or the state of the mind, the other could be inferred by a person who sufficiently understood the correspondence. If it is held that there is no causal interaction between mind and brain, this is merely a new form of the pre-established harmony. But if causation is regarded—as it usually is by empiricists—as nothing but invariable sequence or concomitance, then the supposed correspondence of brain and mind tautologically involves causal interaction. The whole question of the dependence of mind on body or body on mind has been involved in quite needless obscurity owing to the emotions involved. The facts are quite plain. Certain observable occurrences are commonly called "physical", certain others "mental"; sometimes "physical" occurrences appear as causes of "mental" ones, sometimes vice versa. A blow causes me to feel pain, a volition causes me to move my arm. There is no reason to question either of these causal connections, or at any rate no reason which does not apply to all causal connections equally.

These considerations remove one set of difficulties that stand in the way of acceptance of the physical theory of perception.

The common-sense arguments in favour of the physical causation of perceptions are so strong that only powerful prejudices could have caused them to be questioned. When we shut our eyes we do not see, when we stop our ears we do not hear, when we are under an anaesthetic we perceive nothing. The appearance that a thing presents can be altered by jaundice, short sight, microscopes, mists, etc. The time at which we hear a sound depends upon our distance from its physical point of origin. The same is true of what we see, though the velocity of light is so great that, where terrestrial objects are concerned, the time between an occurrence and our seeing of it is inappreciable. If it is by a divine illumination that we perceive objects, it must be admitted that the illumination adapts itself to physical conditions.

There are, however, two objections to the physical causation of perceptions. One is that it makes it impossible, or at least very difficult, to suppose that external objects are what they seem to be; the other is that it seems to make it doubtful whether the occurrences that we call "perceptions" can really be a source of knowledge as to the physical world. The first of these may be ignored as having only to do with prejudices, but the second is more important.

The problem is this: Every empiricist holds that our knowledge as to matters of fact is derived from perception, but if physics is true there must be so little resemblance between our percepts and their external causes that it is difficult to see how, from percepts, we can acquire a knowledge of external objects. The problem is further complicated by the fact that physics has been inferred from perception. Historically, physicists started from naïve realism, that is to say, from the belief that external objects are exactly as they seem; on the basis of this assumption, they developed a theory which made matter something quite unlike what we perceive. Thus their conclusion contradicted their premiss, though no one except a few philosophers noticed this. We therefore have to decide whether, if physics is true, the hypothesis of naïve realism can be so modified that there shall be a valid inference from percepts to physics. In a word: If physics is true, is it possible that it should be known?

Let us first try to define what we are to mean by the hypothesis that physics is true. I want to adopt this hypothesis only to the extent to which it appeals to educated common sense. We find that the theories of physicists constantly undergo modification, so that no prudent man of science would expect any physical theory to be quite unchanged a hundred years hence. But when theories change, the alteration usually has only a small effect so far as observable phenomena are concerned. The *practical* difference between Einstein's theory of gravitation and Newton's is very minute, though the theoretical difference is very great. Moreover, in every new theory there are some parts that seem pretty certain, while others remain very speculative. Einstein's substitution of space-time for space and time represents a change of language for which there are the same sort of grounds of simplicity as there were for the Copernican change of language. This part of Einstein's theory may be accepted with considerable confidence. But the view that the universe is a three-dimensional sphere of finite diameter remains speculative; no one would be surprised if evidence were found which would lead astronomers to give up this way of speaking.

Or, again, take the physical theory of light. No one doubts that light travels at the rate of roughly 300,000 kilometers per second, but whether it consists of waves, or of particles called photons, is a matter as to which dispute has been possible. In the case of sound, on the other hand, the wave theory may be accepted as firmly established.

Every physical theory which survives goes through three stages. In the first stage, it is a matter of controversy among specialists; in the second stage, the specialists are agreed that it is the theory which best fits the available evidence, though it may well hereafter be found incompatible with new evidence; in the third stage, it is thought very unlikely that any new evidence will do more than somewhat modify it.

When I say that I shall assume physics to be true, I mean that I shall accept those parts of physics which have reached the third stage, not as certain, but as more probable than any philosophical speculation, and therefore proper to be accepted by philosophers as a premiss in their arguments.

Let us now see what the most certain parts of physics have to say that is relevant to our present problem.

The great physical discoveries of the seventeenth century were made by means of two working hypotheses. One of these was that causal laws in the physical world need only take account of matter and motion, matter being composed of particles persisting through time but continuously changing their positions in space. It was assumed that, so far as physics is concerned, there is no need to take account of anything about a particle except its position in space at various times; that is to say, we might suppose particles to differ only in position, not in quality. At first, this was hardly more than a definition of the word "physics"; when it was necessary to take account of qualitative differences, we were concerned with a different subject, called "chemistry". During the present century, however, the modern theory of the atom has reduced chemistry, theoretically, to physics. This has enormously extended the scope of the hypothesis that different particles of matter differ only in position.

Does this hypothesis apply also to physiology, or is the behaviour of living matter subject to laws different from those governing dead matter? Vitalists maintain the latter view, but I think the former has the greater weight of authority in its favour. What can be said is that, wherever a physiological process is understood, it is found to follow the laws of physics and chemistry, and that, further, there is no physiological process which is clearly not explicable by these laws. It is therefore the best hypothesis that physiology is reducible to physics and chemistry. But this hypothesis has not nearly the same degree of certainty as the reduction of chemistry to physics.

I shall assume henceforth that the first of the seventeenth-century working hypotheses, which may be called the hypothesis of the homogeneity of matter, applies throughout the physical world, and to living as well as dead matter. I shall not constantly repeat that this theory is not *certainly* true; this is to be taken as said once for all. I assume the theory because the weight of evidence, though not conclusive, seems to me strongly in its favour.

The second of the working hypotheses of the seventeenth century may be called the hypothesis of the independence of causes; it is embodied in the parallelogram law. In its simplest form it says such things as: If you walk for a minute on the deck of a moving ship, you will reach the same point, relatively to the water, as you would if first you stood still for a minute while the ship moved, and then the ship stood still for a minute while you did your walk on the deck. More generally, when a body is subject to several forces, the result of their all acting at once for a given length of time is the same as would be the result of their all acting by turns, each for the given length of time—or rather, if the given length of time is very short this will be nearly true, and the shorter the time the more nearly true it will become. For instance, the moon is attracted both by the earth and by the sun; in one second, it will move very nearly as if, for one second, it were not attracted by either, but went on moving as before, then for another second it were to move as if (starting from rest) it were attracted by the earth only, then for another second as if (starting from rest) it were attracted by the sun only. If we take a shorter time than a second this will be more nearly true, approaching the limit of complete truth as the period of time is indefinitely diminished.

This principle is of the utmost importance technically. It enables us, when we have studied the effects of a number of separate forces each acting singly, to calculate the effect of their all acting together. It is the basis of the mathematical methods employed in traditional physics. But it must be said that it is not self-evident, except in simple cases like that of the man walking on the deck of the ship. In other cases, it is to be believed if it works, but we ought not to be surprised if we find that it sometimes does not work. In the quantum theory of the atom it has had to be abandoned, though this is perhaps not definitive. However that may be, this second working hypothesis is much less securely established than the first. It holds, at least approximately, over a wide field, but there is no good ground for believing that it holds universally.

The present century has somewhat modified the assumptions of physics. First, there is a four-dimensional manifold of events, instead of the two manifolds of space and time; second, causal laws do not suffice to determine individual events, but only statistical distributions; third, change is probably discontinuous. These modifications would be more important to us than they are, but for the fact that the second and third only apply effectively to microscopic phenomena, while the physical occurrences, such as speaking, which are associated with "mental" events, are macroscopic. Therefore if a human body works wholly in accordance with physical laws, it will still be correct to use the laws of classical physics to determine what a man will say, and generally what will be the large-scale motions of his body.

This brings us to the problem of the relation of mind and matter, since perception is commonly considered "mental" while the object perceived and the stimulus to perceiving are considered "physical". My own belief is that there is no difficulty whatever about this problem. The supposed difficulties have their origin in bad metaphysics and bad ethics. Mind and matter, we are told, are two substances, and are utterly disparate. Mind is noble, matter is base. Sin consists in subjection of the mind to the body. Knowledge, being one of the noblest of mental activities, cannot depend upon sense, for sense marks a form of subjection to matter, and is therefore bad. Hence the Platonic objection to identifying knowledge with perception. All this, you may think, is antiquated, but it has left a trail of prejudices hard to overcome.

Nevertheless, the distinction of mind and matter would hardly have arisen if it had not some foundation. We must seek, therefore, for one or more distinctions more or less analogous to the distinction between mind and matter. I should define a "mental" occurrence as one which can be known without inference. But let us examine some more conventional definitions.

We cannot use the Cartesian distinction between thought and extension, if only on Leibniz's ground, that extension involves plurality and therefore cannot be an attribute of a single substance. But we might try a somewhat analogous distinction. Material things, we may say, have spatial relations, while mental things do not. The brain is in the head, but thoughts are not—so at least philosophers assure us. This point of view is due to a confusion between different meanings of the word "space". Among the things that I see at a given moment there are spatial relations which are a part of my percepts; if percepts are "mental", as I should contend, then spatial relations which are ingredients of percepts are also "mental". Naïve realism identifies my percepts with physical things; it assumes that the sun of the astronomers is what I see. This involves identifying the spatial relations of my percepts with those of physical things. Many people retain this aspect of naïve realism although they have rejected all the rest.

But this identification is indefensible. The spatial relations of physics hold between electrons, protons, neutrons, etc., which we do not perceive; the spatial relations of visual percepts hold between things that we do perceive, and in the last analysis between coloured patches. There is a rough correlation between physical space and visual space, but it is very rough. First: depths become indistinguishable when they are great. Second: the timing is different; the place where the sun seems to be now corresponds to the place where the physical sun was eight minutes ago. Third: the percept is subject to changes which the physicist does not attribute to changes in the object, e.g. those brought about by clouds, telescopes, squinting, or closing the eyes. The correspondence between the percept and the physical object is therefore only approximate, and it is no more exact as regards spatial relations than it is in other respects. The sun of the physicist is not identical with the sun of my percepts, and the 93,000,000 miles that separate it from the moon are not identical with the spatial relation between the visual sun and the visual moon when I happen to see both at once.

When I say that something is "outside" me, there are two different things that I may mean. I may mean that I have a percept which is outside the percept of my body in perceptual space, or I may mean that there is a physical object which is outside my body as a physical object in the space of physics. Generally there is a rough correspondence between these two. The table that I see is outside my body as I see it in perceptual space, and the physical table is outside my physical body in physical space. But sometimes the correspondence fails. I dream, say, of a railway accident: I see the train falling down an embankment, and I hear the shrieks of the injured. These dream-objects are genuinely and truly "outside" my dream body in my own perceptual space. But when I wake up I find that the whole dream was due to a noise in my ear. And when I say that the noise is in my ear, I mean that the physical source of the sound that I experience is "in" my ear as a physical object in physical space. In another sense, we might say that all noises are in the ear, but if we confuse these two senses the result is an inextricable tangle.

Generalizing, we may say that my percept of anything other than my body is "outside" the percept of my body in perceptual space, and if the perception is not misleading the physical object is "outside" my physical body in physical space. It does not follow that my percept is outside my physical body. Indeed, such a hypothesis is *prima facie* meaningless, although, as we shall see, a meaning can be found for it, and it is then false.

We can now begin to tackle our central question, namely, what do we mean by a "percept", and how can it be a source of knowledge as to something other than itself?

What is a "percept"? As I use the word, it is what happens when, in common-sense terms, I see something or hear something or otherwise believe myself to become aware of something through my senses. The sun, we believe, is always there, but I only sometimes see it: I do not see it at night, or in cloudy weather, or when I am otherwise occupied. But sometimes I see it. All the occasions on which I see the sun have a certain resemblance to each other, which enabled me in infancy to learn

to use the word "sun" on the right occasions. Some of the resemblances between different occasions when I see the sun are
obviously in me; for example, I must have my eyes open and turn
in the right direction. These, therefore, we do not regard as
properties of the sun. But there are other resemblances which, so
far as common sense can discover, do not depend upon us; when
we see the sun, it is almost always round and bright and hot. The
few occasions when it is not are easily explicable as due to fog or
to an eclipse. Common sense therefore says: there is an object
which is round and bright and hot; the kind of event called
"seeing the sun" consists in a relation between me and this object,
and when this relation occurs I am "perceiving" the object.

But at this point physics intervenes in a very awkward way. It
assures us that the sun is not "bright" in the sense in which we
usually understand the word; it is a source of light-rays which have
a certain effect upon eyes and nerves and brains, but when this
effect is absent because the light-rays do not encounter a living
organism, there is nothing that can be properly called "brightness".
Exactly the same considerations apply to the words "hot" and
"round"—at least if "round" is understood as a perceptible
quality. Moreover, though you see the sun now, the physical
object to be inferred from your seeing existed eight minutes ago;
if, in the intervening minutes, the sun had gone out, you would
still be seeing exactly what you are seeing. We cannot therefore
identify the physical sun with what we see; nevertheless what we
see is our chief reason for believing in the physical sun.

Assuming the truth of physics, what is there in its laws that
justifies inferences from percepts to physical objects? Before we
can adequately discuss this question, we must determine the
place of percepts in the world of physics. There is here a peculiarity: physics never mentions percepts except when it speaks of
empirical verification of its laws; but if its laws are not concerned
with percepts, how can percepts verify them? This question
should be borne in mind during the following discussions.

The question of the position of percepts in the causal chains of
physics is a different one from that of the cognitive status of
percepts, though the two are interconnected. At the moment I am
concerned with the location of percepts in causal chains. Now
a percept—say hearing a noise—has a series of antecedents, which
travel in space-time from the physical source of the noise through

the air to the ears and brain. The experience which we call "hearing the noise" is as nearly as can be determined simultaneous with the cerebral term of the physical causal chain. If the noise is of the kind to call forth a bodily movement, the movement begins almost immediately after "hearing the noise". If we are going to fit "hearing the noise" into a physical causal chain, we must therefore connect it with the same region of space-time as that of the accompanying cerebral events. And this applies also to the noise as something perceived. The only region of space-time with which this noise has any direct connection is the present state of the hearer's brain; the connection with the physical source of the sound is indirect. Exactly the same argument applies to things seen.

I am anxious to minimize the metaphysical assumptions to be made in this connection. You may hold that mind and matter interact, or that, as the Cartesians contended, they run in parallel series, or that, as materialists believe, mental occurrences are mere concomitants of certain physical occurrences, determined by them but having no reciprocal influence on physical events. What you hold in these respects has no bearing on the point that I am making. What I am saying is something which is obvious to educated common sense, namely that, whether we consider the percept cr the simultaneous state of the brain, the causal location of either is intermediate between occurrences in afferent nerves constituting the stimulus, and occurrences in efferent nerves constituting the reaction.

This applies not only to the perceiving, which we naturally regard as "mental", but to what we experience when we perceive. That is to say, it applies not only to "seeing the sun", but also to the sun, if we mean by "the sun" something that a human being can experience. The astronomer's sun is inferred, it is not hot or bright, and it existed eight minutes before what is called seeing it. If I see the sun and it makes me blink, what I see is not 93,000,000 miles and eight minutes away, but is causally (and therefore spatio-temporally) intermediate between the light-waves striking the eye and the consequent blinking.

The dualistic view of perception, as a relation of a subject to an object, is one which, following the leadership of William James, empiricists have now for the most part abandoned. The distinction between "seeing the sun" as a mental event, and the immediate object of my seeing, is now generally rejected as invalid, and in this view I concur. But many of those who take the view that I take on this point nevertheless inconsistently adhere to some form of naïve realism. If my seeing of the sun is identical with the sun that I see, then the sun that I see is not the astronomer's sun. For exactly the same reasons, the tables and chairs that I see, if they are identical with my seeing of them, are not located where physics says they are, but where my seeing is. You may say that my seeing, being mental, is not in space; if you do, I will not argue the point. But I shall none the less insist that there is one, and only one, region of space-time with which my seeing is always causally bound up, and that is my brain at the time of the seeing. And exactly the same is true of all objects of sense-perception.

We are now in a position to consider the relation between a physical occurrence and the subsequent occurrence popularly regarded as seeing it. Consider, say, a flash of lightning on a dark night. The flash, for the physicist, is an electrical discharge, which causes electromagnetic waves to travel outward from the region where it has taken place. These waves, if they meet no opaque matter, merely travel further and further; but when they meet opaque matter their energy undergoes transformations into new forms. When they happen to meet a human eye connected with a human brain, all sorts of complicated things happen, which can be studied by the physiologist. At the moment when this causal process reaches the brain, the person to whom the brain belongs "sees" the flash. This person, if he is unacquainted with physics, thinks that the flash *is* what takes place when he "sees" the flash; or rather, he thinks that what takes place is a relation between himself and the flash, called "perceiving" the flash. If he is acquainted with physics, he does not think this, but he still holds that the sort of thing that takes place when he "sees" the flash gives an adequate basis for knowledge of the physical world.

We can now at last tackle the question: How, and to what extent, can percepts be a source of knowledge as to physical objects? A percept, we have agreed, comes at the end of a causal chain which starts at the object. (Of course no causal chain really has either a beginning or an end. From another point of view the percept is a beginning; it begins the reaction to a stimulus.) If the percept is to be a source of knowledge of the object, it must be possible to infer the cause from the effect, or at least to infer some characteristics of the cause. In this backward inference from effect to cause, I shall for the present assume the laws of physics.

If percepts are to allow inferences to objects, the physical world must contain more or less separable causal chains. I can see at the present moment various things—sheets of paper, books, trees, walls, and clouds. If the separateness of these things in my visual field is to correspond to a physical separateness, each of them must start its own causal chain, arriving at my eye without much interference from the others. The theory of light assures us that this is the case. Light-waves emanating from a source will, in suitable circumstances, pursue their course practically unaffected by other light-waves in the same region. But when light-waves encounter a reflecting or refracting object this independence of the medium disappears.

This is important in deciding *what* the object is that we are supposed to see. In the daytime, practically all the light that reaches the eye comes ultimately from the sun, but we do not say that we are seeing only the sun. We are seeing the last region after which the course of the light was virtually unimpeded until it reached the eye. When light is reflected or scattered, we consider, as a rule, that it makes us see the last object from which it is reflected or scattered; when it is refracted, we consider that we are still seeing the previous source, though inaccurately. Reflected light, however, is not always taken as giving perception of the reflector; it is not so taken when the reflection is accurate, as in a mirror. What I see when I shave I consider to be my own face. But when sunlight is reflected on an outdoor landscape it gives me much more information about the things in the landscape than about the sun, and I therefore consider that I am perceiving the things in the landscape.

In a lesser degree similar things may be said about sound. We distinguish between hearing a sound and hearing an echo of it. If the sun were as chromatically noisy as it is bright, and if terrestrial things were resonant only to certain of its notes, we should say that we were hearing the things, not the sun, when they gave characteristic sound-reflections.

The other senses do not give the same kind of perception of distant objects or of intermediate links in causal chains, because they are not concerned with physical processes having the peculiar kind of independence that is characteristic of wave motions.

From what we have been saying it is clear that the relation of a percept to the physical object which is supposed to be perceived is vague, approximate, and somewhat indefinite. There is no *precise* sense in which we can be said to perceive physical objects.

The question of perception as a source of knowledge can be merged in a wider question: How far, and in what circumstances, can one stage in a physical process be a basis for inferring an earlier stage? Clearly this can only happen in so far as the process in question is independent of other processes. That processes can be thus independent is perhaps surprising. We see the separate stars because the light that starts from each travels on through regions full of other trails of light, and yet retains its independence. When this independence fails, we see a vague blur, like the milky way. In the case of the milky way, the independence does not fail till we reach the physiological stage; that is why telescopes can separate the different stars of the milky way. But the independence of the light from different parts of one star cannot be restored by telescopes; that is why stars have no measurable apparent magnitude.

Our perceptive apparatus, as studied by the physiologist, can to some extent be ignored by the physicist, because it can be treated as approximately constant. It is not of course really constant. By squinting I can see two suns, but I do not imagine that I have performed an astronomical miracle. If I close my eyes and turn my face to the sun, I see a vague red glare; this change in the sun's appearance I attribute to myself, not to the sun. Things look different when I see them out of the corner of my eye from what they do when I focus on them. They look different to short-sighted and to long-sighted people. And so on. But common sense learns to distinguish these subjective sources of variation in the percept from those that are due to variation in the physical object. Until we learn to draw, we think that a rectangular object always looks rectangular; and we are right, in the sense that an animal inference causes us to judge it to be rectangular.

Science deals with these matters by assuming a normal observer who is to some extent a fiction, like the economic man, but not so completely a fiction as to be practically useless. When a normal observer sees a difference between two objects, for example that one looks yellow and the other looks blue, this difference is assumed to have its source in a difference in the objects, not in the subjective perceptive apparatus of the observer. If, in a given case, this assumption is erroneous, it is held that multiplicity of observations by a multitude of observers will correct it. By such methods, the physicist is enabled to treat our perceptive apparatus as the source of a *constant* error, which, because it is constant, is for many purposes negligible.

The principles which justify the inference from percepts to physical objects have not been sufficiently studied. Why, for example, when a number of people see the sun, should we believe that there is a sun outside their percepts, and not merely that there are laws determining the circumstances in which we shall have the experience called "seeing the sun"?

Here we come up against a principle which is used both by science and by common sense, to the effect that, when a number of phenomena in separated parts of space-time are obviously causally interconnected, there must be some continuous process in the intervening regions which links them all together. This principle of spatio-temporal continuity needs to be re-examined after we have considered the inference from perceptual to physical space. In the meantime, it can be accepted as at least a first step towards formalizing inference from perceptual to physical objects.

I will conclude with a summary of the present Chapter.

Our main question was: If physics is true, how can it be known, and what, besides physics, must we know to infer physics? This problem arises through the physical causation of perception, which makes it probable that physical objects differ greatly from percepts; but if so, how can we infer physical objects from percepts? Moreover, since perceiving is considered to be "mental" while its causes are "physical", we are confronted with the old problem of the relation between mind and matter. My own belief is that the "mental" and the "physical" are not so disparate as is generally thought. I should define a "mental" occurrence as one which some one knows otherwise than by inference; the distinction between "mental" and "physical" therefore belongs to theory of knowledge, not to metaphysics.

One of the difficulties which have led to confusion was failure to distinguish between perceptual and physical space. Perceptual space consists of perceptible relations between parts of percepts, whereas physical space consists of inferred relations between inferred physical things. What I see may be outside my percept of my body, but not outside my body as a physical thing.

Percepts, considered causally, are between events in afferent nerves (stimulus) and events in efferent nerves (reaction); their location in causal chains is the same as that of certain events in the brain. Percepts as a source of knowledge of physical objects can only serve their purpose in so far as there are separable, more or less independent, causal chains in the physical world. This only happens approximately, and therefore the inference from percepts to physical objects cannot be precise. Science consists largely of devices for overcoming this initial lack of precision on the assumption that perception gives a first approximation to the truth.

Chapter V

TIME IN EXPERIENCE

THE purpose of this Chapter is to consider those features of crude experience which form the raw material of the concept of time, which has to go through a long elaboration before it is fit to appear in physics or history. There are two sources of our belief in time; the first is the perception of change within one specious present, the other is memory. When you look at your watch, you can see the second-hand moving, but only memory tells you that the minute-hand and hour-hand have moved. Shakespeare's timepieces had no second-hand, as appears from the lines:

> Ah! yet doth beauty, like a dial hand,
> Steal from his figure, and no pace perceiv'd.

"Pace perceiv'd" is only possible when the motion is so rapid that, though the beginning and end are noticeably different, the lapse of time is so short that both are parts of one sensation. No sensation, not even that caused by a flash of lightning, is strictly instantaneous. Physiological disturbances die down gradually, and the length of time during which we see a flash of lightning is much greater than the length of time occupied by the physical phenomenon.

The relation of "preceding", or of "earlier-and-later", is an element in the experience of perceiving a change, and also in the experience of remembering. Strictly speaking, we ought also to add immediate expectation, but this is of less importance. When I see a rapid movement, such as that of a falling star, or of cloud-shadows in a landscape, I am aware that one part of the movement is earlier than another, in spite of the whole being comprised within one specious present; if I were not aware of this, I should not know whether the movement had been from A to B or from B to A, or even that change had occurred. When a movement is sufficiently rapid we do not perceive change: if you spin a penny very efficiently, it takes on the appearance of a diaphanous sphere. If a motion is to be perceived, it must be neither too fast nor too slow. If it satisfies this condition, it provides experiences from which it is possible to obtain ostensive definitions of the words for temporal relations: "preceding", "succeeding", "before", "after", "earlier", "later". When these words have come to be understood, we can understand such sentences as "A precedes B" even when A and B are not part of one specious present, provided we know what is meant by "A" and what by "B".

But one specious present is a very small part of one man's life, and for longer periods of time within our own experience we rely upon memory. In fact, of course, we rely upon a great deal besides memory. In regard to past engagements noted in my diary, I can infer their time-order and their distance from the present by the dates at which they are recorded. This, however, is a process presupposing considerable knowledge, whereas I am concerned at present with the data upon which our knowledge concerning time is based. Within limits, and with a considerable risk of error, we can place our memories in a time-order by the way they "feel". Suppose we have just had a conversation, beginning amicably, but ending in a violent quarrel, and suppose the person with whom we were conversing has flounced out of the room in a rage. We can go over the whole conversation in retrospect, thinking "at this point I said the wrong thing", or "at that point the remark he allowed himself was unpardonable". Our memory, in fact, is not of a *heap* of events, but of a *series*, and often there can be no reasonable doubt that the time-order supplied by our memory is correct.

There is here, however, a complication which has been too often overlooked. All my recollections occur *now*, not at the times when the recollected events occurred. The time-order of the past events, in so far as I can know it by means of memory, must be connected with a quality of my recollections: some must *feel* recent and others must *feel* remote. It must be by means of this felt quality of recentness or remoteness that I place remembered events in a series when I am relying upon memory alone. In travelling from percepts towards "the dark backward and abysm of time", the present contents of my mind have an order, which I believe to be correlated, roughly at any rate, with the objective time-order of the events to which my recollections refer. This order in the present contents of my mind, which, by means of expectation, may be extended into the future, may be called "subjective" time. Its relations to objective time are difficult, and demand discussion.

St. Augustine, whose absorption in the sense of sin led him to excessive subjectivity, was content to substitute subjective time for the time of history and physics. Memory, perception, and expectation, according to him, made up all that there is of time. But obviously this won't do. All his memories and all his expectations occurred at about the time of the fall of Rome, whereas mine occur at about the time of the fall of industrial civilization, which formed no part of the Bishop of Hippo's expectations. Subjective time might suffice for a solipsist of the moment, but not for a man who believes in a real past and future, even if only his own. My momentary experience contains a space of perception, which is not the space of physics, and a time of perception and recollection, which is not the time of physics and history. My past, as it occurred, cannot be identified with my recollections of it, and my objective history, which was in objective time, differs from the subjective history of my present recollections, which, objectively, is all *now*.

That memory is in the main veridical is, in my opinion, one of the premisses of knowledge. What this premiss asserts is, or implies, broadly speaking, that a present recollection is as a rule correlated with a past event. Obviously this is not logically necessary. I might have come into existence a few moments ago, complete with just those recollections which I then had. If the whole world came into existence then, just as it then was, there will never be anything to prove that it did not exist earlier; in fact, all the evidence that we now have in favour of its having existed earlier, we should then have. This illustrates what I mean by saying that memory is a premiss, for we are none of us prepared for a moment to entertain the supposition that the world began five minutes ago. We do not entertain the supposition, because we are persuaded that, as a rule, when we recollect, something resembling our present recollection occurred at a time which is objectively past.

I said a moment ago that the general trustworthiness of memory is a premiss of human knowledge. We might find at a later stage that it can be subsumed under a wider premiss, but for the present this possibility may be ignored. What does, however, need to be considered at this stage is the relation of confidence in particular memories to the postulate that memory is trustworthy as a rule, or in certain specified circumstances.

When I remember something, I do not first take note of my present state of mind, then reflect that memory is usually veridical, and finally infer that something like what I am recollecting occurred in the past. On the contrary, what happens when I remember *is* belief that something happened in the past. What I am concerned with in this Chapter is (*a*) analysis of such beliefs, and (*b*) statement of what is meant when such a belief is said to be true. Neither of these questions is as simple as seems to be generally supposed.

Memories often float through the mind as mere images, unaccompanied by belief, but I am concerned only with memories that are believed. Let us take a concrete illustration. Suppose I have seen my child very nearly run over by a motor-car, but in fact unhurt, and suppose that in the following night I have a nightmare in which the child is killed. When I wake up, I think, with inexpressible relief: "*This* did not occur; *that* occurred."

A good deal of clarification is necessary before we can arrive at the core of the problems raised by this illustration. To begin with, when we say "this did not occur", we are not denying that the nightmare occurred; in so far as we are remembering the nightmare as a private experience, our memory is quite correct. The nightmare, however, did not have the context that waking experiences have: it had no context whatever in the life of the child, or of any person except myself and such persons as had to listen while I related it, and in my own life its context sharply ended when I woke, instead of being prolonged through years of sorrow. This is the sort of thing we mean by saying that the nightmare was only a dream.

But all this is irrelevant to our problem of memory, and I have only mentioned it in order to make clear what is relevant and what is not. When I remember the nightmare, my memory is veridical; I am only misled if I suppose the nightmare to have had the sort of context that a similar waking experience would have had. An error of memory occurs only when we believe that, in the past, we had some experience which in fact we did not have, and when, further, we believe this in the specific way that is called "remembering", as opposed to the way that comes when we read records of forgotten events, or have to listen to aunts relating our exploits as children. Such errors of memory undoubtedly occur. I will not insist upon George IV remembering that he was at the battle of Waterloo; coming nearer home, I know that when, too late, I have thought of a witty retort, I find a tendency to remember that I actually made it, which I only resist by a considerable moral effort. When two people independently report an acrimonious conversation, each will usually falsify the truth in a way favourable to his self-esteem. And even memories having little emotional interest can often be proved by records to be inaccurate.

But the most convincing examples of false memories are supplied by dreams, though not by the nightmare which I supposed a moment ago. Let us alter the nightmare: I now do not dream that I see the child killed, but that, having seen this, it is my duty to tell the child's mother what has happened. This is just as much a nightmare, but now the false belief in my dream is not merely as to the context of my experience, but as to my very own past experience. When I dream that I *see* the child run over, I do have the experience, though it does not have its usual concomitants; but when I dream that I *saw* the child run over, I never did have the experience that in my dream I am remembering. This is a genuine case of false memory, and shows that memory alone cannot make it certain that what is remembered really occurred, however much we may whittle down what is remembered to its core of purely personal experience.

This example, I hope, will make it clear what I mean by "subjective" time, and what is the problem of its relation to objective time. In dreams, as in waking life, there is a difference between perceiving and remembering. The perceiving and the remembering do really occur in dreams, and so far as the perceiving is concerned we do not have to suppose that dreams deceive us as to our own experiences: what, in dreams, we see and hear, we do in fact see and hear, though, owing to the unusual context, what we see and hear gives rise to false beliefs. Similarly what we remember in dreams we do really remember, that is to say, the experience called "remembering" does occur. In the dream, this remembering has a quality differing from that of dream-perception, and in virtue of this quality the remembering is referred to the past. But the quality is not that of genuine pastness which belongs to the events of history; it is that of subjective pastness, in virtue of which the present remembering is judged (falsely) to refer to something that is objectively past.

This quality of subjective pastness belongs to waking memories as well as to those of dreams, and is what makes them subjectively distinguishable from perceptions. It is a quality which is capable of degrees: our memories *feel* more remote or less remote, and can be arranged in a series by this qualitative difference. But since all our memories are *now* from the point of view of history, this subjective time-order is wholly distinct from the objective time-order, though we hope that there is a certain degree of correspondence between the two.

I can perceive a remembering, but I cannot perceive what is remembered. Remembering consists of remembering "something". I want now to analyse remembering, and especially to consider this relation to "something". In short: what do we mean when, thinking of some past occurrence, we judge *"that* occurred"? What can "that" be?

The difficulty is that, to know what we mean by "that occurred", the word "that" must refer to some present content of the mind, whereas, if the word "occurred" is justified, the word "that" must refer to something in the past. Thus it would seem that the word "that" must refer to something which is both past and present. But we are in the habit of thinking that the past is dead, and that nothing past can also be present. What, then, do we mean when we judge "that occurred"?

There are two different possible answers, connected with the two different theories as to proper names which we considered in an earlier chapter. If we consider that, in describing the structure of the world, the terms which must be merely named must include "events", which are uniquely defined by their spatio-temporal position, and are logically incapable of recurring, then we must say that the phrase "that occurred" is inaccurate, and should be replaced by "something very like that occurred". If, on the other hand, we hold that an "event" can be defined as a bundle of qualities, each and all of which may recur, then "that occurred" may be completely accurate. If, for example, I see a rainbow on two occasions, and I see some shade of colour near the middle on one occasion, I probably saw the very same shade on the other occasion. If, then, remembering the earlier rainbow while I am seeing the later one, I say, of some shade of colour that I am now seeing, "that occurred on the previous occasion", what I say may be exactly true.

Either of these answers will solve the particular difficulty with which we have been immediately concerned, and for the present I shall not attempt to decide between them. They leave open the question what is meant by the word "occurred"; I shall deal with this when I come to consider public time.

It should be observed that what we mean by "the past" in the historical sense is understood by us in virtue of the experience of succession within one specious present. It is this experience that makes us understand the word "precedes". We can then understand: "if y is in the specious present, x precedes y". We can therefore understand what is meant by saying that x precedes everything in the specious present, i.e. that x is in the past. The essential point is that the time that occurs in the specious present is objective, not subjective.

We can now sum up the discussion of this Chapter.

There are two sources for our knowledge of time. One is the perception of succession within one specious present, the other is memory. Remembering can be perceived, and is found to have a quality of greater or less remoteness, in virtue of which all my present memories can be placed in a time-order. But this time is subjective, and must be distinguished from historical time. Historical time has to the present the relation of "preceding", which I know from the experience of change within one specious present. In historical time, all my present memories are *now*, but in so far as they are veridical they point to occurrences in the historical past. There is no *logical* reason why any memories should be veridical; so far as logic can show, all my present memories might be just what they are if there had never been any historical past. Our knowledge of the past therefore depends upon some postulate which is not to be discovered by mere analysis of our present rememberings.

Chapter VI

SPACE IN PSYCHOLOGY

PSYCHOLOGY is concerned with space, not as a system of relations among material objects, but as a feature of our perceptions. If we could accept naïve realism, this distinction would have little importance: we should perceive material objects and their spatial relations, and the space that characterizes our perceptions would be identical with the space of physics. But in fact naïve realism cannot be accepted, percepts are not identical with material objects, and the relation of perceptual to physical space is not identity. What the relation is, I shall consider presently; I am concerned, to begin with, only with space as it appears in psychology, ignoring all questions of physics.

It is clear that experience is what has led us to believe in the existence of spatial relations. Psychology is concerned to examine what experiences are relevant, and by what process of inference or construction we pass from such experiences to the space of common sense. Since a great part of the process occurs in early infancy, and is no longer remembered in later years, it is a somewhat difficult matter of observation and inference to discover the character of the original experiences which give rise to the habits that adult common sense takes for granted. To take only the most obvious instance: we place things touched and things seen in one space, automatically and without reflection, but babies under the age of about three months seem unable to do so. That is to say, they do not know how to touch an object that they see and that is within their reach. It is only through frequent accidental contacts that they gradually learn the movements necessary to produce a tactile sensation when a visual sensation is given. Chickens, on the other hand, can do this from birth.

We have to separate the crude material of sensation from the supplementation that it has acquired through experience and habit. When you see (let us say) an orange, you do not have merely a visual experience, but also expectations of touch, smell, and taste. You would have a violent shock of surprise if you found that it felt like putty, or smelt like a bad egg, or tasted like a beef-steak. You would be even more surprised if, like Macbeth's dagger, it proved incapable of being touched. Such surprises show that expectations of non-visual sensations are part of what spontaneously happens to you when you have a visual sensation of a familiar kind. In the chicken, apparently, such expectations are in part due to its innate constitution. In human beings this happens much less, if at all; our expectations seem to be generated, mainly if not wholly, by experience. A visual sensation has at first, it would seem, a certain purity, and only gradually, through frequent collocations, acquires the penumbra of expectations connected with other senses that it has in adult life. And the same is true of other senses.

It follows that the unitary space of common sense is a construction, though not a deliberate one. It is part of the business of psychology to make us aware of the steps in this construction.

When we examine our momentary visual field, stripping it, as far as we can, of all the adjuncts derived from experience, we find that it is a complex whole in which the parts are interrelated in various ways. There are relations of right and left, up and down; there are also relations which we learn to interpret as depth. These relations all belong to the sensational datum. The best way to become aware of the sensational element in visual perceptions of depth is by the use of the stereoscope. When you look at the two separate photographs that are going to be seen together in the stereoscope, they both look flat, as they are; but when you see the combination in the stereoscope, you get the impression that things "stand out", and that some are nearer than others. As a judgment this would of course be mistaken; the photographs are just as flat as they were before. But it is a genuine quality of the visual datum, and very instructive as a help in showing how we arrive visually at estimates of depth.

By means of the three relations right-and-left, up-and-down, seeming-far-and-seeming-near, your momentary visual field can be arranged in a three-dimensional manifold. But far-and-near, estimated visually, is not capable of distinguishing except when one of the distances is very short; we cannot "see" that the sun is further off than the moon, or even than clouds which are not obscuring it.

Other senses than sight supply other elements which contribute to the common-sense construction of space. When a part of the body is touched, we can tell, within limits, what part it is, without needing to look. (On the tongue or the finger-tips we can tell pretty accurately, on the back only vaguely.) This implies that touches in one part have a quality not belonging to touches in another part, and that the qualities appropriate to different parts have relations enabling us to arrange them in a two-dimensional order. Experience teaches us to connect sensations of touch with the visual sensations of seeing different parts of the body.

Not only static sensations, such as we have mentioned, but also sensations of movement are involved in constructing common-sense space. Sensations of movement are of two sorts, active and passive—active when we have a feeling of muscular exertion, passive when the observed change seems independent of ourselves. When we move a part of our body and see it move, we have active and passive sensations at the same time. What I am calling passive sensations are only relatively passive; there is always the activity of attention, involving adjustment of the sense organs, except in the case of rather violent sensations. When you unexpectedly hit your head against a low doorway you are almost wholly passive, whereas when you listen carefully to a very faint sound the element of activity is considerable. (I am speaking of activity and passivity as elements in sensations, and am not inquiring into their causal status.)

Movement is essential in enlarging our conception of space beyond our own immediate neighbourhood. The distance from where we are to some place may be estimated as an hour's walk, three hours by train, or twelve hours by aeroplane. All such estimates assume fixed places. You can tell how long it takes from London to Edinburgh, because both retain fixed positions on the earth's surface, but you cannot tell how long it will take to reach Mr. Jones, because he may move while you are on the way. All distances above a rather small minimum depend upon the assumption of immobility; it is partly the fact that this assumption is never quite true that necessitated the special theory of relativity, in which distance is between events, not bodies, and is a space-time distance, not a purely spatial distance. But such considerations take us beyond the scope of common sense.

It is to be observed that the spatial relations given in sensation are always between data of the same sense. There is a spatial relation between two parts of the same visual field, or between two simultaneous pin-pricks on different parts of the hand; such spatial relations are within the realm of sensation, and are not learnt by experience. But between the tactual sensation of a pin-prick and the visual sensation of seeing the pin there is no direct sensational spatial relation, but only a correlation which human beings learn by experience. When you both see and feel a pin touching your hand it is only experience that enables you to identify the point of contact seen and the point of contact felt by touch. To say that they are the same place is convenient, but in psychology it is not strictly accurate: what is accurate is that they are correlated places in two different spaces, visual and tactual. It is true that in *physical* space only one place is involved, but this place lies outside our direct experience, and is neither visual nor tactual.

The construction of one space in which all our perceptual experiences are located is a triumph of pre-scientific common sense. Its merit lies in its convenience, not in any ultimate truth that it may be supposed to possess. Common sense, in attributing to it a degree of non-conventional truth beyond what it actually has a right to claim, is in error, and this error, uncorrected, adds greatly to the difficulty of a sound philosophy of space.

An even more serious error, committed not only by common sense but by many philosophers, consists in supposing that the space in which perceptual experiences are located can be identified with the inferred space of physics, which is inhabited mainly by things which cannot be perceived. The coloured surface that I see when I look at a table has a spatial position in the space of my visual field; it exists only where eyes and nerves and brain exist to cause the energy of photons to undergo certain transformations. (The "where" in this sentence is a "where" in physical space.) The table as a physical object, consisting of electrons, positrons, and neutrons, lies outside my experience, and if there is a space which contains both it and my perceptual space, then in that space the physical table must be wholly external to my perceptual space. This conclusion is inevitable if we accept the view as to the physical causation of sensations which is forced on us by physiology and which we considered in an earlier chapter.

The conception of one unitary space, Kant's "infinite given whole", is one which must be abandoned. The crude material available for empirical constructions contains several kinds of relations—more especially those between parts of one visual field or parts of one tactual field—each of which arranges its field in a manifold having the properties that pure mathematicians need for a geometry. By means of correlations—more especially between the visual and tactual place of an object which I simultaneously see and touch—the various spaces generated by relations of parts of single sensational fields can be amalgamated into one space. To the making of this space experience of correlations is necessary; the kinds of relations given in single experiences no longer suffice.

The common-sense world results from a further correlation, combined with an illegitimate identification. There is a correlation between the spatial relations of unperceived physical objects and the spatial relations of visual or other sensational data, and there is an identification of such data with certain physical objects. For example: I am sitting in a room, and I see—or at least common sense thinks I see—spatial relations between the pieces of furniture that it contains. I know that on the other side of the door there is a hall and a staircase. I believe that the spatial relations of things beyond the door—e.g. the relation "to-the-left-of"— are the same as those between the bits of furniture that I see; and further, I identify what I see with physical objects which can exist unseen, so that, if I am content with common sense, there is no gulf between the visual furniture and the unseen hall beyond the door. The two accordingly are thought to fit into one space, of which part is perceived while the rest is inferred.

But in fact, if physics and physiology are to be believed, I do not "see" the furniture in my room except in a Pickwickian sense. When I am said to "see" a table, what really happens is that I have a complex sensation which is, in certain respects, similar in structure to the physical table. The physical table, consisting of electrons, positrons, and neutrons, is inferred, and so is the space in which it is located. It has long been a commonplace in philosophy that the physical table does not have the qualities of the sensational table: it has no colour, it is not warm or cold in the sense in which we know warmth and cold by experience, it is not hard or soft if "hard" and "soft" mean qualities given in tactile sensations, and so on. All this, I say, has long been a commonplace, but it has a consequence that has not been adequately recognized, namely that the space in which the physical table is located must also be different from the space that we know by experience.

We say that the table is "outside" me, in a sense in which my own body is not. But in saying this we have to guard against an ambiguity due to the necessity of distinguishing between physical and psychological space. The visual table is "outside" my body in visual space, if "my body" is interpreted as what I see, and not as what physics takes to be my body. The physical table is "outside" my body if my body is interpreted as in physics, but has no direct or obvious spatial relation to my body as a visual object that I experience. When we come to consider the hall on the other side of the door, which I cannot see, we are wholly confined to the physical sense: the hall is outside my physical body in physical space, but is not, in any obvious sense, outside my sensational body in psychological space, because there is no sensational hall, and therefore the hall has no location whatever in psychological space. Thus while there are two senses in which the table is "outside" me, there is only one sense in which the hall is "outside" me.

There is a further source of confusion, which is due to the fact that there are two quite divergent ways of correlating psychological and physical space. The obvious way is to correlate the place of the sensational table in psychological space with the place of the physical table in physical space, and for most purposes this is the more important correlation. But there is a quite different relation between the two kinds of space, and this other relation must be understood if confusions are to be avoided. Physical space is wholly inferential, and is constructed by means of causal laws. Physics starts with a manifold of events, some of which can be collected into series by physical laws; for example, the successive events constituting the arrival of a light-ray at successive places are bound together by the laws of the propagation of light. In such cases we use the denial of action at a distance, not as a physical principle, but as a means of *defining* space-time order. That is to say, if two events are connected by a causal law, so that one is an effect of the other, any third event which is a cause of the one and an effect of the other is to be placed between the two in space-time order.

Consider now a single causal sequence, beginning with an external stimulus, say to the eye, continuing along afferent nerves to the brain, producing first a sensation and then a volition, followed by a current along efferent nerves and finally a muscular movement. This whole series, considered as one causal sequence, must, in physical space-time, occupy a continuous series of positions, and since the physiological terms of the series end and begin in the brain, the "mental" terms must begin and end in the brain. That is to say, considered as part of the manifold of events ordered in space-time by causal relations, sensations and volitions must be located in the brain. A point in space-time, following the theory to be developed in a subsequent chapter, is a class of events, and there is no reason why some of these events should not be "mental". Our feeling to the contrary is only due to obstinate adherence to the mind-matter dualism.

We can now sum up the above discussion. When I have the experience called "seeing a table", the visual table has, primarily, a position in the space of my momentary visual field. Then, by means of experienced correlations, it has a position in a space which embraces all my perceptual experiences. Next, by means of physical laws it is correlated with a place in physical space-time, namely the place occupied by the physical table. Finally, by means of psychophysical laws it is related to another place in physical space-time, namely the place occupied by my brain as a physical object. If the philosophy of space is to avoid hopeless confusions, these different correlations must be kept carefully disentangled.

In conclusion, it should be observed that the twofold space in which percepts are located is closely analogous to the twofold time of memories. In subjective time, memories are in the past; in objective time, they are now. Similarly, in subjective space my percept of a table is over there, but in physical space it is here.

Chapter VII

MIND AND MATTER

COMMON SENSE believes that we know something about mind, and something about matter; it holds, further, that what we know of both is enough to show that they are quite different kinds of things. I hold, on the contrary, that whatever we know without inference is mental, and that the physical world is only known as regards certain abstract features of its space-time structure—features which, because of their abstractness, do not suffice to show whether the physical world is, or is not, different in intrinsic character from the world of mind.

I will begin with an attempt to state the common-sense point of view as clearly as is possible in view of the confusions that are essential to it.

Mind—so common sense might say—is exhibited by persons who do and suffer various things. Cognitively, they perceive, remember, imagine, abstract, and infer; on the side of the emotions, they have feelings that are pleasurable and feelings that are painful, and they have sentiments, passions, and desires; volitionally, they can will to do something or will to abstain from doing something. All these occurrences can be perceived by the person to whom they happen, and all are to be classified together as "mental" events. Every mental event happens "to" some person, and is an event in his life.

But in addition to perceiving "thoughts"—so common sense holds—we also perceive "things", and events which are outside ourselves. We see and touch physical objects; we hear sounds which are also heard by other people, and therefore are not in us; when we smell a bad drain, other people do so too, unless they are plumbers. What we perceive, when it is outside ourselves, is called "physical"; this term includes both "things" which are "matter", and events, such as a noise or a flash of lightning.

Common sense also allows inferences to what is not perceived, at any rate by us, e.g. the centre of the earth, the other side of the moon, the thoughts of our friends, and the mental events that have produced historical records. An inferred mental event can be known without inference by the person to whom it happens. An inferred physical thing or event may or may not have been perceived by some one; some physical things, such as the centre of the earth, are held to have been never perceived.

This common-sense view, while on the whole acceptable as regards mental events, requires radical alteration where physical events are concerned. What I know without inference when I have the experience called "seeing the sun" is not the sun, but a mental event in me. I am not immediately aware of tables and chairs, but only of certain effects that they have on me. The objects of perception which I take to be "external" to me, such as coloured surfaces that I see, are only "external" in my private space, which ceases to exist when I die—indeed my private visual space ceases to exist whenever I am in the dark or shut my eyes. And they are not "external" to "me", if "me" means the sum-total of my mental events; on the contrary, they are among the mental events that constitute me. They are only "external" to certain other percepts of mine, namely those which common sense regards as percepts of my body; and even to these they are "external" only for psychology, not for physics, since the space in which they are located is the private space of psychology.

In considering what common sense regards as perception of external objects, there are two opposite questions to be considered: first, why must the datum be regarded as private; second, what reason is there to take the datum as a sign of something which has an existence not dependent upon me and my perceptive apparatus?

The reasons for regarding the datum—say in sight or touch—as private, are twofold. On the one hand there is physics, which, starting with the intention of doing its best for naïve realism, arrives at a theory of what goes on in the physical world which shows that there is no ground for supposing the physical table or chair to resemble the percept except in certain abstract structural respects. On the other hand there is the comparison of what different people experience when, according to common sense, they perceive the same thing. If we confine ourselves to the sense of sight, when two people are said to see the same table there are differences of perspective, differences of apparent size, differences in the way light is reflected, and so on. Thus at most the projective properties of the table are the same for a number of percipients, and even these are not quite the same if there is a refracting medium such as a steaming kettle, or our old friend the water that makes a stick look bent. If we consider, as common sense does, that the "same" object can be perceived by both sight and touch, the object, if it is to be really the same, must be still further removed from the datum, for a complex sight-datum and a complex touch-datum differ in intrinsic quality, and cannot be similar except in structure.

Our second question is more difficult. If the datum in my perceptions is always private to me, why do I nevertheless regard it as a sign by means of which I can infer a physical "thing" or event which is a cause of my percept if my body is suitably placed, but does not form part of my immediate experience except partially in exceptional cases?

When we begin to reflect, we find ourselves with an unshakeable conviction that some of our sensations have causes external to our own body. Headache, toothache, and stomachache, we are willing to admit, have internal causes, but when we stub our toe or run into a post in the dark or see a flash of lightning we cannot easily make ourselves doubt that our experience has an external source. It is true that we sometimes come to think that this belief was mistaken, for instance if it occurs in dreams, or when we have a buzzing in the ears which sounds like the hum of telegraph wires. But such cases are exceptional, and common sense has discovered ways of dealing with them.

What chiefly confirms us in our belief that most sensations have physical causes is, on the one hand, the quasi-publicity of many sensations, and, on the other hand, the fact that, if regarded as arising spontaneously, they seem completely erratic and unaccountable.

As regards quasi-publicity, the argument is the opposite of that which proves the privacy of data: although two neighbouring men do not have exactly the same visual data, they have data which are very similar, and although visual and tactual *qualities* are different, the structural properties of an object seen are approximately identical with those of the same object touched. If you have models of the regular solids, the one which you can see to be a dodecahedron will be correctly named by an educated blind man after feeling it. Apart from the publicity concerned with different percipients, there is also what may be called temporal publicity in one man's experience. I know that by taking suitable measures I can see St. Paul's at any time; I know that the sun and moon and stars recur in my visual world, and so do my friends and my house and my furniture. I know that the differences between the times when I see these objects and the times when I do not are easily explicable as due to differences in me or my environment which do not imply any change in the objects. Such considerations confirm the common-sense belief that there are, in addition to mental events, things which are sources of similar percepts in different observers at one time, and often of the same observer at different times.

As regards the irregularity of a world consisting only of data, this is an argument to which it is difficult to give precision. Roughly speaking, many sensations occur without any fixed antecedents in our own experience, and in a manner which suggests irresistibly that, if they have causes, these causes lie partly outside our experience. If you are hit on the head by a tile falling off a roof while you are walking below, you will experience a sudden violent pain which cannot be explained causally by anything of which you were aware before the accident happened. It is true that there are some extreme psycho-analysts who maintain that accidents only happen to people who have grown tired of life through reflecting on their sins, but I do not think such a view has many adherents. Consider the inhabitants of Hiroshima when the bomb burst: it cannot be that they had all reached a point in their psychological development which demanded disaster as the next step. To explain such an occurrence causally, we must admit purely physical causes; if they are rejected, we must acquiesce in causal chaos.

Such arguments may be reinforced by the considerations set forth above in the chapter on solipsism, showing that we must choose between two alternatives: either (a) no inferences from data to other events are to be admitted as valid, in which case we know far less than most solipsists suppose, and in fact a great deal less than we can force ourselves to regard as the minimum of our knowledge, or (b) there are principles of inference which allow us to infer things outside our own experience.

Belief in the physical causation of sensations is also reinforced by the fact that, if this belief is rejected, there remains no reason for the acceptance of science in its broad outlines, while the refusal of such acceptance does not seem rational.

Such are the broad considerations which lead us to look for a way of systematizing and rationalizing our common-sense propensity to infer physical causes of sensations.

The inferences from experiences to the physical world can, I think, all be justified by the assumption that there are causal chains, each member of which is a complex structure ordered by the spatio-temporal relation of compresence (or of contiguity); that all the members of such a chain are similar in structure; that each member is connected with each other by a series of contiguous structures; and that, when a number of such similar structures are found to be grouped about a centre earlier in time than any of them, it is probable that they all have their causal origin in a complex event which is at that centre and has a structure similar to the structure of the observed events. I shall, at a later stage, endeavour to give greater precision to this assumption, and to show reasons for accepting it. For the present, to avoid verbiage, I shall treat it as though it were unquestionably correct, and on this basis I shall return to the relations between mental and physical events.

When, on a common-sense basis, people talk of the gulf between mind and matter, what they really have in mind is the gulf between a visual or tactual percept and a "thought"—e.g. a memory, a pleasure, or a volition. But this, as we have seen, is a division within the mental world; the percept is as mental as the "thought". Slightly more sophisticated people may think of matter as the unknown cause of sensation, the "thing-in-itself" which certainly does not have the secondary qualities and perhaps does not have the primary qualities either. But however much they may emphasize the unknown character of the thing-in-itself, they still suppose themselves to know enough of it to be sure that it is very different from a mind. This comes, I think, of not having rid their imaginations of the conception of material things as something hard that you can bump into. You can bump into your friend's body, but not into his mind; therefore his body is different from his mind. This sort of argument persists imaginatively in many people who have rejected it intellectually.

Then, again, there is the argument about brain and mind.

When a physiologist examines a brain, he does not see thoughts, therefore the brain is one thing and the mind which thinks is another. The fallacy in this argument consists in supposing that a man can see matter. Not even the ablest physiologist can perform this feat. His percept when he looks at a brain is an event in his own mind, and has only a causal connection with the brain that he fancies he is seeing. When, in a powerful telescope, he sees a tiny luminous dot, and interprets it as a vast nebula existing a million years ago, he realizes that what he sees is different from what he infers. The difference from the case of a brain looked at through a microscope is only one of degree: there is exactly the same need of inference, by means of the laws of physics, from the visual datum to its physical cause. And just as no one supposes that the nebula has any close resemblance to a luminous dot, so no one should suppose that the brain has any close resemblance to what the physiologist sees.

What, then, do we know about the physical world? Let us first define more exactly what we mean by a "physical" event. I should define it as an event which, if known to occur, is inferred, and which is not known to be mental. And I define a "mental" event (to repeat) as one with which some one is acquainted otherwise than by inference. Thus a "physical" event is one which is either totally unknown, or, if known at all, is not known to any one except by inference—or, perhaps we should say, is not known to be known to any one except by inference.

If physical events are to suffice as a basis for physics, and, indeed, if we are to have any reason for believing in them, they must not be *totally* unknown, like Kant's things-in-themselves. In fact, on the principle which we are assuming, they are known, though perhaps incompletely, so far as their space-time structure is concerned, for this must be similar to the space-time structure of their effects upon percipients. E.g. from the fact that the sun looks round in perceptual space we have a right to infer that it is round in physical space. We have no right to make a similar inference as regards brightness, because brightness is not a structural property.

We cannot, however, infer that the sun is *not* bright—meaning by "brightness" the quality that we know in perception. The only legitimate inferences as regards the physical sun are structural; concerning a property which is not structural, such as brightness, we must remain completely agnostic. We may perhaps say that it is unlikely that the physical sun is bright, since we have no knowledge of the qualities of things that are not percepts, and therefore there seems to be an illimitable field of choice of possible qualities. But such an argument is so speculative that perhaps we ought not to attach much weight to it.

This brings us to the question: Is there any reason, and if so what, for supposing that physical events differ in quality from mental events?

Here we must, to begin with, distinguish events in a living brain from events elsewhere. I will begin with events in a living brain.

I assume, for reasons which will be given in Part IV, that a small region of space-time is a collection of compresent events, and that space-time regions are ordered by means of causal relations. The former assumption has the consequence that there is no reason why thoughts should not be among the events of which the brain consists, and the latter assumption leads to the conclusion that, in physical space, thoughts are in the brain. Or, more exactly, each region of the brain is a class of events, and among the events constituting a region thoughts are included. It is to be observed that, if we say thoughts are in the brain, we are using an ellipsis. The correct statement is that thoughts are among the events which, as a class, constitute a region in the brain. A given thought, that is to say, is a member of a class, and the class is a region in the brain. In this sense, where events in brains are concerned, we have no reason to suppose that they are not thoughts, but, on the contrary, have strong reason to suppose that at least some of them are thoughts. I am using "thoughts" as a generic term for mental events.

When we come to events in parts of physical space-time where there are no brains, we have still no positive argument to prove that they are not thoughts, except such as may be derived from observation of the differences between living and dead matter coupled with inferences based on analogy or its absence. We may contend, for instance, that habit is in the main confined to living matter, and that, since memory is a species of habit, it is unlikely that there is memory except where there is living matter. Extending this argument, we can observe that the behaviour of living matter, especially of its higher forms, is much more dependent on its past history than that of dead matter, and that, therefore, the whole of that large part of our mental life that depends upon habit is presumably only to be found where there is living matter. But such arguments are inconclusive and limited in scope. Just as we cannot be *sure* that the sun is not bright, so we cannot be *sure* that it is not intelligent.[1] We may be right in thinking both improbable, but we are certainly wrong if we say they are impossible.

I conclude that, while mental events and their qualities can be known without inference, physical events are known only as regards their space-time structure. The qualities that compose such events are unknown—so completely unknown that we cannot say either that they are, or that they are not, different from the qualities that we know as belonging to mental events.

[1] I do not wish the reader to take this possibility too seriously. It is of the order of "pigs might fly", dealt with by Mr. Crawshay-Williams in *The Comforts of Unreason*, p. 193.

PART IV

SCIENTIFIC CONCEPTS

Chapter I

INTERPRETATION

IN all that has been said hitherto about the world of science, everything has been taken at its face value. I am not saying merely that we have taken the attitude of believing what men of science tell us, for this attitude, up to a point, is the only rational one for any man who is not a specialist on the matter in question. In saying that this attitude is rational, I do not mean that we should feel sure of the truth of what we are told, for it is generally admitted that probably in due course corrections will be found necessary. What I do mean is that the best scientific opinion of the present time has a better chance of truth, or of approximate truth, than any differing hypothesis suggested by a layman. The case is analogous to that of firing at a target. If you are a bad shot you are not likely to hit the bull's eye, but you are nevertheless more likely to hit the bull's eye than to hit any other equal area. So the scientist's hypothesis, though not likely to be quite right, is more likely to be right than any variant suggested by an unscientific person. This, however, is not the point with which we are concerned in this chapter.

The matter with which we are now to be concerned is not truth, but *interpretation*. It often happens that we have what seems adequate reason to believe in the truth of some formula expressed in mathematical symbols, although we are not in a position to give a clear definition of the symbols. It happens also, in other cases, that we can give a number of different meanings to the symbols, all of which will make the formula true. In the former case we lack even one definite interpretation of our formula, whereas in the latter we have many. This situation, which may seem odd, arises in pure mathematics and in mathematical physics; it arises even in interpreting common-sense statements such as "my room contains three tables and four chairs". It will thus appear that there is a large class of statements, concerning each of which, in some sense, we are more certain of its truth than of its meaning. "Interpretation" is concerned with such statements; it consists in finding as precise a meaning as possible for a statement of this sort, or, sometimes, in finding a whole system of possible meanings.

Let us take first an illustration from pure mathematics. Mankind have long been convinced that $2 + 2 = 4$; they have been so firmly convinced of this that it has been taken as the stock example of something certain. But when people were asked what they meant by "2", "4", " $+$ ", and " $=$ ", they gave vague and divergent answers, which made it plain that they did not know what these symbols meant. Some maintained that we know each of the numbers by intuition, and therefore have no need to define them. This might seem fairly plausible where small numbers were concerned, but who could have an intuition of 3,478,921? So they said we had an intuition of 1 and $+$; we could then define "2" as "$1 + 1$", "3" as "$2 + 1$", "4" as "$3 + 1$", and so on. But this did not work very well. It enabled us to say that $2 + 2 = (1 + 1) + (1 + 1)$, and that $4 = \{(1 + 1) + 1\} + 1$ and we then needed a fresh intuition to tell us that we could rearrange the brackets, in fact to assure us that, if l, m, n are three numbers, then

$$(l + m) + n = l + (m + n)$$

Some philosophers were able to produce this intuition on demand, but most people remained somewhat sceptical of their claims, and felt that some other method was called for.

A new development, more germane to our problem of interpretation, was due to Peano. Peano started with three undefined terms, "0", "finite integer (or number)" and "successor of", and concerning these terms he made five assumptions, namely:

(1) 0 is a number;
(2) If a is a number, the successor of a (i.e. $a + 1$) is a number;
(3) If two numbers have the same successor, the two numbers are identical;
(4) 0 is not the successor of any number;
(5) If s be a class to which belongs 0 and also the successor of every number belonging to s, then every number belongs to s.

The last of these assumptions is the principle of mathematical induction.

Peano showed that by means of these five assumptions he could prove every formula in arithmetic.

But now a new trouble arose. It was assumed that we need not know what we meant by "o", "number", and "successor", so long as we meant something satisfying the five assumptions. But then it turned out that there were an infinite number of possible interpretations. For instance, let "o" mean what we commonly call "1", and let "number" mean what we commonly call "number other than o"; then all the five assumptions are still true, and all arithmetic can be proved, though every formula will have an unexpected meaning. "2" will mean what we usually call "3", but "2 + 2" will not mean "3 + 3"; it will mean "3 + 2", and "2 + 2 = 4" will mean what we usually express by "3 + 2 = 5". In like manner we could interpret arithmetic on the assumption that "o" means "100", and "number" means "number greater than 99". And so on.

So long as we remain in the region of arithmetical formulae, all these different interpretations of "number" are equally good. It is only when we come to the empirical uses of numbers in enumeration that we find a reason for preferring one interpretation to all the others. When we buy something in a shop, and the attendant says "three shillings, please", his "three" is not a mere mathematical symbol, meaning "the third term after the beginning of some series"; his "three", in fact, is not capable of being defined by its *arithmetical* properties. It is obvious that his interpretation of "three" is, outside arithmetic, preferable to all the others that Peano's system leaves possible. Such statements as "men have 10 fingers", "dogs have 4 legs", "New York has 10,000,000 inhabitants", require a definition of numbers which cannot be derived from the mere fact that they satisfy the formulae of arithmetic. Such a definition is, therefore, the most satisfactory "interpretation" of number-symbols.

The same sort of situation arises whenever mathematics is applied to empirical material. Take, for example, geometry, considered not as a logical exercise in deducing consequences from arbitrarily assumed axioms, but as a help in land surveying, map making, engineering, or astronomy. Such practical uses of geometry involve a difficulty which, though sometimes admitted in a perfunctory manner, is never allowed anything like its due weight. Geometry, as set forth by the mathematicians, uses points, lines, planes, and circles, but it is a platitude to say that no such objects are to be found in nature. When, in surveying, we use the process of triangulation, it is admitted that our triangles do not have accurate straight lines for their sides nor exact points at their corners, but this is glozed over by saying that the sides are *approximately* straight and the corners *approximately* points. It is not at all clear what this means, so long as it is maintained that there are no exact straight lines or points to which our rough-and-ready lines and points approximate. We may mean that sensible lines and points have approximately the properties set forth in Euclid's definitions and axioms, but unless we can say, within limits, how close the approximation is, such a view will make calculation vague and unsatisfactory.

This problem of the exactness of mathematics and the inexactness of sense is an ancient one, which Plato solved by the fantastic hypothesis of reminiscence. In modern times, like some other unsolved problems, it has been forgotten through familiarity, like a bad smell which you no longer notice because you have lived with it so long. It is clear that, if geometry is to be applied to the sensible world, we must be able to find definitions of points, lines, planes, etc., in terms of sensible data, or else we must be able to infer from sensible data the existence of unperceived entities having the properties that geometry needs. To find ways, or a way, of doing one or other of these things is the problem of the empirical interpretation of geometry.

There is also a non-empirical interpretation, which leaves geometry within the sphere of pure mathematics. The assemblage of all ordered trios of real numbers forms a three-dimensional Euclidean space. With this interpretation, all Euclidean geometry is deducible from arithmetic. Every non-Euclidean geometry is capable of a similar arithmetical interpretation. It can be proved that Euclidean geometry, and every form of non-Euclidean geometry, can be applied to every class having the same number of terms as the real numbers; the question of the number of dimensions, and whether the resulting geometry is Euclidean or non-Euclidean, will depend upon the ordering relation that we select; an infinite number of ordering relations exist (in the logical sense), and only reasons of empirical convenience can lead us to select some one among them for special attention. All this is relevant in considering what interpretation of pure geometry had better be adopted by the engineer or the physicist. It shows that, in an empirical interpretation, the ordering relation, and not only the terms ordered, must be defined in empirical terms.

Very similar considerations apply to time, which, however, so far as our present question is concerned, is not so difficult a problem as space. In mathematical physics, time is treated as consisting of instants, though the perplexed student is assured that instants are mathematical fictions. No attempt is made to show him why fictions are useful, or how they are related to what is not fictitious. He finds that by the use of these fairy tales it is possible to calculate what really happens, and after a time he probably ceases to trouble himself as to why this is the case.

Instants were not always regarded as fictions; Newton thought them as "real" as the sun and moon. When this view was abandoned, it was easy to swing to the opposite extreme, and to forget that a fiction which is useful is not likely to be a *mere* fiction. There are degrees of fictiveness. Let us, for the moment, regard an individual person as something in no degree fictive; what, then, shall we say of the various aggregates of persons to which he belongs? Most people would hesitate to regard a family as a fictitious unit, but what about a political party or a cricket club? What about the assemblage of persons called "Smith", to which we will suppose our individual to belong? If you believe in astrology, you will attach importance to the assemblage of persons born under a certain planet; if you do not, you will regard such an assemblage as fictive. These distinctions are not logical; from the logical point of view, all assemblages of individuals are equally real or equally fictive. The importance of the distinctions is practical, not logical: there are some assemblages about which there are many useful things to be said, and others about which this is not the case.

When we say that instants are *useful* fictions, we must be supposed to mean that there are entities to which, as to individual people, we feel inclined to attach a high degree of "reality" (whatever that may mean), and that, in comparison with them, instants have that lesser degree of "reality" that cricket clubs have in relation to their members; but we wish also to say that about instants, as about families as opposed to "artificial" aggregates of people, there are many practically important things to say.

All this is very vague, and the problem of interpretation is that of substituting something precise, remembering always that, however we define "instants", they must have the properties required in mathematical physics. Given two interpretations which both satisfy this requisite, the choice between them is one of taste and convenience; there is not one interpretation which is "right" and others that are "wrong".

In classical physics, the technical apparatus consists of points, instants, and particles. It is assumed that there is a three-term relation, that of occupying a point at an instant, and what occupies a point at an instant is called a "particle". It is also assumed technically that particles are indestructible, so that whatever occupies a point at a given instant occupies *some* point at every other instant. When I say that this is assumed, I do not mean that it is asserted to be a fact, but that the technique is based on the assumption that no harm will come of treating it as a fact. This is still held to be the case in macroscopic physics, but in microscopic physics "particles" have been gradually disappearing. "Matter" in the old sense is no longer needed; what is needed is "energy", which is not defined except as regards its laws and the relation of changes in its distribution to our sensations, more especially the relation of frequencies to colour-perceptions.

Broadly speaking, we may say that the fundamental technical apparatus of modern physics is a four-dimensional manifold of "events" ordered by space-time relations, which can be analysed into a spatial and a temporal component in a number of ways, the choice between which is arbitrary. Since the calculus is still used, it is still technically assumed that space-time is continuous, but it is not clear how far this assumption is more than a mathematical convenience. Nor is it clear that "events" have that precise location in space-time that used to characterize a particle at an instant. All this makes the question of the interpretation of modern physics very difficult, but in the absence of *some* interpretation we cannot say what is being asserted by the quantum physicists.

"Interpretation", in its logical aspect, is somewhat different from the rather vague and difficult concept which we considered at the beginning of this Chapter. We were there concerned with symbolic statements which are known to have a connection with observable phenomena, and to lead to results which observation confirms, but are somewhat indeterminate in meaning except in so far as their connection with observation defines them. In this case we can say, as we said at the beginning of this Chapter, that we are pretty sure our formulae are true, but not at all sure what they mean. In logic, however, we proceed differently. Our formulae are not regarded as "true" or "false", but as hypotheses containing variables. A set of values of the variables which makes the hypotheses true is an "interpretation". The word "point", in geometry, may be interpreted as meaning "ordered triad of real numbers", or, as we shall see, as meaning what we shall call "complete complex of compresence"; it may also be interpreted in an infinite number of other ways. What all the ways have in common is that they satisfy the axioms of geometry.

We often have, both in pure and applied mathematics, collections of formulae all logically deducible from a small number of initial formulae, which may be called "axioms". These axioms may be regarded as hostages for the whole system, and we may concentrate our attention exclusively upon them. The axioms consist partly of terms having a known definition, partly of terms which, in any interpretation, will remain variables, and partly of terms which, though as yet undefined, are intended to acquire definitions when the axioms are "interpreted". The process of interpretation consists in finding a constant signification for this class of terms. The signification may be given by a verbal definition, or may be given ostensively. It must be such that, with this interpretation, the axioms become *true*. (Before interpretation, they are neither true nor false.) It thus follows that all their consequences are also true.

Suppose, for example, we wish to interpret the formulae of arithmetic. In Peano's five axioms (given above) there are: first, logical terms, such as "is a" and "is identical with", of which the meaning is supposed known; second, variables, such as a and s, which are to remain variables after interpretation; third, the terms "o", "number", and "successor of", for which an interpretation is to find a constant meaning which makes the five axioms true. As we saw, there are an infinite number of interpretations satisfying these conditions, but there is only one among them which also satisfies empirical statements of enumeration, such as "I have 10 fingers". In this case, therefore, there is one interpretation which is very much more convenient than any of the others.

As we saw in the case of geometry, a given set of axioms may be capable of two sorts of interpretation, one logical and one empirical. All nominal definitions, if pushed back far enough, must lead ultimately to terms having only ostensive definitions, and in the case of an empirical science the empirical terms must depend upon terms of which the ostensive definition is given in perception. The astronomer's sun, for instance, is very different from what we see, but it must have a definition derived from the ostensive definition of the word "sun" which we learnt in childhood. Thus an empirical interpretation of a set of axioms, when complete, must always involve the use of terms which have an ostensive definition derived from sensible experience. It will not, of course, contain *only* such terms, for there will always be logical terms; but it is the presence of terms derived from experience that makes an interpretation empirical.

The question of interpretation has been unduly neglected. So long as we remain in the region of mathematical formulae, everything appears precise, but when we seek to interpret them it turns out that the precision is partly illusory. Until this matter has been cleared up, we cannot tell with any exactitude what any given science is asserting.

Chapter II

MINIMUM VOCABULARIES

IN the present chapter we shall be concerned with a linguistic technique which is very useful in the analysis of scientific concepts. There are as a rule a number of ways in which the words used in a science can be defined in terms of a few among them. These few may have ostensive definitions, or may have nominal definitions in terms of words not belonging to the science in question, or—so long as the science is not "interpreted" in the sense considered in the last chapter—they may be left without either ostensive or nominal definition, and regarded merely as a set of terms having the properties which the science ascribes to its fundamental terms. Such a set of initial words I call a "minimum vocabulary" for the science in question, provided that (a) every other word used in the science has a nominal definition in terms of these words, and (b) no one of these initial words has a nominal definition in terms of the other initial words.

Everything said in a science can be said by means of the words in a minimum vocabulary. For whenever a word occurs which has a nominal definition, we can substitute the defining phrase; if this contains words with a nominal definition, we can again substitute the defining phrase, and so on, until none of the remaining words have nominal definitions. In fact, definable terms are superfluous, and only undefined terms are indispensable. But the question which terms are to be undefined is in part arbitrary. Take, for example, the calculus of proposition, which is the simplest and most completed example of a formal system. We can take "or" and "not" as undefined, or "and" and "not"; instead of two such undefined terms, we can take one, which may be "not this or not that" or "not this and not that". Thus in general we cannot say that such-and-such a word *must* belong to the minimum vocabulary of such-and-such a science, but at most that there are one or more minimum vocabularies to which it belongs.

Let us take geography as an example. I shall assume the vocabulary of geometry already established; then our first distinctively geographical need is a method of assigning latitude and longitude. For this it will suffice to have as part of our minimum vocabulary "Greenwich", "the North Pole", and "West of"; but clearly any other place would do as well as Greenwich, and the South Pole would do as well as the North Pole. The relation "west of" is not really necessary, for a parallel of latitude is a circle on the earth's surface in a plane perpendicular to the diameter passing through the North Pole. The remainder of the words used in physical geography, such as "land" and "water", "mountain" and "plain", can now be defined in terms of chemistry, physics, or geometry. Thus it would seem that it is the two words "Greenwich" and "North Pole" that are needed in order to make geography a science concerning the surface of the earth, and not some other spheroid. It is owing to the presence of these two words (or two others serving the same purpose) that geography is able to relate the discoveries of travellers. It is to be observed that these two words are involved wherever latitude and longitude are mentioned.

As this example illustrates, a science is apt to acquire a smaller minimum vocabulary as it becomes more systematic. The ancients knew many geographical facts before they knew how to assign latitudes and longitudes, but to express these facts they needed a larger number of undefined words than we need. Since the earth is a spheroid, not a sphere, "North-Pole" need not be undefined: we can define the two Poles as the extremities of the earth's shortest diameter, and the North Pole as the Pole nearer to Greenwich. In this way we can manage with "Greenwich" as the only undefined term peculiar to geography. The earth itself is defined as "that spheroid whose surface is formed of land and water bounded by air, and on whose surface Greenwich is situated". But here we seem to reach a dead end in the way of diminishing our minimum vocabulary: if we are to be sure that we are talking about the earth, we must mention some place on its surface or having a given geometrical relation to it, and the place must be one which we can recognize. Therefore although "New York" or "Moscow" or "Timbuctoo" would do just as well as "Greenwich", *some* place must be included in any minimum vocabulary for geography.

One further point is illustrated by our discussion of Greenwich, and that is, that the terms which are officially undefined in a science may not be identical with those that are undefined for a given person. If you have never seen Greenwich, the word "Greenwich" cannot, for you, have an ostensive definition; therefore you cannot understand the word unless it has a nominal definition. In fact, if you live in a place called "P", then for you "P" takes the place of Greenwich, and your official longitude, for you, defines the meridian of Greenwich, not the longitude of P. Such considerations, however, are pre-scientific, and are usually ignored in the analysis of scientific concepts. For certain purposes, they cannot be ignored, particularly when we are considering the relation of science to sensible experience; but as a rule there is little danger in ignoring them.

Let us consider next the question of minimum vocabularies for astronomy. Astronomy consists of two parts, one a kind of cosmic geography, the other an application of physics. Statements as to the size and orbits of the planets belong to cosmic geography, whereas Newton's and Einstein's theories of gravitation belong to physics. The difference is that, in the geographical part, we are concerned with statements of fact as to what is where, while in the part which is physics we are concerned with laws. As I shall presently be considering physics on its own account, let us consider first the geographical part of astronomy. In this part, so long as it is in an elementary stage, we need proper names for the sun, the moon, the planets, and all the stars and nebulae. The number of proper names required can, however, be steadily reduced as the science of astronomy advances. "Mercury" can be defined as meaning "the planet nearest the sun", "Venus" as "the second planet", "the earth" as "the third planet", and so on. Constellations are defined by their co-ordinates, and the several stars in a constellation by their order of brightness.

On this system, "the sun" will remain part of our minimum vocabulary, and we shall need what is necessary for defining celestial co-ordinates. "The Pole Star" will not be necessary, since it may be defined as "the star without diurnal revolution", but we shall need some other heavenly body to fulfil the function which Greenwich fulfils in terrestrial geography. In this way official astronomy could get on with (it would seem) only two proper names, "the sun" and (say) "Sirius". "The moon", for instance, can be defined as "the body whose co-ordinates on such-

and-such a date are so-and-so." With this vocabulary we can, in a sense, state everything that the astronomer wishes to say, just as, with Peano's three undefined terms, we can state all arithmetic.

But just as Peano's system proves inadequate when we come to counting, so our official astronomy proves inadequate when we attempt to link it to observation. There are two essential propositions which it fails to include, namely "that is the sun" and "that is Sirius". We have, it appears, formed a vocabulary for astronomy in the abstract, but not for astronomy as a record of observations.

Plato, who was interested in astronomy solely as a body of laws, wished it to be wholly divorced from sense; those who were interested in the actual heavenly bodies that happen to exist would, he said, be punished in the next incarnation by being birds. This point of view is not nowadays adopted by men of science, but it, or something very like it, is to be found in the works of Carnap and some other logical positivists. They are not, I think, conscious of holding any such opinion, and would vehemently repudiate it; but absorption in words, as opposed to what they mean, has exposed them to Platonic temptation, and led them down strange paths towards perdition, or what an empiricist must consider such. Astronomy is not *merely* a collection of words and sentences; it is a collection of words and sentences chosen, from others that were linguistically just as good, because they described a world connected with sensible experience. So long as sensible experience is ignored, no reason appears for concerning ourselves with a large body having just so many planets at just such distances from it. And the sentences in which sensible experience breaks in are such as "that is the sun".

Every advanced empirical science has two aspects: on the one hand, it consists of a body of propositions interconnected in various ways, and often containing a small selection from which all the others can be deduced; on the other hand, it is an attempt to describe some part or aspect of the universe. In the former aspect, the truth or falsehood of the several propositions is not in question, but only their mutual connections. For example, if gravitation varied directly as the distance, planets (if any) would revolve round the sun (if it existed) in ellipses of which the sun would occupy the centre, not a focus. This proposition is not part of descriptive astronomy. There is a similar statement, also not part of descriptive astronomy, saying that if gravitation varies inversely as the square of the distance, planets (if any) will go round the sun (if any) in ellipses of which the sun will occupy a focus. This is different from the two statements: gravitation varies inversely as the square of the distance, and planets revolve in ellipses round the sun in a focus. The former statement is a hypothetical; the two latter assert both the antecedent and the consequent of the previous hypothetical. What enables them to do this is the appeal to observation.

The appeal to observation is made in statements such as "that is the sun"; such statements, therefore, are essential to the truth of astronomy. Such statements never appear in any finished exposition of an astronomical theory, but they do appear while a theory is being established. For instance, after the eclipse observations in 1919, we were told that the photographs of certain stars appeared with such-and-such a displacement towards the sun. This was a statement as to the positions of certain dots on a photographic plate, as observed by certain astronomers at a certain date; it was a statement not primarily belonging to astronomy, but to biography, and yet it constituted the evidence for an important astronomical theory.

The vocabulary of astronomy, it thus appears, is wider if we consider it as a body of propositions deriving truth, or at least probability, from observation, than it is if we treat it as a purely hypothetical system whose truth or falsehood does not concern us. In the former case we must be able to say "that is the sun", or something of the sort; in the latter case, no such necessity arises.

Physics, which we must next consider, is in a different position from geography and astronomy, since it is not concerned to say what exists where, but only to establish general laws. "Copper conducts electricity" is a law of physics, but "there is copper in Cornwall" is a fact of geography. The physicist as such does not care where there is copper, so long as there is enough in his laboratory.

In the earlier stages of physics the word "copper" was necessary, but now it has become definable. "Copper" is "the element whose atomic number is 29", and this definition enables us to deduce many things about the copper atom. All the elements can be defined in terms of electrons and protons, or at any rate of electrons, positrons, neutrons, and protons. (Perhaps a proton consists of a neutron and a positron.) These units themselves can be defined by their mass and electric charge. In the last analysis, since mass is a form of energy, it would seem that energy, electric charge, and space-time co-ordinates are all that physics needs; and owing to the absence of the geographical element the co-ordinates can remain purely hypothetical, i.e. there need be no analogue of Greenwich. Physics as a "pure" science—i.e. apart from methods of verification—would seem, therefore, to require only a four-dimensional continuum containing distributions of varying amounts of energy and electricity. Any four-dimensional continuum will do, and "energy" and "electricity" need only be quantities whose mode of change of distribution is subject to certain assigned laws.

When physics is brought to this degree of abstraction it becomes a branch of pure mathematics, which can be pursued without reference to the actual world, and which requires no vocabulary beyond that of pure mathematics. The mathematics, however, are such as no pure mathematician would have thought of for himself. The equations, for instance, contain Planck's constant h, of which the magnitude is about $6 \cdot 55 \times 10^{-27}$ erg secs. No one would have thought of introducing just this quantity if there had not been experimental reasons for doing so, and as soon as we introduce experimental reasons the whole picture is changed. The four-dimensional continuum is no longer a mere mathematical hypothesis, but the space-time continuum to which we have been led by successive refinements of the space and time with which we are familiar in experience. Electricity is no longer just any quantity, but the thing measured by the observable behaviour of our electrical instruments. Energy, though highly abstract, is a generalization arrived at by means of completely concrete experiments such as those of Joule. Physics as verifiable, therefore, uses various empirical concepts in addition to those purely abstract concepts that are needed in "pure" physics.

Let us consider in more detail the definition of such a term as "energy". The important point about energy is its constancy, and the chief step in establishing its constancy was the determination of the mechanical equivalent of heat. This was effected by observation, for example of thermometers. If, then, we mean by "physics" not merely the body of physical laws, but these together with the evidence for their truth, then we must include in "physics" Joule's perceptions when he looked at thermometers. And what do we mean by "heat"? The plain man means a certain kind of sensation, or its (to him) unknown cause; the physicist means a rapid agitation of the minute parts of bodies. But what has led the physicist to this definition? Only the fact that, when we *feel* heat, there is reason to think that such agitation is occurring. Or take the fact that friction causes heat: our primary evidence for this fact is that when we have seen friction we can feel heat. All the non-mathematical terms used in physics considered as an experimental science have their origin in our sensible experience, and it is only on this account that sensible experience can confirm or confute physical laws.

It thus appears that, if physics is regarded as a science based on observation, not as a branch of pure mathematics, and if the evidence for physical laws is held to be part of physics, then any minimum vocabulary for physics must be such as to enable us to mention the experiences upon which our physical beliefs are based. We shall need such words as "hot", "red", "hard", not only to describe what physics asserts to be the condition of bodies that give us these sensations, but also to describe the sensations themselves. Suppose I say, for instance: By "red" light I mean light of such-and-such a range of wave-lengths. In that case the statement that light of such wave-lengths makes me see red is a tautology, and until the nineteenth century people were uttering meaningless noises when they said that blood is red, because nothing was known of the correlation of wave-lengths with sensations of colour. This is absurd. It is obvious that "red" has a meaning independent of physics, and that this meaning is relevant in collecting data for the physical theory of colours, just as the pre-scientific meaning of "hot" is relevant in establishing the physical theory of heat.

The main conclusion of the above discussion of minimum vocabularies is that every empirical science, however abstract, must contain in any minimum vocabulary words descriptive of our experiences. Even the most mathematical terms, such as "energy", must, when the chain of definitions is completed until we reach terms of which there is only an ostensive definition, be found to depend for their meaning upon terms directly descriptive of experiences, or even, in what may be called the "geographical" sciences, giving names to particular experiences. This conclusion, if valid, is important, and affords great assistance in the work of interpreting scientific theories.

Chapter III

STRUCTURE

IN the present chapter we shall be concerned with a purely logical discussion which is essential as a preliminary to any further steps in the interpretation of science. The logical concept which I shall endeavour to explain is that of "structure".

To exhibit the structure of an object is to mention its parts and the ways in which they are interrelated. If you were learning anatomy, you might first learn the names and shapes of the various bones, and then be taught where each bone belongs in the skeleton. You would then know the structure of the skeleton in so far as anatomy has anything to say about it. But you would not have come to an end of what can be said about structure in relation to the skeleton. Bones are composed of cells, and cells of molecules, and each molecule has an atomic structure which it is the business of chemistry to study. Atoms, in turn, have a structure which is studied in physics. At this point orthodox science ceases its analysis, but there is no reason to suppose that further analysis is impossible. We shall have occasion to suggest the analysis of physical entities into structures of events, and even events, as I shall try to show, may be regarded with advantage as having a structure.

Let us consider next a somewhat different example of structure, namely sentences. A sentence is a series of words, arranged in order by the relation of earlier and later if the sentence is spoken, and of left to right if it is written. But these relations are not really between words; they are between *instances* of words. A word is a class of similar noises, all having the same meaning or nearly the same meaning. (For simplicity I shall confine myself to speech as opposed to writing.) A sentence also is a class of noises, since many people can utter the same sentence. We must say, then, not that a sentence is a temporal series of words, but that a sentence is a class of noises, each consisting of a series of noises in quick temporal succession, each of these latter noises being an instance of a word. (This is a necessary but not a sufficient characteristic of a sentence; it is not sufficient because some series of words are not significant.) I will not linger on the distinction between different parts of speech, but will go on to the next stage in analysis, which belongs no longer to syntax, but to phonetics. Each instance of a word is a complex sound, the parts being the separate letters (assuming a phonetic alphabet). Behind the phonetic analysis there is a further stage: the analysis of the complex physiological process of uttering or hearing a single letter. Behind the physiological analysis is the analysis of physics, and from this point onward analysis proceeds as in the case of the bones.

In the above account I passed hastily over two points that need elucidation, namely that words have *meaning* and sentences have *significance*. "Rain" is a word, but "raim" is not, though both are classes of similar noises. "Rain is falling" is a sentence, but "rain snow elephant" is not, though both are series of words. To define "meaning" and "significance" is not easy, as we saw in discussing the theory of language. The attempt is not necessary so long as we confine ourselves strictly to questions of structure. A word acquires meaning by an external relation, just as a man acquires the property of being an uncle. No post mortem, however thorough, will reveal whether the man was an uncle or not, and no analysis of a set of noises (so long as everything external to them is excluded) will show whether this set of noises has meaning, or significance if the set is a series of what seem to be words.

The above example illustrates that an analysis of structure, however complete, does not tell you all that you may wish to know about an object. It tells you only what are the parts of the object and how they are related to each other; it tells you nothing about the relations of the object to objects that are not parts or components of it.

The analysis of structure usually proceeds by successive stages, as in both the above examples. What are taken as unanalysed units in one stage are themselves exhibited as complex structures in the next stage. The skeleton is composed of bones, the bones of cells, the cells of molecules, the molecules of atoms, the atoms of electrons, positrons, and neutrons; further analysis is as yet conjectural. Bones, molecules, atoms, and electrons may each be treated, for certain purposes, as if they were unanalysable units devoid of structure, but at no stage is there any positive reason to suppose that this is in fact the case. The ultimate units so far reached may at any moment turn out to be capable of analysis. Whether there must be units incapable of analysis because they are destitute of parts, is a question which there seems no way of deciding. Nor is it important, since there is nothing erroneous in an account of structure which starts from units that are afterwards found to be themselves complex. For example, points may be defined as classes of events, but that does not falsify anything in traditional geometry, which treated points as simples. Every account of structure is relative to certain units which are, for the time being, treated as if they were devoid of structure, but it must never be assumed that these units will not, in another context, have a structure which it is important to recognize.

There is a concept of "identity of structure" which is of great importance in relation to a large number of questions. Before giving a precise definition of this concept I will give some preliminary illustrations of it.

Let us begin with linguistic illustrations. Suppose that, in any given sentence, you substitute other words, but in a way which still leaves the sentence significant; then the new sentence has the same structure as the original one. Suppose, e.g., you start with "Plato loved Socrates"; for "Plato" substitute "Brutus", for "loved" substitute "killed", and for "Socrates" substitute "Caesar". You thus arrive at the sentence "Brutus killed Caesar", which has the same structure as "Plato loved Socrates". All sentences having this structure are called "dyadic-relation sentences". Similarly from "Socrates is Greek" you could have passed to "Brutus is Roman" without change of structure; sentences having this structure are called "subject-predicate sentences". In this way sentences can be classified by their structure; there are in theory an infinite number of structures that sentences may have.

Logic is concerned with sentences that are true in virtue of their structure, and that always remain true when other words are substituted, so long as the substitution does not destroy significance. Take, for example, the sentence: "If all men are mortal and Socrates is a man, then Socrates is mortal." Here we may substitute other words for "Socrates", "man", and "mortal", without destroying the truth of the sentence. It is true that there are other words in the sentence, namely "if-then" (which must count as one word), "all", "are", "and", "is", "a". These words must not be changed. But these are "logical" words, and their purpose is to indicate structure; when they are changed, the structure is changed. (All this raises problems, but it is not necessary for our present purpose to go into them.) A sentence belongs to logic if we can be sure that it is true (or that it is false) without having to know the meanings of any of the words except those that indicate structure. That is the reason for the use of variables. Instead of the above sentence about Socrates and man and mortal, we say: "If all α's are β's and x is an α, then x is a β." Whatever x and α and β may be, this sentence is true; it is true in virtue of its structure. It is in order to make this clear that we use "x" and "α" and "β" instead of ordinary words.

Let us take next the relation of a district to a map of it. If the district is small, so that the curvature of the earth can be neglected, the principle is simple: east and west are represented by right and left, north and south by up and down, and all distances are reduced in the same proportion. It follows that from every statement about the map you can infer one about the district, and vice versa. If there are two towns, A and B, and the map is on the scale of an inch to the mile, then from the fact that the mark "A" is ten inches from the mark "B" you can infer that A is ten miles from B, and conversely; and from the direction of the line from the mark "A" to the mark "B" you can infer the direction of the line from A to B. These inferences are possible owing to identity of structure between the map and the district.

Now take a somewhat more complicated illustration: the relation of a gramophone record to the music that it plays. It is obvious that it could not produce this music unless there were a certain identity of structure between it and the music, which can be exhibited by translating sound-relations into space-relations, or vice versa—e.g. what is nearer to the centre on the record corresponds to what is later in time in the music. It is only because of the identity of structure that the record is able to cause the music. Very similar considerations apply to telephones, broadcasting, etc.

We can generalize such examples so as to deal with the relations of our perceptual experiences to the external world. A wireless set transforms electromagnetic waves into sound waves; a human organism transforms sound waves into auditory sensations. The electromagnetic waves and the sound waves have a certain similarity of structure, and so (we may assume) have the sound waves and the auditory sensations. Whenever one complex structure causes another, there must be much the same structure in the cause and in the effect, as in the case of the gramophone record and the music. This is plausible if we accept the maxim "same cause, same effect" and its consequence, "different effects, different causes". If this principle is regarded as valid, we can infer from a complex sensation or series of sensations the structure of its physical cause, but nothing more, except that relations of neighbourhood must be preserved, i.e. neighbouring causes have neighbouring effects. This argument is one which needs much amplification; for the moment I am merely mentioning it by way of anticipation, in order to show one of the important applications of the concept of structure.

We can now proceed to the formal definition of "structure". It is to be observed that structure always involves relations: a mere class, as such, has no structure. Out of the terms of a given class many structures can be made, just as many different sorts of houses can be made out of a given heap of bricks. Every relation has what is called a "field", which consists of all the terms that have the relation to something or to which something has the relation. Thus the field of "parent" is the class of parents and children, and the field of "husband" is the class of husbands and wives. Such relations have two terms, and are called "dyadic". There are also relations of three terms, such as jealousy and "between"; these are called "triadic". If I say "A bought B from C for D pounds", I am using a "tetradic" relation. If I say "A minds B's love for C more than D's hatred of E", I am using a "pentadic" relation. To this series of kinds of relation there is no theoretical limit.

Let us in the first instance confine ourselves to dyadic relations. We shall say that a class α ordered by the relation R has the same structure as a class β ordered by the relation S, if to every term in α some one term in β corresponds, and vice versa, and if when two terms in α have the relation R, then the corresponding terms in β have the relation S, and vice versa. We may illustrate by the similarity between a spoken and a written sentence. Here the class of spoken words in the sentence is α, the class of written words in the sentence is β, and if one spoken word is earlier than another, then the written word corresponding to the one is to the left of the written word corresponding to the other (or to the right if the language is Hebrew). It is in consequence of this identity of structure that spoken and written sentences can be translated into each other. The process of learning to read and write is the process of learning which spoken word corresponds to a given written word and vice versa.

A structure may be defined by several relations. Take, for instance, a piece of music. One note may be earlier or later than another, or simultaneous with it. One note may be louder than another, or higher in pitch, or differing through a wealth or poverty of harmonics. All the relations of this kind that are musically relevant must have analogues in a gramophone record if it is to give a good reproduction. In saying that the record must have the same structure as the music, we are not concerned with only one relation R between the notes of the music and one corresponding relation S between the corresponding marks on the record, but with a number of relations such as R and a number of corresponding relations such as S. Some maps use different colours for different altitudes; in that case, different positions on the map correspond to different latitudes and longitudes, while different colours correspond to different elevations. The identity of structure in such maps is greater than in others; that is why they are able to give more information.

The definition of identity of structure is exactly the same for relations of higher orders as it is for dyadic relations. Given, for example, two triadic relations R and S, and given two classes α and β of which α is contained in the field of R while β is contained in the field of S, we shall say that α ordered by R has the same structure as β ordered by S if there is a way of correlating one member of α to one of β, and vice versa, so that, if a_1, a_2, a_3 are correlated respectively with b_1, b_2, b_3, if R relates a_1, a_2, a_3 (in that order), then S relates b_1, b_2, b_3 (in that order), and vice versa. Here, again, there may be several relations such as R, and several such as S; in that case, there is identity of structure in various respects.

When two complexes have the same structure, every statement about the one, in so far as it depends only on structure, has a corresponding statement about the other, true if the first was true, and false if the first was false. Hence arises the possibility of a dictionary, by means of which statements about the one complex can be translated into statements about the other. Or, instead of a dictionary, we may continue to use the same words, but attach different meanings to them according to the complex to which they are referred. This sort of thing happens in interpreting a sacred text or the laws of physics. The "days" in the Biblical account of the Creation are taken to mean "ages", and in this way Genesis is reconciled with geology. In physics, assuming that our knowledge of the physical world is only as to the structure resulting from the empirically known relation of "neighbourhood" in the topological sense, we have immense latitude in the interpretation of our symbols. Every interpretation that preserves the equations and the connection with our perceptive experiences has an equal claim to be regarded as *possibly* the true one, and may be used with equal right by the physicist to clothe the bare bones of his mathematics.

Take, for example, the question of waves *versus* particles. Until recently it was thought that this was a substantial question: light must consist either of waves or of little packets called photons. It was regarded as unquestionable that matter consisted of particles. But at last it was found that the equations were the same if both matter and light consisted of particles, or if both consisted of waves. Not only were the equations the same, but all the verifiable consequences were the same. Either hypothesis, therefore, is equally legitimate, and neither can be regarded as having a superior claim to truth. The reason is that the physical world can have the same structure, and the same relation to experience, on the one hypothesis as on the other.

Considerations derived from the importance of structure show that our knowledge, especially in physics, is much more abstract and much more infected with logic than it used to seem. There is however a very definite limit to the process of turning physics into logic and mathematics; it is set by the fact that physics is an empirical science, depending for its credibility upon relations to our perceptive experiences. The further development of this theme must be postponed until we come to the theory of scientific inference.

Chapter IV

STRUCTURE AND MINIMUM VOCABULARIES

THE reader will remember that, in relation to a given body of knowledge, a minimum vocabulary is defined as one having the two properties (1) that every proposition in the given body of knowledge can be expressed by means of words belonging to the minimum vocabulary, (2) that no word in this vocabulary can be defined in terms of other words in it. In the present chapter I wish to show the connection of this definition with structure.

The first thing to notice is that a minimum vocabulary cannot contain names for complexes of which the structure is known. Take (say) the name "France". This denotes a certain geographical region, and can be defined as "all places within such-and-such boundaries". But we cannot conversely define the boundaries in terms of "France". We want to be able to say "this place is on the boundaries of France", which requires a name for this place, or for constituents which compose it. "This place" enters into the definition of "France", but "France" does not enter into the definition of "this place".

It follows that every discovery of structure enables us to diminish the minimum vocabulary required for a given subject-matter. Chemistry used to need names for all the elements, but now the various elements can be defined in terms of atomic structure, by the use of two words, "electron" and "proton" (or perhaps three words, "electron", "positron", and "neutron"). Any region in space-time can be defined in terms of its parts, but its parts cannot be defined in terms of it. A man can be defined by enumerating, in the right temporal order, all the events that happen to him, but the events cannot be defined in terms of him. If you wish to speak both about complexes and about the things that are in fact their constituents, you can always achieve it without names for the complexes, if you know their structure. In this way analysis simplifies, systematizes, and diminishes your initial apparatus.

The words required in an empirical science are of three sorts. There are, first, proper names, which usually denote some continuous portion of space-time; such are "Socrates", "Wales", "the sun". Then there are words denoting qualities or relations; instances of qualities are "red", "hot", "loud", and instances of relations are "above", "before", "between". Then there are logical words, such as "or", "not", "some", "all". For our present purposes we may ignore logical words, and concentrate upon the other two kinds.

It is usually taken for granted that the analysis of something that has a proper name consists in dividing it into spatio-temporal parts. Wales consists of counties, the counties consist of parishes, each parish consists of the church, the school, etc. The church in turn has parts, and so we can continue (it is thought) until we reach points. The odd thing is that we never do reach points, and that the familiar building thus seems to be composed of an infinity of unattainable and purely conceptual constituents. I believe this view of spatio-temporal analysis to be mistaken.

Qualities and relations are sometimes analysable, sometimes not. I do not believe that "before", as we know it in experience, can be analysed; at any rate I do not know any analysis of it that I am willing to accept. But in some cases the analysis of a relation is obvious. "Grandparent" means "parent of parent", "brother" means "son of parent", and so on. All family relationships can be expressed by means of the three words "spouse", "male", and "parent"; this is a minimum vocabulary in this subject-matter. Adjectives (i.e. words denoting qualities) are often complex in their meaning. Milton calls the woodbine "well-attired", which is a word of which the meaning is very complex. So is such a word as "famous". Words such as "red", which come nearer to simplicity, do not achieve it; there are many shades of red.

Whenever the analysis of a quality or relation is known, the word for that quality or relation is unnecessary in our "basic English".

When we have words for every thing, quality, and relation that we cannot analyse, we can express all our knowledge without the need of any other words. In practice this would be too lengthy, but in theory nominal definitions are unnecessary.

If the world is composed of simples, i.e. of things, qualities, and relations that are devoid of structure, then not only all our knowledge, but all that of Omniscience, could be expressed by means of words denoting these simples. We could distinguish in the world a stuff (to use William James's word) and a structure. The stuff would consist of all the simples denoted by names, while the structure would depend on relations and qualities for which our minimum vocabulary would have words.

This conception can be applied without assuming that there is anything absolutely simple. We can define as "relatively simple" whatever we do not know to be complex. Results obtained by using the concept of "relative simplicity" will still be true if complexity is afterwards found, provided we have abstained from asserting absolute simplicity.

If we allow denotative as opposed to structural definitions, we can, at least apparently, content ourselves with a much smaller apparatus of names. All places in space-time can be indicated by their co-ordinates, all colours by their wave-lengths, and so on. We have already seen that the assignment of space-time co-ordinates requires a few proper names, say "Greenwich", "the Pole Star", and "Big Ben". But this is a very small apparatus compared to names for all the different places in the universe. Whether this way of defining spatio-temporal places enables us to say all that we know about them, is a difficult question, to which I shall return shortly. Before discussing it, it will be well to examine more closely the questions that arise concerning qualities.

Consider the definition of the word "red". We may define it (1) as any shade of colour between two specified extremes in the spectrum, or (2) as any shade of colour caused by wave-lengths lying between specified extremes, or (3) (in physics) as waves having wave-lengths between these extremes. There are different things to be said about these three definitions, but there is one thing to be said about all of them.

What is to be said about all of them is that they have an artificial, unreal, and partly illusory precision. The word "red", like the word "bald", is one which has a meaning that is vague at the edges. Most people would admit that, if a man is not bald, the loss of one hair will not make him so; it follows by mathematical induction that the loss of all his hairs will not make him so, which is absurd. Similarly, if a shade of colour is red, a very tiny change will not make it cease to be red, from which it follows that all shades of colour are red. The same sort of thing happens when we use wave-lengths in our definition, since lengths cannot be accurately measured. Given a length which, by the most careful measurements, appears to be a metre, it will still appear to be a metre if it is very slightly increased or diminished; therefore every length appears to be a metre, which again is absurd.

It follows from these considerations that any definition of "red" which professes to be precise is pretentious and fraudulent.

We shall have to define "red", or any other vague quality, by some such method as the following. When the colours of the spectrum are spread out before us, there are some that everybody would agree to be red, and others that everybody would agree to be not red, but between these two regions of the spectrum there is a doubtful region. As we travel along this region, we shall begin by saying "I am nearly certain that that is red", and end by saying "I am nearly certain that that is not red", while in the middle there will be a region where we have no preponderant inclination either towards *yes* or towards *no*. All empirical concepts have this character—not only obviously vague concepts such as "loud" or "hot", but also those that we are most anxious to make precise, such as "centimetre" and "second".

It might be thought that we could make "red" precise by confining the term to those shades that we are certain are red. This, however, though it diminishes the area of uncertainty, does not abolish it. There is no precise point in the spectrum where you are sure that you become uncertain. There will still be three regions, one where you are certain that you are certain the shade is red, one where you are certain that you are uncertain, and an intermediate region where you are uncertain as to whether you are certain or uncertain. And these three regions, like the previous ones, will have no sharp boundaries. You have merely adopted one of the innumerable techniques which diminish the area of vagueness without ever wholly abolishing it.

The above discussion has proceeded on the assumption of continuity. If all change is discrete—and we do not know that it is not—then complete accuracy is theoretically possible. But if there is discontinuity it lies, for the present, far below the level of sensible discrimination, so that discreteness, even if it should exist, would be useless as a help in defining empirically given qualities.

Let us now ignore the problem of vagueness, and revert to our three definitions. But we will now adapt them so as to be definitions of a given shade of colour. This introduces no new difficulties, since, as we have seen, the definition of "red" as a band of colours requires a definition of the precise shades that form its boundaries.

Let us suppose that I am seeing a certain coloured patch, and that I call the shade of the patch "C". Physics tells me that this shade of colour is caused by light of wave-length λ. I may then define "C" as: (1) the shade of any patch that is indistinguishable in colour from the patch I am seeing now; or (2) as the shade of any visual sensation caused by electromagnetic waves of wave-length λ; or (3) as electromagnetic waves of wave-length λ. When we are concerned only with physics, without regard to the methods by which its laws are verified, (3) is the most convenient definition. We use it when we speak of ultra-violet light, and when we say that the light from Mars is red, and when, during a sunset, we say that the sun's light is not really red, but only looks red because of intervening mist. Physics, *per se*, has nothing to say about sensations, and if it uses the word "colour" (which it need not do), it will wish to define it in a way that is logically independent of sensation.

But although physics as a self-contained logical system does not need to mention sensations, it is only through sensations that physics can be *verified*. It is an empirical law that light of a certain wave-length causes a visual sensation of a certain kind, and it is only when such laws are added to those of physics that the total becomes a verifiable system. The definition (2) has the defect of concealing the force of the empirical law which connects wave-length with sensation. Names for colours were used for thousands of years before the undulatory theory of light was invented, and it was a genuine discovery that wave-lengths grow shorter as we travel along the spectrum from red to violet. If we define a shade of colour by its wave-length, we shall have to add that sensations caused by light of the same wave-length all have a recognizable similarity, and that there is a lesser degree of similarity when the wave-lengths differ, but only by a little. Thus we cannot express all that we know on the subject without speaking about shades of colour as known directly in visual sensation, independently of any physical theory as to light-waves.

It would seem, therefore, that if we wish for clarity in exhibiting the empirical data which lead us to accept physics, we shall do well to adopt our first definition of a shade of colour, since we shall certainly need some way of speaking about what this definition defines, without having to make the detour through physics that is involved in mentioning wave-lengths.

It remains, however, an open question whether the raw material in our definitions of colours should be a given shade of colour (wherever it may occur), or a given patch of colour, which can only occur once. Let us develop both hypotheses.

Suppose I wish to give an account of my own visual field throughout a certain day. Since we are concerned only with colour, depth may be ignored. I have therefore at each moment a two-dimensional manifold of colours. I shall assume that my visual field can be divided into areas of finite size, within each of which the colour is sensibly uniform. (This assumption is not essential, but saves verbiage.) My visual field, on this assumption, will consist of a finite number of coloured patches of varying shape. I may start by giving a name to each patch, or by giving a name to each shade of colour. We have to consider whether there are any reasons for preferring one of these courses to the other.

If I start by giving a name to each patch, I proceed to the definition of a shade of colour by means of a relation of colour-similarity between patches. This similarity may be greater or less; we suppose that there is an extreme degree of it which may be called "exact likeness". This relation is distinguished by being transitive, which is not the case with minor degrees of resemblance. For the reasons already given, we can never be sure that, in any given case, there is exact colour-likeness between two patches, any more than we can be sure that a given length is exactly a metre. However, we can invent techniques which approximate more and more closely to what would be needed for establishing exact likeness.

We define the shade of colour of a given patch as the class of patches having exact colour-likeness to it. Every shade of colour is defined in relation to a "this"; it is "the shade of colour of *this* patch". To each "this", as we become aware of it, we give a name, say "P"; then "the shade of P" is defined as "all patches having exact colour-likeness to P".

The question now arises: given two patches which are indistinguishable in colour, what makes me think them two? The answer is obvious: difference of spatio-temporal position. But though this answer is obvious, it does not dispose of the problem. For the sake of simplicity, let us suppose that the two patches are parts of one visual field, but are not in visual contact with each other. Spatial position in the momentary visual field is a quality, varying according to distance from the centre of the field of vision, and also according as the region in question is above or below, to the right or to the left, of the centre. The various qualities that small portions of the visual field may have are related by relations of up-and-down, right-and-left. When we move our eyes, the qualities associated with a given physical object change, but if the various physical objects have not moved, there will be no *topological* change in the part of the visual field which is common to both occasions. This enables common sense to ignore the subjectivity of visual position.

Concerning these visual positional qualities we have exactly the same alternatives as in the case of shades of colour. We may give a name to each quality, considered as something which is the same on different occasions, or we may give a name to each instance of the quality, and connect it with other instances of the same quality by the relation of exact likeness. Let us concentrate on the quality that distinguishes the centre of the field of vision, and let us call this quality "centrality". Then on one view there is a single quality of centrality, which occurs repeatedly, while on the other view there are many particulars which have exact positional likeness, and the quality of centrality is replaced by the class of these particulars.

When we now repeat, in relation to the particulars which are instances of centrality, the question as to how we distinguish one of these particulars from another, the answer is again obvious: we distinguish them by their position in time. (There cannot be two simultaneous instances of centrality in one person's experience.) We must therefore now proceed to analyse difference of position in time.

In regard to time, as in regard to space, we have to distinguish objective and subjective time. Objective space is that of the physical world, whereas subjective space is that which appears in our percepts when we view the world from one place. So objective time is that of physics and history, while subjective time is that which appears in our momentary view of the world. In my present state of mind there are not only percepts, but memories and expectations; what I remember I place in the past, what I expect I place in the future. But from the impartial stand-point of history my memories and expectations are just as much *now* as my percepts. When I remember, something is happening to me now which, if I remember correctly, has a certain relation to what happened at an earlier time, but what happened then is not itself in my mind now. My memories are placed in a time-order, just as my visual perceptions are placed in a space-order, by intrinsic qualities, which may be called "degrees of remoteness". But however high a degree of remoteness a memory may possess, it is still, from the objective historical point of view, an event which is happening *now*.

I said a moment ago that there could not be two simultaneous instances of centrality in one person's experience, but in a certain sense this may be false. If, when my eyes are open, I remember some previous visual experience, there will be one instance of centrality in my percepts and another in my memory, and these are both now in historical time. But they are not both now in the time of my present subjective experience. Thus the correct statement is: two instances of centrality cannot be simultaneous in historical time if they are *perceptual* parts of one man's experience, and they cannot in any case be simultaneous in the subjective time of a single experience composed of percepts and memories and expectations.

There is a certain difficulty in the conception of a time which, in a sense, is wholly *now*, and a space which, in a sense, is wholly *here*. Yet these conceptions seem unavoidable. The whole of my psychological space is *here* from the standpoint of physics, and the whole of my psychological time is *now* from the standpoint of history. Like Leibniz's monads, we mirror the universe, though very partially and very inaccurately; in my momentary mirroring there is a mirror-space and a mirror-time, which have a correspondence, though not an exact one, with the impersonal space and time of physics and history. From the objective standpoint, the space and time of my present experience are wholly confined within a small region of physical space-time.

We must now return from this digression to the question whether we are to assume one quality of centrality which can exist at various times, or a number of instances of it, each of which exists only once. It begins to be obvious that the latter hypothesis will entail great unnecessary complications, which the former hypothesis avoids. We can bring the question to a head by asking what can be meant by "this". Let us suppose "this" to be some momentary visual datum. There is a sense in which it may be true to say "I have seen this before", and there is another sense in which this cannot be true. If I mean by "this" a certain shade of colour, or even a certain shade of a certain shape, I may have seen it before. But if I mean something dated, such as might be called an "event", then clearly I cannot have seen it before. Just the same considerations apply if I am asked "do you see this anywhere else"? I may be seeing the same shade of colour somewhere else, but if in the meaning of "this" I include position in visual space, then I cannot be seeing it somewhere else. Thus what we have to consider is spatio-temporal particularity.

If we take the view—which I think the better one—that a given quality, such as a shade of colour, may exist in different places and times, then what would otherwise be instances of the quality become complexes in which it is combined with other qualities. A shade of colour combined with a given positional quality cannot exist in two parts of one visual field, because the parts of the field are defined by their positional qualities. There is a similar distinction in subjective time: the complex consisting of a shade of colour together with one degree of remoteness cannot be identical with the complex consisting of the same shade of colour and another degree of remoteness. In this way "instances" can be replaced by complexes, and by this replacement a great simplification can be effected.

It results from the above discussion that a possible minimum vocabulary for describing the world of my experience can be constructed as follows. Names are given to all the qualities of experiences, including such qualities of visual space and remembered time as we have been considering. We also have to have words for experienced relations, such as right-and-left in one visual field, and earlier-and-later in one specious present. We do not need names for space-time regions, such as "Socrates" or "France", because every space-time region can be defined as a complex of qualities or a system of such complexes. "Events", which have dates and cannot recur, are capable of being regarded as always complex; whatever we do not know how to analyse is capable of occurring repeatedly in various parts of space-time.

When we pass outside our own experience, as we do in physics, we need no new words. Definitions of things not experienced must be denotational. Qualities and relations, if not experienced, can only be known by means of descriptions in which all the constants denote things that are experienced. It follows that a minimum vocabulary for what we experience is a minimum vocabulary for all our knowledge. That this must be the case is obvious from a consideration of the process of ostensive definition.

Chapter V

TIME, PUBLIC AND PRIVATE

THE purpose of this Part is to provide possible interpretations of the concepts of science, in terms of possible minimum vocabularies. It will not be asserted that no other interpretations are possible, but it is hoped that, in the course of the discussion, certain common characteristics of all acceptable interpretations will emerge. In the present chapter we shall be concerned to interpret the word "time".

Most people will be inclined to agree with St. Augustine: "What, then, is time? If no one asks of me, I know: if I wish to explain to him who asks, I know not." Philosophers, of course, have learned to be glib about time, but the rest of mankind, although the subject feels familiar, are apt to be aware that a few questions can reduce them to hopeless confusion. "Does the past exist? No. Does the future exist? No. Then only the present exists? Yes. But within the present there is no lapse of time? Quite so. Then time does not exist? Oh I wish you wouldn't be so tiresome." Any philosopher can elicit this dialogue by a suitable choice of interlocuter.

Sir Isaac Newton, who understood the Book of Daniel, also knew all about time. Let us hear what he has to say on the subject in the Scholium following the initial definitions in the *Principia*:

"I do not define time, space, place and motion, as being well known to all. Only I must observe, that the vulgar conceive those quantities under no other notions but from the relation they bear to sensible objects. And thence arise certain prejudices, for the removal of which, it will be convenient to distinguish them into absolute and relative, true and apparent, mathematical and common. Absolute, true, and mathematical time, of itself, and from its own nature flows equably without regard to anything external, and by another name is called duration: relative, apparent, and common time, is some sensible external (whether accurate or unequable) measure of duration by the means of motion, which is commonly used instead of true time; such as an hour, a day, a month, a year."

He goes on to explain that days are not all of equal length, and that perhaps there is nowhere in nature a truly uniform motion, but that we arrive at absolute time, in astronomy, by correction of "vulgar" time.

Sir Isaac Newton's "absolute" time, although it remained embedded in the technique of classical physics, was not generally accepted. The theory of relativity has provided reasons, within physics, for its rejection, though these reasons leave open the possibility of absolute space-time. But before relativity Newton's absolute time was already widely repudiated, though for reasons which had nothing to do with physics. Whether, before relativity, these reasons had any validity is a question which I think we shall find it worth while to examine.

Although Newton says that he is not going to define time because it is well known, he makes it clear that only "vulgar" time is well known, and that mathematical time is an inference. In modern terms, we should rather call it an adjustment than an inference. The process of arriving at "mathematical" time is essentially as follows: there are a number of periodic motions—the rotations and revolutions of the earth and the planets, the tides, the vibrations of a tuning fork, the heart beats of a healthy man at rest—which are such that, if one of them is assumed to be uniform, all the others are approximately uniform. If we take one of them, say the earth's rotation, as uniform by definition, we can arrive at physical laws—notably the law of gravitation—which explain the phenomena, and show why the other periodic motions are approximately uniform. But unfortunately the laws so established are only approximate, and, what is more, they show that the earth's rotation should suffer retardation by tidal friction. This is self-contradictory if the earth's rotation is taken as the measure of time; we therefore seek a different measure, which shall also make our physical laws approximate more nearly to exact truth. It is found convenient not to take any actual motion as *defining* the measure of time, but to adopt a compromise measure which makes physical laws as accurate as possible. It is this compromise measure that serves the purposes for which Newton invoked "absolute" time. There is no reason, however, to suppose that it represents a physical reality, for the choice of a measure of time is conventional, like the choice between the Christian and the Mohammedan eras. We choose, in fact, the measure which gives the greatest attainable simplicity to the statement of physical laws, but we do so on grounds of convenience, not because we think that this measure is more "true" than any other.

A frequent ground of objection to Newton's "absolute" time has been that it could not be observed. This objection, on the face of it, comes oddly from men who ask us to believe in electrons and protons and neutrons, quantum transitions in atoms, and what not, none of which can be observed. I do not think that physics can dispense with inferences that go beyond observation. The fact that absolute time cannot be observed is not, by itself, fatal to the view that it should be accepted; what is fatal is the fact that physics can be interpreted without assuming it. Whenever a body of symbolic propositions which there is reason to accept can be interpreted without inferring such-and-such unobserved entities, the inference from the body of propositions in question to these supposed entities is invalid, since, even if there are no such entities, the body of propositions may be true. It is on this ground, and not merely because "absolute" time cannot be observed, that Newton was mistaken in inferring it from the laws of physics.

While the rejection of Newton's view is a commonplace, few people seem to realize the problems that it raises. In physics there is an independent variable t, the values of which are supposed to form a continuous series, and each to be what is commonly called an "instant". Newton regarded an instant as a physical reality, but the modern physicist does not. Since, however, he continues to use the variable t, he must find some interpretation for its values, and the interpretation must serve the technical purposes that were served by Newton's "absolute" time. This problem of the interpretation of "t" is the one that concerns us in this chapter. In order to simplify the approach to it, we will at first ignore relativity and confine ourselves to time as it appears in classical physics.

We shall continue to give the name "instant" to a value of the variable t, but we shall look for an interpretation of the word "instant" in terms of physical data, that is to say, we shall expect the word to have a definition, and not to belong to a minimum physical vocabulary. All that we require of the definition is that instants, so defined, should have the formal properties demanded of them by mathematical physics.

In seeking a definition of "instant" or "point", the material to be used depends upon the theory we adopt as to "particulars" or proper names. We may take the view that when, for instance, a given shade of colour appears in two separated locations, there are two separate "particulars", each of which is an "instance" of the shade of colour, and is a subject of which qualities can be predicated, but which is not *defined* by its qualities, since another precisely similar particular might exist elsewhere. Or we may take the view that a "particular" is a bundle of coexisting qualities. The discussions of the preceding chapter, as well as the earlier discussion of proper names, inclined us to the latter view. I shall, however, in this and the two following chapters, hypothetically adopt the former view, and in Chapter VIII I shall show how to interpret what has been said in terms of the latter view. For the moment, therefore, I take as raw material "events", which are to be imagined as each occupying a finite continuous portion of space-time. It is assumed that two events can overlap, and that no event recurs.

It is clear that time is concerned with the relation of earlier and later; it is generally held also that nothing of which we have experience has a merely instantaneous existence. Whatever is earlier or later than something else I shall call an "event". We shall want our definition of "instant" to be such that an event can be said to exist "at" certain instants and not at certain others. Since we have agreed that events, so far as known to us, are not merely instantaneous, we shall wish to define "instant" in such a way that every event exists at a continuous stretch of the series of instants. That instants must form a series defined by means of the relation of earlier and later is one of the requisites that our definition must fulfil. Since we have rejected Newton's theory, we must not regard instants as something independent of events, which can be occupied by events as hats occupy hat-pegs. We are thus compelled to search for a definition which makes an instant a structure composed of a suitable selection of events. Every event will be a member of many such structures, which will be the instants during which it exists: it is "at" every instant which is a structure of which the event is a member.

A date is fixed with complete precision if it is known concerning every event in the world whether it wholly preceded that date, or will wholly come after it, or was in existence at that date. To this statement some one might object that, if the world were to remain without change for (say) five minutes, there would be no way of fixing a date within these five minutes if the above view were adopted, for every event wholly preceding one part of the five minutes would wholly precede every other part, every event wholly subsequent to any part of the five minutes would be wholly subsequent to every other part, and every event existing at any part of the five minutes would exist throughout the whole of them. This, however, is not an objection to our statement, but only to the supposition that time could go on in an unchanging world. On the Newtonian theory this would be possible, but on a relational theory of time it becomes self-contradictory. If time is to be defined in terms of events, it must be impossible for the universe to be unchanging for more than an instant. And when I say "impossible" I mean *logically* impossible.

Although we cannot agree with Newton that "time" does not need to be defined, it is obvious that temporal statements demand *some* undefined term. I choose the relation of earlier-and-later, or of wholly-preceding. Between two events *a* and *b* three temporal relations are possible: *a* may be wholly before *b*, or *b* may be wholly before *a*, or *a* and *b* may overlap. Suppose you wish to fix as accurately as possible some date within the duration of *a*. If you say that your date is also to be within the duration of *b*, you fix the date somewhat more accurately than by merely saying that it is within the duration of *a*, unless it so happens that *a* and *b* both began and ended together. Suppose now there is a third event *c* which overlaps with both *a* and *b*— that is to say, in ordinary language (to which we are not yet entitled), there is a period of time during which *a* and *b* and *c* all exist. This period, in general, will be shorter than that during which both *a* and *b* exist. We now look for a fourth event *d* which overlaps with *a* and *b* and *c*, i.e., in ordinary language, exists during some part of the time during which *a* and *b* and *c* all exist; the time during which *a* and *b* and *c* and *d* all exist is, in general, shorter than that during which any three of them all exist. In this way, step by step, we get nearer to an exact date.

Let us suppose this process carried on as long as possible, i.e. until there is no event remaining which overlaps with all the events already in our group. I say that, when this stage has been reached, the group of events that has been constructed may be defined as an "instant". To prove that this assertion is legitimate I only have to show that "instants", so defined, have the mathematical properties that physics demands. I do not have to show that this is what people commonly mean when they speak of "instants", though it might be desirable to complete the argument by showing that they commonly mean nothing.

An "instant", as I propose to define the term, is a class of events having the following two properties: (1) all the events in the class overlap; (2) no event outside the class overlaps with every member of the class. This group of events, as I shall show, does not persist for a finite time.

To say that an event persists for a finite time can only mean, on a relational view of time, that changes occur while it exists, i.e. that the events which exist when it begins are not all identical with the events existing when it ends. This amounts to saying that there are events which overlap with the given event but not with each other. That is to say: "*a* lasts for a finite time" means "there are two events *b* and *c* such that each overlaps with *a* but *b* wholly precedes *c*".

We may apply the same definition to a group of events. If the members of the group do not all overlap, the group as a whole has no duration, but if they all overlap, we shall say that the group as a whole lasts for a finite time if there are at least two events which overlap with every member of the group although one of them wholly precedes the other. If this is the case, change occurs while the group persists; if not, not. Now if a group constitutes an "instant" as above defined, no event outside the group overlaps all the members of the group, and no event inside the group wholly precedes any other event inside the group. Therefore the group as a whole does not last for a finite time. And therefore it may suitably be defined as an "instant".

Instants will form a series ordered by a relation defined in terms of the relation "wholly preceding" among events. One instant is earlier than another if there is a member of the first instant which wholly precedes a member of the second, i.e. if some event "at" the first instant wholly precedes some event "at" the second instant. It will be observed that being "at" an instant is the same thing as being a member of the class which is the instant.

According to the above definition, it is logically impossible

289

for the world to remain unchanging throughout a finite time. If two instants differ, they are composed (at least in part) of different members, and that means that some event existing at the one instant does not exist at the other.

Our theory makes no assumption as to whether there are or are not events that exist only at one instant. Such events, if any, would have the characteristic that any two events overlapping with them would overlap with each other. In general, the "duration" of an event means "the class of those instants of which the event in question is a member". It is generally assumed that an event occupies a continuous stretch of the series of instants; this assumption, formally, is embodied in the "axiom" that nothing wholly precedes itself. But this axiom is not necessary.

Something has already been said concerning the quantitative measurement of time, but it may be well to re-state the view to which we are led by physics. The quantitative measurement of time is conventional except to this extent, that a larger measure must be applied to a whole than to a part. We must assign a larger measure to a year than to any month in *that* year, but we might, if convenient, assign to that year a smaller measure than to a month in some other year. It turns out, however, that this is not convenient. Historically, astronomers started with the assumption that the day and the year were each of constant length; then it turned out that, if the sidereal day was constant, the solar day was not, but the year was. If the sidereal day was constant by definition, a large number of other periodic occurrences were approximately constant; this led to dynamical laws which suggested that it would be more convenient to treat the sidereal day as not *exactly* constant owing to tidal friction. The laws *could* be formulated with *any* measure of time, but naturally astronomers and physicists preferred the measure which made the statement of the laws simplest. As this so very nearly agreed with the "natural" measures of days and years, its conventional character was not perceived, and it could be supposed that what was being defined was Newton's "true" or "mathematical" time, believed to have physical reality.

I have been speaking so far as if there were, as used to be thought, one cosmic time for the whole universe. Since Einstein, we know that this is not the case. Each piece of matter has its own local time. There is very little difference between the local time of one piece of matter and that of another unless their relative velocity is an appreciable fraction of the velocity of light. The local time of a given piece of matter is that which will be shown by a perfectly accurate chronometer which travels with it. Beta-particles travel with velocities that do not fall very far short of that of light. If we could place a chronometer on a beta-particle, and make the particle travel in a closed path, we should find, when it returned, that the chronometer would not agree with one that had remained throughout stationary in the laboratory. A more curious illustration (which I owe to Professor Reichenbach) is connected with the possibility of travel to the stars. Suppose we invented a rocket apparatus which could send a projectile to Sirius with a velocity ten elevenths of that of light. From the point of view of the terrestrial observer the journey would take about 55 years, and one might therefore suppose that if the projectile carried passengers who were young when they started, they would be old when they arrived. But from their point of view the journey will only have taken about 11 years. This will not only be the time taken as measured by their clocks, but also the time as measured by their physiological processes—decay of teeth, loss of hair, etc. If they looked and felt like men of 20 when they started, they will look and feel like men of 31 when they arrive. It is only because we do not habitually come across bodies travelling with a speed approaching that of light that such odd facts remain unnoticed except by men of science.

If two pieces of matter (say the earth and a comet) meet and part and meet again, and if in the interval their relative velocity has been very great, the physicists (if any) who live on the two pieces of matter will form different estimates of the lapse of time between the two meetings, but they will agree as to which of the two meetings was the earlier and which the later. "Earlier" and "later", therefore, as applied to two events happening to one piece of matter, have no ambiguity: if there are several pieces of matter to which both the given events happen, one of the events will be earlier for all of them, and the other will be later for all of them.

The construction of "instants" as classes of events, given above, is to be held, for the present, as applying only to events happening to one piece of matter—primarily the body of a given observer. The extension to cosmic time, which can be made in many ways, all equally legitimate, is a matter which I shall not deal with at present.

Instead of basing our construction on the events happening to a given body, we may base it on those happening to a given mind or forming part of a given experience. If the mind is mine, I can experience occurrences of the sort expressed by the words "A wholly precedes B", for example, when I am listening to successive strokes of a clock striking the hour. If A is an event that I experience, everything that overlaps with A or wholly precedes A or wholly succeeds A will constitute "my" time, and only events belonging to "my" time will be involved in the construction of "instants" belonging to "my" time.[1] The linking up of my time with yours will thus remain a problem to be considered.

We may define a "biography" as a collection of events such that, of any two, either they overlap or there is one that wholly precedes the other. For the present I shall assume that, when a biography has a psychological definition, it also has a physical definition—i.e. the time-series constituted out of events that I experience is identical with the time-series constructed out of events that happen to my brain, or some part of it. Accordingly, I shall speak of the "biography" of a piece of matter, not only of the "biography" connected with some person's experience.

What has been said so far can now be summed up in a series of definitions.

An "event" is something which precedes or follows or overlaps something.

The "biography" to which an event belongs is all the events that it precedes or follows or overlaps.

An "instant" is a collection of events belonging to one biography, and having the two properties that (a) any two events in the collection overlap, (b) no event outside the collection overlaps with *all* the members of the collection.

An event is said to "exist at" an instant if it is a member of that instant.

One instant is said to be "earlier" than another if there is an event at the one which wholly precedes some event at the other.

---

[1] "My" time in the above sense is not to be confused with the subjective time of Part III, Chapter V.

A "time-series of a given instant" is a series of instants, of which the given instant is one, and having the property that, of any two, one is earlier than the other.

A "time-series" is a time-series of some instant.

It is not assumed that an instant can only belong to one time-series, nor that an event can only belong to one biography. But it is assumed that, if *a* wholly precedes *b*, then *a* and *b* are not identical. This is an assumption which we shall have to examine, and perhaps modify, at a later stage.

As the above construction of time-series is the simplest example of a kind of procedure which will be frequently employed, I shall spend a few moments in setting forth the reasons for its adoption.

We start from the fact that, although physicists reject Newton's absolute time, they continue to employ the independent variable *t*, of which the values are said to be "instants". The values of *t* are held to form a series ordered by a relation called "earlier-and-later". It is held also that there are occurrences called "events", which include as a sub-class everything that we can observe. There are two observable temporal relations among events: they may overlap, as when I hear a clock striking while I see its hands pointing to twelve o'clock; or one may precede another, as when I still remember the previous stroke of the clock while I am hearing the present stroke. These are the data of our problem.

Now if we are to use the variable *t* without assuming Newton's absolute time, we must find a way of *defining* the class of values of *t*, that is to say, "instants" must not form part of our minimum vocabulary, which, so far as it is not merely that of logic, must consist of words whose meaning is known by experience.

Definitions are of two sorts, which may be called respectively "denotational" and "structural". An example of a denotational definition is "the tallest man in the United States". This is certainly a definition, since there must be one and only one person to whom it applies, but it defines the man merely by his relations. Generally, a "denotational" definition is one which defines an entity as the only one having a certain relation, or certain relations, to one or more known entities. On the other hand, when what we want to define is a structure composed of known elements, we can define it by mentioning the elements and the relations constituting the structure; this is what I call a "structural" definition. If what I am defining is a class, it may be only necessary to mention the structure, since the elements may be irrelevant. For example, I can define an "octagon" as "a plane figure having eight sides"; this is a structural definition. But I might also define it as "a polygon of which all known examples are in the following places", then giving a list. This would be a "denotational" definition.

A denotational definition is not complete without a proof of the existence of the object denoted. "The man over 10 feet tall" is, in logical form, just as good as "the tallest man in the United States", but it probably denotes no one. "The square root of 2" is a denotational definition, but until our own day there was no proof that it denoted anything; now we know that it is equivalent to the structural definition "the class of those rationals whose squares are less than 2", and thereby the question of "existence" (in the logical sense) is solved. Owing to the possible doubt about "existence", denotational definitions are often unsatisfactory.

In the particular case of our variable t, a denotational definition is excluded by our rejection of absolute time. We must therefore seek a structural definition. This implies that instants must have a structure, and that the structure must be built out of known elements. We have, as data of experience, the relations "overlapping" and "preceding", and we find that by means of these we can build structures having the formal properties that mathematical physicists demand of "instants". Such structures, therefore, fulfil all required purposes without the need of any *ad hoc* assumption. This is the justification of our definitions.

Chapter VI

SPACE IN CLASSICAL PHYSICS

IN this chapter we shall be concerned with space as it appears in classical physics. That is to say, we shall be concerned to find an "interpretation" (not necessarily the only possible one) for the geometrical terms used in physics. Much more complicated and difficult problems arise in regard to space than in regard to time. This is partly because of problems introduced by relativity. For the present, however, we will ignore relativity, and treat space as separable from time after the manner of pre-Einsteinian physics.

For Newton, space, like time, was "absolute", that is to say, it consisted of a collection of points, each devoid of structure, and each one of the ultimate constituents of the physical world. Each point was everlasting and unchanging; change consisted in its being "occupied" sometimes by one piece of matter, sometimes by another, and sometimes by nothing. As against this view, Leibniz contended that space was only a system of relations, the terms of the relations being material and not merely geometrical points. Although both physicists and philosophers tended more and more to take Leibniz's view rather than Newton's, the technique of mathematical physics continued to be Newtonian. In the mathematical apparatus, "space" is still an assemblage of "points", each defined by three co-ordinates, and "matter" is an assemblage of "particles", each of which occupies different points at different times. If we are not to agree with Newton in ascribing physical reality to points, this system requires some interpretation in which "points" have a structural definition.

I have used the word "physical reality", which may be held to savour too much of metaphysics. What I mean can be expressed, in a form more acceptable to modern taste, by means of the technique of minimum vocabularies. Given a collection of names, it may happen that some of the things named have a structural definition in terms of others; in that case, there will be a minimum vocabulary not containing the names for which definitions can be substituted. For example, every French human being has a proper name, and "the French nation" may also be regarded as a proper name, but it is an unnecessary one, since we can say: "the French nation" is defined as "the class consisting of the following individuals (here follows the list)". Such a method is only applicable to finite classes, but there are other methods not subject to this limitation. We can define "France" by its geographical boundaries, and then define "French" as "born in France".

To this process of substituting structural definitions for names there are obviously limits in practice, and perhaps (though this may be questioned) there are also limits in theory. Assuming, for the sake of simplicity, that matter consists of electrons and protons, we could, in theory, give a proper name to each electron and each proton; we could then define an individual human being by mentioning the electrons and protons composing his body at various times; thus names for individual human beings are theoretically superfluous. Speaking generally, whatever has a discoverable structure does not need a name, since it can be defined in terms of the names of its ingredients and the words for their relations. On the other hand, whatever has no known structure needs a name if we are to be able to express all our knowledge concerning it.

It is to be observed that a denotational definition does not make a name superfluous. E.g. "the father of Alexander the Great" is a denotational definition, but does not enable us to express the fact which contemporaries could have expressed by "that is Alexander's father", where "that" functions as a name.

When we deny Newton's theory of absolute space, while continuing to use what we call "points" in mathematical physics, our procedure is only justified if there is a structural definition of "point" and (in theory) of particular points. Such a definition must proceed by methods similar to those that we employed in defining "instants". This, however, is subject to two provisos: first, that our manifold of points is to be three-dimensional, and second, that we have to define a point at an instant. To say that a point P at one time is identical with a point Q at another time is to say something which has no definite meaning except a conventional one which depends upon a choice of material axes. As this matter has to do with relativity, I shall not consider it further at present, but shall confine myself to the definition of points at a given instant, ignoring the difficulties connected with the definition of simultaneity.

In what follows I lay no stress on the particular method of constructing points that I have adopted. Other methods are possible, and some of these may be preferred. What is important is only that such methods can be devised. In defining instants, we used the relation of "overlapping" in a temporal sense—a relation which holds between two events when (in ordinary language) there is a time during which both exist. In defining points, we use the relation of "overlapping" in a spatial sense, which is to subsist between two simultaneous events that (in ordinary language) occupy the same region of space, in whole or in part. It is to be observed that events, unlike pieces of matter, are not to be thought of as mutually impenetrable. The impenetrability of matter is a property which results tautologically from its definition. "Events", however, are only defined as terms not assumed to possess a structure, and having spatial and temporal relations such as belong to finite volumes and finite periods of time. When I say "such as", I mean "similar as regards logical properties". But "overlapping" is not itself to be defined logically; it is an empirically known relation, having, in the construction which I advocate, only an ostensive definition.

In a manifold of more than one dimension, we cannot construct anything having the properties required of "points" by means of a two-term relation of "overlapping". As the simplest illustration, let us take areas on a plane. Three areas A, B, C, on a plane may each overlap with the other two, without there being any region common to all three. In the accompanying figure, the circle A overlaps with the rectangle B and the triangle C, and B overlaps with C, but there is no region common to A and B and C. The basis of our construction will have to be a relation of *three* areas, not of two. We shall say that three areas are "copunctual" when there is a region common to all three. (This is an explanation, not a definition.)

We shall assume that the areas with which we are concerned are all either circles, or such shapes as can result from circles by stretching or compressing in a manner which leaves them oval. In that case, given three areas A, B, C which are copunctual, and a fourth area D such that A, B, D are copunctual and also A, C, D and B, C, D, then A, B, C, D all have a common region.

We now define a group of any number of areas as "copunctual" if every triad chosen out of the group is copunctual. A copunctual group of areas is a "point" if it cannot be enlarged without ceasing to be copunctual, i.e. if, given any area X outside the group, there are in the group at least two areas A and B such that A, B, X are not copunctual.

This definition is only applicable in two dimensions. In three dimensions, we must start with a relation of copunctuality between *four* volumes, and the volumes concerned must all be either spheres or such oval volumes as can result from spheres by continuous stretching in some directions and compressing in others. Then, as before, a copunctual group of volumes is one in which every four are copunctual, and a copunctual group is a "point" if it cannot be enlarged without ceasing to be copunctual.

In n dimensions the definitions are the same, except that the original relation of copunctuality has to be between $n + 1$ regions.

"Points" are defined as classes of events by the above methods, with the tacit assumption that every event "occupies" a more or less oval region.

"Events" are to be taken, in the present discussion, as the undefined raw material from which geometrical definitions are to be derived. In another context we may inquire as to what can be meant by an "event", and we may then be able to carry analysis a step further,[1] but for the present we regard the manifold of "events", with their spatial and temporal relations, as empirical data.

The way in which spatial order results from our assumptions is somewhat complicated. I shall say nothing about it here, as I have dealt with it in *Analysis of Matter*, where, also, there is a much fuller discussion of the definition of "points" (Chapters XXVIII and XXIX).

Something must be said about the metrical properties of space. Astronomers, in their popular books, astound us first by telling us how immensely distant many of the nebulae are, and then by telling us that after all the universe is finite, being a three-dimensional analogue of the surface of a sphere. But in their less

[1] See Part II, Chapter III and Part IV, Chapter IV.

popular books they tell us that measurement is merely conventional, and that we could, if we chose, adopt a convention which would make the furthest known nebula in the northern hemisphere nearer to us than the antipodes are. If so, the vastness of the universe is not a fact, but a convenience. I think this is only partially true, but to disentangle the element of convention in measurement is by no means easy. Before attempting it, something must be said about measurement in its elementary forms.

Measurement, even of the distance to remote nebulae, is built up from measurements of distances on the surface of the earth, and terrestrial measurements start with the assumption that certain bodies may be regarded as approximately rigid. If you measure the size of your room, you assume that your foot-rule is not growing appreciably longer or shorter during the process. The ordnance survey of England determines most distances by triangulation, but this process demands that there shall be at least one distance which is measured directly. In fact, a base line on Salisbury Plain was chosen, and was measured carefully in the elementary way in which we measure the size of our room: a chain, which we may take as by definition of unit length, was repeatedly applied to the surface of the earth along a line as nearly straight as possible. This one length having been determined directly, the rest proceeds by the measurement of angles and by calculation: the diameter of the earth, the distance of the sun and moon, and even the distances of the nearer fixed stars, can be determined without any further direct measurement of lengths.

But when this process is scrutinized it is found to be full of difficulties. The assumption that a body is "rigid" has no clear meaning until we have already established a metric enabling us to compare lengths and angles at one time with lengths and angles at another, for a "rigid" body is one which does not alter its shape or size. Then again we need a definition of a "straight line", for all our results will be wrong if the base line on Salisbury Plain and the lines used in triangulation are not straight. It seems, therefore, that measurement presupposes geometry (to enable us to define "straight lines") and enough physics to give grounds for regarding some bodies as approximately rigid, and for comparing distances at one time with distances at another. The difficulties involved are formidable, but are concealed by assumptions taken over from common sense.

Common sense assumes, roughly speaking, that a body *is* rigid if it *looks* rigid. Eels do not look rigid, but steel bars do. On the other hand, a pebble at the bottom of a rippling brook may look as wriggly as an eel, but common sense nevertheless holds it to be rigid, because common sense regards the sense of touch as more reliable than the sense of sight, and if you wade across the brook in bare feet the pebble *feels* rigid. Common sense, in so thinking, is Newtonian: it is convinced that at each moment a body intrinsically has a certain shape and size, which either are or are not the same as its shape and size at another moment. Given absolute space, this conviction has a meaning, but without absolute space it is *prima facie* meaningless. There must, however, be an interpretation of physics which will account for the very considerable measure of success resulting from common-sense assumptions.

As in the case of the measurement of time, three factors enter in: first, an assumption liable to correction; second, physical laws which, on this assumption, are found to be approximately true; third, a modification of the assumption to make the physical laws more nearly exact. If you assume that a certain steel rod, which looks and feels rigid, preserves its length unchanged, you will find that the distance from London to Edinburgh, the diameter of the earth, and the distance of Sirius, are all nearly constant, but are slightly less in warm weather than in cold. It will then occur to you that it will be simpler to say that your steel rod expands with heat, particularly when you find that this enables you to regard the above distances as almost exactly constant, and, further, that you can see the mercury in the thermometer taking up more space in warm weather. You therefore assume that apparently rigid bodies expand with heat, and you do so in order to simplify the statement of physical laws.

Let us get clear as to what is conventional and what is physical fact in this process. It is a physical fact that if two steel rods, neither of which feels either hot or cold, look as if they were of the same length, and if, then, you heat one by the fire and put the other in snow, when you first compare them again the one that has been by the fire looks slightly longer than the one that has been in the snow, but when both have again reached the temperature of your room this difference will have vanished. I am here assuming pre-scientific methods of estimating temperature: a hot body is one that feels hot, and a cold body is one that feels cold. As a result of such rough pre-scientific observations we decide that the thermometer gives an exact measure of something which is measured approximately by our feelings of heat and cold; we can then, as physicists, ignore these feelings and concentrate on the thermometer. It is then a tautology that *my* thermometer rises with an increase of temperature, but it is a substantial fact that all other thermometers likewise do so. This fact states a similarity between the behaviour of my thermometer and that of other bodies.

But the element of convention is not quite as I have just stated it. I do not assume that my thermometer is right by definition; on the contrary, it is universally agreed that every actual thermometer is more or less inaccurate. The ideal thermometer, to which actual thermometers only approximate, is one which, if taken as accurate, makes the general law of the expansion of bodies with rising temperature as exactly true as possible. It is an empirical fact that, by observing certain rules in making thermometers, we can make them approximate more and more closely to the ideal thermometer, and it is this fact which justifies the conception of temperature as a quantity having, for a given body at a given time, some exact value which is likely to be slightly different from that shown by any actual thermometer.

The process is the same in all physical measurements. Rough measurements lead to an approximate law; changes in the measuring instruments (subject to the rule that all instruments for measuring the same quantity must give as nearly as possible the same result) are found capable of making the law more nearly exact. The best instrument is held to be the one that makes the law most nearly exact, and it is assumed that an ideal instrument would make the law quite exact.

This statement, though it may seem complicated, is still not complicated enough. There is seldom only one law involved, and very often the law itself is only approximate. Measurements of different quantities are interdependent, as we have just seen in the case of length and temperature, so that a change in the way of measuring one quantity may alter the measure of another. Laws, conventions, and observations are almost inextricably intertwined in the actual procedure of science. The result of an observation is usually stated in a form which assumes certain laws and certain conventions; if the result contradicts the network of laws and conventions hitherto assumed, there may be considerable liberty of choice as to which should be modified. The stock instance is the Michelson-Morley experiment, where the simplest interpretation was found to involve a radical change in temporal and spatial measurements.

Let us now return to the measurement of distance. There are a number of rough pre-scientific observations which suggest the methods of measurement actually adopted. If you walk or bicycle along a level road with what feels like constant exertion, you will take roughly equal times for successive miles. If the road has to be tarred, the amount of material required for one mile will be about the same as that required for another. If you motor along the road, the time taken for each mile will be about what your speedometer would lead you to expect. If you base trigonometrical calculations on the assumption that successive miles are equal, the results will be in close agreement with those obtained directly by measurement. And so on. All this shows that the numbers obtained by the usual processes of measurement have considerable physical importance, and give a basis for many physical and physiological laws. But these laws, once formulated, give a basis for amending processes of measurement, and for regarding the result of the amended processes as more "accurate", though in fact they are only more convenient.

There is, however, one element in the notion of "accuracy" which is not merely convenient. We are accustomed to the axiom that things that are equal to the same thing are equal to one another. This axiom has a specious and deceptive appearance of obviousness, in spite of the fact that the empirical evidence is against it. You may find that, by the most delicate tests you can apply, A is equal to B, and B to C, but A is noticeably unequal to C. When this happens, we say that A is not *really* equal to B, or B to C. Oddly enough, this tends to be confirmed when the technique of measurement is improved. But the real basis of our belief in the axiom is not empirical. We believe that equality consists in possession of a common property. Two lengths are equal if they have the same *magnitude*, and it is this magnitude that we seek to express when we measure. If we are right in this belief, the axiom is logically necessary. If A and B have the same magnitude, and B and C have the same magnitude, then, of necessity, A and C have the same magnitude, provided that nothing has more than one magnitude.

Although this belief in a magnitude, as a property which several measurable things may have in common, obscurely influences common sense in its conceptions as to what is obvious, it is not a belief which we ought to accept until we have evidence of its truth in the particular subject-matter concerned. The belief that there is such a property of each of a set of terms is logically equivalent to the belief that there is a transitive symmetrical relation which holds between any two terms of the set. (This equivalence is what I formerly called the "principle of abstraction".) Thus in maintaining that there is a set of magnitudes called "distances", what we are maintaining is this: Between any one point-pair and any other, there is either a symmetrical transitive relation or an asymmetrical transitive relation. In the former case, we say that the distance between the one pair of points is equal to the distance between the other pair; in the latter case we say that the first distance is less or greater than the second, according to the sense of the relation. The distance between two points may be defined as the class of point-pairs having to it the relation of equidistance.

This is as far as we can carry the question of the measurement of distance without going into the question of the definition of straight lines, which we must now consider.

The straight line has its common-sense origin as an optical concept. Some lines look straight. If a straight rod is held, end on, against the eye, the part nearest the eye hides all the rest, whereas if the rod is crooked some of it will appear round the corner. There are of course also other common-sense reasons for the concept of straight lines. If a body is rotated, there is a straight line, the axis of rotation, which remains unmoved. If you are standing up in the Underground, you can tell when it goes round a curve by your tendency to overbalance one way or the other. It is also possible, up to a point, to judge straightness by the sense of touch; blind men become almost as good at judging shapes as men who can see.

In elementary geometry straight lines are defined as wholes; their chief characteristic is that a straight line is determinate as soon as two of its points are given. The possibility of regarding distance as a straightforward relation between two points depends upon the assumption that there are straight lines. But in the modern geometry developed to suit the needs of physics there are no straight lines in the Euclidean sense, and "distance" is only definite when the two points concerned are very close together. When the two points are far apart, we must first decide by what route we are to travel from the one to the other, and then add up the many small distances along the route. The "straightest" line between the two is the one that makes this sum a minimum. Instead of straight lines we have to use "geodesics", which are routes from one point to another that are shorter than any slightly different routes. This destroys the simplicity of the measurement of distances, which becomes dependent upon physical laws. The resulting complications in the theory of geometrical measurement cannot be dealt with without examining more closely the connection of physical laws with the geometry of physical space.

Chapter VII

SPACE-TIME

EVERYBODY knows that Einstein substituted space-time for space and time, but people unfamiliar with mathematical physics have usually only a very vague conception as to the nature of the change. As it is an important change in relation to our attempts to conceive the structure of the world, I shall try, in this chapter, to explain those parts of it that have philosophical importance.

Perhaps the best starting-point is the discovery that "simultaneity" is ambiguous when applied to events in different places. Experiments, especially the Michelson-Morley experiment, led to the conclusion that the velocity of light is the same for all observers, however they may be moving. This seemed, at first sight, to be a logical impossibility. If you are in a train which is moving at 30 miles an hour, and you are passed by a train which is moving at 60 miles an hour, its speed relatively to you will be 30 miles an hour. But if it is moving with the velocity of light, its speed relatively to you will be the same as its speed relatively to fixed points on the earth. Beta particles sometimes move with speeds up to 90 per cent of the velocity of light, but if a physicist could move with such a particle, and be passed by a light-ray, he would still judge that the light was moving, relatively to him, at the same rate as if he were at rest in relation to the earth. This paradox is explained by the fact that different observers, all equipped with perfect chronometers, will form different estimates of time-intervals and different judgments as to simultaneity in different places.

It is not difficult to see the necessity for such differences when once it has been pointed out. Suppose an astronomer observes an event in the sun, and notes the time of his observation; he will infer that the event happened about eight minutes before his observation, since that is the length of time that it takes light to travel from the sun to the earth. But now suppose that the earth were travelling very fast towards the sun or away from it. Unless you already knew at what moment, by terrestrial time, the event on the sun took place, you would not know how far the light had

had to travel, and therefore your observation would not enable you to know when the event in the sun had taken place. That is to say, there would be no definite answer to the question: what events on earth were simultaneous with the solar event that you had observed?

From the ambiguity of simultaneity it follows that there is a parallel ambiguity in the conception of distance. If two bodies are in relative motion, their distance apart is continually changing, and in pre-relativity physics there was supposed to be such a quantity as their "distance at a given instant". But if there is ambiguity as to what is the same instant for the two bodies, there is also ambiguity as to "distance at a given instant". One observer will form one estimate, and another will form another, and there is no reason to prefer either estimate. In fact, neither time-intervals nor spatial distances are facts independent of the movements of the observer's body. There is a kind of subjectivity about measurements of time and space separately—not a psychological but a physical subjectivity, since it affects instruments, not only mental observers. It is like the subjectivity of the camera, which takes a photograph from a certain point of view. Photographs from other points of view would look different, and no one among them would have a claim to special accuracy.

There is, however, one relation between two events which is the same for all observers. Formerly there were two, distance in space and lapse of time, but now there is only one, which is called "interval". It is because there is only this one relation of interval, instead of distance and lapse of time, that we have to substitute the one concept of space-time for the two concepts of space and time. But although we can no longer separate space and time, there are still two kinds of interval, one space-like and the other time-like. The interval is space-like if a light-signal, sent out by the body on which one event occurs, reaches the body on which the other event occurs after this other event has taken place. (It is to be observed that there is no ambiguity about the time-order of events on a given body.) It is time-like if a light-signal sent out from one event reaches the body on which the other event occurs before this other event has taken place. Since nothing travels faster than light, we may say that the interval is time-like when one event may have an effect upon the other, or upon something in the same space-time region as the other; when this is not possible, the interval is space-like.

In the special theory of relativity the definition of "interval" is simple; in the general theory it is more complicated.

In the special theory, suppose that an observer, treating himself as motionless, judges the distance between two events to be r, and the lapse of time between them to be t. Then if c is the velocity of light, the square of the interval is

$$c^2\,t^2 - r^2$$

if it is time-like, while if it is space-like it is

$$r^2 - c^2\,t^2$$

It is usually simpler technically to take it as always one of these, in which case the square of the other sort of interval is negative, and the interval is imaginary.

When neither gravitation nor electromagnetic forces are involved, it is found that the interval, as above defined, is the same for all observers, and may therefore be regarded as a genuine physical relation between the two events.

The general theory of relativity removes the above restriction by introducing a modified definition of "interval".

In the general theory of relativity there is no longer a definite "interval" between distant events, but only between events that are very near together. At a great distance from matter the formula for interval approximates to that in the special theory, but elsewhere the formula varies according to the nearness of matter. It is found that the formula can be so adjusted as to account for gravitation, assuming that matter which is moving freely moves in a geodesic, i.e. chooses the shortest or longest route from any one point to a neighbouring point.

It is assumed that, independently of interval, space-time points have an order, so that, along any route, one point can be between two others which are near it. For example, the interval between two different points on one light-ray is zero, but the points still have a temporal order: if a ray travels outward from the sun, the parts near the sun are earlier than the parts farther from it. The space-time order of events is presupposed in the assignment of co-ordinates, for although this is to a great extent conventional it must always be such that neighbouring points have co-ordinates that do not differ much, and that, as points approach closer to each other, the difference between their co-ordinates approaches zero as a limit.

If the physical world is held to consist of a four-dimensional manifold of events, instead of a manifold of persistent moving particles, it becomes necessary to find a way of defining what is meant when we say that two events are part of the history of one and the same piece of matter. Until we have such a definition, "motion" has no definite meaning, since it consists in one thing being in different places at different times. We must define a "particle", or material point, as a series of space-time points having to each other a causal relation which they do not have to other space-time points. There is no difficulty of principle about this procedure. Dynamical laws are habitually stated on the assumption that there are persistent particles, and are used to decide whether two events A and B belong to the biography of one particle or not. We merely retain the laws, and turn the statement that A and B belong to the same biography into a definition of a "biography", whereas before it seemed to be a substantial assertion.

This point perhaps needs some further explanation. Starting from the assumption that there are persistent pieces of matter, we arrive at physical laws connecting what happens to a piece of matter at one time with what happens to it at another. (The most obvious of such laws is the law of inertia.) We now state these laws in a different way: we say that, given an event of a certain kind in a certain small region of space-time, there will be neighbouring events in neighbouring regions which will be related to the given event in certain specific ways. We say that a series of events related to each other in these specific ways is to be called one piece of matter at different times. Thus matter and motion cease to be part of the fundamental apparatus of physics. What is fundamental is the four-dimensional manifold of events, with various kinds of causal relations. There will be relations making us regard the events concerned as belonging to one piece of matter, others making us regard them as belonging to different but interacting pieces of matter, others relating a piece of matter to its "empty" environment (e.g. emission of light), and yet others relating events that are both in empty space, e.g. parts of one light-ray.

The collecting of events into series such as will secure the persistence of matter is only partially and approximately possible. When an atom is pictured as a nucleus with planetary electrons, we cannot say, after a quantum transition, that such-and-such an electron in the new state is to be identified with such-and-such an electron in the old state. We do not even know for certain that the number of electrons in the universe is constant. Mass is only a form of energy, and there is no reason why matter should not be dissolved into other forms of energy. It is energy, not matter, that is fundamental in physics. We do not define energy; we merely discover laws as to the changes in its distribution. And these laws are no longer such as to determine a unique result where atomic phenomena are concerned, though macroscopic occurrences remain statistically determinate with an enormously high degree of probability.

The continuity of space-time, which is technically assumed in physics, has nothing in its favour except technical convenience. It may be that the number of space-time points is finite, and that space-time has a granular structure, like a heap of sand. Provided the structure is fine enough, there will be no observable phenomenon to show that there is not continuity. Theoretically, there might be evidence against continuity, but there could never be conclusive evidence in its favour.

The theory of relativity does not affect the space and time of perception. My space and time, as known in perception, are correlated with those that, in physics, are appropriate to axes that move with my body. Relatively to axes tied to a given piece of matter, the old separation of space and time still holds; it is only when we compare two sets of axes in rapid relative motion that the problems arise which the theory of relativity solves. Since no two human beings have a relative velocity approaching that of light, comparison of their experiences will reveal no such discrepancies as would result if aeroplanes could move as fast as beta particles. In the psychological study of space and time, therefore, the theory of relativity may be ignored.

Chapter VIII

THE PRINCIPLE OF INDIVIDUATION

I SHALL discuss in this Chapter the modern form of a very old problem, much discussed by the scholastics, but still, in our day, far from being definitively solved. The problem, in its broadest and simplest terms, is this: "How shall we define the diversity which makes us count objects as two in a census?" We may put the same problem in words that look different, e.g. "what is meant by a 'particular'?" or "what sort of objects can have proper names?"

Three views have been influentially advocated.

First: a particular is constituted by qualities; when all its qualities have been enumerated, it is fully defined. This is the view of Leibniz.

Second: a particular is defined by its spatio-temporal position. This is the view of Thomas Aquinas as regards material substances.

Third: numerical diversity is ultimate and indefinable. This, I think, would be the view of most modern empiricists if they took the trouble to have a definite view.

The second of the above three theories is reducible to either the first or the third according to the way in which it is interpreted. If we take the Newtonian view, according to which there actually are points, then two different points are exactly alike in all their qualities, and their diversity must be that bare numerical diversity contemplated in the third theory. If, on the other hand, we take —as every one now does—a relational view of space, the second theory will have to say: "If A and B differ in spatio-temporal position, then A and B are two". But here there are difficulties. Suppose A is a shade of colour: it may occur in a number of places and yet be only one. Therefore our A and B must not be qualities, or, if they are, they must be qualities that never recur. If they are not qualities or bundles of qualities, they must be particulars of the sort contemplated in our third theory; if they are qualities or bundles of qualities, it is the first of our three theories that we are adopting. Our second theory, therefore, may be ignored.

The construction of points and instants in our three preceding

Chapters used "events" as its raw material. Various reasons, of which the theory of relativity has been the most influential, have made this procedure preferable to one which, like Newton's, allows "points", "instants", and "particles" as raw material. It has been assumed, in our constructions, that a single event may occupy a finite amount of space-time, that two events may overlap both in space and in time, and that no event can recur. That is to say, if A wholly precedes B, A and B are not identical. We assumed also that, if A wholly precedes B, and B wholly precedes C, then A wholly precedes C. "Events" were provisionally taken as "particulars" in the sense of our third theory. It was shown that, if a raw material of this sort is admitted, space-time points and space-time order can be constructed.

But we are now concerned with the problem of constructing space-time points and space-time order when our first theory is adopted. Our raw material will now contain nothing that *cannot* recur, for a quality can occur in any number of separate places. We have therefore to *construct* something that *does not* recur, and until we have done so we cannot explain space-time order.

We have to ask ourselves: what is meant by an "instance"? Take some definite shade of colour, which we will call "C". Let us assume that it is a shade of one of the colours of the rainbow, so that it occurs wherever there is a rainbow or a solar spectrum. On each occasion of its occurrence, we say that there is an "instance" of C. Is each instance an unanalysable particular, of which C is a quality? Or is each instance a complex of qualities of which C is one? The former is the third of the above theories; the latter is the first.

There are difficulties in either view. Taking first the view that an instance of C is an unanalysable particular, we find that we encounter all the familiar difficulties connected with the traditional notion of "substance". The particular cannot be defined or recognized or known; it is something serving the merely grammatical purpose of providing the subject in a subject-predicate sentence such as "this is red". And to allow grammar to dictate our metaphysic is now generally recognized to be dangerous.

It is difficult to see how something so unknowable as such a particular would have to be can be required for the interpretation of empirical knowledge. The notion of a substance as a peg on which to hang predicates is repugnant, but the theory that we have been considering cannot avoid its objectionable features. I conclude, therefore, that we must, if possible, find some other way of defining space-time order.

But when we abandon particulars in the sense which we have just decided to reject, we are faced, as observed above, with the difficulty of finding something that will not be repeated. A simple quality, such as the shade of colour C, cannot be expected to occur only once. We shall seek to escape this difficulty by considering a "complex" of qualities. What I mean will be most easily understood if stated in psychological terms. If I see something and at the same time hear something else, my visual and auditory experiences have a relation which I call "compresence". If at the same moment I am remembering something that happened yesterday and anticipating with dread a forthcoming visit to the dentist, my remembering and anticipating are also "compresent" with my seeing and hearing. We can go on to form the whole group of my present experiences and of everything compresent with all of them. That is to say, given any group of experiences which are all compresent, if I can find anything else which is compresent with all of them I add it to the group, and I go on until there is nothing further which is compresent with each and all of the members of the group. I thus arrive at a group having the two properties: (a) that all the members of the group are compresent, (b) that nothing outside the group is compresent with every member of the group. Such a group I shall call a "complete complex of compresence".

Such a complex I suppose to consist of constituents most of which, in the natural course of events, may be expected to be members of many other complexes. The shade of colour C, we supposed, recurs every time anybody sees a rainbow distinctly. My recollection may be qualitatively indistinguishable from a recollection that I had yesterday. My apprehension of dental pain may be just what I felt before my last visit to the dentist. All these items of the complex of compresence may occur frequently, and are not essentially dated. That is to say, if A is one of them, and A precedes (or follows) B, we have no reason to suppose that A and B are not identical.

Have we any reason, either logical or empirical, to believe that a complete complex of compresence, as a whole, cannot be repeated? Let us, in the first place, confine ourselves to one person's experience. My visual field is very complex, though probably not infinitely complex. Every time I move my eyes, the visual qualities connected with a given object which remains visible undergo changes: what I see out of the corner of my eyes looks different from what is in the centre of my field of vision. If it is true, as some maintain, that my memory is coloured by my whole past experience, then it follows logically that my total recollections cannot be exactly similar on two different occasions; even if we reject this doctrine, such exact similarity seems very improbable.

From such considerations I think we ought to conclude that the exact repetition of my total momentary experience, which is what, in this connection, I call a "complete complex of compresence", is not logically impossible, but is empirically so exceedingly improbable that we may assume its non-occurrence. In that case, a complete complex of compresence will, so far as one person's experience is concerned, have the formal properties required of "events", i.e.: if A, B, C are complete complexes of compresence, then if A wholly precedes B, A and B are not identical; and if B also wholly precedes C, then A wholly precedes C. We thus have the requisites for defining the time-order in one person's experience.

This, however, is only part, and not the most difficult part, of what we have to accomplish. We have to extend space-time order beyond one person's experience to the experiences of different people and to the physical world. In regard to the physical world, especially, this is difficult.

So long as we confine ourselves to one person's experience, we need only concern ourselves with time. But now we have also to take account of space. That is to say, we have to find a definition of "events" which shall insure that each event has, not merely a unique temporal position, but a unique spatio-temporal position.

So long as we confine ourselves to experiences, there is no fresh difficulty of a serious kind. It may be taken as virtually certain, on empirical grounds, that my visual field, whenever my eyes are open, is not exactly similar to that of any one else. If A and B are looking simultaneously at the same scene, there are differences of perspective; if they change places, A will not see exactly what B was seeing, because of differences of eyesight, changes of lighting meanwhile, and so on. In short, the reasons for supposing that no total momentary experience of A is ever exactly like some total momentary experience of B are of the same kind as the reasons for supposing that no two total momentary experiences of A are ever exactly alike.

This being granted, we can establish a spatial order among percipients by means of the laws of perspective, provided there is any physical object that all the percipients concerned are perceiving. If there is not, a process by means of intermediate links can reach the same result. There are of course complications and difficulties, but they are not such as concern our subject at all closely, and we may safely ignore them.

What can be said about the purely physical world is hypothetical, since physics gives no information except as to structure. But there are reasons for supposing that, at every place in physical space-time, there is at every moment a multiplicity of occurrences, just as there is in a mind. "Compresence", which I take to have a merely ostensive definition, appears in psychology as "simultaneity in one experience", but in physics as "overlapping in space-time". If, as I maintain, my thoughts are in my head, it is obvious that these are different aspects of one relation. However, this identification is inessential to my present argument.

When I look at the stars on a clear night, each star that I see has an effect on me, and has an effect on the eye before it has an effect on the mind. It follows that, at the surface of the eye, something causally connected with each visible star is happening. The same considerations apply to ordinary objects seen in daylight. At this moment I can see white pages covered with writing, some books, an oval table, innumerable chimneys, green trees, clouds, and blue sky. I can see these things because there is a chain of physical causation from them to my eyes and thence to the brain. It follows that what is going on at the surface of my eye is as complex as my visual field, in fact as complex as the whole of what I can see. This complexity must be physical, not merely physiological or psychological; the optic nerve could not make the complex responses that it does make except under the influence of equally complex stimuli. We must hold that, wherever the light of a certain star penetrates, something connected with that star is happening. Therefore in a place where a telescope photographs many millions of stars, many millions of things must be happening, each connected with its own star.

These things are only "experienced" in places where there is a recording nervous system, but that they happen in other places also can be shown by cameras and dictaphones. There is therefore no difficulty of principle in constructing "complexes of compresence", where there are no percipients, on the same principles as we employed in dealing with momentary experiences.

Abandoning speculations about the physical world, about which our knowledge is very limited, let us return to the world of experience. The view which I am suggesting, as preferable to the assumption of such wholly colourless particulars as points of space or particles of matter, may be expressed as follows:

There is a relation, which I call "compresence", which holds between two or more qualities when one person experiences them simultaneously—for example, between high C and vermilion when you hear one and see the other. We can form groups of qualities having the following two properties: (a) all members of the group are compresent; (b) given anything not a member of the group, there is at least one member of the group with which it is not compresent. Any one such complete group of compresent qualities constitutes a single complex whole, defined when its constituents are given, but itself a unit, not a class. That is to say, it is something which exists, not merely because its constituents exist, but because, in virtue of being compresent, they constitute a single structure. One such structure, when composed of mental constituents, may be called a "total momentary experience".

Total momentary experiences, as opposed to qualities, have time relations possessing the desired characteristics. I can see blue yesterday, red to-day, and blue again to-morrow. Therefore, so far as qualities are concerned, blue is before red and red is before blue, while blue, since it occurs yesterday and to-morrow, is before itself. We cannot therefore construct, out of qualities alone, such a relation as will generate a series. But out of total momentary experiences we can do this, provided no total momentary experience ever exactly recurs. That this does not happen is an empirical proposition, but, so far as our experience goes, a well-grounded one. I regard it as a merit in the above theory that it gets rid of what would otherwise be synthetic *a priori* knowledge. That, if A precedes B, B does not precede A, and that, if A precedes B and B precedes C, then A precedes C, are synthetic propositions; moreover, as we have just seen, they are not true if A and B and C are qualities. By making such statements (in so far as they are true) empirical generalizations, we overcome what would otherwise be a grave difficulty in the theory of knowledge.

I come back now to the conception of "instance". An "instance" of a quality, as I wish to use the word, is a complex of compresent qualities of which the quality in question is one. In some cases this view seems natural. An instance of "man" has other qualities besides humanity: he is white or black, French or English, wise or foolish, and so on. His passport enumerates enough of his characteristics to distinguish him from the rest of the human race. Each of these characteristics, presumably, exists in many other instances. There are baby giraffes who have the height mentioned in his passport, and parrots who have the same birthday as he has. It is only the assemblage of qualities that makes the instance unique. Every man, in fact, is defined by such an assemblage of qualities, of which humanity is only one.

But when we come to points of space, instants of time, particles of matter, and such stock-in-trade of abstract science, we feel as if a particular could be a "mere" instance, differentiated from other instances by relations, not by qualities. To some degree, we think this of less abstract objects: we say "as like as two peas", suggesting that between two peas there are no qualitative differences. We think also that two patches of colour may be *merely* two, and may differ only numerically. This way of thinking, I maintain, is a mistake. I should say that, when the same shade of colour exists in two places at once, it is one, not two; there are, however, two complexes, in which the shade of colour is combined with the qualities that give position in the visual field. People have become so obsessed with the relativity of spatial position in physics that they have become oblivious of the absoluteness of spatial position in the visual field. At every moment, what is in the centre óf my field of vision has a quality that may be called "centrality"; what is to the right is "dexter", what to the left "sinister", what above "superior", what below "inferior". These are *qualities* of the visual datum, not relations. It is the complex consisting of one such quality combined with a shade of colour that is distinct from the complex consisting of the same shade elsewhere. In short, the multiplicity of instances of a given shade of colour is formed exactly as the multiplicity of instances of humanity is formed, namely by the addition of other qualities.

As for points, instants, and particles, in so far as they are not logical fictions similar considerations apply. Take first instants. It will be found that what I call a "total momentary experience" has all the formal properties required of an "instant" in my biography. And it will be found that, where there is only matter, the "complete complex of compresence" may serve to define an instant of Einsteinian local time, or to define a "point-instant" in cosmic space-time. Points in perceptual space are defined without any trouble, since the qualities of up-and-down, right-and-left, in their various degrees, have already all the properties that we require of "points". It is indeed this fact, together with perception of depth, that has led us to place such emphasis on the spatial characteristics of the world.

I do not think "particles" can be dealt with quite in the above manner. In any case, they are no longer part of the fundamental apparatus of physics. They are, I should say, strings of events interconnected by the law of inertia. They are no longer indestructible, and have become merely convenient approximations.

I come now to a possible objection to the above theory, which was advanced by Arnauld against Leibniz. If a "particular" is really a complex of qualities, then the statement that such-and-such a particular has such-and-such a quality must, when true, be analytic; at least, so it would seem. Leibniz held (1) that every proposition has a subject and a predicate; (2) that a substance is defined by the total of its predicates; (3) that the soul is a substance. It followed that everything that can be truly said of a given soul consists in mentioning some predicate which is one of those that constitute the given soul. "Cæsar", for example, was a collection of predicates, one of which was "crossing the Rubicon". He was therefore compelled by logic to cross the Rubicon, and there is no such thing as contingency or free will. Leibniz ought, on this point, to have agreed with Spinoza, but he chose not to, for reasons discreditable either to his intellect or to his moral character. The question is: Can I avoid agreeing with Spinoza without equal discredit?

What we have to consider is a subject-predicate proposition expressing a judgment of perception, such as "this is red". What is "this"? Clearly it is not my whole momentary experience; I am not saying "one of the qualities that I am at present experiencing is "redness". The word "this" may be accompanied by a gesture, indicating that I mean what is in a certain direction, say the centre of my visual field. In that case, the core of what I am saying may be expressed by "centrality and redness overlap spatially in my present visual field". It is to be observed that, within the large complex of my total momentary experience, there are smaller complexes constituted by spatial compresence in perceptual space. Whatever quality I see in a certain direction has perceptual-spatial compresence with the visual quality constituting that direction. It would seem that the word "this", accompanied by a gesture, is equivalent to a description, e.g. "what is occupying the centre of my visual field". To say that this description applies to redness is to say something which clearly is not analytic. But since it employs a description instead of a name, it is not quite what we set out to consider.

We were considering what sort of thing could have the formal properties that are required for space-time order. Such a thing must happen in only one time and place; it must not recur, either on another occasion or in another location. So far as time and physical space are concerned, these conditions are satisfied by the "complete complex of compresence", whether this consists of my momentary experiences or of a full group of overlapping physical qualities. (I call such a group "full" when, if anything is added, the members will no longer be all compresent.) But when we come to consider perceptual space, we have no need of an analogous procedure. If I see simultaneously two patches of a given shade of colour, they differ as regards the qualities of up-and-down, right-and-left, and it is by means of these qualities that the patches acquire particularity.

With these preliminaries, let us examine the question of proper names.

It seems preposterous to maintain that "Cæsar crossed the Rubicon" is an analytic proposition. But if it is not, what do we mean by "Cæsar"?

Taking Cæsar as he was, without the limitations due to our ignorance, we may say that he was a series of events, each event being a momentary total experience. If we were to define "Cæsar" by enumerating these events, the crossing of the Rubicon would

THE PRINCIPLE OF INDIVIDUATION

have to come in our list, and "Cæsar crossed the Rubicon" would be analytic. But in fact we do not define "Cæsar" in this way, and we cannot do so, since we do not know all his experiences. What happens in fact is more like this: Certain series of experiences have certain characteristics which make us call such a series a "person". Every person has a number of characteristics that are peculiar to him; Cæsar, for example, had the name "Julius Cæsar". Suppose P is some property which has belonged to only one person; then we can say: "I give the name 'A' to the person who had the property P". In this case, the name "A" is an abbreviation for "the person who had the property P". It is obvious that, if this person also had the property Q, the statement "A had the property Q" is not analytic unless Q is analytically a consequence of P.

This is all very well as regards a historical character, but how about somebody whom I know more intimately, e.g. myself? How about such a statement as "I am hot"? This may, following our earlier analysis, be translated into "heat is one of the qualities that make up I-now". Here "I-now" may be taken as denoting the same complex that is denoted by "my total present momentary experience". But the question remains: how do I know what is denoted by "I-now"? What is denoted is continually changing; on no two occasions can the denotation be the same. But clearly the words "I-now" have in some sense a constant meaning; they are fixed elements in the language. We cannot say that, in the ordinary sense, "I-now" is a name, like "Julius Cæsar", because to know what it denotes we must know when and by whom it is used. Nor has it any definable conceptual content, for that, equally, would not vary with each occasion when the phrase is used. Exactly the same problems arise in regard to the word "this".

But although "I-now" and "this" are not names in quite the ordinary sense, I incline to think that there is a sense in which they must count as names. A proper name, as opposed to a concealed description, can be given to the whole or to any part of what the speaker is at the moment experiencing. When our verbal inventiveness fails, we fall back on "this" for the part of our total momentary experience to which we are specially attending, and upon "I-now" for the total momentary experience. I maintain that I can perceive a complex of compresent qualities without necessarily perceiving all the constituent qualities. I can give the name "this" to such a complex, and then, by attention, observe that redness (say) is one of its constituent qualities. The resulting knowledge I express in the sentence "this is red", which, accordingly, is a judgment of analysis, but not, in the logical sense, an analytic judgment. A complex can be perceived without my being aware of all its parts; when, by attention, I become aware that it has such-and-such a part, this is a judgment of perception which analyses the whole, but is not analytic, because the whole was defined as "this", not as a complex of known parts.

The kind of thing I have in mind is the kind of thing that is emphasized by the Gestalt psychologists. Suppose I possessed a clock which showed not only hours and minutes, but the day of the month, the month of the year, and the year of the Christian era, and suppose that this clock were to function throughout my life. It would then never twice during my life present the same appearance. I might perceive that two appearances of it were different, without being able to say at once in what the difference consisted. Attention might lead me to say: "In this appearance the minute-hand is at the top; in that, it is at the bottom". Here "this" and "that" are merely names, and therefore nothing said about them can be logically analytic.

There is another way of escaping from the conclusion that judgments are analytic when in fact they are obviously empirical. Consider again our clock that never repeats itself. We can define a date unambiguously by means of this clock. Suppose that, when the clock indicates 10 hours 47 minutes on June 15, 1947, I say "I am hot". This can be translated into: "Hotness is compresent with the appearance of the clock that is described as 10 hours 47 minutes, June 15, 1947". This is certainly not analytic.

One way of making clear the scope and purport of our discussion is to put it in terms of "minimum vocabularies". We may ask: "What is, in principle, a minimum vocabulary for describing the world of my sensible experience?" We have to ask ourselves: Can I be content with names of qualities, and words for compresence and for spatial and temporal relations, or do I need also proper names? And in the latter case, what sorts of things will need proper names?

I have suggested that ordinary proper names, such as "Socrates", "France", or "the sun", apply to continuous portions of space-time which happen to interest us, and that space-time is composed of "complete complexes of compresence", which themselves are composed of qualities. According to this theory, an "instance" of (say) a shade of colour is a complex of which that shade is a constituent. The colour itself exists wherever (as we should commonly say) there is something that has that colour. Any collection of compresent qualities may be called a "complex of compresence", but it is only a "complete complex" when it cannot be enlarged without ceasing to be a complex of compresence. Often a complete complex can be rendered definite by mentioning only some of its components; e.g. in the above case of the clock, the complex is determined when we are told what appearance of the clock belongs to it. This is what makes dating convenient.

Subject-predicate propositions expressing judgments of perception occur in two ways. First: if a complex is rendered determinate when only some of its constituent qualities are assigned, we may state that this complex also has such-and-such other qualities; this is illustrated by the statement "I was hot when the clock said 10 hours 47 minutes".

Second: I may perceive a complex without being aware of all its parts; in that case, I may, by attention, arrive at a judgment of perception of the form "P is part of W", where "W" is the proper name of the perceived complex. If such judgments are admitted as irreducible, we need proper names for complexes. But it would seem that the need for such judgments only arises through ignorance, and that, with better knowledge, our whole W can always be described by means of its constituents. I think, therefore, though with some hesitation, that there is no theoretical need for proper names as opposed to names of qualities and of relations. Whatever is dated and located is complex, and the notion of simple "particulars" is a mistake.

As the subject of this Chapter is somewhat difficult, it will perhaps contribute to clarity and to the prevention of misunderstanding to repeat the main points of the above discussion more briefly and less controversially. Let us begin with "compresence".

"Compresence", as I wish to understand the term, applies to the physical world as well as to the world of mind. In the physical world it is equivalent to "overlapping in space-time", but this cannot be taken as its definition, since compresence is needed in defining spatio-temporal position. I wish to emphasize that the relation is to be the very same in physics as in psychology. Just as many things happen simultaneously in my mind, so, we must suppose, many things happen simultaneously in every place in space-time. When we look at the night sky, each star that we can see produces its separate effect, and this is only possible if, at the surface of the eye, things are happening that are connected with each visible star. These different things are all "compresent".

Wherever several things are compresent, they form what I shall call a "complex of compresence". If there are other things compresent with all of them, they can be added to form a larger complex. When it is no longer possible to find anything compresent with all the constituents of the complex, I call the complex "complete". Thus a "complete complex of compresence" is one whose constituents have the two properties (a) that all of them are compresent, (b) that nothing outside the group is compresent with every member of the group.

"I-now" denotes the complete complex of compresence which contains the present contents of my mind. "This" denotes whatever part of this complex I am specially noticing.

Complete complexes of compresence are the subjects of spatio-temporal relations in physical space-time. For empirical, not logical, reasons, it is highly probable that none of them recurs, i.e. that none of them precedes itself, or is north of itself, or west of itself, or above itself.

A complete complex of compresence counts as a space-time point-instant.

A complex which is not complete will, in general, be a part of various complete complexes; so will a single quality. A given shade of colour, for example, is part of every complete complex which is a space-time point at which this shade exists. To say of a quality or of an incomplete complex that it "exists at" such-and-such a space-time point is to say that it is part of the complete complex which is that point.

An incomplete complex occupies a continuous region in space-time if, given any two space-time points of which it is part, there is a continuous route, from the one to the other, consisting wholly of points of which the incomplete complex is part.

Such a complex may be called an "event". It has the property of non-recurrence, but not that of occupying only one space-time point.

The occupation of a continuous region by a given incomplete complex may be defined as follows. A complete complex B is said to be "between" two not too distant complete complexes A and C if what is common to A and C is part of B. A collection of complete complexes is "continuous" (for our purposes) if between any two of its members there are other members of the collection. This, however, is only a rough-and-ready definition; a precise definition could only be given by means of topology.

We can never know that a given complex of compresence is complete, since there may always be something else, of which we are not aware, which is compresent with every part of the given complex. This is another way of saying that we cannot, in practice, define a place or a date exactly.

Certain incomplete complexes have advantages from the point of view of dating. Take, for example, the date in to-day's news-paper together with a 24-hour clock which is going. These two together make a complex which never recurs, and of which the duration is so brief that for most purposes we do not need to notice that it is more than an instant. It is by means of such incomplete complexes that we in fact determine dates.

For determining spatial position, there are similar advantages in the ocular qualities of centrality, up-and-down, and right-and-left. These qualities are mutually exclusive as regards what may be called "private compresence", which is a relation between elements in one total momentary experience. The quality of centrality, for example, has "private compresence" with the colour which is occupying the centre of my visual field. The correlation of places in my private space with places in physical space proceeds on the assumption that, if visual percepts are not privately compresent, the corresponding physical objects are not publicly compresent, but if the visual percepts are privately compresent, the corresponding physical objects may differ in distance from the percipient, though they will agree approximately in direction. Thus private compresence of percepts is a necessary but not sufficient condition for public compresençe of the corresponding physical objects.

It is to be observed that, in general, every increase in the number of qualities combined in a complex of compresence diminishes the amount of space-time that it occupies. A complete complex of compresence will occupy a portion of space-time which has no parts that are portions of space-time; if we assume continuity, such a portion will have the properties that we expect of a point-instant. But there is no reason, either empirical or *a priori*, to suppose either that space-time is continuous, or that it is not; everything known can be explained equally well on either hypothesis. If it is not continuous, a finite number of complexes of compresence will occupy a finite space-time volume, and the structure of space-time will be granular, like that of a heap of shot.

A complex of compresence, as I conceive it, is determinate when the qualities constituting it are given. That is to say, if the qualities q_1, q_2, . . . q_n are all mutually compresent, there is just one complex of compresence, say C, which consists of the combination of these qualities. It is always logically possible for C to occur more than once, but I assume that, if C is sufficiently complex, there will not in fact be recurrence. A few words are necessary to explain what, logically, is meant by "recurrence". Let us, for simplicity, confine ourselves to time in one biography, and let us begin by considering complete complexes.

I assume that, between any two complete complexes belonging to the same biography, there is a relation of earlier-and-later. To suppose that a complete complex can recur is to suppose that a complete complex can have the relation of earlier-and-later to itself. This, I assume, does not happen, or at any rate does not happen within any ordinary period of time. I do not mean to deny dogmatically that history may be cyclic, as some Stoics thought, but the possibility is too remote to need to be taken into account.

Since we can never know that a known complex of compresence is complete—since, in fact, we can be pretty sure that it is not—we use, in practice, for purposes of chronology and geography, such incomplete complexes as either do not recur at all, or recur in a fairly regular manner. The date on a calendar persists for twenty-four hours, and then changes abruptly. Some clocks have a minute-hand that moves with a jerk once a minute; the appearance of such a clock persists for a minute and recurs every twelve hours. If we had sixty such clocks in a circle, and each gave its jerk one second after the one to the left of it, the complex consisting of the appearance of all the sixty would fix the time within one second. By such methods accuracy of dating may be indefinitely increased. Exactly similar remarks apply to methods of determining latitude and longitude.

A complex of compresence, though defined when all its constituent qualities are given, is not to be conceived, like a class, as a mere logical construction, but as something which can be known and named without our having to know all its constituent qualities. The logical point involved may be made clear as follows: the relation earlier-and-later holds, primarily, between two complete complexes of compresence, and only in a derivative and definable sense between partial complexes. In the case of a purely logical structure, a statement about the structure can be reduced to one about its components, but in the case of the time-order this is not possible on the theory of "particulars" adopted in this Chapter. A complex can, therefore, be mentioned in a way which is not reducible to a statement about any or all of its constituents. It is, in fact, the sort of object that is a "this", and that can have a proper name. A given collection of qualities only forms a complex of compresence if the qualities happen to be all mutually compresent; when they are, the complex is something new, over and above the qualities, though necessarily unique when the qualities are given.

According to the above theory, a complex of compresence which does not recur takes the place traditionally occupied by "particulars"; a single such complex, or a string of such complexes causally connected in a certain way, is the kind of object to which it is conventionally appropriate to give a proper name. But a complex of compresence is of the same logical type as a single quality, that is to say, any statement which is significant about either is significant, though probably not true, about the other.

We may agree with Leibniz to this extent, that only our ignorance makes names for complexes necessary. In theory, every complex of compresence can be defined by enumerating its component qualities. But in fact we can perceive a complex without perceiving all its component qualities; in this case, if we discover that a certain quality is a component of it, we need a name for the complex to express what it is that we have discovered. The need for proper names, therefore, is bound up with our way of acquiring knowledge, and would cease if our knowledge were complete.

Chapter IX

CAUSAL LAWS

THE practical utility of science depends upon its ability to foretell the future. When the atomic bombs were dropped, it was expected that large numbers of Japanese would die, and they did. Such highly satisfactory results have led, in our day, to an admiration of science, which is due to the pleasure we derive from the satisfaction of our lust for power. The most powerful communities are the most scientific, though it is not the men of science who wield the power conferred by their knowledge. On the contrary, the actual men of science are rapidly sinking into the position of state prisoners, condemned to slave labour by brutal masters, like subject djinns in the Arabian Nights. But we must not waste any more time upon such pleasant topics. The power of science is due to its discovery of causal laws, and it is causal laws that are to occupy us in this chapter.

A "causal law", as I shall use the term, may be defined as a general principle in virtue of which, given sufficient data about certain regions of space-time, it is possible to infer something about certain other regions of space-time. The inference may be only probable, but the probability must be considerably more than a half if the principle in question is to be considered worthy to be called a "causal law".

I have purposely made the above definition very wide. In the first place, the region to which we infer need not be later than those from which we infer. There are, it is true, some laws—notably the second law of thermodynamics—which allow inferences forwards more readily than backwards, but this is not a general characteristic of causal laws. In geology, for example, the inferences are almost all backwards. In the second place, we cannot lay down rules as to the number of data that may be involved in stating a law. If it should ever become possible to state the laws of embryology in terms of physics, enormously complex data would be required. In the third place, the inference may be only to some more or less general characteristic of the inferred event or events. In the days before Galileo it was known that unsupported heavy bodies fall, which was a causal law; but it was not known how fast they fall, so that when a weight was dropped it was impossible to say accurately where it would be after a given lapse of time. In the fourth place, if the law states a high degree of probability it may be almost as satisfactory as if it stated a certainty. I am not thinking of the probability of the law being true; causal laws, like the rest of our knowledge, may be mistaken. What I am thinking of is that some laws *state* probabilities, for example the statistical laws of quantum theory. Such laws, supposing them completely true, make inferred events only probable, but this does not prevent them from counting as causal laws according to the above definition.

One advantage of admitting laws which only confer probability is that it enables us to incorporate in science the crude generalizations from which common sense starts, such as "fire burns", "bread nourishes", "dogs bark", or "lions are fierce". All these are causal laws, and all are liable to exceptions, so that in a given case they confer only probability. The fire on a plum pudding does not burn you, poisoned bread does not nourish, some dogs are too lazy to bark, and some lions grow so fond of their keepers that they cease to be fierce. But in the great majority of cases the above generalizations will be a sound guide in action. There are a large number of such approximate regularities which are assumed in our every-day behaviour, and it is from them that the conception of causal laws arose. Scientific laws, it is true, are no longer so simple: they have become complicated in the endeavour to give them a form in which they are not liable to exceptions. But the old simpler laws remain valid so long as they are only regarded as asserting probabilities.

Causal laws are of two sorts, those concerned with persistence and those concerned with change. The former kind are often not regarded as causal, but this is a mistake. A good example of a law of persistence is the first law of motion. Another example is the persistence of matter. After the discovery of oxygen, when the process of combustion came to be understood, it was possible to regard all matter as indestructible. It has now become doubtful whether this is quite true, but it remains true for most practical purposes. What appears to be more exactly true is the persistence of energy. The gradual development of laws stating persistence started from the common-sense belief, based on pre-scientific experience, that most solid objects continue to exist until they crumble from old age or are destroyed by fire, and that, when this happens, it is possible to suppose that their small parts survive in a new arrangement. It was this pre-scientific point of view that gave rise to the belief in material substance.

Causal laws concerned with change were found by Galileo and Newton to demand statement in terms of acceleration, i.e. change of velocity in magnitude or direction or both. The greatest triumph of this point of view was the law of gravitation, according to which every particle of matter causes in every other an acceleration directly proportional to the mass of the attracting particle and inversely proportional to the square of the distance between them. But Einstein's form of the law of gravitation made it more analogous to the law of inertia, and, in a sense, a law of persistence rather than a law of change. According to Einstein, space-time is full of what we may call hills; each hill grows steeper as you go up, and has a piece of matter at the top. The result is that the easiest route from place to place is one which winds round the hills. The law of gravitation consists in the fact that bodies always take the easiest route, which is what is called a "geodesic". There is a law of cosmic laziness called the "principle of least action", which states that when a body moves from one place to another it will choose the route involving least work. By means of this principle gravitation is absorbed into the geometry of space-time.

The essential laws of change in modern physics are those of quantum theory, which govern transitions from one form of energy to another. An atom can emit energy in the form of light, which then travels on unchanged until it meets another atom, which may absorb the energy of the light. Such interchanges are governed by certain rules, which do not suffice to say what will happen on a given occasion, but can predict, with a very high degree of probability, the statistical distribution of possible happenings among a very large number of interchanges. This is as near as physics can get at present to the ultimate character of causal laws.

Everything that we believe ourselves to know about the physical world depends entirely upon the assumption that there are causal laws. Sensations, and what we optimistically call "perceptions", are events in us. We do not actually see physical objects, any more than we hear electromagnetic waves when we listen to the wireless. What we directly experience might be all that exists, if we did not have reason to believe that our sensations have external causes. It is important, therefore, to inquire into our belief in causation. Is it mere superstitition, or has it a solid foundation?

The question of the justification of our belief in causality belongs to theory of knowledge, and I shall therefore postpone it for the present. My purpose in this Part is the interpretation of science, not an inquiry into the grounds for supposing science valid. Science assumes causality in some sense, and our present question is: in what sense is causality involved in scientific method?[1]

Broadly speaking, scientific method consists in inventing hypotheses which fit the data, which are as simple as is compatible with this requirement, and which make it possible to draw inferences subsequently confirmed by observation. The theory of probability shows that the validity of this process depends upon an assumption which may be roughly stated as the postulate that there are general laws of certain kinds. This postulate, in a suitable form, can make scientific laws probable, but without it they do not even achieve probability. We have therefore to examine this assumption, to find out the most plausible form in which it is both effective and possibly true.

If there is no limit to the complexity of possible laws, every imaginable course of events will be subject to laws, and therefore the assumption that there are laws will become a tautology. Take, for example, the numbers of all the taxis that I have hired in the course of my life, and the times when I have hired them. We have here a finite set of integers and a finite number of corresponding times. If n is the number of the taxi that I hired at the time t, it is certainly possible, in an infinite number of ways, to find a function f such that the formula

$$n = f(t)$$

is true for all the values of n and t that have hitherto occurred. An infinite number of these formulae will fail for the next taxi that I hire, but there will still be an infinite number that remain true. By the time I die, it will be possible to close the account, and there will still remain an infinite number of possible formulae,

---

[1] The following pages anticipate, in an abbreviated form, the fuller discussions of Parts V and VI.

each of which might claim to be a law connecting the number of a taxi with the time when I hire it.

The merit of this example, for my present purpose, is its obvious absurdity. In the sense in which we believe in natural laws we should say that there is no law connecting the n and t of the above formula, and that, if any suggested formula happens to work, that is a mere chance. If we had found a formula that worked in all cases up to the present, we should not expect it to work in the next case. Only a superstitious person whose emotions are involved will believe an induction of this sort; gamblers at Monte Carlo practise inductions which no man of science would sanction. But it is not altogether easy to state the difference between the inductions of the superstitious gambler and the inductions of the prudent man of science. Obviously there is a difference, but in what does it consist? And is the difference such as to affect logical validity, or does it consist merely in a difference as to the obviousness of the appeal to the emotions? Is the faith in scientific method merely the scientist's superstition appropriate to his kind of gambling? These questions, however, belong to the theory of knowledge. For the present I want to discover not why we believe, but what we believe, when we believe in natural laws.

It is customary to speak of *induction* as what is needed to make the truth of scientific laws probable. I do not think that induction, pure and simple, is fundamental. The above example of the numbers of taxis illustrates this. All past observations as to these numbers are compatible with a number of laws of the form $n = f(t)$, and these will, as a rule, give different values for the next n. We cannot therefore use them all for prediction, and in fact we have no inclination to believe in any of them. Generalizing, we may say: Every finite set of observations is compatible with a number of mutually inconsistent laws, all of which have exactly the same inductive evidence in their favour. Therefore pure induction is invalid, and is, moreover, not what we in fact believe.

Whenever inductive evidence seems to us to make a suggested law very probable, the law is one which had suggested itself more or less independently of the evidence, and had seemed to us in some way likely to be true. When this is the case, subsequent confirmatory evidence is found astonishingly convincing.

This, however, is only partially true. If a law is suggested of which the consequences are very different from what we should expect, and it then is confirmed by observation, we are more prone to believe in it than if its results were commonplace. But in such a case the law itself may seem plausible, although its consequences, when mentioned, are found surprising. Perhaps one of the most important effects of scientific education is to modify the hypotheses that appear *prima facie* probable. It was this cause, not direct negative evidence, that led the belief in witchcraft to decay. If you had a number of outwardly similar boxes, of which some contained gyrostats, and you showed them to a savage, saying that by uttering a magic formula you could make any one of them impossible to turn round, the inductive evidence would soon persuade him that you were right, but a man of educated scientific outlook would search for some other explanation in spite of repeated apparent verifications of your "law".

Induction, moreover, does not validate many of the inferences in which science feels most confidence. We are all convinced that, when a number of people hear a sound simultaneously, their common experience has an external source, which is propagated through the intervening medium by sound waves. There cannot be inductive evidence (unless in some extended sense) for something outside human experience, such as a sound wave. Our experience will be the same whether there really are sound-waves, or, though there are none, auditory sensations occur as they would if there were sound-waves; no inductive evidence can ever favour one of these hypotheses rather than the other. Nevertheless every one in fact accepts the realist alternative—even the idealist philosopher except in his professional moments. We do this on grounds that have nothing to do with induction—partly because we like laws to be as simple as possible, partly because we believe that causal laws must have spatio-temporal continuity, i.e. must not involve action at a distance.

In the establishment of scientific laws experience plays a two-fold part. There is the obvious confirming or confuting of a hypothesis by observing whether its calculated consequences take place, and there is the previous experience which determines what hypotheses we shall think antecedently probable. But behind these influences of experience there are certain vague general expectations, and unless these confer a finite *a priori* probability on certain kinds of hypotheses, scientific inferences are not valid.

In clarifying scientific method it is essential to give as much precision as possible to these expectations, and to examine whether the success of science in any degree confirms their validity. After being made precise the expectations are, of course, no longer quite what they were while they remained vague, but so long as they remain vague the question whether they are true or false is also vague.

It seems to me that what may be called the "faith" of science is more or less of the following sort: there are formulae (causal laws) connecting events, both perceived and unperceived; these formulae exhibit spatio-temporal continuity, i.e. involve no direct unmediated relation between events at a finite distance from each other; a suggested formula having the above characteristics becomes highly probable if, in addition to fitting in with all past observations, it enables us to predict others which are subsequently confirmed and which would be very improbable if the formula were false.

The justification of this "faith", if any, belongs to theory of knowledge. Our present task is completed in having stated it. But there is still need of some discussion as to the origin and growth of this "faith".

There are various possible postulates which can be taken as the basis of scientific method, but it is difficult to state them with the necessary precision. There is the law of causality; there is the uniformity of nature; there is the reign of law: there is the belief in natural kinds, and Keynes's principle of limited variety; and there is structural constancy with spatio-temporal continuity. It ought to be possible, out of all these somewhat vague assumptions, to distil some definite axiom or axioms which, if true, will confer the desired degree of probability on scientific inferences.

The principle of causality appears in the works of almost all philosophers in an elementary form which it never takes in any advanced science. They suppose science to assume that, given any suitable class of events A, there is always some other class of events B such that every A is "caused" by a B; moreover every event belongs to some such class.

Most philosophers have held that "cause" means something different from "invariable antecedent". The difference may be illustrated by Geulincx's two clocks, which both keep perfect time; when one points to the hour, the other strikes, but we do not think that the one has "caused" the other to strike. A non-scientific Fellow of my College lately remarked in despair: "The barometer has ceased to have any effect on the weather". This was felt to be a joke, but if "cause" meant "invariable antecedent" it would not be. It is supposed that when A is *caused* by B the sequence is not merely a fact, but is in some sense *necessary*. This conception is bound up with the controversy about free will and determinism, summed up by the poet in the following lines:

> There was a young man who said: Damn!
> I learn with regret that I am
> A creature that moves
> In predestinate grooves,
> In short, not a bus, but a tram.

As against this view most empiricists have held that "cause" means nothing but "invariable antecedent". The difficulty of this view, and indeed of any suggestion that scientific laws are of the form "A causes B", is that such sequences are seldom invariable, and, even if they are invariable in fact, circumstances can easily be imagined which would prevent them from being so. As a rule, if you tell a man he is a silly fool he will be angry, but he may be a saint, or may happen to die of apoplexy before he has time to lose his temper. If you strike a match on a box it usually lights, but sometimes it breaks or is damp. If you throw a stone in the air it usually falls down again, but it may be swallowed by an eagle under the impression that it is a bird. If you will to move your arm it usually moves, but not if you are paralysed. In such ways all laws of the form "A causes B" are liable to exceptions, since something may intervene to prevent the expected result.

Nevertheless, there are reasons, of which the strength will appear in Part VI, for admitting laws of the form "A causes B", provided that we do so with suitable safeguards and limitations. The concept of more or less permanent physical objects, in its common-sense form, involves "substance", and when "substance" is rejected we have to find some other way of defining the identity of a physical object at different times. I think this must be done by means of the concept "causal line". I call a series of events a "causal line", if given some of them, we can infer something about the others without having to know anything about the environment. For example, if my doors and windows are shut, and at intervals

I notice my dog asleep on the hearthrug, I infer that he was there, or at least somewhere in the room, at the times when I was not noticing him. A photon which travels from a star to my eye is a series of events obeying an intrinsic law, but ceasing to obey this law when it reaches my eye. When two events belong to one causal line, the earlier may be said to "cause" the later. In this way laws of the form "A causes B" may preserve a certain validity. They are important in connection both with perception and with persistence of material objects.

It is the possibility of something intervening that has led physics to state its laws in the form of differential equations, which may be regarded as stating what is tending to happen. And as already explained, classical physics, when presented with several causes acting simultaneously, represents the resultant as a vector sum, so that, in a sense, each cause produces its effect as if no other cause were acting. But in fact the whole conception of "cause" is resolved into that of "law". And laws, as they occur in classical physics, are concerned with tendencies at an instant. What actually happens is to be inferred by taking the vector sum of all the tendencies at an instant, and then integrating to find out the result after a finite time.

All empirical laws are inferred from a finite number of observations, eked out by interpolation and extrapolation. The part played by interpolation is not always adequately realized. Take for example the apparent motions of the planets. We assume that, during the day-time, they pursue a smooth course which fits in easily with their observed courses during the preceding and succeeding nights. It would be a possible hypothesis that planets only exist when they are observed, but this would make the laws of astronomy very complicated. If it is objected that planets can be photographed fairly continuously, the same problem arises as regards the photographs: do they exist when no one is looking at them? This again is a question of interpolation, and the interpolation is justified by the fact that it gives the simplest laws compatible with what has been observed.

Exactly the same principle applies to extrapolation. Astronomy makes assertions, not only about what planets have done at all times since there were astronomers, but about what they will do and what they did before there was any one to notice them. This extrapolation is often spoken of as if it involved some principle other than that involved in interpolation, but in fact the principle is one and the same: to choose the simplest law that fits the known facts.

As a postulate, however, this is open to grave objections. "Simple" is a vague conception. Moreover it often happens that a simple law turns out, after a time, to be *too* simple, and that the correct law is more complicated. But in such cases the simple law is usually *approximately* right. If, therefore, we only assert that a law is approximately right, we cannot be convicted of error when some other law is found to be a still better approximation.

The uniformity of nature, which is a principle sometimes invoked, has no definite meaning except in connection with natural laws. If it is already granted that there are natural laws, the principle of the uniformity of nature states that time and place must not appear explicitly in the formulation of laws: the laws must be the same in one part of space-time as in another. This principle may or may not be true, but in any case it is insufficient as a postulate, since it presupposes the existence of laws.

The existence of natural kinds underlies most pre-scientific generalizations, such as "dogs bark" or "wood floats". The essence of a "natural kind" is that it is a class of objects all of which possess a number of properties that are not known to be logically interconnected. Dogs bark and growl and wag their tails, while cats mew and purr and lick themselves. We do not know why all the members of an animal species should share so many common qualities, but we observe that they do, and base our expectations on what we observe. We should be amazed if a cat began to bark.

Natural kinds are not only of biological importance. Atoms and molecules are natural kinds; so are electrons, positrons, and neutrons. Quantum theory has introduced a new form of natural kinds in its discrete series of energy levels. It is now possible to conceive the ultimate structure of the physical world not as a continuous flux, in the manner of conventional hydrodynamics, but in a more Pythagorean fashion, in which models are derived from analogy with a heap of shot. Evolution, which in Darwin's time "broadened slowly down from precedent to precedent", now takes revolutionary leaps by means of mutants or freaks. Perhaps wars and revolutions have made us impatient of gradualness; however that may be, modern scientific theories are much more jolty and jagged than the smooth cosmic stream of ordered progress imagined by the Victorians.

The bearing of all this on induction is of considerable importance. If you are dealing with a property which is likely to be characteristic of a natural kind, you can generalize fairly safely after very few instances. Do seals bark? After hearing half a dozen do so, you confidently answer "yes", because you are persuaded in advance that either all seals bark or no seals bark. When you have found that a few pieces of copper are good conductors of electricity, you unhesitatingly assume that this is true of all copper. In such cases a generalization has a finite *a priori* probability, and induction is less precarious than in other problems.

Keynes has a postulate by which, in his opinion, inductive arguments might be justified; he calls it the principle of limited variety. It is a form of the assumption of natural kinds. This is one of the expedients in the way of a general assumption which, if true, validates scientific method. I shall have more to say about it at a later stage. What has been said in this chapter is only by way of anticipation.

Chapter X

SPACE-TIME AND CAUSALITY

PHYSICAL events are arranged by physics in a four-dimensional manifold called space-time. This manifold is an improvement on the older manifold of "things" arranged in varying spatial patterns at varying times; and this, in turn, was an improvement upon the manifold resulting from assuming an accurate correspondence between percepts and "things". No doubt physics would like to forget its early history, which, like that of many established institutions, is not so creditable as could be wished. But unfortunately its title to our allegiance is difficult to disentangle from its early association with naive realism; even in its most sophisticated form, it still appears as an emendation, for which naive realism supplies the text.

Perceptual space is a common-sense construction, composed of diverse raw materials. There are visual space-relations: up-and-down, right-and-left, depth up to a certain distance (after which differences of depth become imperceptible). There are the differences in sensations of touch which enable us to distinguish a touch on one part of the body from a touch on another. There is the somewhat vague power of estimating the direction of a sound. Then there are experienced correlations, of which the most important is the correlation of sight and touch; there are observations of movement, and the experience of moving parts of our own body.

Out of such raw materials (the above list does not claim to be complete) common sense constructs a single space containing objects perceived and unperceived, the perceived objects being identified with percepts, according to the principles of naive realism. The unperceived objects, for common sense, are those which we should perceive if we were in the right position and with suitably adjusted sense-organs, together with objects only perceived by others, and objects, such as the interior of the earth, which are perceived by no one but inferred by common sense.

In the passage from the common-sense world to that of physics, certain common-sense assumptions are retained, though in a

337

modified form. For instance, we assume that the furniture of our room continues to exist when we do not see it. Common sense supposes that what continues is just what we see when we look, but physics says that what continues is the external cause of what we see, i.e. a vast assemblage of atoms undergoing frequent quantum transformations. In the course of these transformations they radiate energy, which, when it comes in contact with a human body, has various effects, some of which are called "perceptions". Two simultaneous parts of one visual percept have a certain visual spatial relation which is a component of the total percept; the physical objects which correspond to these parts of my total percept have a relation roughly corresponding to this visual spatial relation. When I say that the relation "corresponds", I mean that it is part of a system of relations having, to some extent, the same geometry as that of visual percepts, and that the location of physical objects in physical space has discoverable relations to the location of perceptual objects in perceptual space.

But this correspondence is by no means exact. Let us take, to simplify our problem, the heavenly bodies as they are and as they appear. As they appear, they do not obviously differ as regards distance from us; they look like bright points or patches on the celestial sphere. That is to say, their position in visual space is defined by only two co-ordinates. But eclipses and occultations soon led to the view that they are not in fact all equi-distant from the earth, though it was a long time before differences of distance among the fixed stars were admitted. To fix the position of a heavenly body relatively to ourselves we need three polar co-ordinates, r, θ, ϕ. It was assumed that θ and ϕ could be the same for the physical star as for the perceived star, but r must be computed; in fact a great deal of astronomy has been concerned with computing r. The assumption that θ and ϕ are the same in visual and physical space is equivalent to the assumption that light travels in straight lines. This assumption, after a time, came to be thought not exactly true, but it is still sufficiently true for a first approximation.

The θ and ϕ of astronomical space, though they have approximately the same numerical measure as the θ and ϕ of visual space, are not identical with the latter. If they were identical, the hypothesis that light does not move exactly in straight lines would be meaningless. This illustrates at once the connection and the difference between visual space when we look at the night sky and astronomical space as constructed by the astronomers. The connection is kept as close as may be, but beyond a point it has to be abandoned if we are to believe in comparatively simple laws governing the real and apparent movements of the heavenly bodies.

Small distances from ourselves are not estimated by the elaborate methods required in astronomy. We can roughly "see" small distances, though the stereoscope produces this effect deceptively. We judge things that touch our body to be close to the part they touch. When things are not touching us, we sometimes can move so as to come in contact with them; the amount of movement required measures, roughly, their initial distance from us. We have thus three common-sense ways of estimating the distance of visual objects on the surface of the earth. Scientific ways of estimating distance use these ways as their foundation, but correct them by means of physical laws inferred by assuming them. The whole process is one of tinkering. If common-sense estimates of distances and sizes are roughly correct, then certain physical laws are roughly correct. If these laws are quite correct, the common-sense estimates must be slightly amended. If the various laws are not exactly compatible, they must be adjusted until the inconsistency ceases. Thus observation and theory interact; what, in scientific physics, is called an observation is usually something involving a considerable admixture of theory.

Let us now abandon the consideration of the stages towards theoretical physics, and compare the finished physical world with the world of common sense. I see, let us suppose, a buttercup and a bluebell; common sense says the buttercup is yellow and the bluebell is blue. Physics says that electromagnetic waves of many different frequencies start from the sun and reach the two flowers; when they reach them, the buttercup scatters the waves whose frequency produces a yellow sensation, and the bluebell those that produce a blue sensation. This difference in the effect of the two flowers is assumed to be due to some difference in their structure. Thus although yellow and blue exist only where there is an eye, the difference between them allows us to infer differences between the physical objects in the directions in which we see yellow and blue respectively.

Common sense constructs a single space containing "things"

339

which combine properties revealed by different senses, such as hot and hard and bright. These "things" are placed by common sense in a three-dimensional space, in which distance cannot be estimated by common-sense methods unless it is small. Physics until recently retained something like "things", but called it "matter", and robbed it of all properties except position in space. The position of a piece of matter in space was roughly identical with that of the corresponding "thing", except that the distance, if great, had to be calculated by rather elaborate scientific methods.

In this picking and choosing among common-sense beliefs, physics has acted without formulated principles, but nevertheless on a subconscious plan which we must try to make explicit. Part of this plan is to retain always as much of the common-sense world as is possible without intolerable complication; another part is to make such non-refutable assumptions as will lead to simple causal laws. This latter procedure is already implicit in the common-sense belief in "things": we do not believe that the visible world ceases to exist when we shut our eyes, and we hold that the cat exists when it is secretly stealing the cream as well as when we are punishing it for doing so. All this is "probable" inference: it is logically possible to suppose that the world consists only of my percepts, and the inference to the common-sense world, as to that of physics, is non-demonstrative. But I do not wish to go behind common sense at present; I wish only to consider the transition from common sense to physics.

Modern physics is further from common sense than the physics of the nineteenth century. It has dispensed with matter, substituting series of events; it has abandoned continuity in microscopic phenomena; and it has substituted statistical averages for strict deterministic causality affecting each individual occurrence. But it has still retained a great deal of which the source is common sense. And there are still continuity and determinism so far as macroscopic phenomena are concerned, and for most purposes there is still matter.

The world of physics contains more than the world of percepts, and in some respects contains more than the world of common sense. But while it exceeds both in quantity, it falls short of both in known qualitative variety. Both common sense and physics supplement percepts by the assumption that things do not cease to exist when unperceived, and by the further assumption that things never perceived can often be inferred. Physics supplements the common-sense world by the whole theory of microscopic phenomena; what it asserts about atoms and their history surpasses what common sense allows itself to infer.

There are two specially important kinds of chains of events: first, those which constitute the history of a given piece of matter; second, those which connect an object with the perception of it. The sun, for instance, has a biography consisting of all that happens in the part of space-time that it occupies; this biography may be said to *be* the sun. It also emits radiations, some of which reach eyes and brains, and cause the sort of occurrence which is called "seeing the sun". Broadly speaking, the former set of events consists of quantum transitions, the latter of radiant energy. There are correspondingly two sets of causal laws, one set connecting events belonging to the same piece of matter, the other connecting parts of the same radiation. There is also a third set of laws, concerning the transition from energy in the atom to radiant energy and vice versa.

Perceiving, as we know it introspectively, appears to be something quite different from the events that physics considers. Therefore if there is to be inference from percepts to physical occurrences, or from physical occurrences to percepts, we need laws which, *prima facie*, are not physical. I incline to think that physics *can* be so interpreted as to include these laws, but for the present I shall not consider this possibility. Our problem is, therefore: taking percepts as we know them in experience, and physical occurrences as asserted by physics, what laws do we know that inter-connect the two and therefore allow inference from one to the other?

In part, the answer is already patent to common sense. We see when light strikes the eye, we hear when sound strikes the ear, we have sensations of touch when the body is in contact with something else, and so on. These laws are not laws of physics or physiology, unless physics is subjected to a radical re-interpretation. They are laws stating the physical antecedents of perceptions. These antecedents are partly outside the percipient's body (except when he is perceiving something in his own body), partly in his sense-organs and nerves, partly in his brain. A failure in any of these antecedents prevents the perception. But conversely, if one of the later antecedents is caused in an unusual way, the percept will be what it would have been if the causation had been usual, and the percipient is liable to be deceived—for example by something seen in a mirror or heard on the wireless, if he is unaccustomed to mirrors and wireless.

Each single inference from a perception to a physical object is therefore liable to be erroneous in the sense of causing expectations that are not fulfilled. It will not *usually* be erroneous in this sense, since the habit of making that sort of inference must have been generated by a number of occasions when the inference was justified. But here a little further precision is necessary. From a practical point of view, an inference from a percept is justified if it gives rise to expectations that are verified. This, however, is all within the realm of percepts. All that strictly follows is that our inferences as to physical objects are consistent with experience, but there may be other hypotheses that are equally consistent.

The justification of our inferences from perception to physical objects depends upon the consistency of the whole system. First, from ordinary perceptions, we arrive at an elementary kind of physics; this suffices to cause us to put in a separate category dreams, mirages, etc., which contradict our elementary physics. We then set to work to improve our elementary physics so as to include the exceptional phenomena; there is, for instance, a perfectly good physical theory of mirages. We learn in this way to be critical, and we form the concept of a "trained observer". We are critical of percepts in the name of laws, and of laws in the name of percepts; gradually, as physics improves, a closer and closer harmony between percepts and laws is established.

But when I say that we become critical of percepts, I must guard against a misunderstanding. Percepts certainly occur, and a theory which has to deny any of them is faulty; but some, being caused in an unusual way, lead common sense into erroneous inferences. Of this the mirage is a good example. If I see a lake which is only a mirage, I see what I see just as truly as if there were a physical lake; I am mistaken, not as to the percept, but as to what it implies. The percept makes me think that if I walk in a certain direction, I shall reach water that I can drink, and in this I am deceived; but my visual percept may be exactly what it would be if there really were water. My physics, if adequate, must explain not only that there is no water, but also why there seems to be water. A mistaken perception is mistaken, not as to the percept itself, but as to its causal correlates and antecedents and consequents; frequently the mistake is in an animal inference. The fact that animal inferences may be mistaken is one reason for classifying them as inferences.

The relation of physical laws to experience is not altogether simple. Broadly speaking, laws can be disproved by experience, but not proved by it. That is to say, they assert more than experience alone would warrant. In the case of the mirage, if I have believed it real, and have also assumed that a large lake will not dry up in a few hours, I can discover that the mirage caused me to have a false belief. But the false belief may have been the belief that the lake could not dry up so quickly. The belief in the persistence of material objects throughout the interval between two occasions when they are observed is one which, as a matter of logic, cannot be proved by observation. Suppose I were to set up the hypothesis that tables, whenever no one is looking, turn into kangaroos; this would make the laws of physics very complicated, but no observation could refute it. The laws of physics, in the form in which we accept them, must not only be in agreement with observation, but must, as regards what is not observed, have certain characteristics of simplicity and continuity which are not empirically demonstrable. In general, we think that physical phenomena are not affected by being observed, although this is not thought to be strictly true as regards the minute phenomena upon which quantum theory is based.

Physics, assuming it perfected, would have two characteristics. In the first place, it would be able to predict percepts; no perception would be contrary to what physics had led us to expect. In the second place, it would assume unobserved physical occurrences to be governed by causal laws as similar as possible to those that we infer from cases of continuous observation. For example, if I watch a moving body, the motion that I see is sensibly continuous; I therefore assume that all motion, whether observed or not, is approximately continuous.

This brings us to the question of causal laws and physical space-time. Physical space-time, as we have seen, is an inference from perceptual space and time; it contains all observed occurrences, and also all unobserved occurrences. But since it is inferential, the location of an occurrence in it is also inferential.

The locating of events in physical space-time is effected by two methods. First, there is a correlation between perceptual space and time and physical space-time, though this correlation is only rough and approximate. Second, the causal laws of physics assign an order to the events concerned, and it is partly by means of them that unobserved events are located in space-time.

A causal law, as I use the term, is any law which, if true, makes it possible, given a certain number of events, to infer something about one or more other events. For example, "planets move in ellipses" is a causal law. If this law is true, since five points determine an ellipse, five data (theoretically) should enable us to calculate the orbit of the planet. Most laws, however, have not this simplicity; they are usually expressed in differential equations. When they are so expressed they assume an order: each event must have four co-ordinates, and neighbouring events are those whose co-ordinates are very nearly the same. But the question arises: how do we assign co-ordinates to events in physical space-time? I maintain that, in doing so, we make use of causal laws. That is to say, the relation of causal laws to space-time order is a reciprocal one. The correct statement is: Events can be arranged in a four-dimensional order such that, when so arranged, they are interconnected by causal laws which are approximately continuous, i.e. events whose co-ordinates differ very little also differ very little. Or rather: Given any event, there is a series of closely similar events, in which the time-co-ordinate varies continuously from rather less to rather more than that of the given event, and in which the space-co-ordinates vary continuously about those of the given event. This principle, apparently, does not hold for quantum transitions, but it holds for macroscopic events, and for all events (such as light-waves) where there is no matter.

The correlation between physical and perceptual space-time, which is only approximate, proceeds as follows. In visual space, if objects are near enough for differences of depth to be perceptible, every visual percept has three polar co-ordinates, which may be called distance, up-and-downness, and right-and-leftness. All these are qualities of the percept, and all are measurable. We may assign the same numerical co-ordinates to the physical object which we are said to be seeing, but these co-ordinates no longer have the same meaning as they have in visual space. It is because they do not have the same meaning that it is possible for the correlation to be only rough—for example, if the object is seen through a refracting medium. But although the correlation is rough, it is very useful in establishing a first approximation to the co-ordinates of events in physical space-time. The subsequent corrections are effected by means of causal laws, of which the refraction of light may again serve as an example.

There is no logical reason why there should be such causal laws, or a known relation establishing such a four-dimensional order among events. The usual argument for the acceptance of physical laws is that they are the simplest hypotheses hitherto devised that are consistent with observation wherever observation is possible. They are not, however, the only hypotheses consistent with observation. Nor is it clear by what right we objectify our preference for *simple* laws.

What physics says about the world is much more abstract than it seems to be, because we imagine that its space is what we know in our own experience, and that its matter is the kind of thing that feels hard when we touch it. In fact, even assuming physics true, what we know about the physical world is very little. Let us first consider theoretical physics in the abstract, and then in relation to experience.

As an abstract system, physics, at present, says something like this: there is a manifold, called the manifold of events, which has a system of relations among its terms by means of which it acquires a certain four-dimensional geometry. There is an extra-geometrical quantity called "energy", which is unevenly distributed throughout the manifold, but of which some finite amount exists in every finite volume. The total of energy is constant. The laws of physics are laws as to the changes in the distribution of energy. To state these laws, we have to distinguish two kinds of regions, those that are called "empty", and those that are said to contain "matter". There are very small material systems called "atoms"; each atom may contain any one of a certain discrete denumerable series of amounts of energy. Sometimes it suddenly parts with a finite amount of energy to the non-material environment, sometimes it suddenly absorbs a finite amount from the environment. The laws as to these transitions from one energy level to another are only statistical. In a given period of time, if not too short, there will be, in a given state of the environment, a calculable number of transitions of each possible kind, the smaller transitions being commoner than the greater.

In "empty space" the laws are simpler and more definite. Parcels of energy that leave an atom spread outward equally in all directions, travelling with the velocity of light. Whether a parcel travels in waves or in little units or in something which is a combination of both, is a matter of convention. Everything proceeds simply until the radiant energy hits an atom, and then the atom may absorb a finite amount of it, with the same individual indeterminacy and statistical regularity as applies to the emission of energy by atoms.

The amount of energy emitted by an atom in a given transition determines the "frequency" of the radiant energy that results. And this in turn determines the kinds of effects that the radiant energy can have upon any matter that it may encounter. "Frequency" is a word associated with waves, but if the wave theory of light is discarded "frequency" may be taken as a measurable but undetermined quality of a radiation. It is measurable by its effects.

So much for theoretical physics as an abstract logical system. It remains to consider how it is connected with experience.

Let us begin with the geometry of space-time. We assume that the position of a point in space-time can be determined by four real numbers, called co-ordinates; it is also generally supposed, though this is not essential, that to every set of four real numbers as co-ordinates (if not too great) a position in space-time corresponds. It will simplify exposition to adopt this supposition. If we do, the number of positions in space-time is the same as the number of real numbers, which is called c. Now of every class of c entities we can assert every kind of geometry in which there is a one-one correspondence between a position and a finite ordered set of real numbers (co-ordinates). Therefore to specify the geometry of a manifold tells us nothing unless the ordering relation is given. Since physics is intended to give empirical truth, the ordering relation must not be a purely logical one, such as might be constructed in pure mathematics, but must be a relation defined in terms derived from experience. If the ordering relation is derived from experience, the statement that space-time has such-and-such a geometry is one having a substantial empirical content, but if not, not.

I suggest that the ordering relation is contiguity or compresence, in the sense in which we know these in sensible experience. Something must be said about these.

Contiguity is a property given in sight and touch. Two portions of the visual field are contiguous if their apparent distances and their angular co-ordinates (up-and-down, right-and-left) differ very little. Two parts of my body are contiguous if the qualities by which I locate a touch in the two parts differ very little. Contiguity is quantitative, and therefore enables us to make series of percepts: if A and B and C are contiguous, but B is more contiguous to both A and C than they are to each other, B is to be put between A and C. There is also contiguity in time. When we hear a sentence, the first and second words are more contiguous than the first and third words. In this way, by means of spatial and temporal contiguity, our experiences can be arranged in an ordered manifold. We may assume that this ordered manifold is a part of the ordered manifold of physical events, and is ordered by the same relation.

For my part, however, I prefer the relation of "compresence". If we use this relation, we suppose that every event occupies a finite amount of space-time, that is to say, no event is confined to a point of space or an instant of time. Two events are said to be "compresent" when they overlap in space-time; this is the definition for abstract physics. But we need, as we saw, a definition derived from experience. As an ostensive definition from experience I should give the following: Two events are "compresent" when they are related in the way in which two simultaneous parts of one experience are related. At any given moment, I am seeing certain things, hearing others, touching others, remembering others, and expecting yet others. All these percepts, recollections, and expectations are happening to me now; I shall say that they are mutually "compresent". I assume that this relation, which I know in my own experience, can also hold between events that are not experienced, and can be the relation by which space-time order is constructed. This will have as a consequence that two events are compresent when they overlap in space-time, which, if space-time order is taken as already determined, may serve, *within physics*, as the definition of compresence.

Compresence is not the same thing as simultaneity, though it implies it. Compresence, as I mean it, is to be taken as known through experience, and having only an ostensive definition. Nor should I define "compresence" as "simultaneity in one person's experience". I should object to this definition on two grounds: first, that it could not be extended to physical occurrences experienced by no one; second, that "experience" is a vague word. I should say that an event is "experienced" when it gives rise to a habit, and that broadly speaking this only happens if the event occurs where there is living matter. If this is correct, "experience" is not a fundamental concept.

The question now arises: can we construct space-time order out of compresence alone, or do we need something further? Let us take a simplified hypothesis. Suppose there are n events, a_1, $a_2, \ldots a_n$, and suppose a_1 is compresent only with a_2, a_2 is compresent with a_1 and a_3, a_3, with a_2 and a_4, and so on. We can then construct the order $a_1, a_2, \ldots a_n$. We shall say that an event is "between" two others if it is compresent with both, but they are not compresent with each other; and, more generally, if a, b, c are three different events, we shall say that b is "between" a and c if the events compresent with both a and c are a proper part of the events compresent with b. This may be taken as the definition of "between". Supplemented by suitable axioms, it will generate the kind of order we want.

It should be observed that we cannot construct space-time order out of Einstein's relation of "interval". The interval between two parts of a light-ray is zero, and yet we have to distinguish between a light-ray that goes from A to B and one that goes from B to A. This shows that "interval" alone does not suffice.

If the above point of view is adopted, points in space-time become classes of events. I have dealt with this subject in "The Analysis of Matter", and in Chapters VI and VIII of this Part, and will therefore say no more about it.

So much for the definition of space-time order in terms of experience. It remains to restate the connection of physical events in the outer world with percepts.

When energy emitted by matter as a result of quantum transitions travels, without further quantum transitions, to a given part of a human body, it sets up a train of quantum transitions which ultimately reach the brain. Assuming the maxim "same cause, same effect", with its consequence, "different effects, different causes", it follows that, if two trains of radiant energy, falling on the same point of the body, cause different percepts, there must be differences in the two trains, and therefore in the quantum transitions that gave rise to them. Assuming the existence of causal laws, this argument seems unobjectionable, and gives a basis for the inference from perceptions to the material source of the process by which they are caused.

I think—though I say this with hesitation—that the distinction between spatial and temporal distance requires the consideration of causal laws. That is to say, if there is a causal law connecting an event A with an event B, then A and B are separated in time, and it is a matter of convention whether we shall also consider them separated in space. There are, however, some difficulties about this view. A number of people may hear or see something simultaneously, and in this case there is a causal connection with no time-interval. But in such a case the connection is indirect, like that connecting brothers or cousins; that is to say, it travels first from effect to cause and then from cause to effect. But how are we to distinguish cause from effect before we have established the time-order? Eddington says we do so by means of the second law of thermodynamics. In a spherical radiation, we take it that it travels *from* a centre, not *to* it. But I, since I wish to connect physics with experience, should prefer to say that we establish time-order by means of memory and our immediate experience of temporal succession. What is remembered is, by definition, in the past; and there are earlier and later within the specious present. Anything compresent with something remembered, but not with my present experience, is also in the past. From this starting-point we can extend the definition of time-order, and the distinction of past and future, step by step to all events. We can then distinguish cause from effect, and say that causes are always earlier than effects.

According to the above theory, there are certain elements that are carried over unchanged from the world of sense to the world of physics. These are: the relation of compresence, the relation of earlier and later, some elements of structure, and differences in certain circumstances—i.e. when we experience different sensations belonging to the same sense, we may assume that their causes differ. This is the residue of naive realism that survives in physics. It survives primarily because there is no positive argument against it, because the resulting physics fits the known facts, and because prejudice causes us to cling to naive realism wherever it cannot be disproved. Whether there are any better reasons than these for accepting physics remains to be examined.

PART V
PROBABILITY

INTRODUCTION

IT is generally recognized that the inferences of science and common sense differ from those of deductive logic and mathematics in a very important respect, namely, that, when the premisses are true and the reasoning correct, the conclusion is only *probable*. We have reasons for believing that the sun will rise to-morrow, and everybody is agreed that, in practice, we can behave as if these reasons justified certainty. But when we examine them we find that they leave some room, however little, for doubt. The doubt that is justified is of three sorts. As regards the first two: on the one hand there may be relevant facts of which we are ignorant; on the other hand, the laws that we have to assume in order to predict the future may be untrue. The former reason for doubt does not much concern us in our present inquiry, but the latter is one which demands detailed investigation. But there is a third kind of doubt, which arises when we know a law to the effect that something happens usually, or perhaps in an overwhelming majority of instances, though not always; in this case we have a right to expect what is usual, though not with complete confidence. For example, if a man is throwing dice, it very seldom happens that he throws double sixes ten times running, although this is not impossible; we have therefore a right to expect that he will not do so, but our expectation ought to be tinged with doubt. All these kinds of doubt involve something that may be called "probability", but this word is capable of different meanings, which it will be important to us to disentangle.

Mathematical probability arises always from a combination of two propositions, of which one may be completely known, while the other is completely unknown. If I draw a card from a pack, what is the chance that it will be an ace? I know completely the constitution of a pack of cards, and I am aware that one card in thirteen is an ace; but I am completely ignorant as to which card I shall draw. But if I say "probably Zoroaster existed", I am saying something about the degree of uncertainty, or of credibility, attaching to the one proposition "Zoroaster existed". This is quite a different concept from that of mathematical probability, although in many cases the two are correlated.

Science is concerned to infer laws from particular facts. An inference of this sort cannot be deductive, unless, in addition to particular facts, there are general laws among our premisses; as a matter of pure logic this is fairly evident. It is sometimes thought that, though particular facts cannot make a general law *certain*, they can make it *probable*. Particular facts can certainly *cause* belief in a general proposition; it is our experience of particular men dying that has caused us to believe that all men are mortal. But if we are justified in believing that all men are mortal, that must be because, as a general principle, certain kinds of particular facts are evidence of general laws. And since deductive logic knows no such principle, any principle which will justify inference from the particular to the general must be a law of nature, i.e. a statement that the actual universe has a certain character which it would be possible for it not to have. I shall undertake the search for some such principle or principles in Part VI; in Part V I shall only contend that induction by simple enumeration is *not* such a principle, and unless severely restricted is demonstrably invalid.

We infer, in science, not only laws, but also particular facts. If we read in the newspaper that the King is dead, we infer that he is dead; if we find that we shall have to make a long railway journey without a chance of a meal, we infer that we shall be hungry. All such inferences can only be justified if it is possible to ascertain *laws*. If there were not general laws, every man's knowledge would be confined to what he himself has experienced. It is more necessary that there should *be* laws than that they should be known. If A is always followed by B, and an animal, seeing A, expects B, the animal may be said to know that B is coming without having knowledge of the general law. But although *some* knowledge of facts as yet unperceived can be acquired in this way, it is impossible to get far without knowledge of general laws. Such laws, in general, state probabilities (in one sense), and are themselves only probable (in another). E.g. it is probable (in one sense) that if you have cancer it is probable (in another sense) that you will die. This state of affairs makes it evident that we cannot understand scientific method without a previous investigation of the different kinds of probability.

Although such an investigation is necessary, I do not think that probability has quite the importance attached to it by some authors. The importance that it has arises in two ways. On the one hand, we need, among the premisses of science, not only data derived from perception and memory, but also certain principles of synthetic inference, which cannot be established by deductive logic or by arguments from experience, since they are presupposed in all inference from experienced facts to other facts or to laws. These premisses may be admitted to be in some degree uncertain, i.e. to have not the highest "degree of credibility". It will be part of our analysis of this form of probability to maintain, in spite of Keynes's adverse opinion, that data and inferential premisses may be uncertain. This is one way in which the theory of probability is relevant, but there is also another. It appears that we frequently know (in some sense of the word "know") that something happens usually, but perhaps not always —e.g. that lightning is followed by thunder. In that case, we have a class of cases A, of which we have reason to believe that most belong to the class B. (In our illustration, A is times shortly after lightning, and B is times when thunder is audible.) In such circumstances, given an instance of the class A concerning which we do not know whether it is an instance of the class B, we have a right to say that it is "probably" a member of the class B. Here "probably" has not the meaning that it has when we are speaking of degrees of credibility, but the quite different meaning that it has in the mathematical theory of probability.

For these reasons, and also because probability-logic is much less complete and incontrovertible than elementary logic, it is necessary to develop the theory of probability in some detail, and to examine various controversial questions of interpretation. It is to be remembered that the whole discussion of probability is of the nature of prolegomena to the investigation of the postulates of scientific inference.

Chapter I

KINDS OF PROBABILITY

ATTEMPTS to establish a logic of probability have been numerous, but to most of them there have been fatal objections. One of the causes of faulty theories has been failure to distinguish—or rather, determination to confound—essentially different concepts which, so far as usage goes, have an equal right to be called "probability". I propose, in this Chapter, to make a preliminary exploration of these different concepts in a discursive manner, leaving to later Chapters the attempt to reach precise definitions.

The first large fact of which we have to take account is the existence of the mathematical theory of probability. There is, among mathematicians who have concerned themselves with this theory, a fairly complete agreement as to everything that can be expressed in mathematical symbols, but an entire absence of agreement as to the interpretation of the mathematical formulae. In such circumstances, the simplest course is to enumerate the axioms from which the theory can be deduced, and to decide that any concept which satisfies these axioms has an equal right, from the mathematician's point of view, to be called "probability". If there are many such concepts, and if we are determined to choose between them, the motives of our choice must lie outside mathematics.

There is one very simple concept which satisfies the axioms of the theory of probability, and which is on other accounts advantageous. Given a finite class B which has n members, and given that m of these belong to some other class A, then we say that, if a member of B is chosen at random, the chance that it will belong to the class A is m/n. Whether this definition is adequate to the uses that we wish to make of the mathematical theory of probability, is a question which we shall have to investigate at a later stage; if it is not, we shall have to look for some other interpretation of mathematical probability.

It must be understood that there is here no question of truth or falsehood. Any concept which satisfies the axioms may be taken to *be* mathematical probability. In fact, it might be desirable to adopt one interpretation in one context, and another in another, for convenience is the only guiding motive. This is the usual situation in the interpretation of a mathematical theory. For example, as we have seen, all arithmetic can be deduced from five axioms enumerated by Peano, and therefore, if all we want of numbers is that they should obey the rules of arithmetic, we may define as the series of natural numbers any series satisfying Peano's five axioms. Now these axioms are satisfied by any progression, and, in particular, by the series of natural numbers starting, not with 0, but with 100, or 1,000, or any other finite integer. It is only if we decide that we want our numbers to serve for enumeration, not only for arithmetic, that we have a motive for choosing the series that starts with 0. Similarly, in the case of the mathematical theory of probability, the interpretation to be chosen may depend upon the purpose we have in view.

The word "probability" is often used in ways that are not, or at least not obviously, capable of interpretation as the ratio of the numbers of two finite classes. We may say: Probably Zoroaster existed, probably Einstein's theory of gravitation is better than Newton's, probably all men are mortal.[1] In these cases, we might maintain that there is evidence of a certain kind, which is known to be conjoined with a conclusion of a certain kind in a large majority of cases; in this way, theoretically, the definition of probability as the ratio of the numbers of two classes might become applicable. It is possible, therefore, that instances such as the above do not involve a new meaning of "probability".

There are, however, two dicta which we are all inclined to accept without much examination, but which, if accepted, involve an interpretation of "probability" which it seems impossible to reconcile with the above definition. The first of these dicta is Bishop Butler's maxim that "probability is the guide of life". The second is the maxim that all our knowledge is only probable, which has been specially emphasized by Reichenbach.

Bishop Butler's maxim is obviously valid according to one very common interpretation of "probability". When—as is usually the case—I am not certain what is going to happen, but I must act upon one or other hypothesis, I am generally well advised to choose the most probable hypothesis, and I am always well advised to take account of probability in making my decision.

[1] Not to be confused with "all men are probably mortal".

But there is an important logical difference between this kind of probability and the mathematical kind, namely that the latter is concerned with propositional functions[1] and the former with propositions. When I say that the chance of a coin coming heads is a half, that is a relation between the two propositional functions "x is a toss of the coin" and "x is a toss of the coin which comes heads". If I am to infer that, in a particular case, the chance of heads is a half, I must state that I am considering the particular case solely as an *instance*. If I could consider it in all its particularity, I should, in theory, be able to decide whether it will fall heads or fall tails, and I should no longer be in the domain of probability. When we use probability as a guide to conduct, it is because our knowledge is inadequate; we know that the event in question is one of a class B of events, and we may know what proportion of this class belongs to some class A in which we are interested. But the proportion will vary according to our choice of the class B; we shall thus obtain different probabilities, all equally valid from the mathematical standpoint. If probability is to be a guide in practice, we must have some way of selecting one probability as *the* probability. If we cannot do this, all the different probabilities remain equally valid, and we shall be left without guidance.

Let us take an instance, in which every sensible man is guided by probability, I mean life insurance. I ascertain the terms on which some company is willing to insure my life, and I have to decide whether insurance on these terms is likely to prove an advantageous bargain, not to insurers in general, but to me.

My problem is different from that of the insurance company, and much more difficult. The insurance company is not interested in my individual case: it offers insurance to all members of a certain class, and need only take account of statistical averages. But I may believe that I have special reasons to expect a long life, or that I am like the Scotchman who died the day after completing his insurance, remarking with his last breath "I always was a lucky fellow". Every circumstance of my health and my way of life is relevant, but some of these may be so uncommon that I can get no reliable help from statistics. At last I decide to

---

[1] I.e. with sentences containing an undefined variable—e.g. "A is a man"—which become propositions when we assign a value to the variable—in the above case "A".

consult a medical man, who, after a few questions, remarks genially: "Oh, I expect you'll live to be 90". I am painfully aware, not only that his judgment is slap-dash and unscientific, but also that he wishes to please me. The probability at which I finally arrive is thus something quite vague and quite incapable of numerical measurement; but it is upon this vague probability that, as a disciple of Bishop Butler, I have to act.

The probability which is the guide of life is not the mathematical kind, not only because it is not relative to arbitrary data, but to all data that bear on the question at issue, but also because it has to take account of something which lies wholly outside the province of mathematical probability, and which may be called "intrinsic doubtfulness". This is what is relevant when it is said that all our knowledge is only probable. Consider for example a distant memory which has grown so dim that we can no longer trust it with any confidence, a star so faint that we are not sure whether we really see it, or a noise so slight that we think it may be only imagined. These are extreme cases, but in a lesser degree the same sort of doubtfulness is very common. If we assert, as Reichenbach does, that all our knowledge is doubtful, we cannot define this doubtfulness in the mathematical way, for in the compiling of statistics it is assumed that we *know* whether or not this A is a B, e.g. whether this insured person has died. Statistics are built up on a structure of assumed certainty as to past instances, and a doubtfulness which is universal cannot be merely statistical.

I think, therefore, that everything we feel inclined to believe has a "degree of doubtfulness", or, inversely, a "degree of credibility". Sometimes this is connected with mathematical probability, sometimes not; it is a wider and vaguer conception. It is not, however, purely subjective. There is a cognate subjective conception, namely, the degree of conviction that a man feels about any of his beliefs, but "credibility", as I mean it, is objective in the sense that it is the degree of credence that a *rational* man will give. When I add up my accounts, I give some credence to the result the first time, considerably more if I get the same result the second time, and almost full conviction if I get it a third time. This increase of conviction goes with an increase of evidence, and is therefore rational. In relation to any proposition about which there is evidence, however inadequate, there is a corresponding "degree of credibility", which is the same as the degree of credence given by a man who is rational. (This latter may perhaps be regarded as a definition of the word "rational".) The importance of probability in practice is due to its connection with credibility, but if we imagine this connection to be closer than it is, we bring confusion into the theory of probability.

The connection between credibility and subjective conviction is one that can be studied empirically; we need not, therefore, have any views on this subject in advance of the evidence. A conjurer, for instance, can arrange circumstances in a manner known to himself but calculated to deceive his audience; he can thus acquire data as to how to cause untrue convictions, which are likely to be useful in advertising and propaganda. We cannot so easily study the relation of credibility to truth, because we commonly accept a high degree of credibility as sufficient evidence of truth, and if we do not do so we can no longer discover any truths. But we can discover whether propositions having high credibility form a mutually consistent set, since the set contains the propositions of logic.

I suggest, as a result of the above preliminary discussion, that two different concepts each, on the basis of usage, have an equal claim to be called "probability". The first of these is mathematical probability, which is numerically measurable and satisfies the axioms of the probability-calculus; this is the sort that is involved in the use of statistics, whether in physics, in biology, or in the social sciences, and is also the sort that we *hope* is involved in induction. This sort of probability has to do always with classes, not with single cases except when they can be considered *merely* as instances.

But there is another sort, which I call "degree of credibility". This sort applies to single propositions, and takes account always of all relevant evidence. It applies even in certain cases in which there is no known evidence. The highest degree of credibility to which we can attain applies to most perceptive judgments; varying degrees apply to judgments of memory, according to their vividness and recentness. In some cases the degree of credibility can be inferred from mathematical probability, in others it cannot; but even when it can it is important to remember that it is a different concept. It is this sort, and not mathematical probability, that is relevant when it is said that all our knowledge is only probable, and that probability is the guide of life.

Both kinds of probability demand discussion. I shall begin with mathematical probability.

Chapter II

MATHEMATICAL PROBABILITY

IN this Chapter I propose to treat the theory of probability as a branch of pure mathematics, in which we deduce the consequences of certain axioms without seeking to assign this or that interpretation[1] to them. It is to be observed that, while interpretation, in this field, is controversial, the mathematical calculus itself commands the same measure of agreement as any other branch of mathematics. This situation is in no way peculiar. The interpretation of the infinitesimal calculus was for nearly two hundred years a matter as to which mathematicians and philosophers debated; Leibniz held that it involved actual infinitesimals, and it was not till Weierstrass that this view was definitely disproved. To take an even more fundamental example: there has never been any dispute as to elementary arithmetic, and yet the definition of the natural numbers is still a matter of controversy. We need not be surprised, therefore, that there is doubt as to the definition of probability though there is none (or very little) as to the calculus of probability.

Following Johnson and Keynes, we will denote by "p/h" the undefined notion: "The probability of p given h". When I say that this notion is undefined, I mean that it is only defined by the axioms or postulates about to be enumerated. Anything satisfying these axioms is an "interpretation" of the calculus of probability, and it is to be expected that there will be many possible interpretations. No one of these is more correct or more legitimate than another, but some may be more *important* than others. So, in finding an interpretation of Peano's five axioms for arithmetic, the interpretation in which the first number is o is more important than that in which it is 3781; it is more important because it enables us to identify the interpretation of the formalist conception with the conception recognized in enumeration. But for the present we will ignore all questions of interpretation, and proceed with the purely formal treatment of probability.

The axioms or postulates required are given in much the same

---

[1] As to "interpretation", see Part IV, Chapter I.

way by different authors. The following statement is taken from Professor C. D. Broad.[1] The axioms are:

I. Given p and h, there is only one value of p/h. We can therefore speak of "*the* probability of p given h".

II. The possible values of p/h are all the real numbers from 0 to 1, both included. (In some interpretations we confine the possible values to *rational* numbers; this is a question I shall discuss later.)

III. If h implies p, then $p/h = 1$. (We use "1" to denote certainty.)

IV. If h implies not-p, then $p/h = 0$. (We use "0" to denote impossibility.)

V. The probability of both p and q given h is the probability of p given h multiplied by the probability of q given p and h, and is also the probability of q given h multiplied by the probability of p given q and h.

This is called the "conjunctive" axiom.

VI. The probability of p and/or q given h is the probability of p given h *plus* the probability of q given h *minus* the probability of both p and q given h.

This is called the "disjunctive" axiom.

It is immaterial, for our purposes, whether these axioms are all *necessary*; what concerns us is only that they are *sufficient*.

Some observations are called for as regards these axioms. It is obvious that II, III, and IV embody, in part, conventions which might easily be changed. If, when they are adopted, the measure of a given probability is x, we might equally well adopt as its measure any number $f(x)$ which increases as x increases; for 1 and 0 in III and IV we should then substitute $f(1)$ and $f(0)$.

According to the above axioms, a proposition which must be true if the data are true is to have the probability 1 in relation to the data, and one which must be false if the data are true is to have the probability 0 in relation to the data.

It is important to observe that our fundamental concept p/h is a relation of two propositions (or conjunctions of propositions), not a property of a single proposition p. This distinguishes probability as it occurs in the mathematical calculus from probability as required as a guide to practice, for the latter kind has to belong to a proposition in its own right, or, at least, in relation

[1] *Mind*, N.S. No. 210, p. 98.

to data which are not arbitrary, but determined by the problem and the nature of our knowledge. In the calculus, on the contrary, the choice of the data h is wholly arbitrary.

Axiom V is the "conjunctive" axiom. It gives the chance that each of two events will happen. For example: if I draw two cards from a pack, what is the chance that they are both red? Here "h" represents the datum that the pack consists of 26 red cards and 26 black ones; "p" stands for the statement "the first card is red" and "q" for the statement "the second card is red". Then "$(p$ and $q)/h$" is the chance that both are red, p/h is the chance that the first is red, "$q/$ (p and h)" is the chance that the second is red, given that the first is red. Obviously $p/h = 1/2$, $q/(p$ and $h) = 25/51$. Thus by the axiom the chance that both are red is $\frac{1}{2} \cdot \frac{25}{51}$.

Axiom VI is the "disjunctive" axiom. In the above illustration, it gives the chance that at least one of the cards is red. It says that the chance that at least one is red is the chance that the first is red *plus* the chance that the second is red (when it is not given whether the first is red or not) *minus* the chance that both are red. This is $\frac{1}{2} + \frac{1}{2} - \frac{1}{2} \cdot \frac{25}{51}$, using the result obtained above by the use of the conjunctive axiom.

It is obvious that, by means of Axioms V and VI, given the separate probabilities of any finite collection of events, we can calculate the probability of their all happening, or of at least one of them happening.

From the conjunctive axiom it follows that

$$p/(q \text{ and } h) = \frac{(p/h) \times q/(p \text{ and } h)}{q/h}$$

This is called the "principle of inverse probability". Its utility may be illustrated as follows. Let p be some general theory, and q an experimental datum relevant to p. Then p/h is the probability of the theory p on the previously known data, q/h is the probability of q on the previously known data, and $q/(p$ and $h)$ is the probability of q if p is true. Thus the probability of the theory p after q has been ascertained is got by multiplying the previous probability of p by the probability of q given p, and dividing by the previous probability of q. In the most useful case, the theory p will be one which implies q, so that $q/(p$ and $h) = 1$. In that case,

$$p/(q \text{ and } h) = \frac{p/h}{q/h}$$

That is to say, the new datum q increases the probability of p in proportion to the antecedent improbability of q. In other words, if our theory implies something very astonishing, and the astonishing thing is then found to happen, that greatly increases the probability of our theory.

This principle may be illustrated by the discovery of Neptune regarded as a confirmation of the law of gravitation. Here $p =$ the law of gravitation, $h =$ all relevant facts known before the discovery of Neptune, $q =$ the fact that Neptune was found in a certain position. Thus q/h was the antecedent probability that a hitherto unknown planet would be found in a certain small region of the heavens. Let us take this to be m/n. Then after the discovery of Neptune the probability of the law of gravitation was n/m times as great as before.

It is obvious that this principle is of great importance in judging the bearing of new evidence on the probability of a scientific theory. We shall find, however, that it proves somewhat disappointing, and does not yield such good results as might have been hoped.

There is an important proposition, sometimes called Bayes's theorem, which is as follows. Let $p_1, p_2, \ldots . p_n$ be n mutually exclusive possibilities, of which some one is known to be true; let h be the general data, and q some relevant fact. We wish to know the probability of one possibility p_r, given q, when we know the probability of each p_r before q was known, and also the probability of q given p_r, for every r. We have

$$p_r/(q \text{ and } h) = [q/(p_r \text{ and } h) . p_r/h]/\sum_1^n[q/(p_r \text{ and } h) . p_r/h]$$

This proposition enables us, for example, to solve the following problem: We are given $n + 1$ bags, of which the first contains n black balls and no white ones, the second contains $n - 1$ black balls and one white one, the $(r + 1)^{th}$ contains $n - r$ black balls and r white ones. One bag is chosen, but we do not know which; m balls are drawn from it, and are found to be all white; what is the probability that the rth bag has been chosen? Historically, this problem is important in connection with Laplace's pretended proof of induction.

Take next Bernoulli's law of large numbers. This states that if, on each of a number of occasions, the chance of a certain event occurring is p, then, given any two numbers δ and ϵ, however small, the chance that, from a certain number of occasions onward, the proportion of occasions on which the event occurs will ever differ from p by more than ϵ, is less than δ.

Let us illustrate by the case of tossing a coin. We suppose that heads and tails are equally probable. I say that, in all likelihood, after you have tossed often enough, the proportion of heads will never again depart from $1/2$ by more than ϵ, however small ϵ may be; I say further that, however small δ may be, the chance of such a departure anywhere after the nth toss is less than δ, provided n is sufficiently great.

As this proposition is of great importance in the applications of probability, for instance to statistics, let us spend a little longer in familiarizing ourselves with exactly what it asserts in the above case of tossing a coin. I assert first, let us say, that from some point onwards, the percentage of heads will always remain between 49 and 51. You dispute my assertion, and we decide to test it empirically as far as this is possible. The theorem then asserts that, the longer we go on, the more likely we are to find my assertion borne out by the facts, and that, as the number of tosses is increased, this likelihood approaches certainty as a limit. You are convinced by experiment, we will suppose, that from some point onwards the percentage of heads remains always between 49 and 51, but I now assert that, from some further point onwards, it will always remain between 49·9 and 50·1. We repeat our experiment, and again you are convinced after a time, though probably after a longer time than before. After any given number of throws, there is a chance that my assertion may not be verified, but this chance diminishes as the number of throws increases, and can be made less than any assigned chance, however small, by going on long enough.

The above proposition is easy to deduce from the axioms, but cannot, of course, be adequately tested empirically, since it involves infinite series. If the tests we can make seem to confirm it, the opponent can always say they would not have done so if we had gone on longer; and if they seem not to confirm it, the supporter of the theorem can equally say that we have not gone on long enough. The theorem cannot, therefore, be either proved or disproved by empirical evidence.

The above are the principal propositions in the pure theory

of probability that are important in our inquiry. I will, however, say something more on the subject of the $n + 1$ bags, containing n balls each, some white and some black, the $r + 1^{th}$ bag containing r white balls and $n - r$ black balls. The data are as follows: I know that the bags have these varying numbers of white and black balls, but there is no way of distinguishing them from the outside. I choose one bag at haphazard, and draw from it, one by one, m balls which I do not replace after drawing them. They turn out to be all white. In view of this fact, I want to know two things: first, what is the chance that I have chosen the bag that has only white balls? second, what is the chance that the next ball I draw will be white?

We proceed as follows. Let h be the fact that the bags are constituted in the above manner, and q the fact that m white balls have been drawn; also let p_r be the hypothesis that we have chosen the bag containing r white balls. It is obvious that r must be at least as great as m, i.e.

If r is less than m, then $p_r/qh = 0$ and $q/p_r h = 0$.

After some calculation, it turns out that the chance that we have

chosen the bag in which all the balls are white is $\dfrac{m + 1}{n + 1}$.

We now want to know the chance that the next ball will be white. After some further calculation, it turns out that this

chance is $\dfrac{m + 1}{m + 2}$.

Note that this is independent of n, and that, if m is large, it is very nearly 1.

I have not, in the above outline, included any arguments on the subject of induction, which I postpone to a later stage. I shall first consider the adequacy of a certain interpretation of probability, in so far as this can be considered independently of the problems connected with induction.

Chapter III

THE FINITE-FREQUENCY THEORY

IN this Chapter we are concerned with a certain very simple interpretation of "probability". We have, first, to show that it satisfies the axioms of Chapter II, and then to consider, in a preliminary way, how far it can be made to cover ordinary uses of the word "probability". I shall call it "the finite frequency theory", to distinguish it from another form of frequency theory which we shall consider later.

The finite frequency theory starts from the following definition:

Let B be any finite class, and A any other class. We want to define the chance that a member of B chosen at random will be a member of A, e.g. that the first person you meet in the street will be called Smith. We define this probability as the number of B's that are A's divided by the total number of B's. We denote this by the symbol A/B.

It is obvious that a probability so defined must be a rational fraction or o or 1.

A few illustrations will make the purport of this definition clear. What is the chance that an integer less than 10, chosen at random, will be a prime? There are 9 integers less than 10, and 5 of them are primes; therefore the chance is 5/9. What is the chance that it rained in Cambridge on my birthday last year, assuming that you do not know when my birthday is? If m was the number of days on which it rained, the chance is $m/365$. What is the chance that a man whose name occurs in the London telephone book will be called Smith? To solve this problem, you must first count the entries under the name "Smith", and then count all the entries, and divide the former number by the latter. What is the chance that a card drawn at random from a pack will be a spade? Obviously 13/52, i.e. 1/4. If you have drawn a spade, what is the chance that you will draw another? The answer is 12/51. In a throw of two dice, what is the chance that the numbers will add up to 8? There are 36 ways in which the dice may fall, and in 5 of these the numbers add up to 8, so the chance is 5/36.

It is obvious that, in a number of elementary cases, the above definition gives results that accord with usage. Let us now inquire whether probability, so defined, satisfies the axioms.

The letters p and q and h, which occur in the axioms, must now be taken to stand for classes or propositional functions, not for propositions. Instead of "h implies p" we shall have "h is contained in p"; "p and q" will stand for the common part of the two classes p and q, while "p or q" will be the class of all terms that belong to either or both of the two classes p and q.

Our axioms were:

I. There is only one value of p/h. This will be true unless h is null, in which case $p/h = 0/0$. We shall therefore assume that h is not null.

II. The possible values of p/h are all the real numbers from 0 to 1. In our interpretation, they will be only the *rational* numbers, unless we can find a way of extending our definition to infinite classes. This cannot be done simply, since division does not yield a unique result when the numbers concerned are infinite.

III. If h is contained in p, then $p/h = 1$. In this case, the common part of h and p is h, therefore the above follows from our definition.

IV. If h is contained in not -p, then $p/h = 0$. This is obvious on our definition, since in this case the common part of h and p is null.

V. *The conjunctive axiom.*—This states, on our interpretation, that the proportion of members of h which are members of both p and q is the proportion of members of h that are members of p multiplied by the proportion of members of p and h that are members of q. Suppose the number of members of h is a, the number of members common to p and h is b, and the number of members common to p and q and h is c. Then the proportion of members of h that are members of both p and q is c/a; the proportion of members of h that are members of p is b/a, and the proportion of members of p and h that are members of q is c/b. Thus our axiom is verified, since $c/a = b/a \times c/b$.

VI. *The disjunctive axiom.* This says, on our present interpretation, keeping the above meanings of a, b, and c, and adding that d is the number of members of h that are members of p or q or both, while e is the number of members of h that are members of q, that

$$\frac{d}{a} = \frac{b}{a} + \frac{e}{a} - \frac{c}{a}, \text{ i.e. } d = b + e - c$$

which again is obvious.

Thus our axioms are satisfied if *h* is a finite class which is not null, except that the possible values of a probability are confined to *rational* fractions.

It follows that the mathematical theory of probability is valid on the above interpretation.

We have, however, to inquire as to the *scope* of probability so defined, which is, *prima facie*, much too narrow for the uses that we wish to make of probability.

In the first place, we wish to be able to speak of the chance that some definite event will have some characteristic, not only of the chance that an unspecified member of a class will have it. For example: You have already made a throw with two dice, but I have not seen the result. What is, for me, the probability that you have thrown double sixes? We want to be able to say that it is 1/36, and if our definition does not allow us to say so, it is inadequate. In such a case, we should say that we are considering an event merely as an instance of a certain class; we should say that, if *a* is considered merely as a member of the class B, the chance that it belongs to the class A is A/B. But it is not very clear what is meant by "considering a definite event merely as a member of a certain class". What is involved in such a case is this: We are given some characteristic of an event which, to more complete knowledge than ours, is sufficient to determine it uniquely; but relatively to our knowledge, we have no way of finding out whether it belongs to the class A, though we do know that it belongs to the class B. You, who have thrown the dice, know whether the throw belongs to the class of double sixes, but I do not know this. My only relevant knowledge is that it is one of the 36 possible kinds of throws. Or take the following question: What is the chance that the tallest man in the United States lives in Iowa? Somebody may know who he is; at any rate there is a known method of finding out who he is. If this method has been successfully employed, there is a definite answer not involving probability, namely, either that he does live in Iowa or that he does not. But I have not this knowledge. I can ascertain that the population of Iowa is *m* and that of the United States is *n*, and say that, relative to these data, the probability that he lives in Iowa is *m/n*. Thus when we speak of the probability of a definite event having some characteristic, we must always specify the data relative to which the probability is to be estimated.

We may say generally: Given any object a, and given that a is a member of the class B, we say that, in relation to this datum, the probability that a is an A is A/B as previously defined. This conception is useful because we often know enough about some object to enable us to define it uniquely, without knowing enough to determine whether it has this or that property. "The tallest man in the United States" is a definite description, which applies to one and only one man, but I do not know what man, and therefore for me it is an open question whether he lives in Iowa. "The card I am about to draw" is a definite description, and in a moment I shall know whether this description applies to a red or a black card, but as yet I do not know. It is this very common condition of partial ignorance as to definite objects that makes it *useful* to apply probability to definite objects, and not only to wholly undefined members of classes.

Although partial ignorance is what makes the above form of probability *useful*, ignorance is not involved in the concept of probability, which would still have the same meaning for omniscience as for us. Omniscience would know whether a is an A, but would still be able to say: Relative to the datum that a is a B, the probability that a is an A is A/B.

In the application of our definition to a definite instance, there is a possible ambiguity in certain cases. To make this clear, we must use the language of properties rather than classes. Let the class A be defined by the property ϕ and the class B by the property ψ. Then we say:

The probability that a has the property ϕ given that it has the property ψ is defined as the proportion of things having both the properties ϕ and ψ to those having the property ψ. We denote "a has the property ϕ" by "ϕa". But if a occurs more than once in "ϕa", there will be an ambiguity. E.g. suppose "ϕa" is "a commits suicide", i.e. "a kills a". This is a value of "x kills x", which is the class of suicides; also of "a kills x", which is the class of persons whom a kills; also of "x kills a", which is the class of persons who kill a. Thus in defining the probability of ϕa, if "a" occurs more than once in "ϕa", we must indicate which of its occurrences are to be regarded as values of a variable and which not.

It will be found that we can interpret all elementary theorems in accordance with the above definition.

Take, for example, Laplace's supposed justification of induction:
There are $N + 1$ bags, each containing N balls.

Of the bags, the $r + 1^{th}$ contains r white balls and $N - r$ black
balls. We have drawn from one bag n balls, all white. What is
the chance

(a) that we have chosen the bag in which all are white?

(b) that the next ball will be white?

Laplace says that (a) is $(n + 1)/(N + 1)$ and (b) is $(n + 1)/(n + 2)$.

Let us illustrate by some numerical instances. First: Suppose
there are 8 balls altogether, of which 4 have been drawn, all
white. What are the chances (a) that we have chosen the bag
consisting only of white balls, and (b) that the next ball drawn
will be white?

Let p_r represent the hypothesis that we have chosen the bag
with r white balls. The data exclude p_0, p_1, p_2, p_3. If we have p_4,
there is only one way in which we can have drawn 4 whites, and
there remain 4 ways of drawing a black, none of drawing a white.
If we have p_5, there were 5 ways in which we could have drawn
4 whites, and for each of these there was 1 way of drawing
another white, and 3 of drawing a black; thus from p_5 we get
a contribution of 5 cases where the next is white and 15 where
it is black. If we have p_6, there were 15 ways of choosing 4 whites,
and when they had been chosen there remained 2 ways of choosing
a white and 2 of choosing a black; thus we get from p_6 30 cases
of another white and 30 where the next is black. If we have p_7,
there are 35 ways of drawing 4 whites, and after they have been
drawn there remain 3 ways of drawing a white and one of drawing
a black; thus we get 105 ways of drawing another white and 35
of drawing a black. If we have p_8, there are 70 ways of drawing
4 whites, and when they have been drawn there are 4 ways of
drawing another white and none of drawing a black; thus we get
from p_8 280 cases of a fifth white and none of a black. Adding,
we have $5 + 30 + 105 + 280$, i.e. 420, cases in which the fifth
ball is white, and $4 + 15 + 30 + 35$, i.e. 84, cases in which the
fifth ball is black. Therefore the odds in favour of white are
420 to 84, i.e. 5 to 1; that is to say, the chance of the fifth ball
being white is $5/6$.

The chance that we have chosen the bag in which all the balls
are white is the ratio of the number of ways of choosing 4 white
balls from this bag to the total number of ways of choosing 4

white balls. The former, we have seen, is 70; the latter is $1 + 5 + 15 + 35 + 70$, i.e. 126. Therefore the chance is 70/126, i.e. 5/9.

Both these results are in accordance with Laplace's formula.

To take one more numerical example: suppose there are 10 balls, of which 5 have been drawn, and have been found to be all white. What is the chance of p_{10}, i.e. of our having chosen the bag with only white balls? And what is the chance that the next ball will be white?

p_5 possible in   1 way; if p_5,   no way of another white, 5 of a black.
p_6 ,,   ,,   6 ways; ,, p_6, 1   ,,   ,,   ,, , 4 ,, ,,
p_7 ,,   ,,   21 ,, ; ,, p_7, 2 ways   ,,   ,, , 3 ,, ,,
p_8 ,,   ,,   56 ,, ; ,, p_8, 3 ,,   ,,   ,, , 2 ,, ,,
p_9 ,,   ,,   126 ,, ; ,, p_9, 4 ,,   ,,   ,, , 1 ,, ,,
p_{10} ,,   ,,   252 ,, ; ,, p_{10}, 5 ,,   ,,   ,, , 0 ,, ,,

Thus the chance of p_{10} is $252/[1 + 6 + 21 + 56 + 126 + 252]$, i.e. 252/462, i.e. 6/11.

The ways in which the next ball can be white are

$$6 + 21 \times 2 + 56 \times 3 + 126 \times 4 + 252 \times 5, \text{ i.e. } 1980$$

and the ways in which it can be black are

$$5 + 4 \times 6 + 3 \times 21 + 2 \times 56 + 126, \text{ i.e. } 330.$$

Therefore the odds in favour of white are 1,980 to 330, i.e. 6 to 1, so that the chance of another white is 6/7. This again is in accordance with Laplace's formula.

Let us now take Bernoulli's law of large numbers. We may illustrate it as follows: suppose we toss a coin n times, and put 1 for every time it comes heads, 2 for every time it comes tails, thus forming a number of n digits. We will suppose every possible sequence to come just once. Thus if $n = 2$, we have the four numbers 11, 12, 21, 22; if $n = 3$, we have the 8 numbers 111, 112, 121, 122, 211, 212, 221, 222; if $n = 4$, we have 16 numbers. 1111, 1112, 1121, 1122, 1211, 1212, 1221, 1222, 2111, 2112, 2121
2122, 2211, 2212, 2221, 2222;
and so on. Taking the last of the above lists, we find

    1 number all 1's
    4 numbers with three 1's and one 2
    6   ,,   ,,   two 1's ,, two 2's
    4   ,,   ,,   one 1 ,, three 2's
    1 number all 2's.

These numbers, 1, 4, 6, 4, 1, are the coefficients in $(a + b)^4$. It is easy to prove that, for n digits, the corresponding numbers are the coefficients in $(a + b)^n$. All that Bernoulli's theorem amounts to is that, if n is large, the sum of the coefficients near the middle is very nearly equal to the sum of all the coefficients (which is 2^n). Thus if we take all possible series of heads and tails in a large number of tosses, the immense majority have very nearly the same number of both; the majority and the nearness, moreover, increase indefinitely as the number of throws increases.

Though Bernoulli's theorem is more general and more precise than the above statements with equi-probable alternatives, it is to be interpreted, on our present definition of "probability", in a manner analogous to the above. It is a fact that, if we form all numbers that consist of 100 digits, each of which is either 1 or 2, about a quarter have 49 or 50 or 51 digits that are 1, nearly a half have 48 or 49 or 50 or 51 or 52 digits that are 1, more than half have from 47 to 53 digits that are 1, and about three-quarters from 46 to 54. As the number of digits is increased, the preponderance of cases in which 1's and 2's are nearly evenly balanced increases.

Why this purely logical fact should be regarded as giving us good ground for expecting that, when we toss a penny a great many times, we shall in fact attain an approximately equal number of heads and tails, is a different question, involving laws of nature in addition to logical laws. I mention it now only to emphasize the fact that I am not at present discussing it.

I want to lay stress on the fact that, in the above interpretation, there is nothing about possibility, and nothing which essentially involves ignorance. There is merely a counting of members of a class B and determining what proportion of them also belong to a class A.

It is sometimes contended that we need an axiom of equi-probability—e.g. to the effect that heads and tails are equally probable. If this means that in fact they occur with approximately equal frequency, the assumption is not necessary to the mathematical theory, which, as such, is not concerned with actual occurrences.

Let us now consider possible applications of the finite-frequency definition to cases of probability which might seem to fall outside it.

First: in what circumstances can the definition be extended to infinite collections? Since we have defined a probability as a fraction, and since fractions are meaningless when numerator and denominator are infinite, it will only be possible to extend the definition when there is some means of proceeding to a limit. This requires that the a's, of which we are to estimate the probability of their being b's, should form a series, in fact a progression, so that they are given as $a_1, a_2, a_3, \ldots a_n, \ldots$ where for every finite integer n there is a corresponding a_n and vice versa. We can then denote by "p_n" the proportion of a's up to a_n that belong to b. If, as n increases, p_n approaches a limit, we can define this limit as the probability that an a will be a b.[1] We must, however, distinguish the case in which the value of p_n oscillates about the limit from that in which it approaches the limit from one side only. If we repeatedly toss a coin, the number of heads will be sometimes more than half the total, sometimes less; thus p_n oscillates about the limit $1/2$. But if we consider the proportion of primes up to n, this approaches the limit zero from one side only: for any finite n, p_n is a definite positive fraction, which, for large values of n, is approximately $1/\log n$. Now $1/\log n$ approaches zero as n increases indefinitely. Thus the proportion of primes approaches zero, but we cannot say "no integers are primes"; we may say that the chance of an integer being a prime is infinitesimal, but not zero. Obviously the chance of an integer being a prime is greater than that of its being (say) both odd and even, although the chance is less than any finite fraction, however small. I should say that, when the chance that an a is a b is strictly zero, we can infer "no a is a b", but when the chance is infinitesimal we cannot make this inference.

It is to be observed that, unless we make some assumption about the course of nature, we cannot use the method of proceeding to the limit when we are dealing with a series which is defined empirically. For example, if we toss a given coin repeatedly, and find that the number of heads, as we go on, approaches continually nearer to the limit $1/2$, that does not entitle us to assume that this really would be the limit if we could make our series infinite. It may be, for example, that, if n is the number

---

[1] This limit depends upon the order of the a's, and therefore belongs to them as a series, not as a class.

of tosses, the proportion of heads does not approximate strictly to 1/2 but to

$$\tfrac{1}{2} + \tfrac{1}{4} \sin^2 \frac{n}{N}$$

where N is a number much larger than any that we can reach in actual experiments. In that case, our inductions would begin to be empirically falsified just as we were thinking they were firmly established. Or again, it might happen, with any empirical series, that after a time it became utterly lawless, and ceased in any sense to approach a limit. If, then, the above extension to infinite series is to be used in empirical series, we shall have to invoke some kind of inductive axiom. Without this, there is no reason for expecting the later parts of such a series to continue to exemplify some law which the earlier parts obey.

In ordinary empirical judgments of probability, such, for example, as are contained in the weather forecast, there is a mixture of different elements which it is important to separate. The simplest hypothesis—unduly simplified for purposes of illustration—is that some symptom is observed which, in (say) 90 per cent of the cases in which it has been previously observed, has been followed by rain. In that case, if inductive arguments were as indubitable as deductive ones, we should say "there is a 90 per cent probability of rain". That is to say, the present moment belongs to a certain class (that of moments when the symptom in question is present) of which 90 per cent are moments preceding rain. This is probability in the mathematical sense which we have been considering. But it is not this alone that makes us uncertain whether it will rain. We are also uncertain as to the validity of the inference; we do not feel sure that the symptom in question will, in the future, be followed by rain nine times out of ten. And this doubt may be of two kinds, one scientific, the other philosophical. We may, while retaining full confidence in scientific procedure in general, feel that, in this case, the data are too few to warrant an induction, or that not sufficient care has been taken to eliminate other circumstances which may have also been present and may be more invariable precursors of rain. Or, again, the records may be doubtful: they may have been rendered nearly indecipherable by rain, or have been made by a man who was shortly afterwards certified as insane. Such doubts are within scientific procedure, but there are also the doubts raised by Hume: is inductive procedure valid, or is it merely a habit which makes us comfortable? Any or all of those reasons may make us hesitant about the 90 per cent chance of rain which our evidence inclines us to believe in.

We have, in cases of this sort, a hierarchy of probabilities. The primary level is: Probably it will rain. The secondary level is: Probably the symptoms I noticed are a sign of probable rain. The tertiary level is: Probably certain kinds of events make certain future events probable. Of these three levels, the first is that of common sense, the second that of science, and the third that of philosophy.

In the first stage, we have observed that, hitherto, A has been followed, nine times out of ten, by B; in the past, therefore A has made B probable in the sense of finite frequency. We suppose without reflection, at this stage, that we may expect the same thing in the future.

In the second stage, without questioning the general possibility of inferring the future from the past, we realize that such inferences should be submitted to certain safeguards, such, for example, as those of Mill's four methods. We realize also that inductions, even when conducted according to the best rules, are not always verified. But I think our procedure can still be brought within the scope of the finite frequency theory. We have made in the past a number of inductions, some more careful, some less so. Of those made by a certain procedure, a proportion p have, so far, been verified; therefore this procedure, hitherto, has conferred a probability p upon the inductions that it sanctioned. Scientific method consists largely of rules by means of which p (as tested by the past results of past inductions) can be made to approach nearer to 1. All this is still within the finite frequency theory, but it is now inductions that are the single terms in our estimate of frequency.

That is to say, we have two classes A and B, of which A consists of inductions that have been performed in accordance with certain rules, and B consists of inductions which experience hitherto has confirmed. If n is the number of members of A, and m is the number of members common to A and B, then m/n is the chance that an induction conducted according to the above rules will have, up to the present, led to results which, when they could be tested, were found to be true.

In saying this, we are not using induction; we are merely describing a feature of the course of nature so far as it has been observed. We have, however, found a criterion of the excellence (hitherto) of any suggested rules of scientific procedure, and we have found it within the finite frequency theory. The only novelty is that our units are now inductions, not single events. The inductions are treated as occurrences, and it is only those that have actually occurred that are to be regarded as members of our class A.

But as soon as we argue either that an individual induction which has hitherto been confirmed will, or will probably, be confirmed in the future, or that rules of procedure, which have given, so far, a large proportion of inductions that have been confirmed so far, are likely to give a large proportion of confirmed inductions in the future, we have passed outside the finite frequency theory, since we are dealing with classes of which the numbers are not known. The mathematical theory of probability, like all pure mathematics, though it gives knowledge, does not (at least in one important sense) give anything new; induction, on the other hand, certainly gives something new, and the only doubt is whether what it gives is knowledge.

I do not want, as yet, to examine induction critically; I wish only to make clear that it cannot be brought within the scope of the finite frequency theory, even by the device of considering a particular induction as one of a class of inductions, since tested inductions can only supply *inductive* evidence in favour of a hitherto untested induction. If, then, we say that the principle which validates induction is "probable", we must be using the word "probable" in a different sense from that of the finite frequency theory; the sense in question must, I should say, be what we called "degree of credibility".

I incline to think that, if induction, or whatever postulate we may decide upon as a substitute, is assumed, all precise and measurable probabilities can be interpreted as finite frequencies. Suppose I say, for example: "There is a high probability that Zoroaster existed". To substantiate this statement, I shall have to consider, first, what is the alleged evidence in his case, and then to look out for similar evidence which is known to be either veridical or misleading. The class upon which the probability depends is not the class of prophets, existent and non-existent, for by including the non-existent we make the class somewhat vague; nor can it be the class of existent prophets only, since the question at issue is whether Zoroaster belongs to this class. We shall have to proceed as follows: There is, in the case of Zoroaster, evidence belonging to a certain class A; of all the evidences that belong to this class and can be tested, we find that a proportion p are veridical; we therefore infer, by induction, that there is a probability p in favour of the similar evidence in the case of Zoroaster. Thus frequency plus induction covers this use of probability.

Or suppose we say, like Bishop Butler: "It is probable that the universe is the result of design on the part of a Creator". Here we start with such subsidiary arguments as that a watch implies a watchmaker. There are very many instances of watches known to be made by watchmakers, and none of watches known to be not made by watchmakers. There is in China a kind of marble which sometimes, by accident, produces what appear to be pictures made by artists; I have seen the most astonishing examples. But this is so rare that, when we see a picture, we are justified (assuming induction) in inferring an artist with a very high degree of probability. What remains for the episcopal logician, as he emphasizes by the title of his book, is to prove the analogy; this may be held doubtful, but cannot well be brought under the head of mathematical probability.

So far, therefore, it would seem that doubtfulness and mathematical probability—the latter in the sense of finite frequency—are the only concepts required in addition to laws of nature and rules of logic. This conclusion, however, is only provisional. Nothing definitive can be said until we have examined certain other suggested definitions of "probability".

Chapter IV

THE MISES-REICHENBACH THEORY

THE frequency interpretation of probability, in a form different from that of the previous chapter, has been set forth in two important books, both by German professors who were then in Constantinople.[1]

Reichenbach's work is a development of that of v. Mises, and is in various ways a better statement of the same kind of theory. I shall therefore confine myself to Reichenbach.

After giving the axioms of the probability calculus, Reichenbach proceeds to offer an interpretation which seems to be suggested by the case of statistical correlations. He supposes two series $(x_1, x_2, \ldots x_n, \ldots)$, $(y_1, y_2, \ldots y_n, \ldots)$, and two classes O and P. Some or all of the x's belong to the class O; what interests him is the question: how often do the corresponding y's belong to the class P?

Suppose, for example, you were investigating the question whether a man is predisposed to suicide by having a nagging wife. In this case, the x's are wives, the y's are husbands, the class O consists of naggers, and the class P of suicides. Then given that a wife belongs to the class O, our question is: how often does her husband belong to the class P?

Consider the sections of the two series consisting of the first n terms of each. Suppose that, among the first n x's, there are a terms belonging to the class O, and suppose that, of these, there are b terms such that the corresponding y belongs to the class P. (The corresponding y is the one with the same suffix.) Then we say that, throughout the section from x_1 to x_n, the "relative frequency" of O and P is b/a. (If all the x's belong to the class O, $a = n$, and the relative frequency is b/n.) We denote this relative frequency by "$H_n(O, P)$".

We now proceed to define "the probability of P O", given which we denote by "$W(O, P)$". The definition is:

[1] Richard von Mises, *Wahrscheinlichkeit, Statistik und Wahrheit*, 2nd ed. Vienna, 1936 (1st ed. 1928); Hans Reichenbach, *Wahrscheinlichkeitslehre*, Leiden, 1935. See also the latter's *Experience and Prediction*, 1938.

W(O, P) is the limit of H_n(O, P) as n is indefinitely increased.

This definition can be considerably simplified by the use of a little mathematical logic. In the first place, it is unnecessary to have two series. For both are assumed to be progressions, and there is therefore some one-one correlator of their terms. If this is S, to say that a certain y belongs to a class P is equivalent to saying that the corresponding x belongs to the class of terms having the relation S to some one or other of the members of P. E.g. let S be the relation of wife to husband; then if y is a married man and x is his wife, to say that y is a government official is true if, and only if, x is the wife of a government official.

In the second place, there is no advantage in admitting the case in which not all the x's belong to the class O. The definition is only appropriate if an infinite number of the x's belong to the class O; in that case, those that belong to O form a progression, and the rest can be forgotten. Thus we retain what is essential in Reichenbach's definition if we substitute the following:

Let Q be a progression, and a some class, of which, in the important cases, there are members, in the series of Q, later than any given member. Let m be the number of members of a among the first n members of Q. Then W(Q, a) is defined as the limit of m/n when n is indefinitely increased.

Perhaps through inadvertence, Reichenbach speaks as if the concept of probability were *only* applicable to progressions, and had no application to finite classes. I cannot think he intends this. The human race, for example, is a finite class, and we wish to apply probability to vital statistics, which would be impossible according to the letter of the definition. As a matter of psychological fact, when Reichenbach speaks of the limit for $n =$ infinity, he is *thinking* of the limit as some number which is very nearly approached whenever n is large from an empirical point of view, i.e. when it is not far short of the maximum that our means of observation enable us to reach. He has an axiom or postulate to the effect that, when there is such a number for every large observable n, it is approximately equal to the limit for $n =$ infinity. This is an awkward axiom, not only because it is arbitrary, but because most of the series with which we are concerned outside pure mathematics are not infinite; indeed it may be doubted whether any of them are. We are in the habit of assuming that space-time is continuous, which implies the existence of infinite series; but this assumption has no basis except mathematical convenience.

I shall assume, in order to make Reichenbach's theory as adequate as possible, that, where finite classes are concerned, the definition of the last chapter is to be retained, and that the new definition is only intended as an extension enabling us to apply probability to infinite classes. Thus his H_n (O, P) will be a probability, but one applying only to the first n terms of the series.

What Reichenbach postulates, as his form of induction, is something like this: Suppose we have made N observations as to the correlation of O and P, so that we are in a position to calculate H_n (O, P) for all values of n up to $n = N$, and suppose that, throughout the last half of the values of n, H_n (O, P) always differs from a certain fraction p by less than ϵ, where ϵ is small. Then it shall be posited that, however much we were to increase n, H_n (O, P) would still lie within these narrow boundaries, and therefore W (O, P), which is the limit for $n =$ infinity, will also lie within these boundaries. Without this assumption, we can have no empirical evidence as to the limit for $n =$ infinity, and the probabilities for which the definition is specially designed must remain totally unknown.

In defence of Reichenbach's theory, in face of the above difficulties, two things may be said. In the first place, he may contend that it is not necessary to suppose n to approach infinity indefinitely; for all practical purposes, it suffices if n is allowed to become very large. Suppose, for instance, that we are dealing with vital statistics. It does not matter to an insurance company what will happen to the statistics if they are prolonged for another 10,000 years; at most, the next 100 years concern it. If, when we have accumulated statistics, we assume that frequencies will remain roughly the same until we have ten times as many data as we have now, that is enough for almost all practical purposes. Reichenbach may say that, when he speaks of infinity, he is using a convenient mathematical shorthand, meaning only "a good deal more of the series than we have investigated hitherto". The case is exactly analogous, he might say, to that of the empirical deter-

mination of a velocity. In theory, a velocity can only be determined if there is no limit to the smallness of measureable spaces
and times; in practice, since there is such a limit, the velocity
at an instant can never be known even approximately. We can,
it is true, know with a fair measure of accuracy the *average*
velocity throughout a short time. But even if we assume a postulate
of continuity, the average velocity throughout (say) a second gives
absolutely no indication as to the velocity at a given instant during
that second. All motion might consist of periods of rest separated
by instants of infinite velocity. Short of this extreme hypothesis,
and even if we assume continuity in the mathematical sense, no
finite velocity at an instant is incompatible with any finite average
velocity throughout a finite time, however short, which contains
that instant. For practical purposes, however, this is of no consequence. Except in a few phenomena such as explosions, if we
take the velocity at any instant through a very short measurable
time to be approximately the average velocity during that time,
the laws of physics are found to be verified. "Velocity at an instant", therefore, may be regarded as nothing but a convenient
mathematical fiction.

In like manner, Reichenbach may say, when he speaks of the
limit of a frequency when *n* is infinite, he means only the actual
frequency for very large numbers, or rather this frequency with
a small margin of error. The infinite and the infinitesimal are
equally unobservable, and therefore (he may say) equally irrelevant
to empirical science.

I am inclined to admit the validity of this answer. I only regret
that I do not find it explicitly in Reichenbach's books; I think,
nevertheless, that he must have had it in mind.

The second point in favour of his theory is that it applies to
just the sort of cases in which we wish to use probability arguments. We wish to use these arguments when we have *some* data
as to a certain future event, but not enough to determine its
character in some respect that interests us. My death, for example,
is a future event, and if I am insuring my life I may wish to
know what evidence exists as to the likelihood of death occurring
in some given year. In such a case we always have a number of
individual facts recorded in a series, and we assume that the
frequencies we have found hitherto will more or less continue.
Or take gambling, from which the whole subject took its rise.

We are not interested in the mere fact that there are 36 possible results of a throw with two dice. What we are interested in is the fact (if it be a fact) that in a long series of throws each of these 36 possibilities will be realized an approximately equal number of times. This is a fact which does not follow from the mere existence of 36 possibilities. When you meet a stranger, there are exactly two possibilities: on the one hand, he may be called Ebenezer Wilkes Smith; on the other hand, he may not. But in a long life, during which I have met a great many strangers, I have only once found the former possibility realized. The pure mathematical theory, which merely enumerates possible cases, is devoid of practical interest unless we know that each possible case occurs approximately with equal frequency, or with some known frequency. And this, if we are considering events, not a logical schema, can only be known through actual statistics, the use of which, it may be said, must proceed more or less as in Reichenbach's theory.

This argument, also, I shall admit provisionally; it will be examined afresh when we come to consider induction.

There is an objection of a quite different kind to Reichenbach's theory as he states it, and that has to do with his introducing series where only classes seem to be logically relevant. Let us take an illustration: what is the chance that an integer chosen at random will be a prime? If we take the integers in their natural order, the chance, on his definition, is zero; for if n is an integer, the number of primes less than or equal to n is approximately $n/\log n$ if n is large, so that the chance of an integer less than n being a prime approximates to $1/\log n$, and the limit of $1/\log n$ as n is indefinitely increased is zero. But now suppose we rearrange the integers on the following plan: Put first the first 9 primes, then the first number that is not a prime, then the next 9 primes, and then the second number that is not a prime, and so on indefinitely. When the integers are arranged in this order, Reichenbach's definition shows that the chance of a number selected at random being a prime is $\frac{9}{10}$. We could even arrange the integers so that the chance of a number not being a prime would be zero. To get this result, begin with the first non-prime, i.e. 4, and put after the nth number which is not a prime the n primes next after those already placed; this series begins 4, 1, 6, 2, 3, 8, 5, 7, 11, 9, 13, 17, 19, 23, 10, 29, 31, 37, 41, 43, 12. . . .

In this arrangement, there will be, before the $(n + 1)^{th}$ non-prime, n non-primes and $\frac{1}{2} n (n + 1)$ primes; thus as n increases, the ratio of the number of non-primes to the number of primes approaches o as a limit.

From this illustration it is obvious that, if Reichenbach's definition is accepted, given any class A having as many terms as there are natural numbers, and given any infinite sub-class B, the chance that an A selected at random will be a B will be anything from o to 1 (both included), according to the way in which we choose to distribute the B's among the A's.

It follows that, if probability is to apply to infinite collections, it must apply to series, not to classes. This seems strange.

It is true that, where empirical data are concerned, they are all given in a time-order, and therefore as a series. If we choose to assume that there is going to be an infinite number of events of the kind we are investigating, then we can also decide that our definition of probability is to apply only so long as the events are arranged in temporal sequence. But outside pure mathematics no series are known to be infinite, and most are, as far as we can judge, finite. What is the chance that a man of 60 will die of cancer? Surely we can estimate this without assuming that the number of men who, before time ends, will have died of cancer, is infinite. But according to the letter of Reichenbach's definition this should be impossible.

If probabilities depend upon taking events in their temporal order, rather than in any other order of which they are susceptible, then probability cannot be a branch of logic, but must be part of the study of the course of nature. This is not Reichenbach's view; he holds, on the contrary, that all true logic is probability-logic, and that the classical logic is at fault because it classifies propositions as true or false, not as having this or that degree of probability. He should, therefore, be able to state what is fundamental in probability-theory in abstract logical terms, without introducing accidental features of the actual world, such as time.

There is great difficulty in combining a statistical view of probability with the view, which Reichenbach also holds, that all propositions are only probable in varying degrees that fall short of certainty. The difficulty is that we seem committed to an endless regress. Suppose we say it is probable that a man who has plague will die of it. This means that, if we could ascertain the whole series of men who, from the earliest times till the extinction of the human race, will have suffered from plague, we should find that more than half of them will have died of it. Since the future and much of the past are unrecorded, we assume that the recorded cases are a fair sample. But now we are to remember that all our knowledge is only probable; therefore if, in compiling our statistics, we find it recorded that Mr. A had plague and died of it, we must not regard this item as certain, but only as probable. To find out how probable it is, we must include it in a series, say of official death certificates, and we must find some means of ascertaining what proportion of death certificates are correct. Here a single item in our statistics will be: "Mr. Brown was officially certified to have died, but turned out to be still alive". But this, in turn, is to be only probable, and must therefore be one of a series of recorded official errors, some of which turned out to be not errors. That is to say, we must collect cases where it was falsely believed that a person certified dead had been found to be still alive. To this process there can be no end, if all our knowledge is only probable, and probability is only statistical. If we are to avoid an endless regress, and if all our knowledge is to be only probable, "probability" will have to be interpreted as "degree of credibility", and will have to be estimated otherwise than by statistics. Statistical probability can only be estimated on a basis of certainty, actual or postulated.

I shall return to Reichenbach in connection with induction. For the present, I wish to make clear my own view as to the connection of mathematical probability with the course of nature. Let us take as an illustration a case of Bernoulli's law of large numbers, choosing the simplest possible case. We have seen that, if we make up all possible integers consisting of n digits, each either 1 or 2, then, if n is large—say not less than 1,000—a vast majority of the possible integers have an approximately equal number of 1's and 2's. This is merely an application of the fact that, in the binomial expansion of $(x + y)^n$, when n is large the sum of the coefficients near the middle falls not far short of the sum of all the coefficients, which is 2^n. But what has this to do with the statement that, if I toss a penny often, I shall probably get an approximately equal number of heads and tails? The one is a logical fact, the other, apparently, an empirical fact; what is the connection between them?

With some interpretations of "probability", a statement containing the word "probable" can never be an empirical statement. It is admitted that what is improbable may happen, and what is probable may fail to happen. It follows that what does happen does not show that a previous judgment of probability was either right or wrong; every imaginable course of events is logically compatible with every imaginable anterior estimate of probabilities. This can only be denied by maintaining that what is very improbable does not happen, which we have no right to maintain. In particular, if induction asserts only probabilities, then whatever may happen is logically compatible both with the truth and with the falsehood of induction. Therefore the inductive principle has no empirical content. This is a *reductio ad absurdum*, and shows that we must connect the probable with the actual more closely than is sometimes done.

If we adhere to the finite frequency theory—and so far I have seen no reason for not doing so—we shall say that, if we assert "*a* is an A" to be probably given "*a* is a B", we mean that, in fact, most members of B are members of A. This is a statement of fact, but not a statement about *a*. And if I say that an inductive argument (suitably formulated and limited) makes its conclusion probable, I mean that it is one of a class of arguments, most of which have conclusions that are true.

What, now, can I mean when I say that the chance of heads is a half? To begin with, this, if true, is an empirical fact; it does not follow from the fact that, in tossing a coin, there are only two possibilities, heads and tails. If it did, we could infer that the chance of a stranger being called Ebenezer Wilkes Smith is a half, since there are only two alternatives, that he is so called or that he isn't. With some coins, heads come oftener than tails; with others, tails oftener than heads. When I say, without specifying the coin, that the chance of heads is a half, what do I mean?

My assertion, like all other empirical assertions that pretend to numerical exactitude, must be only approximate. When I say that a man's height is 6 ft. 1 in., I am allowed a margin of error; even if I have said it on oath, I cannot be convicted of perjury if it turns out that I am a hundredth of an inch out. Similarly, I must not be held to have made a false statement about the penny if it turns out that 0·500001 would have been a more accurate estimate than 0·5. It is doubtful, however, whether any evidence could make me think 0·500001 a better estimate than 0·5. In probability, as elsewhere, we take the simplest hypothesis which approximately fits the facts. Take (say) the law of falling bodies. Galileo made a certain number of observations, which fitted more or less with the formula $s = \frac{1}{2}gt^2$. No doubt he could have found a function $f(t)$ such that $s = f(t)$ would have fitted his observations more exactly, but he preferred a simple formula which fitted well enough.[1] In the same way, if I tossed a coin 2,000 times and got 999 heads and 1,001 tails, I should take the chance of heads to be a half. But what exactly should I mean by this statement?

This question shows the strength of Reichenbach's definition. According to him, I mean that, if I continue long enough, the proportion of heads will come, in time, to be permanently very near $\frac{1}{2}$; in fact, it will come to differ from $\frac{1}{2}$ by less than any fraction however small. This is a prophecy; if it is correct, my estimate of the probability is correct, but if not, not. What can the finite frequency theory oppose to this?

We must distinguish between what the probability *is* and what it *probably* is. As to what the probability is, that depends upon the class of tosses we are considering. If we are considering tosses with a given coin, then if, in the whole of its existence, this coin is going to have given m heads out of a total of n tosses, the probability of heads with that coin is m/n. If we are considering coins in general, n will have to be the total number of tosses of coins throughout the past and future history of the world, and m the number of these that will have been heads. We may, to make the problem less vast, confine ourselves to tosses this year in England, or to tosses tabulated by students of probability. In all these cases m and n are finite numbers, and m/n is the probability of heads with the given conditions.

But none of the above probabilities are known. We are therefore driven to make estimates of them, that is to say, to find some way of deciding what they *probably* are. If we are to adhere to the finite frequency theory, this will mean that our series of heads and tails must be one of some finite class of series, and that we must have some relevant knowledge about this whole class. We

[1] Cf. Jeffreys, *Theory of Probability*, and *Scientific Inference*.

will suppose it to have been observed that, in every series of
10,000 or more tosses with a given coin, the proportion of heads
after the $5,000^{th}$ toss has never varied by more than 2ϵ, where ϵ
is small. We can then say: In every observed case, the proportion
of heads after 5,000 tosses with a given coin has always remained
between $p - \epsilon$ and $p + \epsilon$, where p is a constant depending on
the coin. To argue from this to a case not yet observed is a matter
of induction. If this is to be valid, we shall need an axiom to the
effect that (in certain circumstances) a characteristic which is
present in all observed cases is present in a large proportion of
all cases; or, at any rate, we shall need some axiom from which
this results. We shall then be able to infer a probable probability
from observed frequencies, interpreting probability in accordance
with the finite frequency theory.

The above is only an outline suggestion of a theory. The main
point that I wish to emphasize is that, on the theory I advocate,
every probability statement (as opposed to a merely doubtful
statement) is a statement of *fact*, as to some proportion in a series.
In particular, the inductive principle, whether true or false, will
have to assert that, as a fact, most series of certain kinds have,
throughout, any characteristic of a certain sort which is present
in a large number of successive terms of the series. If this is a
fact, inductive arguments may yield probabilities; if not, not.
I do not at present inquire how we are to know whether it is
a fact or not; that is a problem which I shall not consider until
the last section of our inquiry.

It will be seen that, in the above discussion, we have been led
to agree with Reichenbach on many points, while consistently
disagreeing as to the *definition* of probability. The main objection
which I feel to his definition is that the frequency on which it
depends is hypothetical and for ever unascertainable. I disagree
also in distinguishing more sharply than he does between probability and doubtfulness, and in holding that probability-logic is
not logically the fundamental kind, as opposed to certainty-logic.

Chapter V

KEYNES'S THEORY OF PROBABILITY

KEYNES'S *Treatise on Probability* (1921) sets out a theory which is, in a sense, the antithesis of the frequency theory. He holds that the relation used in deduction, namely "*p* implies *q*", is the extreme form of a relation which might be called "*p* more or less implies *h*". "If a knowledge of *h*", he says, "justifies a rational belief in *a* of degree α, we say there is a probability relation of degree α between *a* and *h*". We write this: "*a/h* = α". "Between two sets of propositions there exists a relation, in virtue of which, if we know the first, we can attach to the latter some degree of rational belief." Probability is essentially a relation: "It is as useless to say '*b* is probable' as '*b* is equal' or '*b* is greater than'." From "*a*" and "*a* implies *b*", we can conclude "*b*", that is to say, we can drop all mention of the premiss and simply assert the conclusion. But if *a* is so related to *b* that a knowledge of *a* renders a probable belief in *b* rational, we cannot conclude anything whatever about *b* which has not reference to *a*; there is nothing corresponding to the dropping of a true premiss in demonstrative inference.

Probability, according to Keynes, is a logical relation, which cannot be defined, unless, perhaps, in terms of degrees of rational belief. But on the whole it would seem that Keynes inclines rather to defining "degrees of rational belief" in terms of the probability-relation. Rational belief, he says, is derivative from knowledge: when we have a degree of rational belief in *p*, it is because we know some proposition *h* and also know *p/h* = α. It follows that some propositions of the form "*p/h* = α" must be among our premisses. Our knowledge is partly direct, partly by argument; our knowledge by argument proceeds through direct knowledge of propositions of the form "*p* implies *q*" or "*q/p* = α". In every argument, when fully analysed, we must have direct knowledge of the relation of the premisses to the conclusion, whether it be that of implication or that of probability in some degree. Knowledge of *h* and of *p/h* = α leads to a "rational belief of the appropriate degree" in *p*. Keynes explicitly assumes that all direct knowledge is certain, and that a rational belief which falls short of certainty can only arise through perception of a probability-relation.

Probabilities in general, according to Keynes, are not numerically measurable; those that are so form a very special class of probabilities. He holds that one probability may not be comparable with another, i.e. may be neither greater nor less than the other, nor yet equal to it. He even holds that it is sometimes impossible to compare the probabilities of p and not-p on given evidence. He does not mean that we do not know enough to do this; he means that there actually is no relation of equality or inequality. He thinks of probabilities according to the following geometrical scheme: Take two points, representing the o of impossibility and the 1 of certainty; then numerically measurable possibilities may be pictured as lying on the straight line between o and 1, while others lie on various curved routes from o to 1. Of two probabilities on the same route, we can say that the one nearer 1 is the greater, but we cannot compare probabilities on different routes, except when two routes intersect, which may happen.

Keynes needs, as we have seen, some direct knowledge of probability-propositions. In order to make a beginning in obtaining such knowledge, he examines and emends what is called the "principle of non-sufficient reason", or, as he prefers to call it, the "principle of indifference".

In its crude form, the principle states that if there is no known reason for one rather than another of several alternatives, then these alternatives are all equally probable. In this form, as he points out, the principle leads to contradictions. Suppose, for instance, you know nothing of the colour of a certain book; then the chances of its being blue or not blue are equal, and therefore each is 1/2. Similarly the chance of its being black is 1/2. Therefore the chance of its being blue or black is 1. It follows that all books are either blue or black, which is absurd. Or suppose we know that a certain man inhabits either Great Britain or Ireland, shall we take these as our alternatives, or shall we take England, Scotland, and Ireland, or shall we take each county as equally probable? Or, if we know that the specific gravity of a certain substance lies between 1 and 3, shall we take the intervals 1 to 2 and 2 to 3 as equally probable? But if we consider specific volume, the intervals 1 to 2/3 and 2/3 to 1/3 would be the natural choice, which would make the specific gravity have equal chances of being between 1 and 3/2 or between 3/2 and 3. Such paradoxes can be multiplied indefinitely.

Keynes does not, on this account, totally abandon the principle of indifference; he thinks it can be so stated as to avoid the above difficulties and still be useful. For this purpose, he first defines "irrelevance".

Roughly speaking, an added premiss is "irrelevant" if it does not change the probability; i.e. h_1 is irrelevant in relation to x and h if $x/h_1h = x/h$. Thus, for example, the fact that a man's surname begins with M is irrelevant in estimating his chances of death. The above definition is, however, somewhat too simple, because h_1 might consist of two parts, of which one increased the probability of x while the other diminished it. For example: a white man's chances of life are diminished by living in the tropics, but are increased (or so they say) by being a teetotaller. It may be that the death-rate among white teetotallers in the tropics is the same as that of white men in general, but we should not say that being a teetotaller who lives in the tropics was irrelevant. Therefore we say that h_1 is irrelevant to x/h if there is no part of h_1 which alters the probability of x.

Keynes now states the principle of indifference in the following form: The probabilities of a and b relative to given evidence are equal if there is no relevant evidence relating to a without corresponding evidence relating to b; that is to say, the probabilities of a and b relative to the evidence are equal, if the evidence is symmetrical with respect to a and b.

There is, however, still a somewhat difficult proviso to be added. "We must exclude those cases, in which one of the alternatives involved is itself a disjunction of sub-alternatives *of the same form*." When this condition is fulfilled, the alternatives are called *indivisible* relatively to the evidence. Keynes gives a formal definition of "divisible" as follows: An alternative $\phi(a)$ is divisible, relatively to evidence h, if, given h, "$\phi(a)$" is equivalent to "$\phi(b)$ or $\phi(c)$", where $\phi(b)$ and $\phi(c)$ are incompatible, but each possible, when h is true. It is essential, here, that $\phi(a)$, $\phi(b)$, $\phi(c)$ are all values of the same propositional function.

Keynes thus finally accepts as an axiom the principle that, on given evidence, $\phi(a)$ and $\phi(b)$ are equally probable, if (1) the evidence is symmetrical with respect to a and b, (2) relatively to the evidence, $\phi(a)$ and $\phi(b)$ are indivisible.

To the above theory empiricists might raise a general objection. They might say that the direct knowledge of probability relations which it demands is obviously impossible. Deductive demonstrative logic—so this argument might run—is possible because it consists of tautologies, because it merely re-states our initial stock of propositions in other words. When it does more than this—when, for instance, it infers "Socrates is mortal" from "all men are mortal", it depends upon experience for the meaning of the word "Socrates". Nothing but tautologies can be known independently of experience, and Keynes does not contend that his probability-relations are tautologous. How, then, can they be known? For clearly they are not known by experience, in the sense in which judgments of perception are so known; and it is admitted that some of them are not inferred. They would constitute, therefore, if admitted, a kind of knowledge which empiricism holds to be impossible.

I have much sympathy with this objection, but I do not think we can consider it decisive. We shall find, when we come to discuss the principles of scientific inference, that science is impossible unless we have some knowledge which we could not have if empiricism, in a strict form, were true. In any case, we should not assume dogmatically that empiricism is true, though we are justified in trying to find solutions of our problems which are compatible with it. The above objection, therefore, though it may cause a certain reluctance to accept Keynes's theory, should not make us reject it outright.

There is a difficulty on a question which Keynes seems not to have adequately considered, namely: Does probability in relation to premisses ever confer rational credibility on the proposition which is rendered probable, and, if so, under what circumstances? Keynes says that it is as nonsensical to say "p is probable" as to say "p is equal" or "p is greater than". There is, according to him, nothing analogous to the dropping of a true premiss in deductive inference. Nevertheless, he says that, if we know h, and we also know $p/h = a$, we are entitled to give to p "rational belief in the appropriate degree". But when we do so we are no longer expressing a relation of p to h; we are using this relation to infer something about p. This something we may call "rational credibility", and we can say; "p is rationally credible to the degree a". But if this is to be a true statement about p, not involving mention of h, then h cannot be arbitrary. For suppose $p/h = a$ and $p/h' = a'$, are we, supposing h and h' both known, to give to p the degree a or the degree a' of rational credibility? It is impossible that both answers should be correct in any given state of our knowledge.

If it is true that "probability is the guide of life", then there must be, in any given state of our knowledge, one probability which attaches to p more vitally than any other, and this probability cannot be relative to *arbitrary* premises. We must say that it is the probability which results when h is taken to be all our relevant knowledge. We can say: Given any body of propositions constituting some person's certain knowledge, and calling the conjunction of this body of propositions h, there are a number of propositions, not members of this body, which have probability-relations to it. If p is such a proposition, and $p/h = a$, then a is the degree of rational credibility belonging to p for that person. We must not say that, if h' is some true proposition, short of h, which the person in question knows, and if $p/h' = a'$, then, *for that person*, p has the degree of credibility a'; it will only have this degree of credibility for a person whose relevant knowledge is summed up by h'. All this, however, no doubt Keynes would admit. The objection is, in fact, only to a certain looseness of statement, not to anything essential to the theory.

A more vital objection is as to our means of knowing such propositions as $p/h = a$. I am not now arguing *a priori* that we *cannot* know them; I am merely inquiring how we *can*. It will be observed that if "probability" cannot be defined, there must be probability-propositions which cannot be proved, and which, therefore, if we are to accept them, must be among the premises of our knowledge. This is a general feature of all logically articulated systems. Every such system starts, of necessity, with an initial apparatus of undefined terms and unproved propositions. It is obvious that an undefined term cannot appear in an inferred proposition unless it has occurred in at least one of the unproved propositions; but a defined term need not occur in any unproved proposition. For example: so long as there were held to be undefined terms in arithmetic, there had to be also unproved axioms: Peano had three undefined terms and five axioms. But when numbers and addition are defined logically, arithmetic needs no unproved propositions beyond those of logic. So, in our case, if "probability" can be defined, it may be that all propositions in which the word occurs can be inferred; but if it cannot be defined, there must, if we are to know anything about it, be propositions, containing the word, which we know without extraneous evidence.

It is not quite clear what sort of propositions Keynes would admit as premises in our knowledge of probability. Do we directly know propositions of the form "$p/h = a$"? And when a probability is not numerically measurable, what sort of thing is a? Or do we only know equalities and inequalities, i.e. $p/h < q/h$, or $p/h = q/h$? I incline to think that the latter is Keynes's view. If so, the fundamental facts in the subject are relations of *three* propositions, not of *two*: we ought to start from a triadic relation

$$P(p, q, h)$$

meaning: given h, p is less probable than q. We might then say:

"$p/h = q/h$" means: "Neither $P(p, q, h)$ nor $P(q, p, h)$".

We should assume that P is asymmetrical and transitive with respect to p and q while h is kept constant. Keynes's principle of indifference, if accepted, will then enable us, in certain circumstances, to prove $p/h = q/h$. And from this basis the calculus of probabilities, in so far as Keynes considers it valid, can be built up.

The above definition of equality can only be adopted if p/h and q/h are comparable; if (as Keynes holds possible) neither is greater than the other and yet they are not equal, the definition must be abandoned. We could meet this difficulty by axioms as to the circumstances under which two probabilities must be comparable. When they are comparable they lie on one route between o and 1. On the right-hand side of the above definition of "$p/h = q/h$" we must then add that p/h and q/h are "comparable".

Let us now re-state Keynes's principle of indifference. He is concerned to establish circumstances in which $p/h = q/h$. This will happen, he says, if two conditions (sufficient but not necessary) are fulfilled. Let p be of the form $\phi(a)$ and q of the form $\phi(b)$; then h must be symmetrical with respect to a and b, and $\phi(a)$, $\phi(b)$ must be "indivisible".

When we say that h is symmetrical with respect to a and b, we mean, presumably, that, if h is of the form $f(a, b)$, then

$$f(a, b) \equiv f(b, a).$$

This will happen, in particular, if $f(a, b)$ is of the form $g(a) . g(b)$, which is the case when the information that h gives about a and b consists of separate propositions, one about a and the other about b, and both are values of one propositional function.

We now put $p = \phi(a)$, $q = \phi(b)$, $h = f(a, b)$.

Our axiom must be to the effect that, with a suitable proviso, the interchange of $\phi(a)$ and $\phi(b)$ cannot make any difference. This involves that

$$\phi(a)/f(a, b) = \phi(b)/f(a, b)$$

provided $\phi(a)$ and $\phi(b)$ are comparable with respect to $f(a, b)$. This follows if, as a general principle,

$$\phi a/\psi \, a = \phi b/\psi \, b$$

that is to say, if probability depends not on the particular subject but on propositional functions. There seems hope, along these lines, of arriving at a form of the principle of indifference which might have more self-evidence than Keynes's.

Let us, for this purpose, examine his condition of indivisibility. Keynes defines "$\phi(a)$ is divisible" as meaning that there are two arguments b and c such that "ϕa" is equivalent to "ϕb or ϕc" and ϕb and ϕc cannot both be true, while ϕb, ϕc are both possible given h. I do not think this is quite what he really wishes to say. We get nearer to what he wishes, I think, if we assume a and b and c to be classes, of which a is the sum of b and c. In that case, ϕ must be a function which takes classes as arguments. E.g. let a be an area on a target, divided into two parts b and c. Let "ϕa" be "some point of a is hit" and "ψa" be "some point of a is aimed at". Then ϕa is divisible in the above sense, and we do not have

$$\phi a/\psi a = \phi b/\psi b$$

for obviously $\phi a/\psi a$ is greater than $\phi b/\psi b$.

But it is not clear that our earlier condition, namely that h should be symmetrical with respect to a and b, does not suffice. For now h contains the proposition "b is part of a", which is not symmetrical.

Keynes discusses the conditions for $\phi a/\psi a = \phi b/\psi b$, and gives as an example of failure the case where $\phi x . = . x$ is Socrates. In that case, no matter what ψx may be,

$$\phi(\text{Socrates})/\psi(\text{Socrates}) = 1,$$

while if b is not Socrates, $\phi b/\psi b = 0$.

To exclude this case, I should make the proviso that "ϕx" must not contain "a". To take an analogous case, put

$$\phi x . = . x, \text{ kills } a, \psi x . = . x \text{ inhabits England.}$$

Then $\phi a/\psi a$ is the likelihood of a committing suicide if English, whereas $\phi x/\psi x$, in general, is the likelihood of a being murdered by some Englishman who is named x. Obviously, in most cases, $\phi a/\psi a$ is greater than $\phi b/\psi b$, because a man is more likely to kill himself than to kill another person selected at random.

The essential condition, then, seems to be that "ϕx" must not contain "a" or "b". If this condition is fulfilled, I do not see how we can fail to have

$$\phi a/\psi a = \phi b/\psi b.$$

I conclude that what the principle of indifference really asserts is that probability is a relation between propositional functions, not between propositions. This is what is meant by such phrases as "a random selection". This phrase means that we are to consider a term solely as one satisfying a certain propositional function; what is said is, then, really about the propositional function and not about this or that value of it.

Nevertheless, there remains something substantial which is what really concerns us. Given a probability-relation between two propositional functions ϕx and ψx, we can regard this as a relation between ϕa and ψa, provided "ϕx" and "ψx" do not contain "a". This is a necessary axiom in all applications of probability in practice, for then it is particular cases that concern us.

My conclusion is that the chief *formal* defect in Keynes's theory of probability consists in his regarding probability as a relation between propositions rather than between propositional functions. The application to propositions, I should say, belongs to the *uses* of the theory, not to the theory itself.

Chapter VI

DEGREES OF CREDIBILITY

A. GENERAL CONSIDERATIONS

THAT all human knowledge is in a greater or less degree doubtful is a doctrine that comes to us from antiquity; it was proclaimed by the sceptics, and by the Academy in its sceptical period. In the modern world it has been strengthened by the progress of science. Shakespeare, to represent the most ridiculous extremes of scepticism, says:

> Doubt that the stars are fire,
> Doubt that the sun doth move.

The latter, when he wrote, had already been questioned by Copernicus, and was about to be even more forcibly questioned by Kepler and Galileo. The former is false, if "fire" is used in its chemical sense. Many things which had seemed indubitable have turned out to be in all likelihood untrue. Scientific theories themselves change from time to time, as new evidence accumulates; no prudent man of science feels the same confidence in a recent scientific theory as was felt in the Ptolemaic theory throughout the middle ages.

But although every part of what we should like to consider "knowledge" may be in *some* degree doubtful, it is clear that some things are almost certain, while others are matters of hazardous conjecture. For a rational man, there is a scale of doubtfulness, from simple logical and arithmetical propositions, and perceptive judgments, at one end, to such questions as what language the Myceneans spoke or "what song the Sirens sang", at the other. Whether any degree of doubtfulness attaches to the least dubitable of our beliefs, is a question with which we need not at present concern ourselves; it is enough that any proposition concerning which we have rational grounds for some degree of belief or disbelief can, in theory, be placed in a scale between certain truth and certain falsehood. Whether these limits are themselves to be included, we may leave an open question.

There is a certain connection between mathematical probability and degrees of credibility. The connection is this: When, in relation to all the available evidence, a proposition has a certain mathematical probability, then this measures its degree of credibility. For instance, if you are about to throw dice, the proposition "double sixes will be thrown" has only one thirty-fifth of the credibility attaching to the proposition "double sixes will not be thrown". Thus the rational man, who attaches to each proposition the right degree of credibility, will be guided by the mathematical theory of probability *when it is applicable*.

The concept "degree of credibility", however, is applicable much more widely than that of mathematical probability; I hold that it applies to every proposition except such as neither are data nor are related to data in any way which is favourable or unfavourable to their acceptance. I hold, in particular, that it applies to propositions that come as near as is possible to merely expressing data. If this view is to be logically tenable, we must hold that the degree of credibility attaching to a proposition is itself sometimes a datum. I think we should also hold that the degree of credibility to be attached to a *datum* is sometimes a datum, and sometimes (perhaps always) falls short of certainty. We may hold, in such a case, that there is only one datum, namely, a proposition with a degree of credibility attached to it, or we may hold that the datum and its degree of credibility are two separate data. I shall not consider which of these two views should be adopted.

A proposition which is not a datum may derive credibility from various different sources; a man who wishes to prove his innocence of a crime may argue both from an alibi and from his previous good character. The grounds in favour of a scientific hypothesis are practically always composite. If it is admitted that a datum may not be certain, its degree of credibility may be increased by an argument, or, on the contrary, may be rendered very small by a counter-argument.

The degree of credibility conferred by an argument is not capable of being estimated simply. Take, first, the simplest possible case, namely that in which the premisses are certain and the argument, if valid, is demonstrative. At each step we have to "see" that the conclusion of this step follows from its premisses. Sometimes this is easy, for example if the argument is a syllogism in Barbara. In such a case, the degree of credibility attaching to the connection of premisses and conclusion is almost certainty, and the conclusion has almost the same degree of credibility as the premisses. But in the case of a difficult mathematical argument the chance of an error in reasoning is much greater. The logical connection may be completely obvious to a good mathematician, while to a pupil it is barely perceptible, and that only at moments. The pupil's grounds for believing in the validity of the step are not purely logical; they are in part arguments from authority. These arguments are by no means demonstrative, for even the best mathematicians sometimes make mistakes. On such grounds, as Hume points out, the conclusion of a long argument has less certainty than the conclusion of a short one, for at each step there is some risk of error.

By means of certain simplifying hypotheses, this source of uncertainty could be brought within the scope of the mathematical theory of probability. Suppose it established that, in a certain branch of mathematics, good mathematicians are right in a step in their arguments in a proportion x of all cases; then the chance that they are right throughout an argument of n steps is x^n. It follows that a long argument which has not been verified by repetition runs an appreciable risk of error, even if x is nearly 1. But repetition can reduce the risk until it becomes very small. All this is within the scope of the mathematical theory.

What, however, is not within the scope of that theory is the private conviction of the individual mathematician as he takes each step. This conviction will vary in degree according to the difficulty and complexity of the step; but in spite of this variability it must be as direct and immediate as our confidence in objects of perception. To prove that a certain premiss implies a certain conclusion, we must "see" each step; we cannot prove the validity of the step except by breaking it up into smaller steps, each of which will then have to be "seen". Unless this is admitted, all arguments will be lost in an endless regress.

I have been speaking, so far, of demonstrative inference, but as regards our present question non-demonstrative inference presents no new problem, for, as we have seen, even demonstrative inference, when carried out by human beings, only confers probability on the conclusion. It cannot even be said that reasoning which professes to be demonstrative always confers a higher degree of probability on the conclusion than reasoning which is avowedly only probable; of this there are many examples in traditional metaphysics.

If—as I believe, and as I shall argue in due course—data, as well as results of inference, may be destitute of the highest attainable degree of credibility, the epistemological relation between data and inferred propositions becomes somewhat complex. I may, for instance, think that I recollect something, but find reason to believe that what I seemed to recollect never happened; in that case I may be led by argument to reject a datum. Conversely, when a datum has, *per se*, no very high degree of credibility, it may be confirmed by extraneous evidence; for example, I may have a faint memory of dining with Mr. So-and-So some time last year, and may find that my diary for last year has an entry which corroborates my recollection. It follows that every one of my beliefs may be strengthened or weakened by being brought into relation with other beliefs.

The relation between data and inferences, however, remains important, since the reason for believing no matter what must be found, after sufficient analysis, in data, and in data alone. (I am here including among data the principles used in any inferences that may be involved.) What does result is that the data relevant to some particular belief may be much more numerous than they appear to be at first sight. Take again the case of memory. The fact that I remember an occurrence is evidence, though not conclusive evidence, that the occurrence took place. If I find a contemporary record of the occurrence, that is confirmatory evidence. If I find many such records, the confirmatory evidence is strengthened. If the occurrence is one which, like a transit of Venus, is made almost certain by a well-established scientific theory, this fact must be added to the records as an additional ground for confidence. Thus while there are beliefs which are only conclusions of arguments, there are none which, in a rational articulation of knowledge, are only premises. In saying this, I am speaking in terms of epistemology, not of logic.

Thus an epistemological premiss may be defined as a proposition which has some degree of rational credibility on its own account, independently of its relations to other propositions. Every such proposition can be used to confer some degree of credibility on propositions which either follow from it or stand in a probability relation to it. But at each stage there is some diminution of the original stock of credibility; the case is analogous to that of a fortune which is lessened by death duties on each occasion when it is inherited. Carrying the analogy a little further, we may say that intrinsic credibility is like a fortune acquired by a man's own efforts, while credibility as the result of an argument is like inheritance. The analogy holds in that a man who has made a fortune can also inherit one, though every fortune must owe its origin to something other than inheritance.

In this chapter I propose to discuss credibility, first in relation to mathematical probability, then in relation to data, then in relation to subjective certainty, and finally in relation to rational behaviour.

B. CREDIBILITY AND FREQUENCY

I am now concerned to discuss the question: In what circumstances is the credibility of a proposition a derived from the frequency of ψx given some ϕx? In other words, if "ϕa" is "a is an α", in what circumstances is the credibility of "a is a β" derived from one or more propositions of the form: "A proportion m/n of the members of α are members of β"? This question, we shall find, is not quite so general as the one we ought to ask, but it will be desirable to discuss it first.

It seems clear to common sense that, in the typical cases of mathematical probability, it is equal to degree of credibility. If I draw a card at random from a pack, the degree of credibility of "the card will be red" is exactly equal to that of "the card will not be red", and therefore the degree of credibility of either is $1/2$, if 1 represents certainty. In the case of a die, the degree of credibility of "1 will come uppermost" is exactly the same as that of "2 will come uppermost", or 3 or 4 or 5 or 6. Hence all the derived frequencies of the mathematical theory can be interpreted as derived degrees of credibility.

In this translation of mathematical probabilities into degrees of credibility, we make use of a principle which the mathematical theory does not need. The mathematical theory merely counts cases; but in the translation we have to know, or assume, that each case is equally credible. The need of this principle has long been recognized; it has been called the principle of non-sufficient reason, or (by Keynes) the principle of indifference. We considered this principle in connection with Keynes, but we must now consider it on its own account. Before discussing it, I wish to point out that it is *not* needed in the mathematical theory of probability. In that theory, we only need to know the numbers of various classes. It is only when mathematical probability is taken as a measure of credibility that the principle is required.

What we need is something like the following: "Given an object a, concerning which we wish to know what degree of credibility to attach to the proposition 'a is a β', and given that the only relevant knowledge we have is 'a is an α', then the degree of credibility of 'a is a β' is the mathematical probability measured by the ratio of the number of members common to α and β to the number of members of α".

Let us illustrate this by considering once more the tallest person in the United States, and the chance that he lives in Iowa. We have here, on the one hand, a description d, known to be applicable to one and only one of a number of named persons $A_1, A_2, \ldots A_n$, where n is the number of inhabitants of the United States. That is to say, one and only one of the propositions "$d = A_r$" (where r runs from 1 to n) is known to be true, but we do not know which. If this is really all our relevant knowledge, we assume that any one of the propositions "$d = A_r$" is as credible as any other. In that case, each has a credibility $1/n$. If there are m inhabitants of Iowa, the proposition "d inhabits Iowa" is equivalent to a disjunction of m of the propositions "$d = A_r$", and therefore has m times the credibility of any one of them, since they are mutually exclusive. Therefore it has a degree of credibility measured by m/n.

Of course in the above illustration the propositions "$d = A_r$" are not all on a level. The evidence enables us to exclude children and dwarfs, and probably women. This shows that the principle may be difficult to apply, but does not show that it is false.

The case of drawing a card from a pack comes nearer to realizing the conditions required by the principle. Here the description "d" is "the card I am about to draw". The 52 cards all have what we may regard as names: "2 of spades", etc. We have thus 52 propositions "$d = A_r$", of which one and only one is true, but we have no evidence whatever inclining us to one rather than another. Therefore the credibility of each is $1/52$. This, if admitted, connects credibility with mathematical probability.

We may therefore enunciate, as a possible form of the "principle of indifference", the following axiom:

"Given a description d, concerning which we know that it is applicable to one and only one of the objects a_1, a_2, . . . a_n, and given that we have no knowledge bearing on the question which of these objects the description applies to, then the n propositions '$d = a_r$' ($1 \leqslant r \leqslant n$) are all equally credible, and therefore each has a credibility measured by $1/n$."

This axiom is more restricted than the principle of non-sufficient reason as usually enunciated. We have to inquire whether it will suffice, and also whether we have reason to believe it.

Let us first compare the above with Keynes's principle of indifference, discussed in an earlier chapter. It will be remembered that his principle says: the probabilities of p and q relative to given evidence are equal if (1) the evidence is symmetrical with respect to p and q, (2) p and q are "indivisible", i.e. neither is a disjunction of propositions of the same form as itself. We decided that this could be simplified: what is needed, we said, is that p and q should be values of one propositional function—say $p = \phi(a)$ and $q = \phi(b)$; that "ϕx" should not contain either a or b; and that, if the evidence contains a mention of a, say in the form $\psi(a)$, it must also contain $\psi(b)$, and vice versa, where ψx, in turn, must not mention a or b. This principle is somewhat more general than the one enunciated in the previous paragraph: it implies the latter, but I doubt whether the latter implies it. We may perhaps accept the more general principle, and re-state it as follows:

"Given two propositional functions ϕx, ψx, neither of which mentions a or b, or, if it does so, mentions them symmetrically, then, given ψa and ψb, the two propositions ϕa, ϕb have equal credibility".

This principle, if accepted, enables us to infer credibility from mathematical probability, and makes all the propositions of the mathematical theory available for measuring degrees of credibility in the cases to which the mathematical theory is applicable.

Let us apply the above principle to the case of n balls in a bag, each of which is known to be either white or black; the question is: what is the probability that there are x white balls? Laplace assumed that every value of x from 0 to n is equally likely, so that the probability of a given x is $1/(n + 1)$. From a purely mathematical standpoint, this is legitimate, provided we start from the propositional function:

$$x = \text{the number of white balls.}$$

But if we start from the propositional function:

$$x \text{ is a white ball,}$$

we obtain a quite different result. In this case, there are many ways of choosing x balls. The first ball can be chosen in n ways; when it has been chosen, the next can be chosen in $n - 1$ ways, and so on. Thus the number of ways of choosing x balls is

$$n \text{ times } (n - 1) \text{ times } (n - 2) \text{ times } \ldots \text{ times } (n - x + 1).$$

This is the number of ways in which there can be x white balls. To get the probability of x white balls, we have to divide this number by the sum of the numbers of ways of choosing o white balls, or 1, or 2, or 3, or ... or n. This sum is easily shown to be 2^n. Therefore the chance of exactly x white balls is obtained by dividing the above number by 2^n. Let us call it "$p(n, r)$".

This has a maximum when $x = \frac{1}{2}n$ if n is even, or when $x = \frac{1}{2}n \pm \frac{1}{2}$ if n is odd. Its value when x or $n - x$ is small is very small if n is large. From the purely mathematical point of view, these two very different results are equally legitimate. But when we come to the measurement of degrees of credibility, there is a great difference between them. Let us have some way, independent of colour, by which we can distinguish the balls; e.g. let them be successively drawn out of the bag, and let us call the one first drawn d_1, the one drawn second d_2, and so on. Put "a" for "white" and "b" for "black", and put "ϕa" for "white is the colour of d_1", "ϕb" for "black is the colour of d_1". The evidence is that ϕa or ϕb is true, but not both. This is symmetrical, and therefore, on the evidence, ϕa and ϕb have equal credibility, i.e. "d_1 is white" and "d_1 is black" have equal credibility. The same reasoning applies to $d_2, d_3, \ldots d_n$. Thus in the case of each ball the degrees of credibility of white and black are equal. And therefore, as a simple calculation shows, the degree of credibility of x white balls is $p(n, x)$, where it is assumed that x lies between o and n, both included.

It is to be observed that, in measuring degrees of credibility, we suppose the data not only true, but exhaustive in relation to our knowledge, i.e. we assume that we know nothing relevant except what is mentioned in the data. Therefore for a given person at a given time there is only one right value for the degree of credibility of a given proposition, whereas in the mathematical theory many values are equally legitimate in relation to many different data, which may be purely hypothetical.

In applying the results of the mathematical calculus of probability to degrees of credibility, we must be careful to fulfil two conditions. First, the cases which form the basis of the mathematical enumeration must all be equally credible on the evidence; second, the evidence must include all our relevant knowledge. As to the former of these conditions a few words must be said.

Every mathematical calculation of probability starts from some fundamental class, such as a certain number of tosses of a coin, a certain number of throws of a die, a pack of cards, a collection of balls in a bag. Each member of this fundamental class counts as one. From it we manufacture other logically derivative classes, e.g. a class of n series of 100 tosses of a coin. Out of these n series we can pick out the sub-class of those that consist of 50 heads and 50 tails. Or, starting from a pack of cards, we can consider the class of possible "hands", i.e. selections of 13 cards, and proceed to inquire how many of these contain 11 cards of one suit. The point is that the frequencies that are *calculated* always apply to classes having some structure logically defined in relation to the fundamental class, whereas the fundamental class, for the purposes of the problem, is regarded as composed of members having no logical structure, i.e. their logical structure is irrelevant.

So long as we confine ourselves to the calculation of frequencies, i.e. to the mathematical theory of probability, we can take any class as our fundamental class, and calculate frequencies in relation to it. It is not necessary to make an assumption to the effect that all the members of the class are equally probable; all that we need to say is that, for the purpose in hand, each member of the class is to count as one. But when we wish to ascertain degrees of credibility, it is necessary that our basic class should consist of propositions which are all equally credible in relation to the evidence. Keynes's "indivisibility" is intended to secure this. I should prefer to say that the members of the fundamental class must have "relative simplicity", i.e. they must not have a structure definable in terms of the data. Take, e.g., white and black balls in a bag. Each ball has, in fact, an incredibly complicated structure, since it consists of billions of molecules; but this is quite irrelevant to our problem. On the other hand, a collection of *m* balls chosen from a fundamental class of *n* balls has a logical structure relatively to the fundamental class. If each member of the fundamental class has a name, every sub-class of *m* terms can be defined. All *calculations* of probability have to do with classes which can be defined in terms of the fundamental class. But the fundamental class itself must consist of members which cannot be logically defined in terms of the data. I think that when this condition is fulfilled the principle of indifference is always satisfied.

At this point, however, a caution is necessary. There are two ways in which "*a* is an *α*" may become probable, either (1) because it is certain that *a* belongs to a class most of which are *α*'s, or (2) because it is probable that *a* belongs to a class all of which are *α*'s. For instance, we may say "Mr. A. is probably mortal" if we are sure that most men are mortal, or if we have reason to think it probable that all men are mortal. When we make a throw with two dice, we can say "probably we shall not throw double sixes", because we know that most throws are not double sixes. On the other hand, suppose I have evidence suggesting, but not proving, that a certain bacillus is always present in a certain disease; I may then say, in a given case of this disease, that probably the bacillus in question is present. There is in each case a kind of syllogism. In the first case,

> Most A is B;
> This is an A;
> Therefore this is probably a B.

In the second case,

> Probably all A is B;
> This is an A;
> Therefore this is probably a B.

The second case, however, is more difficult to reduce to a frequency. Let us inquire whether this is possible.

In some cases, this is clearly possible. E.g. most words do not contain the letter Z. Therefore, if some word is chosen at haphazard, it is probable that all its letters are other than Z. Thus if

A = the class of letters in the word in question, and B = the class of letters other than Z, we get a case of our second pseudo-syllogism. The word, of course, must be defined in some way which leaves us in temporary ignorance as to what it is, e.g. the 8,000th word in *Hamlet*, or the third word on p. 248 of the *Concise Oxford Dictionary*. Assuming that you do not at present know what these words are, you will be wise to bet against their containing a Z.

In all cases of our second pseudo-syllogism, it is clear that what I have been calling the "fundamental class" is given as a class of classes, and therefore its logical structure is essential. To generalize the above instance: let κ be a class of classes, such that most of its members are entirely contained in a certain class β; then, from "x is an α" and "α is a κ" we can conclude "x is probably a β". (In the above instance, κ was the class of words, α the class of letters in a certain word, and β the alphabet without Z.) The odd thing is that, denoting by "sum of κ" the class of members of members of κ, our premisses do not suffice to prove that a member of the sum of κ is probably a member of β. For example, let κ consist of the three words STRENGTH, QUAIL, MUCK, together with all words containing no letter occurring in any of these three. Then the sum of κ consists of all the letters of the alphabet, possibly excepting Z.[1] But "x is an α and α is a κ" makes it probable that x is not one of the letters occurring in the above three words, while "x is a member of the sum of κ" does not make this probable. This illustrates the complications that arise when the fundamental class has a structure which is relevant to the probabilities. But in such cases as the above it is still possible to measure credibility by frequency, though less simply.

There is, however, another and more important class of cases, which we cannot adequately discuss except in connection with induction. These are the cases where we have inductive evidence making it probable that all A is B, and we infer that a particular A is probably a B, e.g. probably all men are mortal (*not* all men are probably mortal), therefore Socrates is probably mortal. This is a pseudo-syllogism of our second kind. But if the "probably" in "probably all men are mortal" can be reduced to a frequency,

[1] Whether Z is to be included depends upon whether "ZOO" is allowed to count as a word.

it certainly cannot be so reduced at all simply. I will therefore leave this class of cases to be discussed at a later stage.

There are, we shall find, various examples of degrees of credibility not derivable from frequencies. These I shall now proceed to consider.

C. CREDIBILITY OF DATA

In the present section I propose to advocate an unorthodox opinion, namely, that a datum may be uncertain. There have been hitherto two views: first, that in a proper articulation of knowledge we start from premisses which are certain in their own right, and may be defined as "data"; second, that, since no knowledge is certain, there are no data, but our rational beliefs form a closed system in which each part lends support to every other part. The former is the traditional view, inherited from the Greeks, enshrined in Euclid and theology; the latter is a view first advocated, if I am not mistaken, by Hegel, but most influentially supported, in our day, by John Dewey. The view which I am about to set forth is a compromise, but one somewhat more in favour of the traditional theory than of that advocated by Hegel and Dewey.

I define a "datum" as a proposition which has some degree of rational credibility on its own account, independently of any argument derived from other propositions. It is obvious that the conclusion of an argument cannot derive from the argument a higher degree of credibility than that belonging to the premisses; consequently, if there is such a thing as rational belief, there must be rational beliefs not wholly based on argument. It does not follow that there are beliefs which owe *none* of their credibility to argument, for a proposition may be both inherently credible and also a conclusion from other propositions that are inherently credible. But it does follow that every proposition which is rationally credible in any degree must be so either (*a*) solely in its own right, or (*b*) solely as the conclusion from premisses which are rationally credible in their own right, or (*c*) because it has some degree of credibility in its own right, and also follows, by a demonstrative or probable inference, from premisses which have some degree of credibility in their own right. If all propositions which have any credibility in their own right are certain, case (*c*) has no importance, since no argument can make such propositions more certain. But on the view which I advocate, case (*c*) is of the greatest importance.

The traditional view is adopted by Keynes, and set forth by him in his *Treatise on Probability*, p. 16. He says:

"In order that we may have a rational belief in *p* of a lower degree of probability than certainty, it is necessary that we know a set of propositions *h*, and also know some secondary proposition *q* asserting a probability-relation between *p* and *h*.

"In the above account one possibility has been ruled out. It is assumed that we cannot have a rational belief in *p* of a degree less than certainty except through knowing a secondary proposition of the prescribed type. Such belief can only arise, that is to say, by means of the perception of some probability-relation. . . . All knowledge which is obtained in a manner strictly direct by contemplation of the objects of acquaintance and without any admixture whatever of argument and the contemplation of the logical bearing of any other knowledge on this, corresponds to *certain* rational belief and not to a merely probable degree of rational belief."

I propose to controvert this view. For this purpose I shall consider (1) faint perception, (2) uncertain memory, (3) dim awareness of logical connection.

(1) *Faint perception.*—Consider such familiar experiences as the following. (*a*) You hear an aeroplane going away; at first you are sure you hear it, and at last you are sure you do not hear it, but in the interval there is a period during which you are not sure whether you still hear it or not. (*b*) You are watching Venus during the dawn; at first you see the planet shining brightly, and at last you know that daylight has made it invisible, but between these two times you may be in doubt whether you are still seeing it or not. (*c*) In the course of travel you have attracted a number of fleas; you set to work to get rid of them, and in the end you are sure you have succeeded, but in the meantime you are troubled by occasional doubtful itches. (*d*) By mistake you make tea in a pot that has contained vinegar; the result is appalling. You rinse the pot and try again, but still the offensive flavour is unmistakeable. After a second rinsing you are doubtful whether you still taste the vinegar; after a third you are sure you do not. (*e*) Your drains are out of order, and you call in the plumber. At first, after his visit, you feel sure that the offensive

odour is gone, but gradually, through varying stages of doubt, you become certain that it has returned.

Such experiences are familiar to every one, and must be taken account of in any theory as to the knowledge based on sense-perception.

(2) *Uncertain memory.*—In *The Tempest* (Act I, Scene II), Prospero asks Miranda to look into "the dark backward and abysm of time"; she says "had I not four or five women once that tended me?" and Prospero confirms her doubtful recollection. We all have memories of this kind, about which we do not feel sure. Usually, if it is worth while, we can discover from other evidence whether they are veridical or not, but that is irrelevant to our present thesis, which is that they have a certain degree of credibility on their own account, though this degree may fall far short of full certainty. A recollection which has a fairly high degree of credibility contributes its quota to our grounds for believing in some past occurrence for which we have other evidence. But here a distinction is necessary. The past event I uncertainly remembered has partial credibility in itself; but when I adduce the recollection as a ground for belief, I am no longer treating the past occurrence as a datum, for it is not it but the present recollecting that is my datum. My recollecting confers some credibility on what is recollected; how much credibility, we can more or less ascertain inductively by a statistical inquiry into the frequency of errors of memory. But this is a different matter from past occurrences as data. That such data must be supplied by memory is a thesis which I have argued elsewhere.

(3) *Dim awareness of logical connection.*—Any person whose mathematical abilities are not almost superhuman must, if he has studied mathematics, have often had the experience of being hardly able to "see" a certain step in a proof. The process of following a proof is facilitated by making the steps very small, but however small we make them some of them may remain difficult if the subject-matter is very complex. It is obvious that, if we have made the steps as small as possible, each step must be a datum, for otherwise every attempt at proof would involve an endless regress. Consider, say, a syllogism in Barbara. I say "all men are mortal", and you agree. I say "Socrates is a man", and you agree. I then say "therefore Socrates is mortal", and you say "I don't see how that follows". What, then, can I do?

I can say: "Don't you see that if $f(x)$ is always true, then $f(a)$ is true? and don't you see that therefore if $\phi(x)$ always implies $\psi(x)$, then ϕ (Socrates) implies ψ (Socrates)? and don't you see that I can put 'x is a man' for 'ϕx' and 'x is mortal' for 'ψx'? And don't you see that this proves my point?" A pupil who could follow this but not the original syllogism would be a psychological monstrosity. And even if there were such a pupil, he would still have to "see" the steps of my new argument.

It follows that, when an argument is stated as simply as possible, the connection asserted in every step has to be a datum. But it is impossible that the connection in every step should have the highest degree of credibility, because even the best mathematicians sometimes make mistakes. In fact, our perceptions of the logical connections between propositions, like our sense-perceptions and our memories, can be ordered by their degrees of credibility: in some, we see the logical connection so clearly that we cannot be made to doubt it, while in others our perception of the connection is so faint that we are not sure whether we see it or not.

I shall henceforth assume that a datum, in the sense defined at the beginning of this section, may be uncertain in a greater or less degree. We can, theoretically, make a connection between this kind of uncertainty and the kind derived from mathematical probability, if we suppose that an uncertainty of one kind can be judged greater than, equal to, or less than, one of the other kind. For example, when I think I hear a faint sound, but am not sure, I may theoretically be able to say: The occurrence of this sound has the same degree of rational credibility as the occurrence of double sixes with dice. In some degree, such comparisons could be tested, by collecting evidence of mistakes as to faint sensations and working out their frequency. All this is vague, and I do not see how to make it precise. But at any rate it suggests that the uncertainty of data is quantitative, and can be equal or unequal to the uncertainty derived from a probability inference. I shall assume this to be the case, while admitting that, in practice, the numerical measurement of the uncertainty of a datum is seldom possible. We may say that the uncertainty is a half when the doubt is such as to leave an even balance between belief and disbelief. But such a balance can only be established by introspection, and is incapable of being confirmed by any sort of test.

The admission of uncertainty in data complicates the process of estimating the rational credibility of a proposition. Let us suppose that a certain proposition p has a degree of credibility x on its own account, as a datum; and let us suppose that there is also a conjunction h of propositions, having intrinsic credibility y, from which it follows, by an argument having credibility z, that p has a degree of credibility w. What, then, is the total credibility of p? Perhaps we might be inclined to say that it is $x + yzw$. But h also is sure to have a derived as well as an intrinsic credibility, and this will increase the credibility of x. In fact, the complications will soon become unmanageable. This causes a certain approximation to the theory of Hegel and Dewey.

Given a number of propositions, each having a fairly high degree of intrinsic credibility, and given a system of inferences by virtue of which these various propositions increase each other's credibility, it may be possible in the end to arrive at a body of interconnected propositions having, as a whole, a very high degree of credibility. Within this body, some are only inferred, but none are only premises, for those which are premises are also conclusions. The edifice of knowledge may be compared to a bridge resting on many piers, each of which not only supports the roadway but helps the other piers to stand firm owing to interconnecting girders. The piers are the analogues of the propositions having some intrinsic credibility, while the upper portions of the bridge are the analogues of what is only inferred. But although each pier may be strengthened by the other piers, it is the solid ground that supports the whole, and in like manner it is intrinsic credibility that supports the whole edifice of knowledge.

D. DEGREES OF SUBJECTIVE CERTAINTY

Subjective certainty is a psychological concept, while credibility is at least in part logical. The question whether there is any connection between them is a form of the question whether we know anything. Such a question cannot be discussed on a basis of complete scepticism; unless we are prepared to assert *something*, no argument is possible.

Let us first distinguish three kinds of *certainty*.

(1) A propositional function is certain with respect to another when the class of terms satisfying the second is part of the class

of terms satisfying the first. E.g. "x is an animal" is certain in relation to "x is a rational animal". This meaning of certainty belongs to mathematical probability. We will call this kind of certainty "logical".

(2) A proposition is certain when it has the highest degree of credibility, either intrinsically or as a result of argument. Perhaps no proposition is certain in this sense, i.e. however certain it may be in relation to a given person's knowledge, further knowledge might increase its degree of credibility. We will call this kind of certainty "epistemological".

(3) A person is certain of a proposition when he feels no doubt whatever of its truth. This is a purely psychological concept, and we will call it "psychological certainty".

Short of subjective certainty, a man may be more or less convinced of something. We feel sure that the sun will rise to-morrow, and that Napoleon existed; we are less sure of quantum theory and the existence of Zoroaster; still less sure that Eddington got the number of electrons exactly right, or that there was a king called Agamemnon at the siege of Troy. These are matters as to which there is fairly general agreement, but there are other matters as to which disagreement is the rule. Some people feel no doubt that Churchill is good and Stalin bad, others think the opposite; some people were utterly certain that God was on the side of the Allies, others thought that He was on the side of the Germans. Subjective certainty, therefore, is no guarantee of truth, or even of a high degree of credibility.

Error is not only the absolute error of believing what is false, but also the quantitative error of believing more or less strongly than is warranted by the degree of credibility properly attaching to the proposition believed in relation to the believer's knowledge. A man who is quite convinced that a certain horse will win the Derby is in error even if the horse does win.

Scientific method, broadly speaking, consists of techniques and rules designed to make degrees of belief coincide as nearly as possible with degrees of credibility. We cannot, however, begin to seek such a harmony unless we can start from propositions which are both epistemologically credible and subjectively nearly certain. This suggests a Cartesian scrutiny, but one which, if it is to be fruitful, must have some non-sceptical guiding principle. If there were no relation at all between credibility and subjective certainty, there could be no such thing as knowledge. We assume in practice that a class of beliefs may be regarded as true if (*a*) they are firmly believed by all who have carefully considered them, (*b*) there is no positive argument against them, (*c*) there is no known reason for supposing that mankind would believe them if they were untrue. On this basis, it is generally held that judgments of perception on the one hand, and logic and mathematics on the other, contain what is most certain in our knowledge. We shall see that, if we are to arrive at science, logic and mathematics will have to be supplemented by certain extra-logical principles, of which induction has hitherto (I think mistakenly) been the one most generally recognized. These extra-logical principles raise problems which it will be our business to investigate.

Perfect rationality consists, not in believing what is true, but in attaching to every proposition a degree of belief corresponding to its degree of credibility. In regard to empirical propositions, the degree of credibility changes when fresh evidence accrues. In mathematics, the rational man who is not a mathematician will believe what he is told; he will therefore change his beliefs when mathematicians discover errors in the work of their predecessors. The mathematician himself may be completely rational in spite of making a mistake, if the mistake is one which at the time is very difficult to detect.

Whether we ought to aim at rationality is an ethical question. I shall consider some aspects of it in the following section.

E. PROBABILITY AND CONDUCT

Bishop Butler's statement that probability is the guide of life is very familiar. Let us consider briefly what it can mean, how far it is true, and what is involved in believing it to have the degree of truth that it seems to possess.

Most ethical theories are of one of two kinds. According to the first kind, good conduct is conduct obeying certain rules; according to the second, it is conduct designed to realize certain ends. There are theories which are of neither of these two kinds, but for our purposes we may ignore them.

The first type of theory is exemplified by Kant and the Decalogue. The Decalogue, it is true, is not a pure example of this type of theory, since reasons are given for some of the commandments. You must not worship graven images, because God will be jealous; you should honour your parents, because it diminishes your chances of death. It is of course easy to find reasons against murder and theft, but none are given in the Ten Commandments. If reasons are given, there will be exceptions, and common sense has in general recognized them, but none are admitted in the text.

When ethics is considered to consist of rules of conduct, probability plays no part in it. It is only in the second type of ethical theory, that in which virtue consists in aiming at certain ends, that probability is relevant. So far as the relation to probability is concerned, it makes very little difference what end is chosen. For the sake of definiteness, let us suppose the end to be the greatest possible excess of pleasure over pain, a pleasure and a pain being considered equal when a person who has the choice is indifferent whether he has both or neither. We may designate this end briefly as that of maximizing pleasure.

We cannot say that the virtuous man will act in the way that will *in fact* maximize pleasure, since he may have no reason to expect this result. It would have been a good thing if Hitler's mother had killed him in infancy, but she could not know this. We must therefore say that the virtuous man will act in the way which, so far as his knowledge goes, will *probably* maximize pleasure. The kind of probability that is involved is obviously degree of credibility.

The probabilities concerned are to be estimated by the rules for computing "expectation". That is to say, if there is a probability p that a certain act will have among its consequences a pleasure of magnitude x, this contributes an amount $p x$ to the expectation. Since distant consequences seldom have any appreciable probability, this justifies the practical man in usually confining his attention to the less remote consequences of his action.

There is another consideration: the calculations involved are often difficult, and are most difficult when the felicific properties of two possible actions are nearly equal, in which case the choice is unimportant. Therefore as a rule it is not worth while to determine with any care which action will produce the most pleasure. This is the reason in favour of rules of action, even if our ultimate ethic rejects them: they can be right in the great majority of cases, and save us the trouble and waste of time involved in estimating probable effects. But the rules of action themselves should be carefully justified by their felicific character, and where really important decisions are concerned it may be necessary to remember that the rules are not absolute. Currency reform usually involves something like theft, and war involves killing. The statesman who has to decide whether to reform the currency or to declare war has to go behind rules and do his best to estimate probable consequences. It is only in this sense that probability can be the guide of life, and that only in certain circumstances.

There is, however, another and humbler sense of the dictum, which was perhaps that intended by the Bishop. This is, that we should, in practice, treat as certain whatever has a very high degree of probability. This is merely a matter of common sense, and raises no issue that is of interest to the theory of probability.

Chapter VII

PROBABILITY AND INDUCTION

A. STATEMENT OF THE PROBLEM

THE problem of induction is a complex one, having various aspects and branches. I shall begin by stating the problem of induction by simple enumeration.

I. The fundamental question, to which others are subsidiary, is this: Given that a number of instances of a class α have all been found to belong to a class β, does this make it probable, (a) that the next instance of α will be a β, or (b) that all α's are β's?

II. If either of these is not true universally, are there discoverable limitations on α and β which make it true?

III. If either is true with suitable limitations, is it, when so limited, a law of logic or a law of nature?

IV. Is it derivable from some other principle, such as natural kinds, or Keynes's limitation of variety, or the reign of law, or the uniformity of nature, or what not?

V. Should the principle of induction be stated in a different form, viz.: Given a hypothesis h which has many known true consequences and no known false ones, does this fact make h probable? And if not generally, does it do so in suitable circumstances?

VI. What is the minimum form of the inductive postulate which will, if true, validate accepted scientific inferences?

VII. Is there any reason, and if so what, to suppose this minimum postulate true? Or, if there is no such reason, is there nevertheless reason to *act* as if it were true?

There is need, in these discussions, to remember the ambiguity in the word "probable" as commonly used. When I say that, in certain circumstances, "probably" the next α will be a β, I shall hope to be able to interpret this according to the finite frequency theory. But if I say that the inductive principle is "probably" true, I shall have to be using the word "probably" to express a high degree of credibility. Confusions may easily arise through not keeping these two meanings of the word "probable" sufficiently separate.

418

The discussions upon which we shall be engaged have a history which may be considered to begin with Hume. On a large number of subsidiary points definite results have been obtained; sometimes these points were not recognized, at first, to be subsidiary. But investigation has made it, by now, fairly clear that the technical discussions which reach results throw little light on the main problem, which remains substantially as Hume left it.

B. INDUCTION BY SIMPLE ENUMERATION

Induction by simple enumeration is the following principle: "Given a number n of a's which have been found to be β's, and no a which has been found to be not a β, then the two statements: (a) 'the next a will be a β', (b) 'all a's are β's', both have a probability which increases as n increases, and approaches certainty as a limit as n approaches infinity."

I shall call (a) "particular induction" and (b) "general induction". Thus (a) will argue from our knowledge of the past mortality of human beings that probably Mr. So-and-So will die, whereas (b) will argue that probably all men are mortal.

Before proceeding to more difficult or doubtful points, there are some rather important questions which can be decided without great difficulty. These are:

(1) If induction is to serve the purposes which we expect it to serve in science, "probability" must be so interpreted that a probability-statement asserts a *fact*; this requires that the kind of probability involved should be derivative from truth and false-hood, not an indefinable; and this, in turn, makes the finite-frequency interpretation more or less inevitable.

(2) Induction appears to be invalid as applied to the series of natural numbers.

(3) Induction is not valid as a *logical* principle.

(4) Induction requires that the instances upon which it is based should be given as a series, not merely as a class.

(5) Whatever limitation may be necessary to make the principle valid must be stated in terms of the *intensions* by which the classes a and β are defined, not in terms of extensions.

(6) If the number of things in the universe is finite, or if some finite class is alone relevant to the induction, then induction, for a sufficient n, becomes demonstrable; but in practice this is un-

important, because the *n* concerned would have to be larger than it ever can be in any actual investigation.

I shall now proceed to prove these propositions.

(1) If "probability" is taken as an indefinable, we are obliged to admit that the improbable may happen, and that, therefore, a probability-proposition tells us nothing about the course of nature. If this view is adopted, the inductive principle may be valid, and yet every inference made in accordance with it *may* turn out to be false; this is improbable, but not impossible. Consequently a world in which induction is true is empirically indistinguishable from one in which it is false. It follows that there can never be any evidence for or against the principle, and that it cannot help us to infer what will happen. If the principle is to serve its purpose, we must interpret "probable" as meaning "what in fact usually happens"; that is to say, we must interpret a probability as a frequency.

(2) *Induction in arithmetic.*—It is easy in arithmetic to give examples of inductions which lead to true conclusions, and others which lead to false conclusions. Jevons gives the two instances:

$$5, \ 15, \ 35, \ 45, \ 65, \ 95$$
$$7, \ 17, \ 37, \ 47, \ 67, \ 97$$

In the first row, every number ends in 5 and is divisible by 5; this may lead to the conjecture that every number that ends in 5 is divisible by 5, which is true. In the second row, every number ends in 7 and is prime; this might lead to the conjecture that every number ending in 7 is prime, which would be false.

Or take: "Every even integer is the sum of 2 primes". This is true in every case in which it has been tested, and the number of such cases is enormous. Nevertheless there remains a reasonable doubt as to whether it is *always* true.

As a striking example of failure of induction in arithmetic, take the following:[1]

Put $\pi(x) =$ number of primes $\leqslant x$

$$\mathrm{li}(x) = \int\limits_{0}^{x} \frac{dt}{\log t}$$

[1] See Hardy, *Ramanujan*, pp. 16, 17.

It is known that, when x is large, $\pi(x)$ and li(x) are nearly equal. It is also known that, for every known prime,

$$\pi(x) < \text{li}(x)$$

Gauss conjectured that this inequality always holds. It has been tested for all primes up to 10^7 and for a good many beyond this, and no particular case of its falsity has been discovered. Nevertheless Littlewood proved in 1912 that there are an infinite number of primes for which it is false, and Skewes (*L.M.S. Journal*, 1933) proved that it is false for some number less than

$$10^{10^{10^{34}}}$$

It will be seen that Gauss's conjecture, though it turned out to be false, had in its favour vastly better inductive evidence than exists for even our most firmly rooted empirical generalizations.

Without going so deeply into the theory of numbers, it is easy to construct false inductions in arithmetic in any required number. For instance, no number less than n is divisible by n. We can make n as large as we please, and thus obtain as much inductive evidence as we choose in favour of the generalization: "No number is divisible by n".

It is obvious that any n integers must possess many common properties which most integers do not possess. For one thing, if m is the greatest of them, they all possess the infinitely rare property of being not greater than m. There is therefore no validity in either a general or a particular induction as applied to integers, unless the property to which induction is to be applied is somehow limited. I do not know how to state such a limitation, and yet any good mathematician will have a feeling, analogous to common sense, as to the sort of property that is likely to allow an induction which turns out to be valid. If you have noticed that $1 + 3 = 2^2$, $1 + 3 + 5 = 3^2$, $1 + 3 + 5 + 7 = 4^2$, you will be inclined to conjecture that

$$1 + 3 + 5 + \ldots + (2n - 1) = n^2$$

and this conjecture can easily be proved correct. Similarly if you have noticed that $1^3 + 2^3 = 3^2$, $1^3 + 2^3 + 3^3 = 6^2$,

$1^3 + 2^3 + 3^3 + 4^3 = 10^2$, you may conjecture that the sum of the first n cubes is always a square number, and this again is easily proved. Mathematical intuition is by no means infallible as regards such inductions, but in the case of good mathematicians it seems to be oftener right than wrong. I do not know how to make explicit what guides mathematical intuition in such cases. Meanwhile, we can only say that no known limitation will make induction valid as applied to the natural numbers.

(3) *Induction invalid as a logical principle.*—It is obvious that, if we are allowed to select our class β as we choose, we can easily make sure that our induction shall fail. Let a_1, a_2, . . . a_n be the hitherto observed members of α, all of which have been found to be members of β, and let a_{n+1} be the next member of α. So far as pure logic is concerned, β might consist only of the terms a_1, a_2 . . . a_n; or it might consist of everything in the universe except a_{n+1}; or it might consist of any class intermediate between these two. In any of these cases the induction to a_{n+1} would be false.

It is obvious (an objector may say) that β must not be what might be called a "manufactured" class, i.e. one defined partly by extension. In the sort of cases contemplated in inductive inference, β is always a class known in intension, but not in extension except as regards the observed members a_1, a_2 . . a_n and such other members of β, not members of α, as may happen to have been observed.

It is very easy to make up obviously invalid inductions. A rustic might say: all the cattle I have ever seen were in Herefordshire, therefore probably all cattle are in that county. Or we might argue: No man now alive has died, therefore probably all the men now alive are immortal. The fallacies in such inductions are fairly obvious, but they would not be fallacies if induction were a purely logical principle.

It is therefore clear that, if induction is to be not demonstrably false, the class β must have certain characteristics, or be related in some specific way to the class α. I am not contending that with these limitations the principle must be true; I am contending that without them it must be false.

(4) In empirical material instances come in a time-order, and therefore are always serial. When we consider whether induction is applicable in arithmetic, we naturally think of the numbers as

arranged in order of magnitude. But if we are allowed to arrange them as we like, we can obtain strange results; for instance, as we saw, we can prove that it is infinitely improbable that a number chosen at haphazard will *not* be a prime.

It is essential to the enunciation of particular induction that there should be a *next* instance, which demands a serial arrangement.

If there is to be any plausibility about general induction, we must be given that the *first n* members of α are found to be members of β, not merely that α and β have *n* members in common. This again requires a serial arrangement.

(5) Assuming it admitted that, if an inductive inference is to be valid, there must be some relation between α and β, or some characteristic of one of them, in virtue of which it is valid, it is clear that this relation must be between *intensions*, e.g. between "human" and "mortal", or between "ruminant" and "dividing the hoof". We seek to infer an extensional relation, but we do not originally know the extensions of α and β when we are dealing with empirically given classes of which new members become known from time to time. Everyone would admit "dogs bark" as a good induction; we expect a correlation between the visual appearance of an animal and the noise it makes. This expectation is, of course, the result of another, wider induction, but that is not at the moment the point that concerns me. What concerns me is the correlation of a kind of shape with a kind of noise, both intensions, and the fact that certain intensions seem to us more likely to be inductively related than certain others.

(6) This point is obvious. If the universe is finite, complete enumeration is theoretically possible, and before it has been achieved the ordinary calculus of probability shows that an induction is probably valid. But in practice this consideration has no importance, because of the disproportion between the number of things we can observe and the number of things in the universe.

Let us now revert to the general principle, remembering that we have to seek some limitation which will make it possibly valid. Take particular induction first. This says that, if a random selection of *n* members of α is found to consist wholly of members of β, it is probable that the next member of α will be a β, i.e. most of the remaining α's are β's. This itself need only be probable. We may suppose α to be a finite class, containing (say) N members.

Of these we know that at least n are members of β. If the total number of members of α that are members of β is m, the total number of ways of selecting n terms is $\dfrac{N!}{n!\,(N-n)!}$,[1] and the total number of ways of selecting n terms that are α's is $\dfrac{m!}{n!\,(m-n)!}$. Therefore the chance of a selection consisting wholly of α's is

$$\frac{m!\,(N-n)!}{N!\,(m-n)!}$$

If p_m is the *a priori* likelihood of m being the number of terms common to α and β, then the likelihood after experience is

$$p_m \cdot \frac{m!\,(N-n)!}{N!\,(m-n)!} \bigg/ \sum_{1}^{N} p_m \cdot \frac{m!\,(N-n)!}{N!\,(m-n)!}$$

Let us call this q_m.

If the number of members common to α and β is m, then after withdrawing n α's that are β's there remain $m-n$ β's and $N-n$ not-β's. Therefore, from the hypothesis that α and β have m members in common, we get a probability $q_m \cdot \dfrac{m-n}{N-n}$ of another β. Therefore the total probability is

$$\sum_{n}^{N} q_m \cdot \frac{m-n}{N-n}$$

The value of this depends entirely on the p_m's, which there is no valid way of estimating. If we assume with Laplace that every value of m is equally probable we get Laplace's result, that the chance of the next α being a β is $\dfrac{n+1}{n+2}$. If we assume that, *a priori*, each α is equally likely to be a β and not be a β, we get the value $1/2$. Even with Laplace's hypothesis the *general* induction has only a probability $\dfrac{n+1}{N+1}$, which is usually small.

We need therefore some hypothesis which makes p_m large when m is nearly N. This will have to depend upon the nature of the classes α and β if it is to have any chance of validity.

---

[1] "N!" means the product of all whole numbers from 1 to N.

C. MATHEMATICAL TREATMENT OF INDUCTION

From the time of Laplace onward, various attempts have been made to show that the probable truth of an inductive inference follows from the mathematical theory of probability. It is now generally agreed that these attempts were all unsuccessful, and that, if inductive arguments are to be valid, it must be in virtue of some extra-logical characteristic of the actual world, as opposed to the various logically possible worlds that may be contemplated by the logician.

The first of such arguments is due to Laplace. In its valid, purely mathematical, form, it is as follows:

There are $n + 1$ bags, similar in external appearance, and each containing n balls. In the first, all the balls are black; in the second, one is white and the rest black; in the $(r + 1)^{\text{th}}$, r are white and the rest black. One of these, of which the composition is unknown, is selected, and m balls are withdrawn from it. They prove to be all white. What is the probability (a) that the next ball drawn will be white, (b) that we have chosen the bag consisting wholly of white balls?

The answer is: (a) the chance that the next ball will be white is $\dfrac{m + 1}{m + 2}$; (b) the chance that we have chosen the bag in which all the balls are white is $\dfrac{m + 1}{n + 1}$.

This valid result has a straightforward interpretation on the finite frequency theory. But Laplace infers that if m A's have been found to be B's, the chance that the next A will be a B is $\dfrac{m + 1}{m + 2}$, and the chance that all A's are B's is $\dfrac{m + 1}{n + 1}$. He gets this result by assuming that, given n objects of which we know nothing, the probabilities that $0, 1, 2, \ldots n$ of them are B's are all equal. This, of course, is an absurd assumption. If we replace it by the slightly less absurd assumption that each of the objects has an equal chance of being a B or not a B, the chance that the next A will be a B remains $1/2$, however many A's have been found to be B's.

Even if his argument were accepted, the general induction remains improbable if n is much greater than m, though the particular induction may become highly probable. In fact, however, his argument is only a historical curiosity.

Keynes, in his *Treatise on Probability*, has done the best that can be done for induction on purely mathematical lines, and has decided that it is inadequate. His result is as follows.

Let g be a generalization, x_1, x_2, . . . observed instances favourable to it, and h the general circumstances so far as they are relevant.

Assume $$x_1/h = x_2/h = \text{etc.}$$

Put $$p_n = g/h\, x_1\, x_2\, \ldots\, x_n.$$

Thus p_n is the probability of the general induction after n favourable instances. Write $\bar{g}$ for the negation of g, and p_0 for g/h, the *a priori* probability of the generalization.

Then $$p_n = \frac{p_0}{p_0 + x_1\, x_2\, \ldots\, x_n/g\, h(1 - p_0)}$$

As n increases, this approaches 1 as a limit if

$$\frac{x_1\, x_2\, \ldots\, x_n/g\, h}{p_0}$$

approaches zero as a limit; and this happens if there are finite quantities ϵ and η such that, for all sufficiently great r's,

$$x_r/x_1\, x_2\, \ldots\, x_{r-1}\, \bar{g}\, h < 1 - \epsilon \text{ and } p_0 > \eta$$

Let us consider these two conditions. The first says that there is a quantity $1 - \epsilon$, less than 1, such that, if the generalization is false, the probability of the next instance being favourable will always, after a certain number of favourable instances, be less than this. Consider, as an instance of its failure, the generalization "all numbers are non-prime". As we move up the number-series, primes become rarer, and the chance of the next number after r non-primes being itself a non-prime increases, and approaches certainty as a limit if r is kept constant. This condition, therefore, may fail.

But the second condition, that g must, antecedently to the beginning of the induction, have a probability greater than some finite probability, is more difficult. In general, it is hard to see any way in which this probability can be estimated. What would be the probability of "all swans are white" for a person who had never seen a swan or been told anything about the colour of swans? Such questions are both obscure and vague, and Keynes recognizes that they make his result unsatisfactory.[1]

There is one simple hypothesis which would give the finite probability that Keynes wants. Let us suppose that the number of things in the universe is finite, say N. Let β be a class of n things, and let α be a random selection of m things. Then the number of possible α's is

$$\frac{N!}{m!(N-m)!},$$

and the number of these that are contained in β is

$$\frac{n!}{m!(n-m)!}$$

Therefore the chance of "all α's are β's" is

$$\frac{n!(N-m)!}{N!(n-m)!}$$

which is finite. That is to say, every generalization as to which we have no evidence has a finite chance of being true.

I fear, however, that, if N is as large as Eddington maintained, the number of favourable instances required to make an inductive generalization probable in any high degree would be far in excess of what is practically attainable. This way of escape, therefore, while excellent in theory, will not serve to justify scientific practice.

Induction in the advanced sciences proceeds on a somewhat different system from that of simple enumeration. There is first a body of observed facts, then a general theory consistent with them all, and then inferences from the theory which subsequent observation confirms or confutes. The argument here depends upon the principle of inverse probability. Let p be a general theory, h the previously known data, and q a new experimental datum relevant to p. Then

$$p/q\,h = \frac{(p/h) \cdot (q/p\,h)}{q/h}$$

[1] I shall return to this subject in Part VI, Chapter II.

In the most important case, q follows from p and h, so that $q/p\ h = 1$. In this case, therefore,

$$p/q\ h = \frac{p/h}{q/h}$$

It follows that, if q/h is very small, the verification of q greatly increases the probability of p. This, however, does not have quite the consequences one might hope. We have, putting "$\bar{p}$" for "not-p",

$$q/h = pq/h + \bar{p}q/h = p/h + \bar{p}q/h$$

because, given h, p implies q. Thus if

$$y = \frac{\bar{p}q/h}{p/h},$$

we have

$$p/q\ h = \frac{1}{1+y}$$

This will be a high probability if y is small. Now two circumstances may make y small: (1) if p/h is large, (2) if $\bar{p}\ q/h$ is small, i.e. if q would be improbable if p were false. The difficulties in the way of estimating these two factors are much the same as those that appear in Keynes's discussion. To obtain an estimate of p/h, we shall need some way of evaluating the probability of p antecedently to the special evidence that has suggested it, and it is not easy to see how this can be done. The only thing that seems clear is that, if a suggested law is to have an appreciable probability antecedently to any evidence in its favour, that must be in virtue of a principle to the effect that *some* fairly simple law is bound to be true. But this is a difficult matter, to which I shall return at a later stage.

The probability of $\bar{p}q/h$, in certain kinds of cases, is more possible to estimate approximately. Let us take the case of the discovery of Neptune. In this case, p is the law of gravitation, h is the observations of planetary motions before the discovery of Neptune, and q is the existence of Neptune at the place where calculations showed that it should be. Thus $\bar{p}\ q/h$ is the probability that Neptune would be where it was, given that the law of gravitation was false. Here we must make a proviso as to the sense in which we should use the word "false". It would not be right to take Einstein's theory as showing Newton's to be "false" in the relevant sense. All quantitative scientific theories, when asserted, should be asserted with a margin of error; when this is done, Newton's theory of gravitation remains true of planetary motions.

The following argument looks hopeful, but is not in fact valid.

In our case, apart from p or some other general law, h is irrelevant to q, that is to say, observations of other planets make the existence of Neptune neither more nor less probable than it was before. As for other laws, Bode's law might be held to make it more or less probable that there would be a planet having more or less the orbit of Neptune, but would not indicate the part of its orbit that it had reached at a given date. If we suppose that Bode's law, and any other relevant law except gravitation, conferred a probability x on the hypothesis of a planet roughly in the orbit of Neptune, and suppose the apparent position of Neptune was calculated with a margin of error θ, then the probability of Neptune being found where it was would be $\theta/2\pi$. Now θ was very small, and it cannot be maintained that x was large. Therefore $\bar{p} \, q/h$, which was $x \, \theta/2\pi$, was certainly very small. Suppose we take x to be $1/10$ and θ to be 6 minutes, then

$$\bar{p} \, q/h = \frac{1}{10} \cdot \frac{1}{3,600} = \frac{1}{36,000}$$

Therefore if we suppose that $p/h = 1/36$, we shall have $y = 1/1000$

and
$$p/q \, h = \frac{1,000}{1,001}$$

Thus even if, before the discovery of Neptune, the law of gravitation was as improbable as double sixes with dice, it had afterwards odds of 1000 to 1 in its favour.

This argument, extended to all the observed facts of planetary motions, apparently shows that, if the law of gravitation had even a very small probability at the time when it was first enunciated, it soon became virtually certain. But it does nothing to help us to gauge this initial probability, and therefore would fail, even if valid, to give us a firm basis for the theoretical inference from observation to theory.

Moreover the above argument is open to objection, in view of the fact that the law of gravitation is not the only law which would lead to the expectation of Neptune being where it was. Suppose the law of gravitation to have been true until the time t, where t is any moment subsequent to the discovery of Neptune; then we should still have $q/p'h = 1$, where p' is the hypothesis that the law was true only until the time t. There was therefore better reason to expect the finding of Neptune than would result from pure chance, or from this together with Bode's law. What was rendered highly probable was that the law had held until then. To infer that it would hold in future required a principle not derivable from anything in the mathematical theory of probability. This consideration destroys the whole force of the inductive argument for general theories, unless the argument is reinforced by some principle such as the uniformity of nature is supposed to be. Here again, we find that induction needs the support of some extra-logical general principle not based upon experience.

D. REICHENBACH'S THEORY

The peculiarity of Reichenbach's theory of probability is that induction is involved in the very definition of a probability. His theory is as follows (somewhat simplified).

Given a statistical series, e.g. such as in vital statistics, and given two overlapping classes α and β to which some members of the series belong, we often find that, when the number of items is large, the percentage of members of β that are members of α remains approximately constant. Suppose that, when the number of items exceeds (say) 10,000, it is found that the proportion of recorded β's that are α's is never far from m/n, and that this rational fraction is nearer the average observed proportion than any other. We then "posit" that, however far the series may be prolonged, the proportion will always remain nearly m/n. We define the probability of a β being an α as the limit of the observed frequency when the number of observations is indefinitely increased, and in virtue of our "posit" we assume that this limit exists and is in the neighbourhood of m/n, where m/n is the observed frequency in the largest obtainable sample.

Reichenbach asserts with emphasis that no proposition is certain; all are only probable in varying degrees, and every probability is the limit of a frequency. He admits that, in consequence of this doctrine, the items by means of which the frequency is computed are themselves only probable. Take e.g. the death rate: when a man is judged dead, he may be still alive, therefore every item in mortality statistics is doubtful. This means, by definition, that the record of a death must be one of a series of records, some correct, some erroneous. But those we take to be correct are only probably correct, and must be members of some new series. All this he admits, but he says that at some stage we break off the endless regress, and adopt what he calls a "blind posit".[1] A "blind posit" is a decision to treat some proposition as true although we have no good ground for doing so.

There are in this theory two kinds of "blind posits", namely: (1) the ultimate items in the statistical series which we choose to regard as fundamental; (2) the assumption that the frequency found in a finite number of observations will remain approximately constant however much the number of observations may be increased. Reichenbach considers his theory completely empirical, because he does not assert that his "posits" are true.

I am not now concerned with Reichenbach's general theory, which was considered in an earlier chapter. I am concerned now only with his theory of induction. The gist of his theory of this: If his inductive posit is true, prediction is possible, and if not, not. Therefore the only way in which we can obtain any probability in favour of one prediction rather than another is to suppose his posit true. I am not concerned to deny that some posit is necessary if there is to be any probability in favour of predictions, but I am concerned to deny that the posit required is Reichenbach's.

His posit is this: Given any two classes α and β, and given that instances of α present themselves in a temporal sequence, if it is found that, after a sufficient number of α's have been examined, the proportion that are β's is always roughly m/n, then this proportion will continue however many instances of α may be subsequently observed.

We may observe, in the first place, that this posit is only apparently more general than one applying to the case in which *all* observed α's are β's. For in Reichenbach's hypothesis every segment of the series of α's has the property that about m/n of its members are β's, and the more specialized posit can be applied to the segments. We can therefore confine ourselves to the more specialized posit.

Reichenbach's posit is therefore equivalent to the following: When a large number of α's have been observed, and have all been found to be β's, we shall assume that very nearly all α's

[1] *Experience and Prediction*, p. 401.

are β's. This assumption is necessary (so he maintains) for the *definition* of probability, and for all scientific prediction.

I think this posit can be shown to be false. Suppose a_1, a_2, . . a_n are members of a which have been observed and have been found to belong to a certain class β. Suppose that a_{n+1} is the next a to be observed. If it is a β, substitute for β the class consisting of β without a_{n+1}. For this class the induction breaks down. This sort of argument is obviously capable of extension. It follows that, if induction is to have any chance of validity, a and β must be not *any* classes, but classes having certain properties or relations. I do not mean that induction *must* be valid when there is a suitable relation between a and β, but only that in that case it *may* be valid, whereas in its general form it can be proved to be false.

It might seem evident that a and β must not be what might be called "manufactured" classes. I should call β without a_{n+1}, which occurred above, a "manufactured" class. Broadly speaking, I mean by a "manufactured" class one which is defined, at least in part, by mentioning that such and such a term is, or is not, a member of it. Thus "mankind" is not a manufactured class, but "all mankind except Socrates" is a manufactured class. If a_1, a_2, . . a_{n+1}, are the $n + 1$ members of a first observed, then $a_1, a_2, . . a_n$ have the property of not being a_{n+1}, but we must not inductively infer that a_{n+1} has this property, no matter how great n may be. The classes a and β must be defined by intension, not by mention of their membership. Whatever relation justifies induction must be a relation of *concepts*, and since different concepts may define the same class, it may happen that there are a pair of concepts which are inductively related and respectively define a and β, while other pairs, which also define a and β, are not inductively related. E.g. it may be permissible to infer from experience that featherless bipeds are mortal, but not that rational beings living on earth are mortal, in spite of the fact that the two concepts happen to define the same class.

Mathematical logic, as hitherto developed, aims always at being as extensional as possible. This is perhaps a more or less accidental characteristic, resulting from the influence of arithmetic on the thoughts and purposes of mathematical logicians. The problem of induction, on the contrary, demands intensional treatment. The classes a, β that occur in an inductive inference are, it is true, given in extension so far as the observed instances $a_1, a_2, \ldots a_n$ are concerned, but beyond that point it is essential that, as yet, both classes are only known in intension. E.g. a may be the class of persons in whose blood there are certain bacilli, and β the class of persons showing certain symptoms. It is of the essence of induction that the extensions of these two classes are not known in advance. In practice, we consider certain inductions worth testing, and others not, and we seem to be guided by a feeling as to the kinds of intensions that are likely to be connected.

Reichenbach's posit for induction is therefore both too general and too extensional. Something more limited and intensional is required if it is not to be demonstrably false.

Something must be said about Reichenbach's theory of different levels of frequency, leading up to a set of probabilities which are "blind posits". This is bound up with his doctrine that probability should be substituted for truth in logic. Let us examine the theory in an instance, e.g. the chance that an Englishman of sixty will die within a year.

The first stage is straightforward: accepting the records as accurate, we divide the number who have died within the last year by the total number. But we now remember that each item in the statistics may be mistaken. To estimate the probability of this, we must get some set of similar statistics which has been carefully scrutinized, and discover what percentage of mistakes it contained. Then we remember that those who thought they recognized a mistake may have been mistaken, and we set to work to get statistics of mistakes about mistakes. At some stage in this regress we must stop; wherever we stop, we must conventionally assign a "weight" which will presumably be either certainty or the probability which we guess would have resulted from carrying our regress one stage further.

There are various objections to this procedure considered as a theory of knowledge.

To begin with, the late stages in the regress are usually much more difficult and uncertain than the earlier stages; we are not likely, e.g. to reach the same degree of accuracy in an estimate of mistakes in official statistics as is reached in the official statistics themselves.

Secondly, the blind posits with which we have to start are an attempt to get the best of both worlds: they serve the same purpose as is served in my system by data which may be erroneous, but by calling them "posits" Reichenbach seeks to avoid the responsibility of considering them "true". I cannot see what ground he can have for making one posit rather than another except that he thinks it more likely to be "true"; and since, by his own confession, this does *not* mean (when we are at the stage of blind posits) that there is some known frequency which makes the posit probable, he is committed to some other criterion than frequency for choosing among hypotheses. What this may be, he does not tell us, because he does not perceive its necessity.

Thirdly, when we abandon the purely practical necessity of blind posits to end the endless regress, and consider what, in pure theory, Reichenbach can mean by a probability, we find ourselves entangled in inextricable complications. At the first level, we say the probability that an α will be a β is m_1/n_1; at the second level, we assign to this statement a probability m_2/n_2, by making it one of some series of similar statements; at the third level, we assign a probability m_3/n_3 to the statement that there is a probability m_2/n_2 in favour of our first probability m_1/n_1; and so we go on for ever. If this endless regress could be carried out, the ultimate probability in favour of the rightness of our initial estimate m_1/n_1 would be an infinite product

$$\frac{m_2}{n_2} \cdot \frac{m_3}{n_3} \cdot \frac{m_4}{n_4} \cdots$$

which may be expected to be zero. It would therefore seem that, in choosing the estimate which is most probable at the first level, we are almost sure to be wrong; but in general it will remain the best estimate open to us.

The endless regress in the very definition of "probable" is intolerable. We must, if we are to avoid it, admit that each item in our original statistics is either true or false, and that the value m_1/n_1, obtained for our first probability, is either right or wrong; in fact, we must apply the dichotomy of true-or-false as absolutely to probability judgments as to others. Reichenbach's position is, stated completely, as follows:

There is a proposition p_1, say "this α is a β".
There is a proposition p_2, saying p_1 has the probability x_1.

| ,, | ,, | ,, | p_3, | ,, | p_2 | ,, | ,, | ,, | x_2. |
| ,, | ,, | ,, | p_4, | ,, | p_3 | ,, | ,, | ,, | x_3. |

'I'his series is infinite, and leads (one is to suppose) to a limit-proposition, which alone we have a right to assert. But I do not see how this limit-proposition is to be expressed. The trouble is that, as regards all the members of the series before it, we have no reason, on Reichenbach's principles, to regard them as more likely to be true than to be false; they have, in fact, no probability that we can estimate.

I conclude that the attempt to dispense with the concepts "true" and false" is a failure, and that judgments of probability are not essentially different from other judgments, but fall equally within the absolute true-false dichotomy.

E. CONCLUSIONS

Induction, ever since Hume, has played so large a part in discussions of scientific method that it is important to be clear as to what (if I am not mistaken) the above arguments have established.

First: there is nothing in the mathematical theory of probability to justify us in regarding either a particular or a general induction as probable, however large may be the ascertained number of favourable instances.

Second: if no limitation is placed upon the character of the intensional definition of the classes A and B concerned in an induction, the principle of induction can be shown to be not only doubtful but false. That is to say, given that n members of a certain class A belong to a certain other class B, the values of "B" for which the next member of A does not belong to B are more numerous than the values for which the next member does belong to B, unless n falls not far short of the total number of things in the universe.

Third: what is called "hypothetical induction", in which some general theory is regarded as probable because all its hitherto observed consequences have been verified, does not differ in any essential respect from induction by simple enumeration. For, if p is the theory in question, A the class of relevant phenomena, and B the class of consequences of p, then p is equivalent to "all A is B", and the evidence for p is obtained by a simple enumeration.

Fourth: if an inductive argument is ever to be valid, the inductive

435

principle must be stated with some hitherto undiscovered limitation. Scientific common sense, in practice, shrinks from various kinds of induction, rightly, as I think. But what guides scientific common sense has not, so far, been explicitly formulated.

Fifth: scientific inferences, if they are in general valid, must be so in virtue of some law or laws of nature, stating a synthetic property of the actual world, or several such properties. The truth of propositions asserting such properties cannot be made even probable by any argument from experience, since such arguments, when they go beyond hitherto recorded experience, depend for their validity upon the very principles in question.

It remains to inquire what those principles are, and in what sense, if any, we can be said to know them.

PART VI

POSTULATES OF SCIENTIFIC INFERENCE

Chapter I

KINDS OF KNOWLEDGE

IN seeking the postulates of scientific inference there are two kinds of problems. On the one hand there is analysis of what is generally accepted as valid inference, with a view to discovering what principles are involved; this inquiry is purely logical. On the other hand there is the difficulty that there is, *prima facie*, little reason to suppose these principles true, and still less to suppose them *known* to be true. I think that the question in what sense, if any, these principles can be known, requires an analysis of the concept of "knowledge". This concept is too often treated as though its meaning were obvious and unitary. My own belief is that many philosophical difficulties and controversies arise from insufficient realization of the difference between different kinds of knowledge, and of the vagueness and uncertainty that characterizes most of what we believe ourselves to know. There is another thing which it is important to remember whenever mental concepts are being discussed, and that is our evolutionary continuity with the lower animals. "Knowledge", in particular, must not be defined in a manner which assumes an impassable gulf between ourselves and our ancestors who had not the advantage of language.

What passes for knowledge is of two kinds: first, knowledge of facts; second, knowledge of the general connections between facts. Very closely connected with this distinction is another: there is knowledge which may be described as "mirroring", and knowledge which consists in capacity to handle. Leibniz's monads "mirror" the universe, and in this sense "know" it; but since monads never interact, they cannot "handle" anything external to themselves. This is the logical extreme of one conception of "knowledge". The logical extreme of the other conception is pragmatism, which was first promulgated by Marx in his *Theses on Feuerbach* (1845): "The question whether objective truth belongs to human thinking is not a question of theory, but a practical question. The truth, i.e. the reality and power, of thought must be demonstrated in practice. . . . Philosophers have only *interpreted* the world in various ways, but the real task is to *alter* it."

Both these conceptions, that of Leibniz and that of Marx, are, I suggest, incomplete. Speaking very roughly and approximately, the former is applicable to knowledge of facts, the latter to knowledge of general connections between facts. I am speaking in each case of non-inferential knowledge. Our inquiries in connection with probability have shown us that there must be non-inferential knowledge, not only of facts, but also of connections between facts.

Our knowledge of facts, in so far as it is not inferential, has two sources, sensation and memory. Of these, sensation is the more fundamental, since we can only remember what has been a sensible experience. But although sensation is a *source* of knowledge, it is not itself, in any usual sense, knowledge. When we speak of "knowledge", we generally imply a distinction between the knowing and what is known, but in sensation there is no such distinction. "Perception", as the word is used by most psychologists, is of the nature of knowledge, but it is so because of the adjuncts which are added to pure sensation by experience, or, possibly, by congenital dispositions. But these adjuncts can only count as "knowledge" if there are connections between the sensation and other facts outside my momentary mental state, and these connections must be suitably related to the connection between the pure sensation and the rest of the mental state called a perceiving. The passage from sensation to perception, therefore, involves connections between facts, not only facts. It involves these, however, only if perception is to be regarded as a form of knowledge; as a psychological occurrence, perception is a mere fact, but one which might not be veridical as regards what it adds to sensation. It is only veridical if there are certain connections among facts, e.g. between the visual appearance of iron and hardness.

Memory is the purest example of mirror-knowledge. When I remember a piece of music or a friend's face, my state of mind resembles, though with a difference, what it was when I heard the music or saw the face. If I have sufficient skill, I can play the music or paint the face from memory, and then compare my playing or painting with the original, or rather with something which I have reason to believe closely similar to the original. But we trust our memory, up to a point, even if it does not pass this test. If our friend appears with a black eye, we say "how did you get that injury?" not "I had forgotten that you had a black eye". The tests of memory, as we have already had occasion to notice, are only confirmations; a considerable degree of credibility attaches to a memory on its own account, particularly if it is vivid and recent.

A memory is accurate, not in proportion to the help it gives in handling present and future facts, but in proportion to its resemblance to a past fact. When Herbert Spencer, after fifty years, saw again the lady he had loved as a young man, whom he had imagined still young, it was the very accuracy of his memory which incapacitated him from handling the present fact. In regard to memory, the definition of "truth", and therefore of "knowledge", lies in the resemblance of present imagining to past sensible experience. Capacity for handling present and future facts may be confirmatory in certain circumstances, but can never *define* what we mean when we say that a certain memory is "knowledge".

Sensation, perception, and memory are essentially preverbal experiences; we may suppose that they are not so very different in animals from what they are in ourselves. When we come to knowledge expressed in words, we seem inevitably to lose something of the particularity of the experience that we seek to describe, since all words classify. But here there is an important point that needs to be emphasized: although, in a sense, words classify, the person who uses them need not be doing so. A child learns to respond to stimuli of a certain kind by the word "cat"; this is a causal law, analogous to the fact that a match responds to a certain kind of stimulus by lighting. But the match is not classifying the stimulus as "ignitory", and the child need not be classifying the stimulus when he makes the response "cat". In fact, we get into an endless regress if we do not realize that the use of such a word as "cat" does not *presuppose* classification. No one can utter twice a given instance of the word "cat"; the classifying of the various instances as instances of the word is a process exactly analogous to that of classifying animals as instances of a species. In fact, therefore, classification is later than the beginnings of language. All that is involved in the original activity that looks like classification is a closer similarity in responses to certain stimuli than in the stimuli. Two instances of the word "animal" are more similar than a mouse and a hippopotamus. That is why language helps when we want to consider what all animals have in common.

When I have a memory-picture of some event, what is meant by calling it "true" is in no degree conventional. It is "true" in so far as it has the resemblance which an image has to its prototype. And if the image is felt as a memory, not as mere imagination, it is "knowledge" in the same degree in which it is "true".

But as soon as words are involved, a conventional element enters in. A child, seeing a mole, may say "mouse"; this is an error in convention, like being rude to an aunt. But if a person who is thoroughly master of the language sees a mole for a moment out of the corner of his eye and says "mouse", his error is not conventional, and if he has further opportunities of observation he will say "no, I see it was a mole". Before any verbal statement can be considered to embody knowledge or error, definitions, nominal or ostensive, of all the words involved must be furnished. All ostensive definitions, and therefore all definitions, are somewhat vague. Chimpanzees are certainly apes, but in the course of evolution there must have been animals which were intermediate between apes and men. Every empirical concept is certainly applicable to some objects, and certainly inapplicable to others, but in between there is a region of doubtful objects. In regard to such objects classificatory statements may be more or less true, or may be so near the middle of the doubtful region that it is futile to consider them either true or false.

Scientific technique is largely concerned to diminish this area of uncertainty. Measurements are conducted to so and so many significant figures, and the probable error is given. Sometimes "natural kinds" make error practically impossible. In the existing world, there is probably no animal which is not quite indubitably a mouse or quite indubitably not a mouse; the doubtful cases that must have arisen in the course of evolution no longer exist. In physics, atoms are of a finite number of discrete kinds; "uranium 235" is a concept which is always unambiguously applicable or unambiguously not applicable to a given atom. Speaking generally, the uncertainty due to vagueness is limited and manageable, and exists in only a small proportion of the statements that we wish to make—at any rate where scientific technique is available.

Ignoring vagueness, what is involved when we make such a

statement as "there's a mouse"? A visual sensation causes us to believe that there is, in the direction in which we are looking, an animal with a past and a future, and with whatever characteristics (over and above visual appearance) make up for us the definition of the word "mouse". If we are justified in this very complex belief, there must be in the outer world connections between facts similar to the connections between the visual sensation and the beliefs that it causes. If there are not these connections—if, e.g. the mouse is not "real" but in a film—our beliefs are erroneous. In this way connections between facts are relevant in judging the truth or falsehood of what might pass as judgments of perception.

A part—but not, I think, the whole—of what is asserted when I say "there's a mouse", consists of expectations and hypothetical expectations. We think that, if we continue to watch, we shall either continue to see the mouse, or see it hide in some hole or crack; we should be astonished if it suddenly vanished in the middle of the floor, though in a cinema it could easily be arranged that this should happen. We think that, if we touched it, it would feel like a mouse. We think that, if it moves, it will move like a mouse and not like a frog. If we happen to be anatomists, we may think that if we dissected it we should find the organs of a mouse. But when I say that we "think" all these things, that is altogether too definite. We shall think them if we are asked; we shall be surprised if anything contrary to them occurs; but as a rule what can be developed into these thoughts is something rather vague and unformulated. I think we may say that an object perceived normally arouses two sorts of response, on the one hand certain more or less subconscious expectations, and on the other hand certain impulses to action, though the action may consist only of continued observation. There is a certain degree of connection between these two kinds of response. For instance, continued observation involves expectation that the object will continue to exist; we have no such response to a flash of lightning.

Often expectation is much more definite than it is in such cases as we have been considering. You see a door shutting in the wind, and expect to hear it bang. You see an acquaintance approaching, and expect him to shake hands. You see the sun setting, and expect it to disappear below the horizon. A very large part of daily life is made up of expectations; if we found ourselves in an environment so strange that we did not know what to expect, we should be violently terrified. (See photographs of herds of elephants stampeding at the first sight of an aeroplane.) The desire to know what to expect is a large part of the love of home, and also of the impulse to scientific investigation. Men of science, when compelled to travel, have invented the homogeneity of space because they feel uncomfortable in the thought that "there's no place like home".

Expectations, when reflected upon, involve belief in causal laws. But in their primitive form they seem to involve no such belief, though they are only true in the degree in which the relevant causal laws are true. There are three stages in the development of expectation. In the most primitive stage, the presence of A causes expectation of B, but without any awareness of the connection; in the second stage, we believe "A is present, therefore B will be"; in the third, we rise to the general hypothetical "if A is present, B will be". The passage from the second stage to the third is by no means easy; uneducated people find great difficulty in a hypothetical of which the hypothesis is not known to be true.

Although these three states of mind are different, the condition for the truth of the belief involved is, in general, the same, namely, the existence of a causal connection between A and B. Of course, in the first form, where the presence of A causes the expectation of B, B may *happen* to occur by chance, and the expectation will then be verified; but this will not happen usually unless there is some degree of connection between A and B. In the second form, where we say "A, therefore B", the word "therefore" needs interpreting, but as usually understood it would not be held to be justified if the connection of A and B was fortuitous and for this occasion only. In the third form, the causal law is explicitly asserted.

The question arises: in what circumstances can such beliefs count as "knowledge"? This question is involved in any attempt to answer the question: "In what sense do we know the necessary postulates of scientific inference?"

Knowledge, I maintain, is a matter of degree. We may not know "Certainly A is always followed by B", but we may know "Probably A is usually followed by B", where "probably" is to be taken in the sense of "degree of credibility". It is in this milder form that I shall inquire in what sense, and to what degree, our expectations can count as "knowledge".

We must first consider what we are to mean by "expectation", remembering that we are concerned with something that may exist among dumb animals, and that does not presuppose language. Expecting is a form of believing, and much of what is to be said about it applies to believing in general, but in the present context it is expecting alone that concerns us. The state of expecting, in its more emphatic forms, is one with which we are all familiar. Before a race, you wait expectantly for the pistol shot which is the signal for starting. In a quarry in which blasting operations take place, when an explosion is due you acquire a certain tenseness while waiting for it. When you go to meet a friend at a crowded station, you scan faces with the expected face in your imagination. These various states are partly mental, partly physical; there is adjustment of muscles and sense-organs, and usually also something imagined (which may be only words). At a certain moment, either something happens which gives you the feeling "quite so", or you have the feeling "how surprising". In the former case your expectation was "true", in the latter "false".

Various different physical and mental states may all be expectations of the same event. There may be varying amounts of imagery, varying degrees of muscular adjustment, varying intensities of adaptation of sense-organs. When what is expected is not immediate or not interesting, expectation may consist merely in belief in a certain sentence in the future tense, as, e.g. "there will be an eclipse of the moon to-morrow night". "An expectation of B" may be defined as any state of mind and body such that, if B occurs at the appropriate time, we have the feeling "quite so", and if B does not occur we have the feeling "how surprising". I do not think there is any other way of defining what is in common among all the states that are expectations of a given event.

We have already defined what makes an expectation "true"; it is "true" when it is followed by the "quite-so" feeling. We have now to inquire what makes an expectation "knowledge". Since every case of knowledge is a case of true belief, but not vice versa, we have to inquire what must be added to truth to make a true expectation count as "knowledge".

It is easy to think of cases of true expectation which is not knowledge. Suppose you are impressed by a sage with a long

445

white beard, splendid robes, and a store of oriental wisdom. Suppose he says (and you believe him) that he has the power of foretelling the future. And suppose you toss a coin, he says it will come heads, and it does come heads. You will have had a true expectation, but not knowledge, unless his pretensions were justified. Or, to take a simpler example, suppose you are expecting Mr. X to ring you up on the telephone. The telephone bell rings, but it is not Mr. X. In this case your expectation that the bell would ring, though true, was not knowledge. Or suppose that, being of a sceptical and contrary turn of mind, you expect rain because the weather forecast says it will be fine, and it then rains, it would be an insult to the meteorologists to call your expectation "knowledge".

It is clear that an expectation is not knowledge if it is the result of an argument which has false premisses. If I think that A is almost always followed by B, and therefore, having seen A, I expect B; if, in fact, A is very seldom followed by B, but this happens to be one of the rare cases where it is so followed, then my true expectation of B cannot count as knowledge.

But these are not the really difficult cases. The expectations of animals, and of men except in rare scientific moments, are caused by experiences which a logician might take as premisses for an induction. My dog, when I take out her lead, becomes excited in expectation of a walk. She behaves as if she reasoned: "Taking out the lead (A) has invariably, in my experience, been followed by a walk (B); therefore probably it will be so followed on this occasion". The dog, of course, goes through no such process of reasoning. But the dog is so constituted that, if A has been frequently followed by B in her experience, and B is emotionally interesting, A causes her to expect B. Sometimes the dog is right in this expectation, sometimes wrong. Suppose that, in fact, A is always, or nearly always, followed by B; can we say, in that case, that the dog is right to expect B?

We may carry our question a stage further. Suppose that, although A is in fact always followed by B, this generalization only happens to be right, and most logically similar generalizations are wrong. In that case we must regard it as a stroke of luck for the dog that she has hit on a case in which a fallacious process, by chance, leads to a true result. I do not think that in such a case the dog's expectation can be regarded as "knowledge".

But now let us suppose, not only that A is, in fact, almost always followed by B, but further that the experienced cases of A being followed by B belong to a definable class of cases in which generalization is nearly always in fact true. Shall we, now, admit the dog's expectation as "knowledge"? I am assuming that, although generalizations of the kind considered are *in fact* almost always true, we know of no reason why they should be. My own view is that, in such a case, the dog's expectation should be admitted as "knowledge". And, if so, scientific inductions also are "knowledge", provided the world has certain characteristics. I leave on one side, for the moment, the question whether, and in what sense, we know that it has these characteristics.

We have been, throughout this book, assuming the substantial truth of science, and asking ourselves what are the processes by which we come to know science. We are therefore justified in assuming that animals have become adapted to their environment more or less as biologists say they have. Now animals have, on the one hand, certain congenital propensities, and, on the other hand, an aptitude for the acquisition of habits. Both of these, in a species which succeeds in surviving, must have a certain conformity with the facts of the environment. The animal must eat the right food, mate with a member of its own species, and (among the higher animals) learn to avoid dangers. The habits which it acquires would not be useful unless there were certain causal uniformities in the world. These uniformities need not be absolute: you can poison rats by mixing arsenic with what seems to them attractive food. But unless the food that attracts them were usually wholesome, rats would die out. All the higher animals quickly acquire the habit of looking for food in places where they have found food before; this habit is useful, but only on the assumption of certain uniformities. Thus the survival of animals rests upon their tendency to act in certain ways which owe their advantageous quality to the fact that generalization is more often justified than pure logic would lead us to suppose.

But what, the reader may impatiently ask, have the habits of animals to do with knowledge? According to the traditional conception of "knowledge", nothing; according to the conception that I wish to advocate, everything. In the traditional conception, knowledge, at its best, is an intimate and almost mystical contact between subject and object, of which some may hereafter have complete experience in the beatific vision. Something of this direct contact, we are told to suppose, exists in perception. As for connections between facts, the older rationalists assimilated natural laws to logical principles, either directly or by a détour through God's goodness and wisdom. All this is out of date, except as regards perception, which many still regard as giving direct knowledge, and not as the complex and inaccurate mixture of sensation, habit, and physical causation that I have been arguing it to be. Believing in general, we have seen, has only a rather roundabout relation to what is said to be believed: when I believe, without words, that there is about to be an explosion, it is impossible to say at all accurately what it is that is occurring in me. Believing, in fact, has a complex and somewhat vague relation to what is believed, just as perceiving has to what is perceived.

But what we have now to consider is not belief or knowledge as to particular facts, but as to relations among facts, such as are involved when we believe "if A, then B".

The connections with which I am concerned are such as have a certain generality. Within a complete complex of compresence I can perceive parts having spatial and temporal relations; such relations are among particular perceptual data, and are not what I wish to consider. The relations that I wish to consider are general, like the connection of the dog's lead with a walk. But when I say that they are "general", I do not mean necessarily that they have no exceptions; I mean only that they are true in such a large majority of instances that in each particular case there is a high degree of credibility in the absence of evidence to the contrary as regards that particular case. Such are the generalizations upon which we base our conduct in daily life, e.g. "bread nourishes", "dogs bark", "rattlesnakes are dangerous". It is clear that such beliefs, in the form in which they appear in books on logic, have an ancestry which must, if traced far enough, take us back to the habits of animals. It is this ancestry that I wish to trace.

The purely logical analysis of "dogs bark" soon reaches complexities which make it incredible that ordinary folk can seem to understand anything so remote, mysterious, and universal. The first stage, for the logician, is to substitute: "Whatever x may be, either x is not a dog or x barks". But since dogs only bark sometimes, you have to substitute for "x barks" the statement "there is a time t at which x barks". Then you must substitute one or other of the two alternative definitions of "t" given in Part IV. In the end you will arrive at a statement of enormous length, not only about dogs, but about everything in the universe, and so complicated that it cannot be understood except by a person with a considerable training in mathematical logic. But suppose you have to explain your statement "dogs bark" to such a person, but as he is a foreigner with only a mathematician's knowledge of English, he does not know the word "dog" or the word "bark". What will you do? You will certainly not go through the above logical rigmarole. You will point to your dog and say "dog"; you will then excite him till he barks, and say "bark". The foreigner will then understand you, although, as a logician, he has no business to do so. This makes it clear that the psychology of general propositions is something very different from their logic. The psychology is what does take place when we believe them; the logic is perhaps what ought to take place if we were logical saints.

We all believe that all men are mortal. What happens at a moment when we are actively believing this? Perhaps only a belief that the words are correct, without any thought as to what they signify. But if we try to penetrate to what the words signify, what do we do? We certainly do not see spread out before the mind's eye a vast series of death-beds, one for each man. What we shall really think, if we take the trouble, will probably be something like this: "there's old So-and-So; he's 99, and as vigorous as ever, but I suppose he'll die some day. And young Such-and-Such: in spite of his athletic prowess and his boundless vitality, he won't last for ever. And then there was Xerxes's army, the thought of whose mortality caused him to weep; they are all dead. And I myself, though I find it hard to imagine the world without me, I shall die, but not just yet, I hope. And so on, with whoever you like to mention". Without all this irrelevant detail, it is difficult to grasp a general proposition, except as a form of words of which the interpretation remains vague. In fact, in the above long elucidation, the general proposition never emerges except obscurely in the words "and so on".

I suggest that what really constitutes belief in a general proposition is a mental habit: when you think of a particular man, you think "yes, mortal", provided the question of mortality arises.

That is the real point of the apparently irrelevant detail: it makes you aware of what it is to believe "all men are mortal".

If this is granted, we can allow a preverbal form of a general belief. If an animal has a habit such that, in the presence of an instance of A, it behaves in a manner in which, before the acquisition of the habit, it behaved in the presence of an instance of B, then I shall say that the animal believes the general proposition: "Every instance (or nearly every instance) of A is followed (or accompanied) by an instance of B". That is to say, the animal believes what this form of words signifies.

If this is granted, it becomes obvious that animal habit is essential to the understanding of the psychology and biological origin of general beliefs.

Further, since appropriate habits are what is required for manipulation, the above theory can be brought into relation with the pragmatist theory of "truth", though only as regards general laws, not as regards knowledge of particular facts. There are here, however, various complications and limitations which it is not necessary to our present purpose to examine.

Returning to the definition of "knowledge", I shall say that an animal "knows" the general proposition "A is usually followed by B" if the following conditions are fulfilled:

(1) The animal has had repeated experience of A being followed by B.

(2) This experience has caused the animal to behave in the presence of A more or less as it previously behaved in the presence of B.

(3) A is in fact usually followed by B.

(4) A and B are of such a character, or are so related, that, in most cases where this character or relation exists, the frequency of the observed sequences is evidence of the probability of a general if not invariable law of sequence.

It is evident that the fourth condition raises difficult problems. These will be dealt with in subsequent Chapters.

Chapter II

THE ROLE OF INDUCTION

THE form of inference called "induction by simple enumeration" (which I shall call simply "induction") has occupied, from Francis Bacon to Reichenbach, a very peculiar position in most accounts of scientific inference: it has been considered to be, like the hangman, necessary but unpleasant, and not to be talked of if the subject could possibly be avoided—except by those who, like Hume, refuse to be limited by the canons of good taste. For my part, I hold that the work of Keynes, considered in an earlier Chapter (Part V, Chapter VIII), suggests a change of emphasis, making induction no longer a premiss, but an application of mathematical probability to premisses arrived at independently of induction. Nevertheless, inductive evidence is essential to the justification of accepted generalizations, both those of science and those of daily life. I wish to make clear, in this Chapter, both how induction is useful and why it is not a premiss.

We have seen, in earlier Chapters, how, when we begin to reflect, we find ourselves already believing innumerable generalizations, such as "dogs bark" or "fire burns", which have been *caused* by past experience through the mechanism of the conditioned reflex and habit-formation. When we come to think about our beliefs, if we have a bent towards logic, we wonder whether the cause of our belief can be accepted as a ground for it, and thus, since repetition is the cause, we are led to a desire to justify induction. It has emerged, however, from our earlier inquiries, that we have to find a way of justifying some inductions but not others. To justify induction as such is impossible, since it can be shown to lead quite as often to falsehood as to truth. Nevertheless it remains important as a means of increasing the probability of generalizations in suitable cases. We have a feeling as to what are suitable cases, which, though extremely fallible, suffices to rule out a number of fallacious kinds of induction which logicians can invent but which no sane person would accept. Our purpose must be to substitute for this feeling something which, while not running counter to it, shall be at once more explicit and more reliable.

It is obvious that a conditioned reflex, or "animal induction", is not generated whenever A and B frequently occur together or in quick succession. A and B must be the sort of thing that the animal is inclined to notice. If B is emotionally interesting, a much smaller number of repetitions is required than if it is not. The inductions of animals and savages in regard to matters that vitally concern their welfare are extraordinarily rash; proneness to generalization is much diminished by education. But as against this must be set the fact that a scientific training causes things to be noticed which an animal would never observe. An animal notices when and where it finds food, and is stimulated by the smell of food, but does not notice the chemical ingredients of soil or the effect of fertilizers. An animal also is incapable of hypothesis; it cannot say: "I have noticed several occasions when A has been followed by B; *perhaps* this is always the case, and in any event it is worth while to look out for other instances". But although the man of science, when he is on the look-out for an induction, notices many things that an animal would not notice, he is still limited, as regards the A and B of his induction, to certain kinds of things which seem to him plausible. How far this involuntary and hardly conscious limitation is in line with the limitations that must be imposed on induction to make it valid, is a difficult and obscure question, as to which I do not venture an opinion.

As regards the scientific use of induction, I accept the results reached by Keynes, which were explained in an earlier Chapter. It will perhaps be advantageous, at this stage, to re-state these results.

Keynes supposes some generalization, such as "all A is B", for which, in advance of any observed instances, there is a probability p_0. He supposes, further, that a number of favourable instances $x_1, x_2, \ldots x_n$ are observed, and that no unfavourable instances are observed. The probability of the generalization is to become p_1 after the first favourable instance, p_2 after the first two, and so on, so that p_n is its probability after n favourable instances. We want to know in what circumstances p_n tends to 1 as its limit when n is indefinitely increased. For this purpose we must consider the probability that we should have observed the n favourable instances and no unfavourable ones if the generalization were false. Suppose we call this probability q_n. Keynes shows that p_n tends to 1 as a limit when n increases, if the ratio of q_n to p_0 tends to zero as n increases. This requires that p_0 should be finite, and that q_n should tend to zero as n increases. Induction alone cannot tell us when, if ever, these conditions are fulfilled.

Consider the condition that p_0 should be finite. This means that the suggested generalization "all A is B", before we have observed any instances either favourable or unfavourable, has something to be said in its favour, so that it is at any rate a hypothesis worth examining. The probability p_0, in Keynes's treatment, is relative to the general data h, which, apparently, may include anything except instances of A's that are, or are not, B's. It is very difficult to prevent oneself from thinking of the data as consisting, at least in part, of analogous generalizations which are regarded as well established, and from which we derive inductive evidence in favour of "all A is B". For instance, you want to prove that all copper conducts electricity. Before experimenting with copper you try a number of other elements, and find that each element has a characteristic behaviour in regard to the conduction of electricity. You therefore conclude, inductively, that either all copper conducts electricity, or no copper does so; your generalization, therefore, has an appreciable probability before your observations begin. But since this argument uses induction, it is useless for our purpose. Before we make the induction that all elements have a characteristic behaviour as regards the conduction of electricity, we must ask what was the probability of *this* induction before we had any instances of its truth or falsehood. We may subsume this induction, in turn, under a wider one; we may say: "a large number of properties have been tested, and in regard to each of these every element has been found to have a characteristic behaviour, therefore probably conduction of electricity is also such a property". But to this process of subsuming inductions under wider ones there must in practice be a limit, and wherever we have to stop, in any given state of our knowledge, the data which are summed up in Keynes's h must not be such as to be only relevant if induction is assumed.

We have therefore to seek for principles, other than induction, such that, given certain data not of the form "this A is a B", the generalization "all A is B" has a finite probability. Given such principles, and given a generalization to which they apply, induction can make the generalization increasingly probable, with a probability which approaches certainty as a limit when the number of favourable instances in indefinitely increased. In such an argument, the principles in question are premisses, but induction is not, for in the form in which it is used it is an analytic consequence of the finite-frequency theory of probability.

Our problem, therefore, is to find principles which will make suitable generalizations probable in advance of evidence.

It remains to consider Keynes's other condition, namely that q_n should tend to zero as n increases. Here q_n is the probability that all the first n instances will be favourable although the generalization is false. Suppose—to repeat an earlier illustration—that you are a census officer, concerned to ascertain the names of the inhabitants of a certain Welsh village. The first n inhabitants whom you question are all called Williams. Then q_n is the likelihood of this happening if the inhabitants are not all called Williams. In this case, when n becomes equal to the number of inhabitants of the village, there is no longer any one left who might be not called Williams, and q_n is therefore zero. But such complete enumeration is usually impossible. As a rule, A will be a class of events which keep on happening and cannot be observed until they do, so that A cannot be completely enumerated until the end of time. Nor can we guess how many members A has, nor even whether it is a class with a finite number of members. It is such cases that we have to think of in connection with Keynes's condition that q_n must tend to zero as n increases.

Keynes brings this condition into another form, by making q_n the product of n different probabilities. Suppose Q_1 is the probability that the first A will be a B if the generalization is false, Q_2 the probability that the second A will be a B if the generalization is false and the first A is a B, Q_3 the probability that the third A will be a B if the generalization is false and the first two A's are B's, and so on. Then q_n is the product of $Q_1, Q_2, Q_3, \ldots Q_n$, where Q_n is the probability that the nth A will be a B given that the generalization is false and the first $n - 1$ A's are all B's. If there is any number less than 1 such that all the Q's are less than this number, then the product of n Q's is less than the nth power of this number, and therefore tends to zero as n increases. Thus our condition is satisfied if there is some probability short of certainty, say P, such that, given that the generalization is false and that $n - 1$ A's have been found to be B's, the chance that the nth A will be found to be a B is always less than P provided n is sufficiently great.

It is difficult to see how this condition can fail in empirical material. If it fails, then, if ϵ is any fraction, however small, and n is any number, however large, and if the first n A's are all B's, but not all A's are B's, there is a number m such that the likelihood of the $(n + m)^{th}$ A not being a B is less than ϵ. We may put this in another way. Whatever n may be, let it be given that the first n A's, but not all A's, are B's. If we now arrange the later A's, not in order of their occurrence, but in the order of the probability of their being B's, then the limit of these probabilities is certainty. This is what must happen if the condition fails.

Obviously this condition is less interesting, and much easier to fulfil, than the earlier condition, that our generalization must have a finite probability in advance of favourable instances. If we can find a principle insuring such finite probability in the case of a given generalization, then we have a right to use induction to make the generalization probable. But in the absence of some such principle inductions cannot be accepted as making generalizations probable.

In the above discussion I have followed Keynes in considering only evidence for "all A is B". But in practice, especially in the early stages of an investigation, it is often useful to know that most A is B. Suppose, for instance, there are two diseases, one common and one rare, which have very similar symptoms in their early stages. A medical man, when he comes across these symptoms, will do right to conclude that he probably has to deal with a case of the commoner disease. It very frequently happens that laws which we believe to be without exceptions are discovered by way of prior generalizations which apply to most cases, but not to all. And obviously less evidence is required to establish the probability of "most A is B" than to establish that of "all A is B".

From a practical point of view, the difference is negligible. If it is certain that m/n of the A's are B's, m/n is the probability that the next A will be a B. If it is probable, but not certain, that all A's are B's, it is again probable that the next A will be a B. So far as expectations about the next A are concerned, it therefore comes to the same thing to be sure that most A's are B's, or to think it probable that all A's are B's. The case most likely to occur in practice is that in which it is probable that most A's are B's. This often suffices for rational expectation, and therefore for guidance in practice.

Chapter III

THE POSTULATE OF NATURAL KINDS, OR OF LIMITED VARIETY

IN seeking the postulate or postulates required to make inductive probabilities approach certainty as a limit, there are two desiderata. On the one hand, the postulate or postulates must be sufficient, from a purely logical point of view, to do the work that is asked of them. On the other hand—and this is the more difficult requirement—they must be such that some inferences which depend upon them for their validity are, to common sense, more or less unquestionable. For example: you find two verbally identical copies of the same book, and you assume unhesitatingly that they have a common causal antecedent. In such a case, though every one will admit the inference, the principle which justifies it is obscure, and is only to be discovered by careful analysis. I do not demand that a general postulate arrived at by this method should itself possess any degree of self-evidence, but I do demand that some inferences which, logically, depend upon it, shall be such as any person who understands them, except a sceptical philosopher, will consider so obvious as to be scarcely worth stating. There must, of course, be no positive grounds for regarding a suggested postulate as false. In particular, it should be self-confirmatory, not self-refuting, i.e. inductions which assume it should have conclusions consistent with it.

In the present Chapter I propose to consider a postulate suggested by Keynes, and called by him the "postulate of limited variety". It is closely akin to, if not identical with, an older postulate, that of natural kinds. We shall find that the postulate is adequate logically as a basis for induction. I think, also, that it can be stated in a form in which science to some degree confirms it. It therefore satisfies two of the three requisites of a postulate. But it does not, in my opinion, satisfy the third, namely that of being discoverable, by analysis, as implicit in arguments which we all accept. On this ground, it seems to me necessary to seek other postulates, which I shall do in subsequent Chapters.

Keynes's postulate arises directly out of his discussion of

induction, and is designed to confer on certain generalizations that finite antecedent probability which he has shown to be necessary. Before we consider it, let us examine an argument which might seem to show that no postulate is necessary, since every imaginable generalization has a finite antecedent probability which is never less than a certain minimum.

Let us take a case which arises in real life, and has a certain approximation to pure chance, namely that of passengers on a big liner arriving with their baggage at the custom house. Most pieces of baggage have a number of labels, one showing the name of the owner, and others advertising hotels in which he has stayed. We can then consider the antecedent probability of such a generalization as "every trunk having label A has also label B".

To complete the analogy with logic, let us suppose that there are also negative labels, that no trunk has both the label "A" and the label "not-A", but that every trunk has one or other of these two. In the absence of further information, if we select two labels A and B at haphazard, what is the chance that every trunk having the label A also has the label B? Since every trunk has either the label B or the label not-B, the chance that any given trunk has the label B is a half. (I am assuming that we know nothing about B, and, in particular, that we do not know whether it is a positive or a negative label.) It follows that, if n trunks have the label A, the chance that they all have the label B is 1 in 2^n. This is finite, and if N is the total number of trunks, it is never less than 1 in 2^N.

It follows from the above argument that, if the number of "things" in the universe is some finite number N, the generalization "all A is B" always has an antecedent probability at least as great as $1/2^N$. This is the antecedent probability if everything has the property A; if only some things have this property, the antecedent probability is greater. Therefore in theory a sufficient postulate to add to Keynes's theory of induction would be the assumption that the number of "things" in the universe is finite. This is equivalent to the assumption that the number of space-time points is finite. This, in turn—if we adopt the suggestion of an earlier Chapter, according to which a space-time point is a bundle of compresent qualities—is equivalent to the assumption that the number of qualities is finite.

I have no doubt that this assumption is a logically sufficient postulate. There are, however, two objections to it. One is that science affords no way of deciding whether it is true, so that it is not self-confirmatory; the other is that N would have to be so large that no induction we can actually carry out would achieve any tolerable degree of probability. Let us, therefore, put aside the above suggestion as a mere curiosity, and proceed to consider Keynes's more practical hypothesis.

What Keynes requires is that certain kinds of generalization should be known to have a higher initial probability than belongs to generalizations that are entirely random. He suggests, for this purpose, a postulate to the effect that the qualities things may have fall into groups, and that a group may become determinate when only some of the qualities composing it are given. He supposes:

"That the almost innumerable apparent properties of any given object all arise out of a finite number of generator properties, which we may call $\phi_1, \phi_2, \phi_3, \ldots$. Some arise out of ϕ_1 alone, some out of ϕ_1 in conjunction with ϕ_2, and so on. The properties which arise out of ϕ_1 alone form one group; those which arise out of $\phi_1 \phi_2$ in conjunction form another group, and so on. Since the number of generator properties is finite, the number of groups is also finite. If a set of apparent properties arise (say) out of three generator properties ϕ_1, ϕ_2, ϕ_3 then this set of properties may be said to specify the group $\phi_1 \phi_2 \phi_3$. Since the total number of apparent properties is assumed to be greater than that of the generator properties, and since the number of groups is finite, it follows that, if two sets of apparent properties are taken, there is, in the absence of evidence to the contrary, a finite probability that the second set will belong to the group specified by the first set."

The number of independent groups of the above sort is called the amount of "variety" in the universe, or in whatever part of it is relevant to a particular argument. Keynes's statement of his postulate is as follows:

"As a logical foundation for Analogy, therefore, we seem to need some such assumption as that the amount of variety in the universe is limited in such a way that there is no one object so complex that its qualities fall into an infinite number of independent groups (i.e. groups which might exist independently as well as in conjunction); or rather that none of the objects about which we generalize are as complex as this; or at least that, though some objects may be infinitely complex, we sometimes have a finite probability that an object about which we seek to generalize is not infinitely complex".[1]

It was proved by Nicod that the postulate in the above form is not quite adequate. It is not enough that every object should be of finite complexity; we need that there should be a finite number such that no object has qualities belonging to more than this number of independent groups. I shall consider this emendation made.

We shall, I think, best understand the scope of Keynes's postulate if we take a zoological illustration, say a cow. A cow is an animal, a vertebrate, a mammal, a ruminant, and a member of one species of ruminants. Each of these classificatory words is capable of various definitions which, though differing in intension, give the same extension. How, for example, do we distinguish a cow from other ruminants? Most of us are content with external appearance: a cow is an animal that looks like a cow. This is quite adequate for practical purposes, but a zoologist can enumerate a variety of characteristics common and peculiar to cows, any one of which might be used to define the word "cow". The same applies to "ruminant", "mammal", "vertebrate", and "animal". Each of these words is capable of various definitions that are extensionally equivalent, though we do not know of any reason why they should be so. It is obvious that, if this sort of thing happens often, generalizations have a much greater antecedent probability than they would have if properties were distributed at random.

Let us endeavour to state Keynes's hypothesis in somewhat more detail. He supposes that—either in general or in some specified province—it is possible to pick out a finite set of fundamental properties, such that, when we know which of these properties an individual possesses, we can know (at least in theory) what some, at least, of his other properties are, not because there is a *logical* connection, but because in fact certain properties never occur except in conjunction with certain others, as, for example, all ruminants divide the hoof. The hypothesis is analogous to the Mendelian theory of genes, according to which a finite number of genes determine the whole congenital character

[1] *Treatise on Probability*, Chapter XXII, p. 258.

of an animal or plant. Keynes supposes that there is a finite number of groups of qualities, and that two qualities belonging to the same group have the same extension. If n is the number of such groups, and if two qualities are selected at random, there is a chance $1/n$ that they belong to the same group, and that therefore all individuals possessing either quality possess the other. This suffices to give Keynes the basis that he needs for validating induction.

The postulate, as Keynes points out, can be weakened in various ways without ceasing to be effective. One of these is that we need not suppose that *all* properties belong to such groups as he postulates; it is sufficient if a finite proportion do so. It is sufficient to justify some inductions, though not all, if there is some definable class of properties all of which belong to Keynesian groups. We can more or less distinguish characters distinctive of a species from others which vary from individual to individual. Colour, for example, is known to be very variable among animals, and therefore the stock fallacious induction "all swans are white" was always less reliable than (say) "all swans have long necks". We may call a character "specific" when it belongs to all members of some species, a "species" being a class having a variety of common properties which are found together for no known reason. It is generally held that spatio-temporal position is never a specific character. It is true that marsupials in a wild state only occur in Australia, but they do not cease to be marsupials when they are brought to Zoos elsewhere.

Induction may be needed to determine whether a given character is, or is not, specific; but if we suppose that specific characters are a finite proportion of all characters, this use of induction will be justifiable.

For many purposes it suffices if we can establish that a great majority of A's are B's; we may therefore soften Keynes's postulate by supposing it to say that certain characters are *usually* conjoined. If a "natural kind" is defined by means of a number of properties $A_1, A_2, \ldots A_n$ (not known to be interdependent), we may, for some purposes, consider that an individual which has all these qualities except one is still to be considered a member of the kind—for example, Manx cats are cats in spite of having no tail. Moreover a great many distinctive characters are capable of continuous modification, so that there are border-line cases where we cannot say definitely whether a given character is present or absent. A natural kind is like what in topology is called a neighbourhood, but an intensional, not an extensional, neighbourhood. Cats, for example, are like a star cluster: they are not all in one intensional place, but most of them are crowded together close to an intensional centre. Assuming evolution, there must have been outlying members so aberrant that we should hardly know whether to regard them as part of the cluster or not. This view of natural kinds has the advantage that it needs no modification before incorporation in advanced science.

Such considerations suggest, however, a transformation of Keynes's postulate into something more flexible and less reminiscent of a logical text-book than the principle that he enunciates. It would seem that there must be laws making certain kinds of combination more stable than other kinds, and demanding that, when one character is slightly altered, another shall undergo some correlated slight alteration. This process leads to functional laws of correlation as probably more fundamental than natural kinds.

The above line of thought seems appropriate in biology, but a somewhat different line is suggested by the modern theory of the atom. During the eighteenth and nineteenth centuries it was found that the enormous multiplicity of observed substances could be accounted for by supposing them all composed out of ninety-two elements (some still unobserved). Each element, until our own century, had a number of properties which were found to coexist, though for no known reason. Atomic weight, melting point, appearance, etc., made each element a natural kind, as precisely as in biology before evolution. At last, however, it appeared that the differences between different elements were differences of structure, and were consequences of laws which were the same for all elements. There are still natural kinds— at the moment there are electrons, positrons, neutrons, and protons—but it is hoped that these are not ultimate, and may be reduced to differences of structure. Already in quantum theory their existence is somewhat shadowy and unsubstantial. This suggests that in physics, as in biology since Darwin, the doctrine of natural kinds may prove to have been only a temporary phase.

I conclude that the doctrine of natural kinds, though useful in establishing such pre-scientific inductions as "dogs bark" and "cats mew", is only an approximate and transitional assumption on the road towards fundamental laws of a different kind. Both on this ground and because of its arbitrary character, I cannot accept it as one of the postulates of scientific inference.

Chapter IV

KNOWLEDGE TRANSCENDING
EXPERIENCE

SOME modern empiricists—in particular, the majority of logical positivists—have, in my opinion, misconceived the relation of knowledge to experience. This has arisen, if I am not mistaken, from two errors: first, an inadequate analysis of the concept "experience", and second, a mistake as to what is involved in the belief that some assigned property belongs to some (undetermined) subject. Two specific problems arise, one as regards significance, the other as regards knowledge of what are called "existence propositions", i.e. propositions of the form "something has this property". It is maintained, on the one hand, that a statement is not "significant" unless there is some known method of verifying it; on the other hand, that we cannot know "something has this property" unless we can mention a specific subject that has the property. In the present Chapter I wish to give reasons for rejecting both these opinions.

Before examining the abstract logic of these two problems, let us consider them, for a moment, from a common-sense point of view.

To begin with verification: There are some who maintain that, if atomic warfare is not checked, it may lead to the extermination of life on this planet. I am not concerned to maintain that this opinion is true, but only that it is significant. It is, however, one which cannot be verified, for who would be left to verify it if life were extinct? Only Berkeley's God, whom, I am sure, logical positivists would not wish to invoke. Going backwards instead of forwards, we all believe that there was a time before there was life on the earth. Those who regard verifiability as necessary to significance do not mean to deny such possibilities, but in order to admit them they are compelled to define "verifiability" somewhat loosely. Sometimes a proposition is regarded as "verifiable" if there is any empirical evidence in its favour. That is to say, "all A is B" is "verifiable" if we know of one A that is B and do not know of one that is not B. This view, however, leads to logical absurdities. Suppose there is no single member of A concerning which we know whether it is a B, but there is an object x, not a member of A, which we know to be a B. Let A′ be the class consisting of the class A together with the object x. Then "all A′ is B" is verifiable in terms of the definition. Since this implies "all A is B", it follows that "all A is B" is verifiable. Consequently every generalization of the form "all A is B" is verifiable if there is, anywhere, a single object known to be a B.

Consider now a generalization of a different sort, such as we may wish to make in connection with the doctrine of natural kinds. The generalizations I have in mind are those of the form: "all predicates of the class A are true of the object B". Applying the same definition of "verifiability", this is "verifiable" if some, or at least one, of the predicates of the class A is empirically known to be true of B. If this is not the case, let P be some predicate known to be true of B, and let A′ be the class consisting of the class A together with P. Then "all predicates of the class A′ are true of B" is verifiable, and so, therefore, is "all predicates of the class A are true of B".

From these two processes it follows that, if anything is known to have any predicate, all generalizations are "verifiable". This consequence was not intended, and shows that the above wide definition of "verifiability" is useless. But unless we allow some such wide definition, we cannot escape from paradoxes.

Let us next consider propositions containing the word "some", or an equivalent, e.g. "some men are black", or "some quadrupeds have no tails". As a rule, such propositions are known by means of instances. If I am asked "how do you know that some quadrupeds have no tails?" I may reply "because I once had a Manx cat, and it had no tail". The view which I wish to combat maintains that this is the only way of knowing such propositions. This view has been maintained by Brouwer in mathematics, and is maintained by some other philosophers in regard to empirical objects.

The paradoxes resulting from this opinion are very similar to those resulting from the above doctrine as to verifiability. Take such a proposition as "rain sometimes falls in places where there is no one to see it". No sane person would deny this, but it is impossible to mention a raindrop that has never been noticed. To deny that we know that there are occurrences not observed by any one is incompatible with common sense, but is necessary if we never know such propositions as "there are A's" except when we can mention A's that we have observed. Can any one seriously maintain that the planet Neptune or the Antarctic Continent did not exist until it was discovered? Again only a Berkeleian God will enable us to escape from paradoxes. Or again: we all believe that there is iron in the interior of the earth, but we cannot give instances beyond the depth of the deepest mine.

Adherents of the doctrine that I am combating interpret such facts hypothetically. They say that the statement "there is undiscovered iron" is an abbreviation, and that the full statement should be: "if I did certain things, I should discover iron". Suppose, for the sake of precision, we take the statement "there is iron more than 1,000 miles below the surface of the earth". It is unlikely that anybody will ever find this iron, and, in any case, how can it be known what a person would find? Only by knowing what is there to be found. A hypothetical of which the hypothesis will probably always be false tells us nothing. Or consider: "there was once a world without life". This cannot mean: "If I had been alive then, I should have seen that nothing was alive".

Let us now consider the above two doctrines more formally, from a strictly logical point of view.

A. MEANING AND VERIFICATION

There is a theory that the meaning of a proposition consists in its method of verification. It follows (a) that what cannot be verified or falsified is meaningless, (b) that two propositions verified by the same occurrences have the same meaning.

I reject both, and I do not think that those who advocate them have fully realized their implications.

First: practically all the advocates of the above view regard verification as a *social* matter. This means that they take up the problem at a late stage, and are unaware of its earlier stages. Other people's observations are not data for me. The hypothesis that nothing exists except what I perceive and remember is for me identical, in all its verifiable consequences, with the hypothesis that there are other people who also perceive and remember. If we are to believe in the existence of these other people—as we must do if we are to admit testimony—we must reject the identification of meaning with verification.

"Verification" is often defined very loosely. The only strict meaning of verification is the following: A proposition asserting a finite number of future occurrences is "verified" when all these occurrences have taken place, and are, at some moment, perceived or remembered by some one person. But this is not the sense in which the word is usually employed. It is customary to say that a general proposition is "verified" when all those of its consequences which it has been possible to test have been found to be true. It is always assumed that, in that case, probably the consequences which have not been tested are also true. But this is not the point with which I am concerned at present. The point with which I am concerned at the moment is the theory that two propositions whose verified consequences are identical have the same significance. I say "verified", not "verifiable"; for we cannot know, until the last man perishes, whether the "verifiable" consequences are identical. Take, e.g. "all men are mortal". It may be that on February 9, 1991, an immortal man will be born. The presently verifiable consequences of "all men are mortal" are the same as those of "all men born before the time t are mortal, but not all those born later", where t is any time not more than a century before the present.

If we insist upon using the word "verifiable" rather than "verified", we cannot know that a proposition is verifiable, since this would involve knowledge of an indefinitely long future. In fact, that a proposition is verifiable is itself not verifiable. This is because to state that all the future consequences of a general proposition are true is itself a general proposition of which the instances cannot be enumerated, and no general proposition can be established on purely empirical evidence except one applying to a list of particulars all of which have been observed. E.g. I may say "the inhabitants of such-and-such a village are Mr. and Mrs. A, Mr. and Mrs. B, etc., and their families, all of whom are known to me personally; and all of them are Welsh".[1] But when I cannot enumerate the members of a class,

---

[1] But, as we saw in Part II, Chapter X, such general enumerative statements involve many difficulties.

I cannot, on purely empirical grounds, justify any generalization about its members except what follows analytically from its definition.

There is however still a point to be made in favour of the verifiers. They contend that there is a distinction between two kinds of cases. In one, we have two propositions whose consequences hitherto have been indistinguishable, but whose future consequences may diverge; e.g. "all men are mortal" and "all men born before A.D. 2000 are mortal". In the other, we have two propositions whose observable consequences can never diverge; this is especially the case with metaphysical hypotheses. The hypothesis that the starry heavens exist at all times, and the hypothesis that they only exist when I see them, are exactly identical in all those of their consequences that I can test. It is specially in such cases that meaning is identified with verification, and that, therefore, the two hypotheses are said to have the same significance. And it is this that I am specially concerned to deny.

Perhaps the most obvious case is other people's minds. The hypothesis that there are other people, having thoughts and feelings more or less like my own, does not have the same significance as the hypothesis that other people are only parts of my dreams, and yet the verifiable consequences of the two hypotheses are identical. We all feel love and hate, sympathy and antipathy, admiration and contempt, for what we believe to be real people. The *emotional* consequences of this belief are very different from those of solipsism, though the *verifiable* consequences are not. I should say that two beliefs whose emotional consequences differ have substantially distinct significations.

But this is a practical argument. I should go further, and say, as a matter of pure theory, that you cannot, without incurring an endless regress, seek the significance of a proposition in its consequences, which must be other propositions. We cannot explain what is the significance of a belief, or what makes it true or false, without bringing in the concept "fact", and when this is brought in the part played by verification is seen to be subsidiary and derivative.

B. INFERENTIAL EXISTENCE-PROPOSITIONS

A form of words containing an undetermined variable—for instance, "x is a man"—is called a "propositional function" if, when a value is assigned to the variable, the form of words becomes a proposition. Thus "x is a man" is neither true nor false, but if for "x" I put "Mr. Jones" I get a true proposition, and if I put "Mrs. Jones" I get a false one.

Besides giving a value to "x", there are two other ways of obtaining a proposition from a propositional function. One is to say that the propositions obtained by giving values to "x" are all true; the other is to say that at least one of them is true. If "$f(x)$" is the function in question, we will call the first of these "$f(x)$ always" and the second "$f(x)$ sometimes" (where it is understood that "sometimes" means "at least once"). If "$f(x)$" is "x is not a man or x is mortal", we can assert "$f(x)$ always"; if "$f(x)$" is "x is a man", we can assert "$f(x)$ sometimes", which is what we should commonly express by saying "there are men". If "$f(x)$" is "I met x and x is a man", "$f(x)$ sometimes" is "I met at least one man".

We call "$f(x)$ sometimes" an "existence-proposition", because it says that something having the property $f(x)$ "exists". For instance, if you wanted to say "unicorns exist", you would first have to define "x is a unicorn" and then assert that there are values of x for which this is true. In ordinary language, the words "some", "a", and "the" (in the singular) indicate existence-propositions.

There is one obvious way in which we get to know existence-propositions, and that is by means of instances. If I know "$f(a)$", where a is some known object, I can infer "$f(x)$ sometimes". The question I wish to discuss is whether this is the only way in which such propositions can come to be known. I wish to maintain that it is not.

In deductive logic, there are only two ways in which existence-propositions can be proved. One is the above, when "$f(x)$ sometimes" is deduced from "$f(a)$"; the other is when one existence-proposition is deduced from another, for instance "there are bipeds" from "there are featherless bipeds". What other methods are possible in non-deductive inference?

Induction, when valid, gives another method. Suppose there

are two classes A and B and a relation R, such that, in a number of observed instances, we have (writing "a R b" for "a has the relation R to b")

a_1 is an A. b_1 is a B. a_1 R b_1

a_2 is an A. b_2 is a B. a_2 R b_2

. . . .

a_n is an A. b_n is a B. a_n R b_n

and suppose we have no contrary instances. Then in all observed instances, if a is an A, there is a B to which a has the relation R. If the case is one to which induction applies, we infer that probably every member of A has the relation R to some member of B. Consequently, if a_{n+1} is the next observed member of A, we infer as probable: "there is a member of B to which a_{n+1} has the relation R". We infer this, in fact, in many cases in which we cannot adduce any particular member of B such as we have inferred. To revert to an earlier illustration, we all believe that probably Napoleon III had a father. Not even a solipsist, if he allows himself any views as to his own future, can escape from this sort of induction. Suppose, for instance, that our solipsist suffers from intermittent sciatica, which comes on every evening; he may say, on inductive grounds, "probably I shall be suffering pain at 9 p.m. to-night". This is an inference to the existence of something transcending his present experience. "But", you may say, "it does not transcend his *future* experience". If the inference is valid it does not; but the question is: "how is he to know *now* that the inference is probably valid?" The whole practical utility of scientific inference consists in giving grounds for anticipating the future; when the future has come and has verified the inference, memory has replaced inference, which is no longer needed. We must, therefore, find grounds for trusting the inference *before* it is verified. And I defy the world to find any such grounds for trusting inferences which will be verified, which are not equally grounds for trusting certain inferences which will be neither verified nor falsified, such as the inference to Napoleon III's father.

We are again faced with the question: in what circumstances is induction valid? It is futile to say: "Induction is valid when it infers something which subsequent experience will verify". This is futile, because it would confine induction to cases in which it is useless. We must have reasons, in advance of experience, for expecting something, and exactly similar reasons may lead us to believe in some thing that we cannot experience, for example, the thoughts and feelings of other people. The plain fact is that much too much fuss is made about "experience".

Experience is needed for ostensive definition, and therefore for all understanding of the meanings of words. But the proposition "Mr. A had a father" is completely intelligible even if I have no idea who Mr. A's father was. If Mr. B was in fact Mr. A's father, "Mr. B" is not a constituent of the statement "Mr. A had a father", or, indeed of any statement containing the words "Mr. A's father" but not containing the name "Mr. B". Similarly I may *understand* "there was a winged horse" although there never was one, because the statement means that, putting "fx" for "x has wings and is a horse", I assert "fx sometimes". It must be understood that "x" is not a constituent of "fx sometimes" or of "fx always". In fact, "x" means nothing. That is why beginners find it so hard to make out what it means.

When I infer something not experienced—whether I shall or shall not experience it hereafter—I am never inferring something that I can name, but only the truth of an existence-proposition. If induction is ever valid, it is possible to know existence-propositions without knowing any particular instance of their truth. Suppose, for instance, that A is a class of which we have experienced members, and we infer that a member of A will occur. We have only to substitute "future members of A" for "members of A" to make our inference apply to a class of which we cannot mention any instance.

I incline to think that valid inductions, and, generally, inferences going beyond my personal past and present experience, always depend upon causation, sometimes supplemented by analogy. But this is a subject for later Chapters; in the present Chapter I wished only to remove certain *a priori* objections to a certain kind of inference—objections which, though *a priori*, are urged by those who imagine themselves able to dispense with the *a priori* altogether.

Chapter V

CAUSAL LINES

THE concept "cause", as it occurs in the works of most philosophers, is one which is apparently not used in any advanced science. But the concepts that are used have been developed from the primitive concept (which is that prevalent among philosophers), and the primitive concept, as I shall try to show, still has importance as the source of approximate generalizations and pre-scientific inductions, and as a concept which is valid when suitably limited.

"Cause", as it occurs, for example, in J. S. Mill, may be defined as follows: All events can be divided into classes in such a way that every event of a certain class A is followed by an event of a certain class B, which may or may not be different from A. Given two such events, the event of class A is called the "cause" and the event of class B is called the "effect". If A and B are quantitative, there will usually be a quantitative relation between cause and effect—e.g. a bigger charge of gun-powder, when it explodes, will cause a louder noise. When we have discovered a causal relation, we can, given an A, infer a B. The converse inference, from B to A, is less reliable, because sometimes a variety of causes may all have the same kind of effect. Nevertheless, with proper precautions, backward inference, from effects to causes, is very often possible.

Mill supposes that the law of universal causation, more or less as we have just enunciated it, is proved, or at least rendered extremely probable, by induction. His famous four methods, which are designed, in a given class of cases, to find out what is the cause and what the effect, assume causation, and do not depend upon induction otherwise than as induction is supposed to justify this assumption. But we have seen that induction cannot prove causation unless causation is antecedently probable. As a basis for inductive generalization, however, causation may be something much weaker than it is usually supposed to be. Suppose we start with the assumption that, given some event, it is probable (not certain) that there is some class of events to which it belongs, which is such that most (not necessarily all) members of the class are followed by events of a certain other class. An assumption of this sort may suffice to give a high degree of inductive probability to generalizations of the form "most A's are followed by B's", if a great many instances have been observed of A's being followed by B's and no contrary instances have been observed.

Whether from pure prejudice, or from the influence of tradition, or for some other reason, it is easier to believe that there is a law of nature to the effect that causes are *always* followed by their effects than to the effect that this *usually* happens. We feel that we can imagine, or perhaps even sometimes perceive, a relation "cause-and-effect", which, when it holds, insures *invariable* sequence. The only kind of weakening in the law of causation that it is easy to admit is one that says, not that a causal relation may be not invariable, but that in some cases there may be *no* causal relation. We may find ourselves compelled to admit that quantum transitions and radio-active disintegrations in single atoms have no invariable antecedents; although they are causes, they are not effects, and there is no class of immediate antecedents which can be regarded as their causes. Such a possibility may be admitted without destroying the inductive power of evidence for a causal law, provided it is still held that a large proportion of observable events are both causes and effects. I shall assume this limitation conceded. That is to say, I shall consider the law of causation to assert that causal sequences, when they occur, are invariable, and that they occur frequently, but not that *every* event is a member of *some* invariable causal sequence.

We must ask ourselves: when we assume causation, do we assume a specific relation, cause-and-effect, or do we merely assume invariable sequence? That is to say, when I assert "every event of class A causes an event of class B", do I mean merely "every event of class A is followed by an event of class B", or do I mean something more? Before Hume, the latter view was always taken; since Hume, most empiricists have taken the former.

I am at present only concerned to *interpret* the law of causation, not to inquire into its truth. As a matter of interpretation of what is commonly believed, I do not think that invariable sequence will suffice. Suppose I discovered that throughout the nineteenth century there was only one conchologist whose name began with X, and he married his cook. I could then assert: "All nineteenth-century conchologists whose names began with X married their cooks". But nobody would think this a causal law. Suppose you had lived in the nineteenth century, and been called Ximenes. Suppose further that you had a mild *penchant* for conchology and a very ugly cook. You would not have said to yourself: "I must learn not to take an interest in shells, because I don't want to be compelled to marry this worthy but unattractive female". On the other hand, though Empedocles was (so far as I know) the only man who leapt down the crater of Etna, we consider his fate a quite sufficient reason for not following his example, because we think there was a causal connection between his leap and his death.

Geulincx's two clocks, which both keep perfect time, and of which one always strikes when the other points to the hour, are not such a good example, because there is an indirect causal connection between them. But there are somewhat similar examples in nature, which afford illustrations. Take, for example, two clouds of incandescent gas of a given element. both emit the same spectral lines, but we do not think that either has any effect upon the other. Generally, given any two uniform processes, when one reaches a certain stage, the other also reaches a certain stage, but we do not, in general, infer a causal connection, for instance between the earth's rotation and the period of a Cepheid variable.

It seems clear, therefore, that invariable concomitance or succession is not what we mean by causation: it is implied by causation, but not vice versa. This is not yet to say that causation is a law of nature; it is only a conclusion as to what is meant by "cause" in common parlance.

Belief in causation, whether valid or not, is deeply embedded in language. Consider how Hume, in spite of his desire to be sceptical, allows himself, from the start, to use the word "impression". An "impression" should be something that presses in on one, which is a purely causal conception. The difference between an "impression" and an "idea" should be that the former, but not the latter, has a proximate cause which is external. Hume, it is true, professes to find an intrinsic difference: impressions are distinguished from ideas by their greater "liveliness". But this won't do: some impressions are faint, and some ideas are lively. For my part, I should define an "impression", or a "sensation", as a mental occurrence of which the proximate cause is physical, while an "idea" has a proximate cause which is mental. If, as solipsism maintains, no mental events have external causes, the distinction between "impressions" and "ideas" is a mistake.

In dreams we think we have impressions, but when we wake we usually conclude that we were mistaken. It follows that there is no *intrinsic* character which invariably distinguishes impressions from ideas.

Belief in the external causation of certain kinds of experiences is primitive, and is, in a certain sense, implicit in animal behaviour. It is involved in the concept of "perception". When you "perceive" a table or a person, the sun or the moon, the noise of an explosion or the smell of a bad drain, it is, for common sense, because what you are perceiving is there to be perceived. If you think you are perceiving an object which in fact is not there, you are dreaming, or suffering a hallucination, or misinterpreting a sensation. But it is assumed that such occurrences are sufficiently uncommon, or sufficiently queer, to be incapable of deceiving permanently anybody but a lunatic. Most perceptions, at most times, are taken to be either trustworthy or only momentarily deceptive; persons whose professed perceptions threaten our security by their strangeness are locked up in asylums. Thus common sense, by the help of the law, succeeds in preserving its belief that what seem like perceptions usually have external causes which more or less resemble their effects in perception. I think that common sense is in the right in this belief, except that the resemblance between perception and object is probably less than common sense supposes. This matter has been already considered; at present we are concerned with the part played by the concept of "cause".

The conception of "cause", as we have been considering it, is primitive and. unscientific. In science it is replaced by the conception of "causal laws". The need for this development arises as follows. Suppose we have a common-sense generalization that A causes B—e.g. that acorns cause oaks. If there is any finite interval of time between A and B, something may happen during this time to prevent B—for example, pigs may eat the acorns. We cannot take account of all the infinite complexity of the world, and we cannot tell, except through previous causal knowledge, which among possible circumstances would prevent B. Our law therefore becomes: "A will cause B if nothing happens to prevent B". Or, more simply: "A will cause B unless it doesn't". This is a poor sort of law, and not very useful as a basis for scientific knowledge.

There are three ways in which science overcomes this difficulty; they are those of (1) differential equations, (2) quasi-permanence, (3) statistical regularity. I will say something about each of these in turn.

(1) The use of differential equations is necessary whenever a certain set of circumstances produces a tendency to a certain change in the circumstances, and this change, in turn, alters the tendency to change. Gravitation affords the most familiar example: the earth has at every moment an acceleration towards the sun, but the direction of the sun is continually changing. The law of gravitation, therefore, has to state the tendency to change (acceleration) at each instant, given the configuration at that instant, leaving the total resulting change during a finite time to be calculated. Or take the "curve of pursuit": A man is at one corner of a square field, and his dog is at an adjacent corner. The man walks along the side of the field that does not take him towards the dog; the dog at each instant runs towards his master. What will be the dog's course? Obviously only differential equations will enable us to answer this question since the dog's direction is continually changing.

This interpretation of causal laws is a commonplace of classical dynamics, and need not detain us.

(2) The importance of quasi-permanence is less conventional, and has been less noticed. It may be regarded, in a sense, as an extension of the first law of motion. The first law of motion states that a body which is not interfered with by outside causes will continue to move with uniform velocity in a straight line. This implies, first, that the body will continue to exist, and secondly, that what may be regarded as "small" causes will produce only small changes of direction or velocity. All this is vague, but it establishes what might be called "normal" expectations.

The law of quasi-permanence, as I intend it, is much more general than the first law of motion, and is designed to explain the success of the common-sense notion of "things" and the physical notion of "matter" (in classical physics). For reasons given in earlier Chapters, a "thing" or a piece of matter is not to be regarded as a single persistent substantial entity, but as a string of events having a certain kind of causal connection with each other. This kind is what I call "quasi-permanence". The causal law that I suggest may be enunciated as follows: "Given an event at a certain time, then at any slightly earlier or slightly later time there is, at some neighbouring place, a closely similar event". I do not assert that this happens always, but only that it happens very often—sufficiently often to give a high probability to an induction confirming it in a particular case.

When "substance" is abandoned, the identity, for common sense, of a thing or a person at different times must be explained as consisting in what may be called a "causal line". We normally *recognize* a thing or person by qualitative similarity to a former appearance, but it is not this that *defines* "identity". When a friend returns from years in a Japanese prison, we may say "I should never have known you". Suppose you know two twins whom you cannot tell apart; suppose one of them, in battle, loses an eye, an arm, and a leg. He will then seem much less like his former self than the other twin is, but we nevertheless identify him, not the other twin, with his former self, because of a certain kind of causal continuity. To oneself, personal identity is guaranteed by memory, which generates one kind of "causal line". A given piece of matter at a given moment may belong to more than one causal line; for instance, my arm is always the same arm, though the molecules composing it change. In the one case we are considering anatomical and physiological causal lines, in the other case those of physics.

The conception of "causal lines" is involved, not only in the quasi-permanence of things and persons, but also in the definition of "perception". When I see a number of stars, each produces its separate effect on my retina, which it can only do by means of a causal line extending over the intermediate space. When I see a table or a chair or a page of print, there are causal lines from its parts to the eye. We can carry the chain of causation further back, until we reach the sun—if we are seeing by daylight. But when we go further back than the table or chair or page of print, the causes have no longer any close resemblance to their effects. They are, moreover, not events bound up with only one "thing", but with interactions, e.g. between the sun and the table. Consequently, the experience that I have when I "see a table" can give me much knowledge concerning the table, but not much knowledge concerning earlier parts of the process that ends in my experience. For this reason I am said to be seeing the table, not the sun. But if the sun is reflected in a good mirror I am said to be seeing the sun. Generally, what is said to be perceived, in the kind of experience called a "perception", is the first term in a causal line that ends at a sense-organ.

A "causal line", as I wish to define the term, is a temporal series of events so related that, given some of them, something can be inferred about the others whatever may be happening elsewhere. A causal line may always be regarded as the persistence of something—a person, a table, a photon, or what not. Throughout a given causal line, there may be constancy of quality, constancy of structure, or gradual change in either, but not sudden change of any considerable magnitude. I should consider the process from speaker to listener in broadcasting one causal line: here the beginning and end are similar in quality as well as structure, but the intermediate links—sound waves, electromagnetic waves, and physiological processes—have only a resemblance of structure to each other and to the initial and final terms of the series.

That there are such more or less self-determined causal processes is in no degree logically necessary, but is, I think, one of the fundamental postulates of science. It is in virtue of the truth of this postulate—if it is true—that we are able to acquire partial knowledge in spite of our enormous ignorance. That the universe is a system of interconnected parts may be true, but can only be discovered if some parts can, in some degree, be known independently of other parts. It is this that our postulate makes possible.

(3) On statistical regularity it is not necessary to say much, since it appears to be an inference, not a postulate. Its importance in physics began with the kinetic theory of gases, which made temperature, for example, a statistical concept. Quantum theory has very greatly enhanced its status. It now appears probable that the fundamental regularities of physics are statistical, and are not such as to tell us, even in theory, what an individual atom will do. The difference between this theory and the older

477

individual determinism is unimportant in connection with our present problem, which is that of finding postulates that give the needed basis for inductive inferences. These postulates need not be either certain or universal; we require only a probability that some characteristic occurs usually in a certain class of cases. And this is just as true in quantum mechanics as in classical physics.

Moreover the substitution of statistical for individual regularities has only been found necessary in regard to atomic phenomena, all of which are inferred. All the phenomena that can be observed are macroscopic, and the problem of making such phenomena amenable to science remains what it was.

Chapter VI

STRUCTURE AND CAUSAL LAWS

I⸀T has appeared from previous discussions that induction by simple enumeration is not a principle by which non-demonstrative inference can be justified. I believe, myself, that concentration on induction has very much hindered the progress of the whole inquiry into the postulates of scientific method. In this Chapter I propose to bring out one such postulate, at first in a somewhat vague form, but with increasing precision as the discussion proceeds.

The principle with which I shall be concerned in this Chapter has to do with structure. We find very frequently that many different examples of approximately the same structure exist in different parts of space-time. The anatomy of different human beings is more or less constant: the same bones, the same muscles, the same arteries, and so on, are found in one individual as in another. There is a lesser degree of identity of structure in all mammals, a still lesser degree in all vertebrates, and some degree, for example cell structure, in everything living. There are a number of elements, each of which is characterized by the structure of its nucleus. Coming to artifacts, there are, for example, many copies of a given book; if they are all of the same edition they will be very closely similar in structure.

So far, I have been dealing with what may be called substantial structures, that is to say, structures in which the structural unit may be considered to be a piece of matter, but there are other structures where the unit is an event. Take, for example, a piece of music. You may hear the C Minor Symphony many times, sometimes well performed, sometimes badly. Whenever you hear it, that particular hearing consists of a temporal series of noises. Two different performances are not exactly identical in structure, and it is the minute differences which make the difference between a good performance and a bad one. But they are all very nearly identical in structure, not only with each other, but with the score. The reader will remark that "structure" is a very abstract concept, so abstract that a musical score, a gramophone record, and the actual performance may all have the very same structure. There is thus an actual identity of structure, though not in every minute particular, between all the different examples of a given piece of music, the original manuscript of the composer, the various printed scores, the gramophone records, and the performances. Any competent person who hears a piece of music while following the score is perceiving the identity of structure between what he hears and what he sees.

I come now to another application of the concept of identical structures. We all believe that we live in a common world, peopled not only by sentient beings like ourselves, but also by physical objects. I say we *all* believe this, in spite of the fact that some philosophers have pretended to doubt it. There are on the one hand solipsists who maintain that they alone exist, and make desperate efforts to make others agree with them. Then there are philosophers who hold that all reality is mental, and that while the feelings we experience when we look at the sun are real, the sun itself is a fiction. And as a development of this view there is the theory of Leibniz, according to which the world consists of monads that never interact, and perception is in no degree due to the action of the outer world upon the percipient. In this view we may be said to be all dreaming, but the dreams that we all have are identical in structure. These different views, I say, have been advocated by different philosophers, and I do not think that any of them can be disproved. On the other hand, none of them can be proved, and, what is more, none of them can be believed, not even by their advocates. I am concerned at the moment to search out a principle which, if true, justifies us in adhering to the common-sense belief in a common world of mental and physical objects. Suppose the Prime Minister makes a speech which is broadcast, and suppose a number of people who have listened to the broadcast afterwards compare notes. It will appear that so far as their memory serves they all heard the same structure of sounds, that is to say if you, having a good memory, ask another man with a good memory "what did you hear?" you will hear in reply what is more or less a repetition of what you heard while listening to the broadcast. You think it unlikely that if you and your friend were each enjoying a private hallucination there would be such close similarity between his delusion and yours. You need not, however, rely upon the memory of other people, which is fallible. You could, if you were a philosophic millionaire, have *Hamlet* performed in a theatre in which you were the only live occupant and every other seat was occupied by a cine-camera. When the performance was over you could have the various records thrown upon the screen, and you would find them closely resembling each other and your own memory; you would infer that during the performance something happened at each of the cine-cameras which had the same structure as what was happening at you. Both light and sound have this publicity, that is to say a suitably contrived instrument at any point within a certain region can be made to construct a record identical in structure with what a person in that region hears or sees. The recording instrument may be another person, or may be something purely mechanical like a camera. So far as identity of structure is concerned there is no difference between these two cases.

The conception of an "observer", which is usually taken for granted by men of science, is one of which the use and validity depends upon the postulate that we are considering in this Chapter. To say that many "observers" can observe the "same" occurrence must mean that this occurrence has effects upon the various "observers" which have something in common. If science is to have the publicity that we believe it to have, what these effects have in common must be something which (within limits) enables them to be described in the same words. If these words are as abstract as those of mathematical physics, applicability of the same words involves little, if anything, beyond similarity of space-time structure. Professor Milne (*Relativity, Gravitation and World Structure*, p. 5) makes this similarity a fundamental postulate of physics when he says: "When the inner structure of the system defined is identical from the two points of view (those of different observers), then its description from the two points of view must be identical. This is the essence of the principle of relativity". It is astonishing how much he derives from this postulate.

Whenever there is throughout a certain' neighbourhood and ranged about a centre a group of complex events all identical in structure, as, for example, what different people and cameras see or what different people and gramophone discs hear in a given theatre, we unhesitatingly assume a common causal ancestor for all the different complex events. We do this the more readily, because the different events differ according to the laws of perspective, and the principles of projective geometry enable us to infer the approximate position of the object seen in different perspective by the various spectators. If the object in question is the actor whose performance we have been applauding, he will emphatically agree that he was the cause of the various experiences of the members of the audience, and that they cannot have arisen, as Leibniz supposes, as spontaneous developments in a system of similar dreams.

The same sort of principle occurs in many other connections. Take, for example, the association of a shadow with the object of which it is the shadow. Sometimes, especially at sunset, or when you are standing with others on the edge of a deep narrow valley and your shadow appears on the hill opposite, you may have difficulty in deciding to which person a given shadow belongs, but if you wave your arms and see the shadow wave its arms you conclude that the shadow is yours; that is to say, you assume a certain kind of causal connection between it and yourself. This causal connection you infer from identity of structure in a series of events. In more usual cases you do not need a series of events, because the similarity of shape will be sufficient, this similarity consisting in the identity of the projective properties of the shadow and your own silhouette. Such identity of structure suffices to persuade you that there is a causal connection between yourself and the shadow. Let us take another example from a very different field, that of the brides-in-the-bath murders. A number of middle-aged ladies in different parts of the country, after marrying and insuring their lives in favour of their husbands, mysteriously died in their baths. The identity of structure between these different events led to the assumption of a common causal origin; this origin was found to be Mr. Smith, who was duly hanged.

We have thus two different cases of groups of objects identical in structure: in the one case the structural units are material objects and in the other case they are events. Examples of the former are: atoms of one element, molecules of one compound, crystals of one substance, animals or plants of one species. Examples of the latter are: what different people simultaneously see and hear in one neighbourhood, and what at the same time cameras and gramophone discs record, the simultaneous movements of an object and its shadow, the connection between different performances of the same piece of music, and so on.

We will distinguish the two kinds of structure as "event structures" and "material structures". A house has a material structure and the performance of a piece of music has an event structure. The distinction, however, is not always the relevant one: for example a printed book has a material structure, while the same book read aloud has an event structure. A reporter is a man who has the art of creating a material complex having the same structure as a given event complex.

I suggest, as a principle of inference used unconsciously by common sense, but consciously in science and law, the following postulate: "When a group of complex events in more or less the same neighbourhood and ranged about a central event all have a common structure, it is probable that they have a common causal ancestor". I am using "probable" here in the sense of frequency; I mean that this happens in most cases. As for what I mean by "common causal ancestor", that requires a few words of explanation. I mean that, taking any one of the complex events in question, it has been preceded by other events having the same structure, these events forming a series each of which is temporally and spatially contiguous to the next, and that when such a backward series is formed for each of the complex events in question, the various series all meet at last in one complex event having the given structure and earlier in time than any of the events in the original group. In the case of the people in the theatre, this event is the performance of the actor or actors. In the case of a physical object seen simultaneously by a number of people or photographed simultaneously by a number of cameras, the central original event is the state of that physical object at the time when the light rays which make it visible left it. I want to make it clear that the existence of this central first cause is an inference, although it is one of which common sense is usually unconscious. It is an inference which has stages, and which is involved in regarding noises heard as sometimes expressing the thoughts of persons other than ourselves. If I hear a man utter a sentence, and I then ask other people what sentence was uttered and they repeat just what I heard, and if on another occasion I am absent while he spoke but those who were present again all utter the same words in answer to my question, our principle leads me to place the causal centre of these phenomena not in myself, but in the other person. I know that when I speak and others hear me, the causal centre consisted of certain thoughts and sensations of my own; when I do not hear another man speak but those who heard him all agree as to what he said, I know that I did not have the thoughts and feelings which I should have had if I had uttered the words, but I infer that such thoughts and feelings existed in the causal centre of the connected occurrences, i.e. in the speaker whom I did not hear. This, however, involves the principle of analogy in addition to our present principle.

Before attempting to give more precision to the principle that I am suggesting, I will say a little more about its scope and plausibility. Broadly speaking, what the principle asserts is that coincidences beyond a point are improbable, and become increasingly improbable with every increase in complexity. I once had a pupil who assured me that his name was Hippocrates Apostolos; I found this hard to believe, so I pointed him out to someone who knew him and said: "What is that young man's name?" "Hippocrates Apostolos," he replied. I tried the experiment again and again with the same result, and at last I looked up the University Register. In the end, in spite of the initial improbability of his assertion, I was compelled to believe it. The name being a complex structure, it seemed exceedingly improbable that if everybody I asked had merely invented an answer on the spur of the moment they should all have invented just that answer. If they had said John Smith I should have felt less convinced, because this is a less complex structure. Eddington used to suggest as a logical possibility that perhaps all the books in the British Museum had been produced accidentally by monkeys playing with typewriters. There are here two different kinds of improbability: in the first place some of the books in the British Museum make sense, whereas the monkeys might have been expected to produce only nonsense. In the second place, there are many copies of most books, and two copies are, as a rule, verbally identical. We can here secure plausibility by what is apparently an application of the mathematical theory of probability: given a chance selection of, say, a hundred letters, they will, in the immense majority of cases, not constitute a significant English sentence. Suppose now that a book contains 700,000 letters, the chance that, selected at haphazard, they will all form themselves into significant sentences is infinitesimal. This is the first improbability, but there is a second. Suppose you have in your hands two copies of the same book, and suppose you are considering the hypothesis that the identity between them is due to chance: the chance that the first letter in the two books will be the same is one in twenty-six, so is the chance that the second letter will be the same, and so on. Consequently the chance that all the letters will be the same in two copies of a book of 700,000 letters is the 700,000th power of $\frac{1}{26}$. And now suppose you go to a publisher's stockroom and find not merely two copies of the book in question, but some thousands. The hypothesis of chance becomes exponentially more incredible. You feel obliged, therefore, to invent some hypothesis to account for the similarity between the different volumes. At this moment the publisher who is showing you round says: "that is one of our most successful books, and the author is coming to see me in a few moments; perhaps you would like to meet him". You meet him and say "did you write that book?" He replies "yes". At this point, in spite of having been reduced to scepticism by Hume, it occurs to you that perhaps the noises which seem to issue from the publisher and the author signify what they would signify if you uttered them, and that the many thousands of identical volumes that you have surveyed have a common source in the object which says it is the author. While it is telling you how it came to write the book, you perceive that the facts which have astonished you will cease to be astonishing if there is a law of nature to the following effect: "any complex event tends to. be followed by other complex events identical, or approximately identical, with it in structure, and distributing themselves from next to next throughout a certain region of space-time". By this time the author has finished his speech and you take your leave, saying "pleased to have met you", since your new principle persuaded you, in spite of Hume, that you really have met him, and that he is not merely part of your dream.

The essential point in the principle that I am suggesting is its emphasis on structure. When we examine causal sequences, we find that the quality of an event may change completely in the course of such a sequence, and that the only thing constant is structure. Take, say, broadcasting: a man speaks, and his speech is a certain structure of sounds; the sounds are followed by events in the microphone which are presumably not sounds, these, in turn, are followed by electromagnetic waves, and these, in turn, are transformed back into sounds, which, by a masterpiece of ingenuity, are closely similar to those emitted by the speaker. The intermediate links in this causal chain, however, do not, so far as we know, resemble the sounds emitted by the speaker except in structure. (I should observe that the relations by which the structure is defined are throughout relations involving spatio-temporal contiguity.) Broadcasting was thought a wonderful invention, but, in fact, it is only very slightly more complex than ordinary hearing. Consider what happens when one man speaks and another man hears: the speaker makes certain movements in his mouth, accompanied by breath, which causes waves to proceed through the air from his mouth to the hearer's ear. When these waves reach the ear they cause currents to run along the nerves to the brain, and as these currents reach the brain the hearer has a series of auditory sensations closely similar to those which the speaker himself has if he is not deaf. The only important difference from broadcasting is the omission of the stage of electromagnetic waves; in each case there is a series of occurrences, some of one sort and some of another, but all retaining the same structure, and it is because of the constancy of structure that the speaker is able to communicate with the hearer. It appears generally that, if A and B are two complex structures and A can cause B, then there must be some degree of identity of structure between A and B. It is because of this principle that a complex of sensations can give us information about the complex that caused them. If you see something hexagonal, then, since hexagonality is a structural property, the physical object which has caused your visual sensation must be hexagonal, although its hexagonality will be in a space which is not identical with visual space.

It is to be observed that what we need in addition to actual experience is only a principle giving probability to certain sorts of inductions. What I am suggesting is that we are not merely to seek simple laws such as A causes B, but are to enunciate a principle of the following sort: given two identical structures, it is probable that they have a causal connection of one of two kinds. The first kind consists of those having a common causal ancestor —this is illustrated by the different visual sensations of a number of people looking at a given object, and by the different auditory sensations of a number of people hearing a given speech. The second kind arises where two structures are composed of similar ingredients and there exists a causal law leading such ingredients to arrange themselves in a certain pattern. The most obvious examples of this kind are atoms, molecules, and crystals. The similarities between different animals or plants of a given species may be brought under either head: if we go no further back in time than a generation of the given animals or plants we have a case of the second kind, and we have to suppose that all the sperms of a given species have a certain identity of structure, and so have all the ova. If, however, we take account of evolution, we can trace the similarities to a common ancestry, using the word this time in its literal sense.

Whether a given set of complexes, all having the same structure, are to be considered as of the first or of the second kind is not always an easy question, and does not always have a definite answer, as we have just seen in the case of two animals of the same species. In general, the former kind of complex has events as the units of structure, while the latter has persistent physical objects as its structural units. But this is not universally the distinguishing mark. Take, for example, the relation between writing and speech; the structural units in speech are events, whereas the structural units in writing are material objects, but when there is identity of structure between a spoken and a written discourse either can cause the other, and does so in every case of dictation or reading aloud. The same sort of thing applies to a piece of music or a gramophone record. I think, however, that those cases in which a series of events is represented by a static material structure can only arise where there is some rule for taking the parts of the material structure in a time order and so transforming them again into a series of events. A book in a European language has to be read from left to right and from top to bottom; a gramophone record has to be played with the needle travelling from the circumference towards the centre. Or take an instance where man has not intervened: the interpretation of rocks by geologists as giving a history of the world depends upon taking the rocks from the bottom upwards so that the deepest rocks represent the earliest time.

On the whole it may be said that similarity of structure is taken as showing common causal ancestry whenever the structure is very complex. The similarities of structure which are not so interpreted occur in chemistry and physics, and are all fairly simple. It seems to me that what one may say is as follows: the physical world consists of units of a small number of different kinds, and there are causal laws governing the simpler structures that can be built out of such units, causing such structures to fall into a rather small number of discretely differing kinds. There are also complexes of events which act as causal units, being preceded and followed throughout some finite time by a series of complexes of events all having approximately the same structure and inter-related by spatio-temporal contiguity.

The principle of spatio-temporal contiguity has applications to cases in which structure plays a subordinate role. Take, for example, echoes: anyone hearing an echo of his own shout is incapable of doubting that something has travelled from him to the object from which the echo is reflected and thence back to him. We find that echoes only occur where there is a surface suitable for reflecting sound, and that the time between the emission of a sound and the hearing of the echo is proportional to the distance of such obstacle. It would be extremely difficult to give a plausible account of echoes, either on a solipsistic basis or on the assumption that others' minds exist but lifeless physical objects do not, since mountains give much more resounding echoes than persons do. Or let us consider again an experiment suggested in an earlier chapter. Suppose a man with a gun stationed at a point where many roads meet; suppose that at every hundred metres along each of these roads there is a post, and a man with a flag is stationed at each post up to a distance of a thousand metres. Each of these men with a flag has orders to wave his flag as soon as he hears the sound of the shot. A captive balloon is stationed vertically above the man with the gun and contains an observer who notes the moment at which each flag is waved; he finds that all the flags that are equi-distant from the shot are waved at the same moment, but that the more distant flags are waved later than the nearer ones, and that the time lag is proportional to the distance. All this is explained very simply by the hypothesis that there is a physical process which, when it reaches the ear, causes a sensation of sound, and which travels with a velocity of about five seconds to the mile. Any other hypothesis to account for the observed facts would have to be very elaborate and very artificial. The man in the captive balloon sees first the firing of the gun at the centre, after that he sees successive waving of flags travelling outwards from the centre with a constant velocity. What is convincing to scientific common sense in this experiment is the relation between distance and time which enables us to speak of the velocity of sound.

Similar considerations to those applying to echoes apply to the reflection of light, but in this case the argument for identity of structure has a force which it does not have in the case of sound-echoes. When you see yourself in a mirror it would be preposterous to suggest that the mirror chooses at that moment to look like you without there being any causal connection, and, in fact, the mirror only reflects you when you are in a suitable position, and reflects any movements that you may make while in front of it. The mirror can be stopped from reflecting you by the inter-position of an opaque object, which leads irresistibly to the conclusion that the reflection is due to some process traversing the intervening space between you and the mirror. The time lag which is noticeable between a sound and its echo is too small to be appreciable in the case of terrestrial reflection of light, but on the other hand the argument from identity of structure is very much stronger in the case of light than in that of sound, because the structures that can be reflected are much more complex in the case of light than in the case of sound.

It must be admitted that it is logically possible to confine ourselves to the solipsistic hypothesis, and to deny, in all such cases as we have been considering, everything except our own experiences, but if we do this many phenomena, which realist hypotheses explain by simple laws, become hopelessly irregular and staccato.

I think, therefore, that in the search for empirical laws we may employ the following principles:

I. When a number of similar structures of events exist in regions not widely separated, and are ranged about a centre, there is an appreciable probability that they have been preceded by a central complex having the same structure, and that they have occurred at times differing from a certain time by amounts proportional to their distance from this central structure.

II. Whenever a system of structurally similar events is

found to be connected with a centre in the sense that the time when each event occurs differs from a certain time by an amount proportional to the distance of the event from this centre, there is an appreciable probability that all the events are connected with an event at the centre by intermediate links having spatio-temporal contiguity with each other.

III. When a number of structurally similar systems, such as atoms of this or that element, are found to be distributed in what appears to be a random manner, without reference to a centre, we infer that there are probably natural laws making such structures more stable than others that are logically possible, but that are found to occur rarely or never.

The first two of the above principles apply not only to systems in which the propagation is spherical, as in light and sound waves, but also when it is linear, as in the conduction of electricity along a wire. The causal route may be any continuous curve in space-time. Consider, for instance, the journey of a telegram which is forwarded from one address to another. But in all cases our second principle assumes continuity.

The above three principles, if accepted, will, I think, afford a sufficient *a priori* basis for a large proportion of the inferences that physics bases on observation. I have little doubt that all three principles can be simplified, or perhaps exhibited as consequences of one principle. In the meantime I offer them as a step in the analysis of what is to be presupposed in scientific inference.

The principle of constancy of structure in causal series, which we have been considering, while it has great importance within certain regions, is definitely inapplicable in certain others. Let us consider discursively where it applies and where it is inadequate.

We have seen that the knowledge obtained through perception is only possible in so far as there are more or less independent causal chains proceeding from physical objects to ourselves. We see separate stars because the light from each goes its way regardless of what else may be happening in its neighbourhood. We see separate objects in our environment for the same reason. But the independence of a causal chain is never complete. The light from a star is slightly deflected by gravitation, and completely obscured by cloud or fog. Terrestrial objects are seen more or less vaguely, according to distance, keenness of vision, etc. Sometimes effects of this kind do not alter structures, but only diminish the amount that survives. When you see a distant mountain on a clear day, you may see accurately what you do see in the way of structure, but you see less than if you were nearer. When things are reflected in a good mirror there is no change of structure, except, perhaps, some omission of detail. But when white light is passed through a prism and separated into the colours of the rainbow, there is change of structure, and so there is when a drop of ink falls into a glass of water.

Sometimes the change of structure is much more complete than in the above cases. When a charge of dynamite explodes, all the structures involved are changed except the atoms; when an atomic bomb explodes, even the atoms change. When a plant or animal grows, there is a large degree of constancy of structure, but in the moment of fertilization there is a change which, structurally, is analogous to chemical combination. To such changes our principle of constancy of structure is inapplicable.

Natural processes are of two kinds. On the one hand there are those characterized by some form of *persistence*; on the other hand there are processes of synthesis or dissolution. Persistence is illustrated by "things", light-rays, and sound waves. Synthesis is illustrated by the presumed building up of heavier elements from hydrogen, by chemical combination, and by fertilization. Dissolution is illustrated by radioactivity, chemical analysis, and decay of an animal body after death. In synthesis and dissolution structure changes; in persistence structure remains in some degree constant.

The principle considered in this chapter has to do only with persistence. It is concerned to point out that persistence is a very common feature of natural processes, that structure is what is most apt to persist, and that, when it persists, it fills a certain continuous region of space-time which usually has an origin earlier in time than the rest of the region.

The principle of constancy of structure has a certain analogy to the first law of motion. The first law of motion tells what a piece of matter will do when it is not influenced by its environment; the principle of constancy of structure applies whenever a process is independent of its environment, but also in various other cases. It applies for instance to all the stages that intervene between the oral movements of a speaker whose speech is being broadcast and the auditory sensations of his hearers. It applies to echoes and reflections in mirrors. It applies to every step from an author's thoughts to the printed book. In all these cases, though the environment has various effects upon the process, the effects are such as, broadly speaking, do not affect structure.

From the standpoint of theory of knowledge, the most important application of our principle is to the relation between perception and physical objects. Our principle implies that, in circumstances which occur frequently but not invariably, the structure of a percept is the same as that of each of a series of occurrences leading backward in time to an original occurrence, before which there were not spatio-temporally connected events having the structure in question. This original occurrence is what we are said to "perceive" when it is held that different people can "perceive" the same object.

The sameness of structure between our sensational experiences and their physical causes explains how it comes about that naive realism, though false, gives rise to so little confusion in practice. Given two examples of the same structure, every statement which is true of the one corresponds to a statement which is true of the other; the statement concerning the one is transformed into the statement concerning the other by substituting corresponding terms and corresponding relations. Take, for example, speech and writing, and for the sake of simplicity let us assume a perfect phonetic alphabet. Then to every shape which is a letter a certain sound corresponds, and to the relation left-to-right the relation earlier-to-later corresponds. It is in virtue of this correspondence that we can speak of an "accurate" written report of a speech, in spite of the complete difference of quality between the two. In the same way perception may, in suitable circumstances, give an "accurate" representation of a physical occurrence, although there may be as much difference between the occurrence and the percept as there is between speech and writing.

Given two corresponding statements concerning two examples of the same structure, they may be related by a dictionary giving the words that correspond in the two examples. But there is another method, which, though less desirable, is often employed, and that is, to use the very same words in making a statement about the one example as in making the corresponding statement about the other. We do this habitually as regards speech and writing. The word "word" is used equally for what is spoken and for what is written. So are such words as "sentence", "statement", "question", etc. This plan, which makes all our words ambiguous, is convenient when the difference between the two examples of the same structure is irrelevant to our purpose, and we wish to say things concerning both at once, e.g.: "Discourse is composed of sentences, and sentences of words"—using "discourse" as a word applicable both to speech and writing. And so in a printed book an author may speak of "the *above* statement" or of "an *earlier* statement", though strictly "above" is only applicable to print and "earlier" to speech.

This form of ambiguity is involved when the language of naive realism is used in spite of the fact that it is recognized to be philosophically unjustifiable. In so far as physical objects have the same structure as percepts, a given form of words may be interpreted (in the sense of Part IV, Chapter I) as applying to objects or to percepts, and will be true of both or of neither. We may say of a percept that it is blue, and we may say the same of a light-ray. The word "blue" will have a different meaning as applied to a light-ray from that which it has when applied to a percept, but the meaning, in each case, is part of a system of interpretation, and so long as we adhere to one system the truth or falsehood of our statement is independent, within limits, of the system chosen. It is because there are limits to this principle that philosophy is obliged to reject naive realism. But in spite of the limits the principle is widely applicable, and it is for this reason that naive realism is as plausible as it is.

Chapter VII

INTERACTION

W E have been chiefly concerned, in recent chapters, with a kind of causation that may be called "intrinsic". This is the kind that is interpreted as the persistence of a thing or a process. Owing to the fact that the persistence of things is taken for granted and regarded as involving identity of substance, this form of causation has not been recognized as what it is. It may be stated as follows: "Given an event at a certain time and place, it usually happens that, at every neighbouring time, a closely similar event occurs at some neighbouring place". This principle affords a basis for a great many inductions, but it does not, *prima facie*, enable us to deal with what commonly count as *interactions*, e.g. collisions between billiard balls. It is causal processes of this kind that are to be considered in the present chapter.

Consider two billiard balls which hit each other after each has been moving in a straight line. Each billiard ball persists after the collision, and is regarded as the *same* ball as it was, because it satisfies the above law of intrinsic causation. But there is, so to speak, a higher degree of intrinsic causation when no collision is taking place than when the balls meet. At most times we can say not only that, given the position of a ball at one instant, it will have *some* neighbouring position at a slightly later instant; we can say also that, given the positions of the ball at two neighbouring instants, its position at a third slightly later instant will be approximately collinear with the two earlier positions, and its distance from either will be approximately proportional to the time that has elapsed. That is to say, we have an intrinsic law of *velocity*, not only of *position*. But when there is interaction, there is no such intrinsic law of velocity. This is the purport of the first two laws of motion.

If we assume that, while we are observing the billiard balls, collisions occupy a small portion of the total time involved, it will follow that at most times they are moving approximately in straight lines. What we have to discover is a law determining the new direction in which a ball will move after a collision. If the smallest measurable angle is $1/n^{th}$ of a degree, the number of measurably different directions in which the ball may move is $360n$. Therefore, taking any direction which is determined as accurately as is practically possible, the antecedent probability that the ball will start moving in this direction is $1/360n$. This is finite, though small; therefore induction from observed collisions can make a generalization probable. That is to say, if we assume our law of intrinsic causation, the rest of the mathematical theory of billiards can be developed by means of induction without any further assumption antecedent to experience.

Our law of intrinsic causation, in the course of the above analysis, became enlarged to include velocity as well as position, not always, but at most times. This amounts to assuming that the times when interaction takes place are exceptional. This, however, is perhaps an overstatement. There is at all times an interaction between the billiard table and the billiard ball, which prevents the ball from falling. But as this is constant it can be ignored, in the sense that we can state laws for the movements of the ball without mentioning the table, although, but for the table, these laws would not hold. If the ball collides with another ball, we cannot state laws as to its motions without mentioning the other ball, which is thus, in a sense, causally more important than the table. What we assumed above amounts to this: At most times the approximate laws governing the history of a "thing" do not involve mention of other "things"; the times when such mention is essential are exceptional. But it is not assumed that "intrinsic" laws give more than a first approximation.

"Intrinsic" laws are to be held to apply not only to position and velocity, but also to other matters. A red-hot poker, when taken out of the fire, ceases gradually, not suddenly, to be red-hot. The sound of a bell decays gradually, though swiftly. Very sudden occurrences, such as an explosion or a flash of lightning, are exceptional. Being exceptional, they do not falsify the assumption that, on any given occasion, very sudden change is improbable. And further, change in the direction of change is much more apt to be sudden (more or less) than change of position or quality; this is the case with collisions of billiard balls.

The above suggestions can easily be brought into harmony with atomic theory. An atom, it would seem, is at most times in a steady state, i.e. one in which its history is governed by an intrinsic law;

but the approach of a photon or a neutron or an electron may lead to a more or less sudden change. I do not wish, however, to exaggerate this consonance or to overestimate its importance. Our postulates are concerned more with the beginnings of science than with its advanced results. The theory of impact, for example, was a very early part of dynamics, using a somewhat primitive conception of "matter". I have been suggesting throughout that science necessarily begins with laws which are only first approximations, and only applicable in most cases, but which are completely true so long as they are not stated to be more than this. Our initial postulates must share this character of approximation and probability. They must state that, in given circumstances, what occurs will probably be roughly so-and-so. This suffices for a justifiable expectation, i.e. an expectation having a fairly high degree of intrinsic credibility. As science advances, its laws acquire a higher degree of probability, and also of exactness. A savage can say: "probably the moon will be full to-morrow". An astronomer can say: "Almost certainly, the moon will be full to-morrow between 6h. 38m. and 6h. 39m. G.M.T." But the advance is one of degree, not of kind. And, throughout, the initial probable and approximate assumptions remain indispensable.

It will be observed that I have not introduced a postulate to the effect that there are natural laws. My reason for not doing so is that, in any verifiable form, such a postulate would be either false or a tautology. But let us see what such a postulate could be.

In any verifiable form, it will have to assert that, given a certain number of observations of a suitable sort, there is a discoverable formula from which something can be inferred as to some other phenomena. It will be noticed that the number of observations concerned is necessarily finite, and that none of them can be more exact than is rendered possible by the existing technique of measurement. But here we come up against a difficulty analogous to that which confronted us when we tried to take induction as a postulate. The difficulty is that, given any finite set of observations, there are always an infinite number of formulae verified by all of them. Suppose, for example, we took the recorded positions on the celestial sphere of Mars on Mondays, Jupiter on Tuesdays, and so on throughout the days of the week, a little ingenuity in the use of Fourier series would enable us to construct a number of formulae fitting them all up to the present, but mostly falsified in the future. It is therefore a tautology that there are formulae fitting any casually selected set of quantitative observations, but it is false that a formula which fits past observations affords any ground for predicting the results of future observations.

It is customary to add to the postulate that there are natural laws the explicit or tacit proviso that they must be *simple*. This, however, is both vague and teleological. It is not clear what is meant by "simplicity", and there can be no *a priori* reason for expecting laws to be simple except benevolence on the part of Providence towards the men of science. It would be fallacious to argue inductively that, since the laws we have discovered are simple, therefore probably all laws are simple, for obviously a simple law is easier to discover than a complicated one. It is true that a number of laws that are approximately true are very simple, and no theory of scientific inference is satisfactory unless it accounts for this fact. But I do not think it should be accounted for by making simplicity a postulate.

Let us take an illustration which is historically important, namely the law of falling bodies. Galileo, by a small number of rather rough measurements, found that the distance traversed by a body falling vertically is approximately proportional to the square of the time spent in falling—in other words, that the acceleration is approximately constant. He assumed that, but for the resistance of the air, it would be exactly constant, and when, not long afterwards, the air pump was invented, this assumption appeared to be confirmed. But further observations suggested that acceleration varies slightly with the latitude, and subsequent theory suggested that it also varies with the altitude. Thus the simple law turned out to be only approximate. Newton's gravitation substituted a more complicated law, and Einstein's, in turn, was very much more complicated than Newton's. A similar gradual loss of simplicity has characterized the history of most of the early discoveries of science.

> Nature and Nature's laws lay hid in night.
> God said: "Let Newton be", and all was light.
> It did not last. The Devil, shouting "Ho!
> Let Einstein be", restored the status quo.

This oscillation is typical of the history of science.

Let us take as another illustration the stages from observation to Kepler's first law as applied to Venus.

The crude matter of observation is a bright dot in the sky, continuously present while watched on a given fine evening, and slowly approaching the western horizon. We believe this dot to be the appearance of a "thing", but it may not be: the reflection of a search-light on a cloud may be very similar. The hypothesis that it is the appearance of a "thing" is heightened by the fact that Venus can be seen in many countries at once. To this "thing" we give the name "Hesper". We find that on other occasions there is a morning star, to which we give the name "Phosphor". At last, as an ingenious hypothesis, Hesper and Phosphor are identified; the one star of which both are appearances is called "Venus". This star is supposed to exist at all times, not only when it is visible.

The next step is to attempt to find laws determining the position of Venus on the celestial sphere at different times. To a first approximation, Venus revolves daily with the fixed stars. To advance beyond this point, we assign to Venus angular co-ordinates θ, ϕ determined by relation to the fixed stars. When this is done, the changes in θ and ϕ become slow, and given two observations at not very distant times, the intermediate values of θ and ϕ can be roughly determined by interpolation. The changes in θ and ϕ are approximately regular, but their laws are very complicated.

So far we have been content with the hypothesis that all the heavenly bodies are on the celestial sphere, and all at an equal distance from the earth. But eclipses and occultations and transits lead to the abandonment of this hypothesis. The next step is to suppose that the fixed stars and the several planets each have their own sphere, and each preserve a constant distance from the earth. But this hypothesis also has to be abandoned.

We thus arrive at the following formulation of the problem: Every heavenly body has its position determined by three co-ordinates r, θ, ϕ, of which θ and ϕ are given in observation, but r, the distance from the earth, is inferred. It is assumed that r, like θ and ϕ, may vary with the time. Since r is not observed, we have a free field for the invention of a suitable formula. Certain observations, especially eclipses and occultations and transits, very strongly suggest that Venus is always more distant than the moon, and is sometimes more distant than the sun but sometimes nearer. The problem of planetary theory is to invent a formula for the variation of r which shall be (a) in harmony with such observations, (b) as simple as possible. Epicycles were inferior to Kepler on both counts; Copernicus was superior on (b) but inferior on (a). Since (a) must always outweigh (b) Kepler prevailed.

In the above there are several important steps not made necessary by logic.

1st: Our visual sensations are assumed to have external causes.
2nd: These causes are assumed to persist when they are not causing visual sensations.

(These two steps are involved in giving the name "Venus".)

3rd: The co-ordinate r is wholly outside observation. No possible system of assumed values of r is inconsistent with observed facts, except making r very small.
4th: Kepler's formula for r is the *simplest* that is consistent with observation. This is its *sole* merit.

Observe that induction to the *future* has no special place in this process. The essential thing is inference to *unobserved* times. This is involved in the common-sense assumption of quasi-permanent objects, and therefore in the name "Venus". It is a mistake to say: "Venus has been observed to move in an ellipse hitherto, therefore we infer by induction that it will continue to do so". No such thing has been observed hitherto. The observations are *compatible* with Kepler, but also with a strictly infinite number of other hypotheses.

Mathematical probability does not play any part in the above inferences.

The hypothesis that the heavenly bodies are permanent "things" is not logically necessary. Heraclitus said "the sun is new every day", and probably preferred this view on scientific grounds, since it was difficult to see how the sun could work its way underground during the night from west to east. The hypothesis embodied in Kepler's laws is not *proved* by observation; what observation proves is that the facts are *compatible* with this hypothesis. This may be called the hypothesis of "complete realism". At the other end is the hypothesis of "complete phenomenalism", according to which bright dots exist when observed, but not at other times. Between these two are an infinite number of other hypotheses, e.g. that Venus is "real" but Mars is not, or that Venus is "real" on Mondays, Wednesdays, and Fridays, but not on Tuesdays, Thursdays, and Saturdays. Both extremes and all intermediate hypotheses are consistent with the observed facts; if we choose between them, our choice cannot have any basis in observation alone.

The conclusion to which the above somewhat discursive discussion has seemed to lead is that the fundamental postulate is that of "causal lines". This postulate enables us to infer, from any given event, *something* (though not much) as to what is probable at all neighbouring times and some neighbouring places. So long as a causal line is not entangled with another, a good deal can be inferred, but where there is entanglement (i.e. interaction) the postulate alone allows a much more restricted inference. However, when quantitative measurement is possible, the measurably different possibilities after an interaction are finite in number, and therefore observation plus induction can make a general law highly probable. In this kind of way, step by step, it would seem that scientific generalizations can be justified.

Chapter VIII

ANALOGY

THE postulates hitherto considered have been such as are required for knowledge of the physical world. Broadly speaking, they have led us to admit a certain degree of knowledge as to the space-time structure of the physical world, while leaving us completely agnostic as regards its qualitative character. But where other human beings are concerned, we feel that we know more than this; we are convinced that other people have thoughts and feelings that are qualitatively fairly similar to our own. We are not content to think that we know only the space-time structure of our friends' minds, or their capacity for initiating causal chains that end in sensations of our own. A philosopher might pretend to think that he knew only this, but let him get cross with his wife and you will see that he does not regard her as a mere spatio-temporal edifice of which he knows the logical properties but not a glimmer of the intrinsic character. We are therefore justified in inferring that his scepticism is professional rather than sincere.

The problem with which we are concerned is the following. We observe in ourselves such occurrences as remembering, reasoning, feeling pleasure and feeling pain. We think that stocks and stones do not have these experiences, but that other people do. Most of us have no doubt that the higher animals feel pleasure and pain, though I was once assured by a fisherman that "fishes have no sense nor feeling". I failed to find out how he had acquired this knowledge. Most people would disagree with him, but would be doubtful about oysters and starfish. However this may be, common sense admits an increasing doubt- fulness as we descend in the animal kingdom, but as regards human beings it admits no doubt.

It is clear that belief in the minds of others requires some postulate that is not required in physics, since physics can be content with a knowledge of structure. My present purpose is to suggest what this further postulate may be.

It is clear that we must appeal to something that may be vaguely called "analogy". The behaviour of other people is in many ways analogous to our own, and we suppose that it must have analogous causes. What people say is what we should say if we had certain thoughts, and so we infer that they probably have these thoughts. They give us information which we can sometimes subsequently verify. They behave in ways in which we behave when we are pleased (or displeased) in circumstances in which we should be pleased (or displeased). We may talk over with a friend some incident which we have both experienced, and find that his reminiscences dovetail with our own; this is particularly convincing when he remembers something that we have forgotten but that he recalls to our thoughts. Or again: you set your boy a problem in arithmetic, and with luck he gets the right answer; this persuades you that he is capable of arithmetical reasoning. There are, in short, very many ways in which my responses to stimuli differ from those of "dead" matter, and in all these ways other people resemble me. As it is clear to me that the causal laws governing my behaviour have to do with "thoughts", it is natural to infer that the same is true of the analogous behaviour of my friends.

The inference with which we are at present concerned is not merely that which takes us beyond solipsism, by maintaining that sensations have causes about which *something* can be known. This kind of inference, which suffices for physics, has already been considered. We are concerned now with a much more specific kind of inference, the kind that is involved in our knowledge of the thoughts and feelings of others—assuming that we have such knowledge. It is of course obvious that such knowledge is more or less doubtful. There is not only the general argument that we may be dreaming; there is also the possibility of ingenious automata. There are calculating machines that do sums much better than our schoolboy sons; there are gramophone records that remember impeccably what So-and-so said on such-and-such an occasion; there are people in the cinema who, though copies of real people, are not themselves alive. There is no theoretical limit to what ingenuity could achieve in the way of producing the illusion of life where in fact life is absent.

But, you will say, in all such cases it was the thoughts of human beings that produced the ingenious mechanism. Yes, but how do you know this? And how do you know that the gramophone does *not* "think"?

There is, in the first place, a difference in the causal laws of observable behaviour. If I say to a student "write me a paper on Descartes' reasons for believing in the existence of matter", I shall, if he is industrious, cause a certain response. A gramophone record might be so constructed as to respond to this stimulus, perhaps better than the student, but if so it would be incapable of telling me anything about any other philosopher, even if I threatened to refuse to give it a degree. One of the most notable peculiarities of human behaviour is change of response to a given stimulus. An ingenious person could construct an automaton which would always laugh at his jokes, however often it heard them; but a human being, after laughing a few times, will yawn, and end by saying "how I laughed the first time I heard that joke".

But the differences in observable behaviour between living and dead matter do not suffice to prove that there are "thoughts" connected with living bodies other than my own. It is probably possible theoretically to account for the behaviour of living bodies by purely physical causal laws, and it is probably impossible to refute materialism by external observation alone. If we are to believe that there are thoughts and feelings other than our own, that must be in virtue of some inference in which our own thoughts and feelings are relevant, and such an inference must go beyond what is needed in physics.

I am of course not discussing the history of how we come to believe in other minds. We find ourselves believing in them when we first begin to reflect; the thought that Mother may be angry or pleased is one which arises in early infancy. What I am discussing is the possibility of a postulate which shall establish a rational connection between this belief and data, e.g. between the belief "Mother is angry" and the hearing of a loud voice.

The abstract schema seems to be as follows. We know, from observation of ourselves, a causal law of the form "A causes B", where A is a "thought" and B a physical occurrence. We sometimes observe a B when we cannot observe any A; we then infer an unobserved A. For example: I know that when I say "I'm thirsty", I say so, usually, because I am thirsty, and therefore, when I hear the sentence "I'm thirsty" at a time when I am not thirsty, I assume that some one else is thirsty. I assume this the more readily if I see before me a hot drooping body which goes on to say "I have walked twenty desert miles in this heat with never a drop to drink". It is evident that my confidence in the "inference" is increased by increased complexity in the datum and also by increased certainty of the causal law derived from subjective observation, provided the causal law is such as to account for the complexities of the datum.

It is clear that, in so far as plurality of causes is to be suspected, the kind of inference we have been considering is not valid. We are supposed to know "A causes B", and also to know that B has occurred; if this is to justify us in inferring A, we must know that *only* A causes B. Or, if we are content to infer that A is probable, it will suffice if we can know that in most cases it is A that causes B. If you hear thunder without having seen lightning, you confidently infer that there was lightning, because you are convinced that the sort of noise you heard is seldom caused by anything except lightning. As this example shows, our principle is not only employed to establish the existence of other minds, but is habitually assumed, though in a less concrete form, in physics. I say "a less concrete form" because unseen lightning is only abstractly similar to seen lightning, whereas we suppose the similarity of other minds to our own to be by no means purely abstract.

Complexity in the observed behaviour of another person, when this can all be accounted for by a simple cause such as thirst, increases the probability of the inference by diminishing the probability of some other cause. I think that in ideally favourable circumstances the argument would be formally as follows:

From subjective observation I know that A, which is a thought or feeling, causes B, which is a bodily act, e.g. a statement. I know also that, whenever B is an act of my own body, A is its cause. I now observe an act of the kind B in a body not my own, and I am having no thought or feeling of the kind A. But I still believe, on the basis of self-observation, that only A can cause B; I therefore infer that there was an A which caused B, though it was not an A that I could observe. On this ground I infer that other people's bodies are associated with minds, which resemble mine in proportion as their bodily behaviour resembles my own.

In practice, the exactness and certainty of the above statement must be softened. We cannot be sure that, in our subjective experience, A is the only cause of B. And even if A is the only cause of B in our experience, how can we know that this holds outside our experience? It is not necessary that we should know this with any certainty; it is enough if it is highly probable. It is the assumption of probability in such cases that is our postulate. The postulate may therefore be stated as follows:

If, whenever we can observe whether A and B are present or absent, we find that every case of B has an A as a causal antecedent, then it is probable that most B's have A's as causal antecedents, even in cases where observation does not enable us to know whether A is present or not.

This postulate, if accepted, justifies the inference to other minds, as well as many other inferences that are made unreflectingly by common sense.

Chapter IX

SUMMARY OF POSTULATES

As the outcome of the discussions in previous Chapters of this Part, I suggest that the postulates required to validate scientific method may be reduced to five. It is highly probable that they can be further reduced, but I have not myself succeeded in doing so. The five postulates to which previous analyses have led us may be called:

I. The postulate of quasi-permanence.

II. The postulate of separable causal lines.

III. The postulate of spatio-temporal continuity in causal lines.

IV. The postulate of the common causal origin of similar structures ranged about a centre, or, more simply, the structural postulate.

V. The postulate of analogy.

Each of these postulates asserts that something happens often, but not necessarily always; each therefore justifies, in a particular case, a rational expectation which falls short of certainty. Each has an objective and a subjective aspect: objectively, it asserts that something happens in most cases of a certain sort; subjectively, it asserts that, in certain circumstances, an expectation falling short of certainty in a greater or less degree has rational credibility. The postulates collectively are intended to provide the antecedent probabilities required to justify inductions.

I. *The postulate of quasi-permanence.*

The chief use of this postulate is to replace the common-sense notions of "thing" and "person", in a manner not involving the concept "substance". The postulate may be enunciated as follows:

Given any event A, it happens very frequently that, at any neighbouring time, there is at some neighbouring place an event very similar to A.

506

A "thing" is a series of such events. It is because such series of events are common that "thing" is a practically convenient concept. It is to be observed that, in a series of events which common sense would regard as belonging to one "thing", the similarity need only be between events not widely separated in space-time. There is not very much similarity between a three-months' embryo and an adult human being, but they are connected by gradual transitions from next to next, and are therefore accepted as stages in the development of one "thing".

It will frequently happen—for example, in the case of a drop of water in the sea—that there are, at a given neighbouring time, many neighbouring events similar to A. We can pass by gradual transitions from any one drop in the sea to any other. Our postulate neither affirms nor denies the multiplicity of such events similar to A at a given time; it contents itself with asserting that there is probably at least one such event. Our next postulate, that of causal lines, will enable us to say that, when there are many such events at a given time, there is usually one which has a special connection with A, of the sort which makes us regard it alone as part of the history of the "thing" to which A belongs. This is essential if we are to be able to say that a drop of water in the sea at one time, rather than any other drop, is the "same" as a certain drop at another time. Our present postulate does not suffice to enable us to say this, but gives us a part of what we require.

Our postulate has a subjective and an objective aspect. Suppose you have been looking at the sun, and you then close your eyes. Your subjective condition changes rapidly, but not discontinuously; it passes through the stages of akoluthic sensation, immediate memory, and gradually fading true memory. The sun, we believe, goes through no analogous changes; its changes also, we believe, are gradual, but of quite a different sort. Physical and psychological continuity—for example, that of motion and that of fading memory—have different laws, but both exemplify our postulate.

II. *The postulate of separable causal lines*

This postulate has many uses, but perhaps the most important is in connection with perception, for example in attributing the multiplicity of our visual sensations in looking at the night sky to a multitude of stars as their causes. The postulate may be enunciated as follows:

It is frequently possible to form a series of events such that, from one or two members of the series, something can be inferred as to all the other members.

The most obvious example is motion, particularly unimpeded motion such as that of a photon in interstellar space. But even in the case of impeded motion, so long as the phenomena can be interpreted as a "thing" changing its position, there is an intrinsic causal law, though it tells us less than when the motion is unimpeded. For instance, we can recognize a billiard ball throughout a game of billiards; its motion is continuous, and its changes of appearance are slight. We recognize the billiard ball by means of laws of change which are intrinsic, in the sense that they do not require that we should take account of the effects of other things upon it.

A series of events connected with each other in the manner suggested in the postulate is what I call a "causal line". What makes the inference possible is a "causal law". The first law of motion is an example, provided we give it empirical content by adding that there are many motions in nature which, to a first approximation, are unaffected by outside forces. The motion of light-rays is the most obvious illustration.

Our postulate is involved, however, in the very concept of "motion". This concept requires that something should preserve its identity while changing its position. When we dispense with substance, the "something" will have to be a series of events, and the series must have some characteristic which facilitates the common-sense interpretation as a "thing" with changing states. I suggest that the required characteristic is an intrinsic causal law, i.e. a law which enables us to say something about unobserved members of the series without having to take account of anything else in the world.

As we have seen, when two causal lines interact, for example in the collision of two billiard balls, we need no fresh postulate, but can content ourselves with observation and induction.

Our postulates, with the partial exception of the first, all involve the concept of "cause". I cannot accept the view that causation is merely invariable sequence. This opinion cannot be maintained except with an addendum (which is never made) to the effect that a "cause" must not be too narrowly defined. A statement of the form "A is invariably followed by B" requires that "A" and "B" should be general terms, such as "lightning" and "thunder". But it is possible to multiply the general terms applicable to a given event, or to define them with quantitative precision, until "A" and "B" are descriptions each only applicable to one event in the history of the world. In that case, if A is the earlier, A is invariably followed by B, but in general we should not regard A as the "cause" of B. We only think that A is the cause of B if there are many instances of its being followed by B. In fact, I think, these instances are regarded as evidence of something more than sequence, though not, in general, as conclusive evidence.

Between any two events belonging to one causal line, I should say, there is a relation which may be called one of cause-and-effect. But if we call it so, we must add that the cause does not *completely* determine the effect, even in the most favourable cases. There is always *some* influence, which is also causal, though in a slightly different sense, of the environment on the causal line. A photon in interstellar space is slightly deflected by gravitation from its rectilinear path, and in general the disturbing effect of the environment is much greater than in this case. What our postulate asserts may be re-stated as follows: A given event is very frequently one of a series of events (which may last a fraction of a second or a million years) which has throughout an approximate law of persistence or change. The photon preserves direction and velocity of motion, the billiard ball preserves shape and colour, a foetus develops into an animal of the appropriate species, and so on. In all these cases there is spatio-temporal continuity in the series of events composing a causal line; but this brings us to our third postulate.

III. *The postulate of spatio-temporal continuity*

This postulate is concerned to deny "action at a distance", and to assert that, when there is a causal connection between two events that are not contiguous, there must be intermediate links in the causal chain such that each is contiguous to the next, or (alternatively) such that there is a process which is continuous in the mathematical sense. When a number of people all hear a speaker, it seems obvious that there is a causal connection between what the different auditors hear, and it also seems obvious that, since they are separated in space, there must be a causal process in the intervening regions, such as sound waves are considered to be. Or when you see a given person on a variety of occasions, you do not doubt that he has had a continuous existence during the times when you were not seeing him.

This postulate presupposes causal lines, and is only applicable to them. If you know two twins, A and B, whom you cannot tell apart, and you see one on one occasion and one on another, you cannot assume that a continuous chain connects the two appearances until you have satisfied yourself that it was the same twin on both occasions.

This postulate is not concerned with the evidence for a causal connection but with an inference in cases in which a causal connection is considered to be already established. It allows us to believe that physical objects exist when unperceived, and that it is in virtue of continuous processes in intervening space that percipients in the same neighbourhood have perceptions which appear to be causally interconnected, though not directly caused the one by the other. It also has applications in psychology. For example, we may recollect a given occurrence on various occasions, and in the intervening times there is nothing observable that belongs to the same causal line as the recollections, but we assume that there is *something* (in the brain?) which exists at these intervening times, and makes the causal line continuous.

A great many of our inferences to unobserved occurrences, both in science and in common sense, depend upon this postulate.

IV. *The Structural Postulate*

This postulate is concerned with certain circumstances in which inference to a probable causal connection is warranted. The cases concerned are those in which a number of structurally similar occurrences are grouped about a centre. The phrase "grouped about a centre" is intentionally vague, but in certain cases it is capable of a precise meaning. Suppose a given object to be simultaneously seen by a number of people and photographed by a number of cameras. The visual percepts and the photographs can be arranged by the laws of perspective, and by the same laws the position of the object seen and photographed

can be determined. In this instance the sense in which the percepts and photographs are ",grouped about a centre" is precisely
definable. When a number of people hear the same sound, there
is an equally precise definition if there is an accurate method of
determining when they hear it, for it is found that the times
when they hear it differ from a given time by amounts proportional
to their distance from a certain point; in that case, the point
at the given time is the space-time centre or origin of the sound.
But I wish to employ the phrase also in cases (such as smells)
where no such precision is possible.

Of the three-fold postulate enunciated in Chapter VI, part
has been absorbed into our third postulate, and part is not at
present relevant. What remains is as follows:

*When a number of structurally similar complex events are ranged
about a centre in regions not widely separated, it is usually the
case that all belong to causal lines having their origin in an event
of the same structure at the centre.*

We say that this is "usually" the case, and the inference in a
given instance is therefore only probable. But the probability
can be increased in various ways. It is increased if the structure
is very complex (e.g. a long printed book). It is increased if there
are many examples of the complex structure, e.g. when six million
people listen to the Prime Minister's broadcast. It is increased
by regularity in the grouping about a centre, as in the case of a
very loud explosion heard by many observers, who note the time
when they hear it.

It seems likely that the above postulate could be analysed into
several simpler postulates, and that the above ways of increasing
probabilities would then become demonstrable. But though I
believe this to be possible, I have not succeeded in doing it.

The uses of this postulate have been sufficiently set forth in
Chapter VI.

V. *The Postulate of Analogy*

The postulate of analogy may be enunciated as follows:

*Given two classes of events A and B, and given that, whenever
both A and B can be observed, there is reason to believe that A*

causes B, then if, in a given case, A is observed, but there is no way of observing whether B occurs or not, it is probable that B occurs; and similarly if B is observed, but the presence or absence of A cannot be observed.

In connection with this postulate, it is necessary to recall what was said on the subject of observed negative facts in Part II, Chapter IX. By looking out of the window you can observe that it is not raining; this is different from not observing that it is raining, which can be achieved by shutting the eyes. The postulate is concerned with the second kind of non-observation, not with the first, and there must be some reason for supposing that the unobserved fact, if it occurs, will be unobservable. Suppose, for example that a barking dog is running after a rabbit, and for a moment is hidden by a bush. The bush accounts for your not seeing the dog, and allows you to infer that the bark, which you still hear, is still associated with what you saw a moment ago. When the dog emerges from the bush, you think your belief is confirmed.

The non-perception of other minds is more analogous to that of the dog in the bush than is generally thought. We do not see an object if an opaque body is between it and us, i.e. if no causal line leads from it to our eyes. We feel a touch on any part of the body because causal lines travel along the nerves to the brain from the part touched. If the nerves are cut, we feel nothing; the effect is exactly analogous to that of an opaque body in the case of sight. When some one else's body is touched we feel nothing, because no nerves travel from his body to our brain. Probably in time physiologists will be able to make nerves connecting the bodies of different people; this will have the advantage that we shall be able to feel another man's tooth aching. In the meantime, there are understandable reasons for the impossibility of observing the bodily sensations of others, and therefore the fact that we do not observe them is no reason for supposing that they do not occur. It is only in cases where some such reason for non-observability exists that our postulate can legitimately be applied.

Let us take as an illustration of our postulate the connection of certain kinds of visual appearance with the expectation of hardness. There is a certain kind of tactile sensation which leads us to call the body touched "hard". The word "hard" is a causal word: it denotes that property of an object in virtue of which it causes a certain kind of tactile sensation. Our previous postulates enable us to infer that there is such a property, which bodies possess while they are causing the appropriate sensations. But our previous postulates do not enable us to infer that bodies sometimes have this property when they are not being touched. But now we find that, when a body is both seen and touched, hardness is associated with a certain kind of visual appearance, and our postulate allows us to infer that hardness is probably associated with this visual appearance even when the body concerned is not being touched.

As appears from the above discussion, this postulate has many uses in addition to that of allowing us to infer mental occurrences connected with bodies other than our own.

The above postulates are probably not stated in their logically simplest form, and it is likely that further investigation would show that they are not all necessary for scientific inference. I hope and believe, however, that they are sufficient. There are certain epistemological problems connected with them which I shall consider in the next chapter; these problems do not depend upon the exact form of the postulates, and would remain the same even if the postulates were much modified.

The postulates, in the form in which I have enunciated them, are intended to justify the first steps towards science, and as much of common sense as can be justified. My main problem in this Part has been epistemological: what must we be supposed to know, in addition to particular observed facts, if scientific inferences are to be valid? In dealing with this problem, it is not science in its most advanced and technical form that we have to examine, for advanced science is built on elementary science, and elementary science is built on common sense. The progress of science is from generalizations that are vague and liable to exceptions to others that are more nearly precise and have fewer exceptions. "Unsupported bodies in air fall" is a primitive generalization; the Psalmist noted that sparks are an exception, and nowadays he might have added balloons and aeroplanes. But without this crude and partly untrue law, we should never have arrived at the law of gravitation. Premisses for theory of knowledge are always different from premisses for logic, and it is premisses for theory of knowledge that I have been trying to discover.

In what sense can we be said to "know" the above postulates, or whatever substitutes may hereafter be found preferable? Only, I think, in a sense which takes account of the discussion of kinds of knowledge in Chapter I of this Part. Knowledge of general connections between facts is more different than is usually supposed from knowledge of particular facts. Knowledge of connections between facts has its biological origin in animal expectations. An animal which experiences an A expects a B; when it evolves into a primitive man of science it sums up a number of particular expectations in the statement "A causes B". It is biologically advantageous to have such expectations as will usually be verified; it is therefore not surprising if the psychological laws governing expectations are, in the main, in conformity with the objective laws governing expected occurrences.

We may state the matter as follows. The physical world has what may be called "habits", i.e. causal laws; the behaviour of animals has habits, partly innate, partly acquired. The acquired habits are generated by what I call "animal inference", which occurs where there are the data for an induction, but not in all cases where there are such data. Owing to the world being such as it is, certain kinds of inductions are justified and others are not. If our inductive propensities were perfectly adapted to our environment, we should only be prone to an induction if the case were of the sort which would make the induction legitimate. In fact, all except men of science are too prone to induction when one of the characters concerned is interesting, and too little prone to it when both characters are not easy to notice. When both characters are interesting, the popular mind finds the impulse to induction irresistible: comets foretell the death of princes, because both are felt to be noteworthy. But even in animal induction there are elements of validity. The inference from smell to edibility is usually reliable, and no animal makes any of the absurd inductions which the logician can invent to show that induction is not always valid.

Owing to the world being such as it is, certain occurrences are sometimes, in fact, evidence for certain others; and owing to animals being adapted to their environment, occurrences which are, in fact, evidence of others tend to arouse expectation of those others. By reflecting on this process and refining it, we arrive at the canons of inductive inference. These canons are valid if the world has certain characteristics which we all believe it to have. The inferences made in accordance with these canons are self-confirmatory and are not found to contradict experience. Moreover, they lead us to think it probable that we shall have mental habits such as these canons will on the whole justify. since such mental habits will be biologically advantageous.

I think, therefore, that we may be said to "know" what is necessary for scientific inference, given that it fulfils the following conditions: (1) it is true, (2) we believe it, (3) it leads to no conclusions which experience confutes, (4) it is logically necessary if any occurrence or set of occurrences is ever to afford evidence in favour of any other occurrence. I maintain that these conditions are satisfied. If, however, any one chooses to maintain solipsism of the moment, I shall admit that he cannot be refuted, but shall be profoundly sceptical of his sincerity.

Chapter X

THE LIMITS OF EMPIRICISM

MPIRICISM may be defined as the assertion "all synthetic knowledge is based on experience". I wish to consider what, exactly, this statement can signify, and whether it is wholly true, or only true with certain limitations.

Before the assertion acquires definiteness, we must define "synthetic", "knowledge", "based on", and "experience". With the exception of the word "synthetic", these terms have been more or less defined in previous chapters, but I will recapitulate, briefly and dogmatically, the conclusions of our earlier discussions. With regard to the word "synthetic", the precise definition is difficult, but for our purposes we may define it negatively as any proposition which is not part of mathematics or deductive logic, and is not deducible from any proposition of mathematics or deductive logic. Thus it excludes not only "2 and 2 are 4" but also "two apples and two apples are four apples". But it includes not only all statements of particular facts, but also all generalizations which are not logically necessary, such as "all men are mortal" or "all copper conducts electricity".

"Knowledge", as we have seen, is a term incapable of precision. All knowledge is in some degree doubtful, and we cannot say what degree of doubtfulness makes it cease to be knowledge, any more than we can say how much loss of hair makes a man bald. When a belief is expressed in words, we have to realize that all words outside logic and mathematics are vague: there are objects to which they are definitely applicable, and objects to which they are definitely inapplicable, but there are (or at least may be) intermediate objects concerning which we are uncertain whether they are applicable or not. When a belief is not expressed in words, but only displayed in non-verbal behaviour, there is a great deal more vagueness than is usually the case when it is expressed in language. It is even doubtful what behaviour can be regarded as expressing a belief: going to the station to catch a train clearly does express a belief; sneezing clearly does not; but putting up your arm to ward off a blow is an intermediate case which inclines towards "yes", and blinking when something approaches the eye is an intermediate case which inclines towards "no".

But let us leave these difficulties in the definition of "knowledge", as there are others that are perhaps more important in the present context.

"Knowledge" is a sub-class of true beliefs. We have just seen that "belief" is not easy to define, and "true" is a very difficult term. I shall not, however, repeat what was said about this term in Part II, as the really important question for us is what must be added to truth in order to make a belief an instance of "knowledge".

It is agreed that everything inferred from a piece of knowledge by a demonstrative argument is knowledge. But since inferences start from premises, there must be knowledge which is un-inferred if there is to be any knowledge. And since most inferences are non-demonstrative, we have to consider when such an inference makes its conclusion a piece of "knowledge", granted that we know the premises.

This second question has sometimes a precise answer. Given an argument which, from known premises, confers a probability p on a certain conclusion, then, if the premises embrace all the known relevant evidence, the conclusion has a degree of credibility measured by p, and we may say that we have "uncertain knowledge" of the conclusion, the uncertainty being measured by $1 - p$. Since all knowledge (or almost all) is doubtful, the concept "uncertain knowledge" must be admitted.

But such precision is seldom possible. We do not usually know any mathematical measure of the probability conferred by a non-demonstrative inference, and we hardly ever know the degree of doubtfulness of our premises. Nevertheless, the above gives a kind of ideal towards which we can approximate in estimating the doubtfulness of a conclusion of a non-demonstrative argument. The supposed absolute concept "knowledge" should be replaced by the concept "knowledge with degree of certainty p", where p will be measured by mathematical probability when this can be ascertained.

We have next to consider knowledge of premises. These are *prima facie* of three kinds: (1) knowledge of particular facts, (2) premises of deductive inference, (3) premises of non-deductive inference. I shall ignore (2), which has little relevance to our problems, and does not involve any of the difficulties in which we are interested in this inquiry. But both (1) and (3) involve the fundamental issues with which we have been concerned.

That knowledge of particular facts must depend upon perception is one of the most essential tenets of empiricism, and it is one which I have no inclination to dispute. It was not admitted by those philosophers who accepted the ontological argument, or by those who thought the characteristics of the created world deducible from God's goodness. Such views, however, are now rare. Most philosophers now admit that knowledge of particular facts is only possible if the facts are perceived or remembered, or inferred by a valid argument from such as are perceived or remembered. But when this is admitted many difficulties remain. "Perception", as we saw in Part III, is a vague and slippery concept. The relation of perception to memory is not easy to define. And the question what is a valid argument, when the argument is non-demonstrative, involves all the problems of Part VI. But before considering argument, let us concentrate on the part played by perception and memory in generating knowledge.

Confining ourselves for the present to verbal knowledge, we may consider perception and memory in relation to (a) understanding of words, (b) understanding of sentences, (c) knowledge of particular facts. We are here in the region of Locke's polemic against innate ideas and Hume's principle "no idea without an antecedent impression".

As regards the understanding of words, we may confine ourselves to such as are defined ostensively. Ostensive definition consists in the repeated use of a certain word by a person A at times when what the word means is occupying the attention of another person B. (We may take it that A is a parent and B a child.) It must be possible for A to surmise with a high degree of probability what B is attending to. This is easiest in the case of objects perceived by the public senses, especially sight and hearing. It is slightly more difficult in such matters as toothache, earache, stomachache, etc. It is still more difficult in regard to "thoughts", such as recollections, the multiplication table, etc. Consequently children do not learn to talk about these as early as they learn to talk about cats and dogs. But in all such cases perception of the object which is what the word means is still, in some sense, essential to understanding the word.

At this point it is desirable to recapitulate certain theories that have been set forth in Part II.

There is a distinction between "object words" and "syntax words". "Cat", "dog", "Stalin", "France" are object words; "or", "not", "than", "but" are syntax words. An object word can be used in an exclamatory manner, to indicate the presence of what it means; this is, indeed, its most primitive use. A syntax word cannot be so used. During a Channel crossing, when first Cap Grisnez comes in sight, one may exclaim "France!", but there are no circumstances in which it would be appropriate to exclaim "than!"

Syntax words can only be verbally defined in terms of other syntax words; therefore in any language which has a syntax there must be undefined syntax words. The question arises: what is the process of ostensive definition in the case of a syntax word? Is there any way of pointing out what it means, in the way in which one can point out a cat or a dog?

Let us take the word "not" as it enters into the life of a child learning to talk. It is, I think, derivative from the word "no", which most children learn very soon. The word "no" is intended to be associated with the expectation of unpleasant feelings, so that an act otherwise attractive can be rendered unattractive by the utterance of this word. I think "not" is only "no" confined to the sphere of belief. "Is that sugar?" "No, it is salt, so if you sprinkle it on your plum tart you will experience a disagreeable taste." There are ideas which it is advantageous to act upon, and others which it is disadvantageous to act upon. The word "not" means, initially, "disadvantageous to act upon". More simply: "Yes" means "pleasure this way", and "no" means "pain that way". (The pleasure and pain may be due to social sanctions established by the parents.) And so "not" will be initially only a negative imperative applied to beliefs.

But this seems still somewhat remote from what the logician means by "not". Can we fill in the intervening stages in the child's linguistic development?

I think we may say that "not" means something like: "You do right to reject the belief that . . ." And "rejection" means, primarily, a movement of aversion. A belief is an impulse towards some action, and the word "not" inhibits this impulse.

Why this curious theory? Because the world can be described without the use of the word "not". If the sun is shining, the statement "the sun is shining" describes a fact which takes place independently of the statement. But if the sun is not shining, there is not a fact *sun-not-shining* which is affirmed by the true statement "the sun is not shining". Now clearly I can believe, and believe truly, that the sun is not shining. But if "not" is unnecessary for a complete description of the world, it must be possible to describe what is happening when I believe that the sun is not shining without using the word "not". I suggest that what is happening is that I am inhibiting the impulses generated or constituted by the belief that the sun is shining. This state of affairs is also called a belief, and is said to be "true" when the belief that the sun is shining is false. A perceptive belief is true when it has certain causal antecedents, and false when it has others; "true" and "false" are both positive predicates. Thus the word "not" is eliminated from our fundamental apparatus.

A similar treatment may be applied to the word "or".

There is more difficulty about the words "all" and "some". Either of these may be defined in terms of the other and negation, since "$f(x)$ always" is the negation of "not-$f(x)$ sometimes" and "$f(x)$ sometimes" is the negation of "not-$f(x)$ always". It is easy to prove the falsehood of "$f(x)$ always" or the truth of "$f(x)$ sometimes", but it is not easy to see how we can prove the truth of "$f(x)$ always" or the falsehood of "$f(x)$ sometimes". But at the moment I am not concerned with the truth or falsehood of such propositions, but with how we come to understand the words "all" and "some".

Take, say, the proposition "some dogs bite". You have observed that this, that, and the other dog bite; you have observed other dogs which, so far as your experience went, did not bite. If, now, in the presence of a certain dog, some one says to you "that dog bites", and you believe him, you will be prompted to certain actions. Some of these actions depend on the particular dog, others do not. Those acts which will occur whatever dog it is may be said to constitute the belief "some dogs bite". The belief "no dogs bite" will be the rejection of this. Thus beliefs expressed by using the words "all" and "some" contain no constituents not contained in beliefs in whose verbal expression these words do not occur.

This disposes of the understanding of logical words.

We may sum up this discussion of vocabulary as follows.

Some words denote objects, others express characteristics of our belief-attitude; the former are object-words, the latter syntax-words. An object-word is understood either through a verbal definition or through an ostensive definition. Verbal definitions must, in the last resort, employ only words having an ostensive definition. An ostensive definition consists in the establishment of an association through the hearing of closely similar sounds whenever the object to be defined is present. It follows that an ostensive definition must apply to a class of similar sensible occurrences; to nothing else is the process applicable. An ostensive definition can never apply to anything not experienced.

Passing now to the understanding of sentences, it is clear that every statement that we can understand must be capable of being expressed in words having ostensive definitions, or derived from a statement so expressed by means of syntax words.

The consequences of this principle are, however, not quite so far-reaching as is sometimes thought. I have never seen a winged horse, but I can understand the statement "there is a winged horse". For, if A is an object which I have named, I can understand "A is a horse" and "A has wings"; therefore I can understand "A is a winged horse"; therefore I can understand "something is a winged horse". The same principle shows that I can understand "the world existed before I was born". For I can understand "A is earlier than B" and "B is an event in my own life"; therefore I can understand "if B is an event in my own life, A is earlier than B", and I can understand the statement that this is true of every B, for some A; and this is the statement "the world existed before I was born".

The only disputable point in the above is the assertion that I can understand the statement "A is an event in my own life". There are various ways of defining my own life, all equally suitable to our purpose. The following will do. "My life" consists of all events that are connected with *this* by a finite number of memory-links backward or forward, i.e. remembering or being remembered. Various other possible definitions will make the statement in question equally understandable.

Similarly, given a definition of "experience", we can understand the statement "there are events that I do not experience" and even "there are events which no one experiences". Nothing in the principle connecting our vocabulary with experience excludes such a statement from intelligibility. But whether any reason can be found for supposing such a statement true, or for supposing it false, is another question.

To illustrate, take the proposition "there is matter perceived by no one". The word "matter" may be defined in various ways, in all of which the terms used in the definition have ostensive definitions. We shall simplify our problems if we consider the proposition "there are events perceived by no one". Clearly this is intelligible if the word "perceive" is intelligible. A piece of matter, in my opinion, is a set of events; therefore we can understand the hypothesis that there is matter perceived by no one. (A piece of matter may be said to be perceived when one of its constituent events is connected with a percept by a causal line.)

The reason that we can understand sentences that, if true, deal with matters lying outside experience, is that such sentences, when we can understand them, contain variables (i.e. "all" or "some" or an equivalent), and that variables are not constituents of the propositions in whose linguistic expression they occur. Take (say) "there are men whom I have never heard of". This says: "the propositional function 'x is human and I have not heard of x' is sometimes true". Here "x" is not a constituent; no more are the names of the men I have not met. But to the principle that words which I can understand derive their meaning from my experience there is no need to admit any exceptions whatever. This part of empiricist theory appears to be true without any qualification.

It is otherwise with knowledge of truth and falsehood, as opposed to knowledge of the meanings of words. We must now turn our attention to this kind of knowledge, which, in fact, alone strictly deserves the name of "knowledge".

Taking the question first as one of logic, we have to ask ourselves: "Do we ever know, and if so how, (1) propositions of the form '$f(x)$ always', (2) propositions of the form '$f(x)$ sometimes' in cases where we know no proposition of the form '$f(a)$'?" We will call the former "universal" propositions and the latter "existence" propositions. A proposition of the form "$f(a)$", in which there are no variables, we will call a "particular" proposition.

As a matter of logic, universal propositions, if inferred, can only be inferred from universal propositions, while existence-propositions can be inferred either from other existence propositions or from particular propositions, since "$f(a)$" implies "$f(x)$ sometimes". If we know "$f(x)$ sometimes" without knowing any proposition of the form "$f(a)$", I shall call "$f(x)$ sometimes" an "unexemplified" existence-proposition.

I shall assume, on the basis of previous discussions, that we have knowledge of some universal propositions and also of some unexemplified existence propositions. We have to inquire whether such knowledge can be wholly based on experience.

(1) *Universal propositions.*—It would seem natural to say that what we learn by perception is always particular, and that therefore, if we have any universal knowledge, this must be, at least in part, derived from some other source. But the reader may remember that doubt was thrown on this view by the discussions in Part II, Chapter X. We there decided that there are negative perceptive judgments, and that these sometimes imply negative universals. E.g. if I am listening to the B.B.C., I can make the negative perceptive judgment "I did not hear pippiness", and infer "I heard no pips". We saw that every empirical enumerative judgment, such as "I have just three children", involves a process of the above kind. This is connected with the doctrine developed in Part IV, Chapter VIII, on the principle of individuation. The rule is simple: if the absence of a certain quality can be perceived, we can infer the absence of all complexes of which this quality is a constituent. There are therefore some universal propositions which empiricism will allow us to know. Unfortunately they are all negative, and do not nearly coincide with all the general propositions that we believe ourselves to know.

Universal propositions based on perception alone apply only to a definite period of time, during which there has been continuous observation; they cannot tell us anything about what happens at other times. In particular, they can tell us nothing about the future. The whole *practical* utility of knowledge depends upon its power of foretelling the future, and if this is to be possible we must have universal knowledge not of the above sort.

But universal knowledge of a different kind is only possible if some such knowledge is known without inference; this is obvious as a matter of logic. Consider, for example, induction in its crude form. It is supposed by those who believe in it that, given n observed facts $f(a)_1, f(a_2) \ldots f(a_n)$, and no observed fact not-$f(b)$, the universal proposition "$f(x)$ always" has a probability which approaches certainty as n increases. But in the statement of this principle "a_1", "a_2" $\ldots$ "a_n" and "f" are variables, and the principle is a universal proposition. It is only by means of this universal proposition that the champions of induction believe themselves able to infer "$f(x)$ always" in the case of a particular "f".

Induction, we have seen, is not quite the universal proposition that we need to justify scientific inference. But we most certainly do need *some* universal proposition or propositions, whether the five canons suggested in an earlier chapter or something different. And whatever these principles of inference may be, they certainly cannot be logically deduced from facts of experience. Either, therefore, we know something independently of experience, or science is moonshine.

It is nonsense to pretend that science can be valid practically but not theoretically, for it is only valid practically if what it predicts happens, and if our canons (or some substitute) are not valid, there is no reason to believe in scientific predictions.

There are some things to be said to soften the harshness of the above conclusion. We need only more or less know our postulates; subjectively they may be only certain habits according to which we infer; we need only know their instances, not their general form; they all state only that something is *usually* the case. But although this softens the sense in which we must know them, there is only a limited possibility of softening the sense in which they must be true; for if they are not in fact true, the things that we expect will not happen. They may be approximate, and usual rather than invariable; but with these limitations they must represent what actually occurs.

(2) *Unexemplified existence-propositions*.[1]—There are here two different cases: (a) when there is no example in my experience, (b) when there is no example in all human experience.

(a) If you say "I saw a kingfisher to-day", and I believe you, I am believing an existence-proposition of which I know no

[1] I am here summarizing the argument of Chapter III of this Part.

example. So I am if I believe "there was a king of Persia called Xerxes", or any other fact of history before my time. The same applies to geography: I believe in Cape St. Vincent because I have seen it, but in Cape Horn only from testimony.

Inference to unexemplified existence-propositions of this sort is, I think, always dependent upon causal laws. We have seen that where testimony is involved, we depend upon our fifth postulate, which involves "cause". Other postulates as well are involved in any attempt to test the truthfulness of witnesses. All verification of testimony is only possible within the framework of a common public world, for the knowledge of which our postulates (or equivalents) are necessary. We cannot therefore know such existence-propositions as the above unless adequate postulates are assumed.

(b) Per contra, no more in the way of postulates is required to justify belief in existence-propositions not exemplified in any human experience than to justify belief when they are only not exemplified in my own experience. In principle, my grounds for believing that the earth existed before there was life on it are of just the same sort as my grounds for believing that you saw a kingfisher when you say you did. My grounds for believing that rain sometimes falls where there is no one to see it are better than my grounds for believing you when you say you saw a kingfisher; so are my grounds for believing that the summit of Mount Everest exists at times when it is invisible.

We must therefore conclude that both kinds of unexemplified existence-propositions are necessary for ordinary knowledge, that there is no reason to regard one kind as easier to know than the other, and that both require, if they are to be known, the very same postulates, namely those that allow us to infer causal laws from the observed course of nature.

We can now sum up our conclusions as to the degree of truth in the doctrine that all our synthetic knowledge is based on experience.

In the first place, this doctrine, if true, cannot be known, since it is a universal proposition of just the sort that experience alone cannot prove. This does not prove that the doctrine is not true; it proves only that it is either false or unknowable. This argument, however, may be regarded as logic-chopping; it is more interesting to inquire positively into the sources of our knowledge.

All particular facts that are known without inference are known by perception or memory, that is to say, through experience. In this respect, the empiricist principle calls for no limitation.

Inferred particular facts, such as those of history, always demand experienced particular facts among their premisses. But since, in deductive logic, one fact or collection of facts cannot imply any other fact, the inferences from facts to other facts can only be valid if the world has certain characteristics which are not logically necessary. Are these characteristics known to us by experience? It would seem not.

In practice, experience leads us to generalizations, such as "dogs bark". As a starting-point for science, it suffices if such generalizations are true in a large majority of cases. But although experience of barking dogs suffices to *cause* belief in the generalization "dogs bark", it does not, by itself, give any ground for believing that this is true in untested cases. If experience is to give such a ground, it must be supplemented by causal principles such as will make certain kinds of generalization antecedently plausible. These principles, if assumed, lead to results which are in conformity with experience, but this fact does not logically suffice to make the principles even probable.

Our knowledge of these principles—if it can be called "knowledge"—exists at first solely in the form of a propensity to inferences of the kind that they justify. It is by reflecting upon such inferences that we make the principles explicit. And when they have been made explicit, we can use logical technique to improve the form in which they are stated, and to remove unnecessary accretions.

The principles are "known" in a different sense from that in which particular facts are known. They are known in the sense that we generalize in accordance with them when we use experience to persuade us of a universal proposition such as "dogs bark". As mankind have advanced in intelligence, their inferential habits have come gradually nearer to agreement with the laws of nature which have made these habits, throughout, more often a source of true expectations than of false ones. The forming of inferential habits which lead to true expectations is part of the adaptation to the environment upon which biological survival depends.

But although our postulates can, in this way, be fitted into a framework which has what we may call an empiricist "flavour", it remains undeniable that our knowledge of them, in so far as we do know them, cannot be based upon experience, though all their verifiable consequences are such as experience will confirm. In this sense, it must be admitted, empiricism as a theory of knowledge has proved inadequate, though less so than any other previous theory of knowledge. Indeed, such inadequacies as we have seemed to find in empiricism have been discovered by strict adherence to a doctrine by which empiricist philosophy has been inspired: that all human knowledge is uncertain, inexact, and partial. To this doctrine we have not found any limitation whatever.

INDEX